IF FOUND, please notify and arrange return to owner. This text is an important study guide for the owner's career and/or exam preparation.

Name: _____

Address: _____

City, State, ZIP: _____

Telephone: (_____) _____ E-mail: _____

D1540427

Gleim Publications, Inc., offers five university-level study manuals:

Auditing & Systems Exam Questions and Explanations	$19.95
Business Law/Legal Studies Exam Questions and Explanations	19.95
Federal Tax Exam Questions and Explanations	19.95
Financial Accounting Exam Questions and Explanations	19.95
Cost/Managerial Accounting Exam Questions and Explanations	19.95

Exam Prep Software also available @ $20 each

The following is a list of Gleim examination review books:

CIA Review: Part I, Internal Audit's Role in Governance, Risk, and Control	$29.95
CIA Review: Part II, Conducting the Internal Audit Engagement	29.95
CIA Review: Part III, Business Analysis and Information Technology	29.95
CIA Review: Part IV, Business Management Skills	29.95

CIA Test Prep software ($49.95 per section) is also available to complement your study.

CMA/CFM Review: Part 1, Economics, Finance, and Management	$26.95
CFM Review: Part 2CFM, Corporate Financial Management	26.95
CMA Review: Part 2CMA, Financial Accounting and Reporting	26.95
CMA/CFM Review: Part 3, Mgmt. Reporting, Analysis, and Behavioral Issues	26.95
CMA/CFM Review: Part 4, Decision Analysis, Information Systems, and Management Controls	26.95

CMA/CFM Test Prep software ($44.95 per section) and *CMA/CFM Review* audios ($69.95 per section) are also available to complement your study.

CPA Review: Financial	$39.95
CPA Review: Auditing	39.95
CPA Review: Business	39.95
CPA Review: Regulation	39.95

CPA Test Prep software ($49.95 per section) and *CPA Review* audios ($89.95 per section) are also available to complement your study.

EA Review: Part 1, Individuals	$29.95
EA Review: Part 2, Sole Proprietorships and Partnerships	29.95
EA Review: Part 3, Corporations, Fiduciaries, Estate and Gift Tax, and Trusts	29.95
EA Review: Part 4, IRS Administration and Other Topics	29.95

EA Test Prep software ($49.95 per section) is also available to complement your study.

Order forms are provided at the back of this book or contact us at www.gleim.com or (800) 87-GLEIM.

All orders must be prepaid. Shipping and handling charges will be added to all orders. Library and company orders may be purchased on account. Add applicable sales tax to shipments within Florida. All payments must be in U.S. funds and payable on a U.S. bank. Please write or call for prices and availability of all foreign country shipments. Orders will usually be shipped the day your request is received. Allow 10 days for delivery in the United States. Please contact us if you do not receive your shipment within 2 weeks.

Gleim Publications, Inc. guarantees the immediate refund of all resalable texts and unopened software and audios purchased directly from Gleim Publications, Inc. if they are returned within 30 days. Shipping and handling charges are nonrefundable. Returns of books purchased from bookstores and other resellers should be made to the respective bookstore or reseller.

Groundwood Paper and Highlighters — This book is printed on high quality groundwood paper. It is lightweight and easy to recycle. We recommend that you purchase a highlighter specifically designed to be non-bleed-through (e.g., Avery *Glidestick*™) at your local office supply store.

REVIEWERS AND CONTRIBUTORS

Garrett Gleim, B.S., University of Pennsylvania, is one of our vice presidents. Mr. Gleim coordinated the production staff, reviewed the manuscript, and provided production assistance throughout the project.

Grady M. Irwin, J.D., is a graduate of the University of Florida College of Law, and he has taught in the University of Florida College of Business. Mr. Irwin provided substantial editorial assistance throughout the project.

Bruce S. Masingil, B.S., Florida International University, is our book production assistant. Mr. Masingil provided assistance throughout the project.

John F. Rebstock, CIA, is a graduate of the Fisher School of Accounting at the University of Florida and has passed the CPA exam. Mr. Rebstock specializes in ensuring that our questions and Knowledge Transfer Outlines are user-friendly. Mr. Rebstock reviewed portions of the manuscript.

A PERSONAL THANKS

This manual would not have been possible without the extraordinary effort and dedication of Charon Benton, Julie Cutlip, Jean Marzullo, Danielle Pablo, Teresa Soard, and Dawn Western, who typed the entire manuscript and all revisions, and drafted, scanned, and laid out the diagrams and illustrations in this book.

The authors also appreciate the production and editorial assistance of Matthew Carty, Katharine Cicatelli, Laura Heston, Jenny Jacob, Chino Leong, Kevin McKinley, Nico Medina, Shane Rapp, Christina Smart, Jessica Sturgeon, and April Woodbury.

The authors also appreciate the critical reading assistance of Kendra Brewer, Jose Carrasco, Christopher North, Dhruven Parikh, Christopher Pavilonis, and Keith Williams.

Finally, we appreciate the encouragement, support, and tolerance of our families throughout this project.

ELEVENTH EDITION

PART IV

BUSINESS MANAGEMENT SKILLS

by

Irvin N. Gleim, Ph.D., CPA, CIA, CMA, CFM

with the assistance of
Grady M. Irwin, J.D.

ABOUT THE AUTHOR

Irvin N. Gleim is Professor Emeritus in the Fisher School of Accounting at the University of Florida and is a member of the American Accounting Association, Academy of Legal Studies in Business, American Institute of Certified Public Accountants, Association of Government Accountants, Florida Institute of Certified Public Accountants, The Institute of Internal Auditors, and the Institute of Management Accountants. He has had articles published in the *Journal of Accountancy, The Accounting Review,* and *The American Business Law Journal* and is author/coauthor of numerous accounting and aviation books and CPE courses.

Gleim Publications, Inc.
P.O. Box 12848
University Station
Gainesville, Florida 32604
(800) 87-GLEIM or (800) 874-5346
(352) 375-0772
FAX: (352) 375-6940
Internet: www.gleim.com
E-mail: admin@gleim.com

This is the second printing of the eleventh edition of *CIA Review: Part IV, Business Management Skills*. Please e-mail update@gleim.com with CIA IV 11-2 included in the subject or text. You will receive our current update as a reply. Updates are available until the next edition is published.

EXAMPLE:

To: update@gleim.com
From: your e-mail address
Subject: CIA IV 11-2

ISSN: 1547-8076

ISBN: 1-58194-334-2

Copyright © 2004 by Gleim Publications, Inc.

Second Printing: July 2004

ALL RIGHTS RESERVED. No part of this material may be reproduced in any form whatsoever without express written permission from Gleim Publications, Inc.

ACKNOWLEDGMENTS FOR PART IV

The author is grateful for permission to reproduce the following materials copyrighted by The Institute of Internal Auditors: Certified Internal Auditor Examination Questions and Suggested Solutions, excerpts from *The Practice of Modern Internal Auditing, Statements of Responsibilities of Internal Auditors, Code of Ethics, Standards for the Professional Practice of Internal Auditing, Professional Standards Practice Releases*, and *Statements on Internal Auditing Standards*, copyright © 1980 - 1998 by The Institute of Internal Auditors, Inc.

The authors also appreciate and thank the Institute of Certified Management Accountants for permission to use questions from past CMA examination, copyright © 1982 - 1990 by the Institute of Management Accountants.

Visit our website (www.gleim.com) for the latest updates and information on all of our products.

This publication is designed to provide accurate and authoritative information with regard to the subject matter covered. It is sold with the understanding that the publisher is not engaged in rendering legal, accounting, or other professional service.

If legal advice or other expert assistance is required, the services of a competent professional person should be sought.

(From a declaration of principles jointly adopted by a Committee of the American Bar Association and a Committee of Publishers.)

TABLE OF CONTENTS

PREFACE

The purpose of this book is to help **you** prepare **yourself** to pass Part IV of the CIA examination. The overriding consideration is to provide an inexpensive, effective, and easy-to-use study program. This manual

1. Defines topics tested on Part IV of the CIA examination.

2. Includes all recent changes in Part IV of the CIA program.

3. Explains how to optimize your grade by analyzing how the CIA exam is constructed and graded.

4. Suggests exam taking techniques to help you maximize your exam score.

5. Outlines all of the subject matter tested on Part IV of the CIA exam in 10 easy-to-use study units, including all relevant authoritative pronouncements.

6. Reorganizes past exam questions according to the subunits within each of the 10 study units and presents an intuitively appealing explanation of each objective question answer.

7. Provides an opportunity for professional accountants to obtain CPE credit while preparing to pass the CIA exam. See the opposite page for more information.

Even though Gleim's four-volume *CIA Review* constitutes a complete self-study program for the CIA exam, candidates should consider enrolling in a formal review program. Local IIA chapters throughout the world have, in the past, coordinated CIA review programs and will probably continue to do so. In addition, all candidates should invest in our *CIA Test Prep* software, which is a powerful supplemental study aid to any review books or courses. Also, new in July 2004, is our audio series available on CD or cassette. Similar audios for CPA candidates and CMA candidates were well-received, so we have added this option for CIA candidates to consider. Call (800) 87-GLEIM for more information.

Thank you for your interest in our materials. We deeply appreciate the thousands of letters and suggestions we have received from CIA, CMA, CFM, and CPA candidates and accounting students during the last four decades.

Please send us your suggestions, comments, and corrections concerning *CIA Review: Part IV*. The last page in this book has been designed to help you note corrections and suggestions throughout your study process. It is imperative that we receive your feedback after you take the CIA exam. We pledge to continue to improve the product (with your suggestions, we hope) in the twelfth and subsequent editions.

The outline format and spacing and the question and answer formats are designed to facilitate learning, understanding, and readability. Please read the introduction of this book carefully.

To continue providing our customers with first-rate service, we request that questions about our books and software be sent to us via <u>mail</u>, <u>e-mail</u>, or <u>fax</u>. The appropriate staff member will give each question thorough consideration and a prompt response. Questions concerning orders, prices, shipments, or payments will be handled via telephone by our competent and courteous customer service staff.

Good Luck on the Exam,

Irvin N. Gleim

July 2004

EARN CPE CREDITS WHILE STUDYING FOR THE CIA EXAM

The Gleim approach to CPE is both interactive and intense. You should be continually challenged to answer each question correctly. When you answer a question incorrectly or have difficulty, you should pursue a complete understanding by reading the answer explanation and consulting reference sources as necessary.

We offer CPE credit online that correlates with this Eleventh Edition text. Visit www.gleim.com/accounting/cpe/onlinecpe for more information.

Most of the questions in the study guide were taken from various professional examinations. Each question is revised, adapted, etc., to provide broader, up-to-date coverage of the internal auditing body of technical knowledge. In addition, publisher questions cover material added since examinations became "closed."

Finally, we ask for any supplemental comments, reactions, suggestions, etc., that you may have as you complete our CPE program. Please attach them to the online Course Evaluation or send an e-mail to cpeinfo@gleim.com.

To continue providing our customers with first-rate service, we request that questions about our books and software be sent to us via mail, e-mail, or fax. The appropriate staff member will give each question thorough consideration and a prompt response. Questions concerning orders, prices, shipments, or payments will be handled via telephone by our competent and courteous customer service staff.

Thank you for your interest, and we look forward to hearing from you.

Best Wishes in Your CPE Endeavors,

Irvin N. Gleim

July 2004

NEW!

GLEIM'S *CIA AUDIO REVIEW*

Now You Can:
- Study while you commute.
- Learn while you excercise.
- Excel on the exam.

With

GLEIM's CIA Audio Reviews

GLEIM's CIA Audio Reviews:

- Consist of one 20-45 minute review for each of the 40 Study Units in **GLEIM's** CIA Review series.

- Explain the core concepts to give you a frame of reference for details covered in the books and software.

- Reinforce topics already studied, as well as prepare you for those that you have not yet covered.

Only
$69⁹⁵
Per Part

GLEIM
KNOWLEDGE
TRANSFER
SYSTEMS

www.gleim.com • (800) 87-GLEIM

PREPARING FOR AND TAKING THE CIA EXAM

ABOUT THE CIA EXAM

Introduction

CIA is the acronym for Certified Internal Auditor. The CIA designation is international, with the examination administered in numerous countries. The CIA exam has been administered by The Institute of Internal Auditors since 1974. The exam consists of four 3 1/2-hour parts that are given on the third Thursday and its preceding Wednesday in May and November. Each part consists of 125 four-answer multiple-choice questions.

Part I	The Internal Audit Activity's Role in Governance, Risk, and Control	Wednesday	8:30 - 12:00	3 1/2 hours
Part II	Conducting the Internal Audit Engagement	Wednesday	1:30 - 5:00	3 1/2 hours
Part III	Business Analysis and Information Technology	Thursday	8:30 - 12:00	3 1/2 hours
Part IV	Business Management Skills	Thursday	1:30 - 5:00	3 1/2 hours
				14 hours

Please note as you read through this introduction that CIA program rules and prices are subject to change. Please visit The IIA website at www.theiia.org for the most up-to-date information.

Internal Auditing

Internal auditing is an independent, objective assurance and consulting activity designed to add value and improve an organization's operations. It helps an organization accomplish its objectives by bringing a systematic, disciplined approach to evaluate and improve the effectiveness of risk management, control, and governance processes.

Internal auditing reviews the reliability and integrity of information, compliance with policies and regulations, the safeguarding of assets, the economical and efficient use of resources, and established operational goals and objectives. Internal audits encompass financial activities and operations including systems, production, engineering, marketing, and human resources.

The Institute of Internal Auditors (IIA)

The IIA was organized in 1941 to develop the professional status of internal auditing. The organization's headquarters was in New York City until 1972, when it moved to Altamonte Springs, about 5 miles north of Orlando, Florida.

The IIA has an annual budget of approximately $17 million and employs a full-time staff of 100+. Presently, more than 45,000 individuals have attained The Institute of Internal Auditors' CIA designation.

The IIA has chapters in more than 200 metropolitan areas and has affiliated national institutes in many countries around the world. The chapters and institutes hold regular meetings, seminars, and conferences that encourage members to network with peers, develop professional contacts, and stay informed about current issues and practices in internal auditing.

The Institute of Internal Auditors' mission is to be the primary international professional association, organized on a worldwide basis, dedicated to the promotion and development of the practice of internal auditing.

The IIA is committed to:

- Providing, on an international scale, comprehensive professional development activities, standards for the practice of internal auditing, and certification.
- Researching, disseminating, and promoting to its members and to the public throughout the world, knowledge and information concerning internal auditing, including internal control and related subjects.
- Establishing meetings worldwide in order to educate members and others as to the practice of internal auditing as it exists in various countries throughout the world.
- Bringing together internal auditors from all countries to share information and experiences in internal auditing and promoting education in the field of internal auditing.

IIA annual dues in the United States and Canada:

1.	Regular Member	$115
2.	Sustaining	$50
3.	Educational Member	$65
4.	Life Member	$2,100
5.	Retired Member	$30
6.	Student Member	$30

For non-Chapter members outside the United States, Canada, and the Caribbean nations, dues are $115. These members are also required to pay a $30 bank collection charge for drafts drawn on banks outside the U.S., Canada, and the Caribbean. Applicants, except students and sustaining members, must also pay an application fee of $25.

CIA Board of Regents

The Board of Regents is a special committee of The Institute of Internal Auditors established to direct the certification program for internal auditors as established and/or modified by The IIA's Board of Directors.

The Board of Regents consists of at least nine regents. The regents are appointed by the Chairman of the Board of Directors to serve 3-year terms. Membership on the Board of Regents rotates, with two or three regents being appointed each year. The responsibilities of the Board of Regents include

- a. Define the common body of knowledge for the Certified Internal Auditor examination and other Institute certification examinations.
- b. Define the education, experience, character, examination, and other program requirements relating to The Institute certifications.
- c. Define continuing professional education (CPE) requirements for Institute certifications.
- d. Maintain the quality and security of examinations.
- e. Promote The Institute's certifications globally.

IIA Certification Department

The Vice President of the Learning Center and the Certification Department staff, who are located in The IIA's Florida offices, administer the program. They undertake all of the day-to-day work with respect to the Board of Regents' responsibilities.

The chair of the Board of Regents divides the members into subcommittees. Each subcommittee is responsible for one part of the exam; i.e., each subcommittee makes the initial recommendations concerning the content and grading of its part of the examination to the Board of Regents as a whole.

Well-Planned Evolution Rather than Abrupt Change

One of the responsibilities of The IIA Board of Regents is to continually update and enhance the sources of exam questions, which in their entirety constitute the **common body of knowledge**.

At the same time, the scope and content of the CIA exam appear to evolve so as to be predictable to CIA candidates. Addition of new topics and deletion of currently tested topics are announced at least one year in advance so candidates may plan and prepare accordingly.

Pass rates on the exam are low enough to give the examination credibility relative to the CMA and CPA exams but are high enough to encourage accounting and auditing professionals to participate in the CIA certification program. Everyone, including The IIA Board of Directors, the Board of Regents, the certification staff, CIAs, noncertified internal auditors, and the accounting/auditing profession in general, is interested in the continual upgrading and improvement of the CIA exam.

Objectives and Content of the CIA Examination

The CIA exam tests a candidate's knowledge and ability regarding the current practice of internal auditing. It enables candidates and prospective managers to adapt to professional changes and challenges by:

- Addressing nearly all management skills.
- Focusing on the principles of management control.
- Measuring a candidate's understanding of risk management and internal controls.

The exam tests candidates' knowledge and ability with respect to the current state of the art of internal auditing practice. The **common body of knowledge**, referred to in The IIA's materials, is reflected in this edition of *CIA Review*.

THE IIA'S CIA CONTENT SPECIFICATION OUTLINES

Part I: The Internal Audit Activity's Role in Governance, Risk, and Control

A.	Comply with the IIA's Attribute Standards	20%
B.	Establish a risk-based plan to determine the priorities of the internal audit activity	20%
C.	Understand the internal audit activity's role in organizational governance	15%
D.	Perform other internal audit roles and responsibilities	5%
E.	Governance, risk, and control knowledge elements	20%
F.	Plan Engagements	20%

Part II: Conducting the Internal Audit Engagement

A.	Conduct Engagements	30%
B.	Conduct Specific Engagements	30%
C.	Monitor Engagement Outcomes	10%
D.	Fraud Knowledge Elements	10%
E.	Engagement Tools	20%

Part III: Business Analysis and Information Technology

A.	Business Processes	20%
B.	Financial Accounting and Finance	20%
C.	Managerial Accounting	15%
D.	Regulatory, Legal, and Economics	10%
E.	Information Technology (IT)	35%

Part IV: Business Management Skills

A.	Strategic Management	25%
B.	Global Business Environments	20%
C.	Organizational Behavior	25%
D.	Management Skills	25%
E.	Negotiating	5%

The IIA publishes Content Specification Outlines (CSOs) that outline topics covered on the CIA exam. The percentage coverage of each exam part is indicated to the right of each topic. (Note that The IIA "percentage coverage" is given in ranges, e.g., 15-25%, as presented in Appendix A. On page 4, we present the midpoint of each range to simplify and provide more relevant information to CIA candidates, e.g., 20% instead of 15-25%.) We continually adjust the content of our books and software to changes in The IIA's CSOs.

Appendix A contains the CSOs in their entirety. Remember that we have studied and restudied the CSOs in developing our *CIA Review* books and software. Accordingly, you do not need to spend time with Appendix A. Rather, it should give you confidence that Gleim's *CIA Review* is the best review source available to help you PASS the CIA exam. The CSOs refer to proficiency and awareness levels. The IIA definitions of these levels are presented below.

> **Proficiency** -- Candidate is able to exhibit the competency in understanding and applying the subject matter in the workplace on a regular basis with skill and expertise.

> **Awareness** -- Candidate exhibits awareness and knowledge. Candidate is able to define terms, recognize issues, and recall facts about the issues.

Gleim Study Unit Listing

We believe our 10 study unit titles better describe the content of each part of the CIA exam. Our study unit titles and content also reflect feedback from CIA candidates. Please use the last page in this book to give us feedback after each exam. Thank you.

LISTING OF GLEIM STUDY UNITS

Part I: Internal Audit's Role in Governance, Risk, and Control

1. Introduction to Internal Auditing
2. Charter, Independence, & Objectivity
3. Standards & Proficiency
4. Internal Audit Roles & Responsibility
5. Control I
6. Control II
7. Planning & Supervising the Engagement
8. Managing the Internal Audit Activity I
9. Managing the Internal Audit Activity II
10. Engagement Procedures

Part II: Conducting the Internal Audit Engagement

1. Engagement Information
2. Working Papers
3. Communicating Results and Monitoring Progress
4. Specific Engagements
5. Information Technology I
6. Information Technology II
7. Statistics and Sampling
8. Other Engagement Tools
9. Ethics
10. Fraud

Part III: Business Analysis and Information Technology

1. Business Performance
2. Managing Resources & Pricing
3. Financial Accounting -- Basic Concepts
4. Financial Accounting -- Assets, Liabilities, and Equity
5. Financial Accounting -- Special Topics
6. Finance
7. Managerial Accounting
8. Regulatory, Legal, & Economic Issues
9. Information Technology I
10. Information Technology II

Part IV: Business Management Skills

1. Structural Analysis and Strategies
2. Industry and Market Analysis
3. Environments and Strategic Decisions
4. Global Business Issues
5. Motivation and Communications
6. Organizational Structure & Effectiveness
7. Managing Groups
8. Influence and Leadership
9. Time Management
10. Conflict and Negotiation

Admission to the CIA Program

Anyone who satisfies these character, educational, and professional requirements may sit for the examination.

1. **Bachelor's degree or equivalent**. Candidates must have an undergraduate (4-year) degree or its equivalent from an accredited college-level institution.

   a. Educational programs outside the United States and the qualifications of candidates who have completed most but not all of a degree program are evaluated by The IIA's Board of Regents to determine equivalency.

   b. IIA affiliates have been given the authority to recommend educational and experience criteria for their countries to ensure adequate consideration of cultural and societal differences around the world. In addition, certain international professional designations (such as Chartered Accountant) may be accepted as equivalent to a bachelor's degree.

   c. A major in accounting is not required.

2. **Character reference**. CIA candidates must exhibit high moral and professional character and must submit a character reference from a responsible person such as a CIA, supervisor, manager, or educator. The character reference must accompany the candidate's application.

3. **Work experience**. Candidates are required to have 24 months of internal auditing experience (or the equivalent) prior to receiving the CIA certificate. However, a candidate may sit for the exam before completing the work experience requirements, but (s)he will not be certified until the experience requirement is met.

   a. An advanced academic degree beyond the bachelor's or work experience in related business professions (such as accounting, law, finance) can be substituted for one year of work experience (1-year maximum).

   b. Equivalent work experience means experience in audit/assessment disciplines, including external auditing, quality assurance, compliance, and internal control.

   c. Full-time college or university-level teaching in the subject matter of the examination is considered equivalent to work experience. Two years of teaching equals one year of internal auditing work experience.

   d. Work experience must be verified by a CIA or the candidate's supervisor. An Experience Verification Form is available on The IIA website or in the CIA brochure for use in verifying professional experience. This may accompany the candidate's application or be submitted later when criteria have been met.

If you have questions about the acceptability of your work experience, contact The IIA Certification Department at certification@theiia.org or by fax at (407) 937-1101. If you do not possess a bachelor's degree and are unsure whether your educational achievements or professional designation qualify as equivalents to a bachelor's degree, you should submit related educational/professional information with your application and include a cover letter requesting review by the Board of Regents. Include a complete description of your situation. Please submit these materials to

Certification Department
The Institute of Internal Auditors
247 Maitland Avenue
Altamonte Springs, FL 32701-4201

You will receive a response from The IIA as soon as the certification staff or the Board of Regents evaluates your request. Applicants for equivalency may be registered for the exam pending review but should expect a separate letter regarding the outcome of the review. Applicants who do not receive an equivalency status letter within four weeks of submission of the application and equivalency request should contact The IIA.

How to Register and Apply for the CIA Exam

You must complete a Certified Internal Auditor Program Registration/Application Form for entrance into the CIA program. The application form is available for download or automatic transfer at www.theiia.org. All documents and fees must be filed to arrive at The Institute on or before March 31 for the May examination and September 30 for the November examination. Submit the following items:

1. A copy of your diploma, transcripts, or other proof of completion of a degree program. This must be submitted with the application form.

2. A Character Reference Form (also available at The IIA's website www.theiia.org)

3. Verification of professional work experience (can be submitted later when the criteria have been met). Visit The IIA website to obtain an experience verification form (www.theiia.org).

The candidate must sign the registration form agreeing to abide by The IIA Code of Ethics. Each registrant is responsible for making timely delivery of the required fees and forms. **The Institute cannot guarantee a candidate's right to sit for the examination if procedures are not followed.** If sending via mail, the application should be mailed to the IIA's Atlanta address as shown on the application.

Candidates must reapply each exam cycle for any remaining parts. A candidate may initially take one, two, three, or all four parts of the examination. A candidate may reapply to repeat any parts failed by submitting the registration form that accompanies the grade letter by using the reapplication form on The IIA website (www.theiia.org), or by contacting The IIA's Customer Service Center -- e-mail: custserv@theiia.org, fax: (407) 937-1101, or telephone: (407) 937-1100. The candidate must also pay the appropriate examination fee. A candidate may take as few as one part at subsequent sittings during the two-year eligibility period.

Each person enrolled in the CIA program is responsible for providing timely written notice of any change of address to the IIA Customer Service Center.

Eligibility Period for the Exam

A candidate has an initial eligibility period of two years (five examinations) after his/her first registration is approved. The eligibility period is subsequently extended for two years each time a candidate sits for a part. A candidate's eligibility will expire only if the candidate does not take a single exam part within any two-year period. If eligibility expires, the candidate loses credit for any part or parts previously passed and must reregister for consideration as a candidate for future examinations.

Professional Recognition Credit for Part IV

The IIA offers a Part IV Professional Recognition Credit for qualified professional certifications. Registered candidates and new CIA candidates who have successfully completed the examination requirements for many designations are eligible to receive credit for Part IV of the CIA exam. Please visit The IIA's website (www.theiia.org) for a complete list of certifications approved for credit. Hence, candidates who attain the credit for Part IV and pass Parts I, II, and III satisfy the examination requirement for the CIA designation.

The CIA exam is a **nondisclosed** exam. **Nondisclosed** means that exam questions and solutions are NOT released after each examination. In order to keep our books and software up-to-date and relevant to CIA candidates, we request feedback on our books and software after each CIA exam. We need to know what topics need to be added or enhanced. Note that we are not asking for information about CIA questions, per se. Rather, we are asking for feedback on our books and software. This approach has been approved by The IIA.

Special Student Examination Fee

The registration fee is the charge for enrolling candidates in the CIA program. The CIA examination is available to full-time students at reduced fees (half price). For them, the member registration fee is $30 (instead of $60), plus a fee of $35 (instead of $70) per part. Students may sit only one time for each part at this special rate.

1. To be eligible for the reduced rate, the student must

    a. Be a full-time student as defined by the institution in which the student is enrolled (a minimum of 12 semester hours or its equivalent for undergraduate students and 9 semester hours for graduate students).
    b. Register for and take the CIA exam while enrolled in school.
    c. Be enrolled as a senior in an undergraduate program or as a graduate student.

2. In addition to the requirements above, the following items should be submitted to the Certification Department of The Institute of Internal Auditors while the student is still enrolled in school:

    a. A Certified Internal Auditor Examination Registration/Application Form *(with school address substituted for business address)*
    b. A completed and signed Full-Time Student Status Form in lieu of a transcript
    c. A completed and signed Character Reference Form
    d. Payment for the $35 examination fee for each part, plus $30 registration fee

Fees for Full-Time Educators

Educators are invited to take the examination free of charge. Along with the required CIA Examination Application Form, educators should include a letter attesting to their college- or university-level teaching. These are submitted for approval of The IIA's Academic Relations Committee. Letters must

1. Be printed on the university's letterhead
2. Specify the courses taught during each semester or quarter
3. Verify that the candidate had a full-time appointment for each academic year submitted
4. Be signed by the dean of the college of business administration

IIA Refund and Deferral Policy

The registration fee is neither refundable nor transferable. The examination fee is refundable with a written request. A $25 processing fee will be charged. Candidates must notify The IIA in writing (via mail, fax, or e-mail) in order to make changes to their registration, such as changing examination sites, changing the examination parts being taken, deferring to sit at a later examination, or canceling the registration. Payment of any required fees is due at the time the change is made.

Deferrals or changes may be made at no cost if written notice is received by the registration deadline (March 31 and September 30). A $25 fee will be charged for deferrals, changes, or cancelations received after the deadline. This fee increases to $70 on the Wednesday of the week before the examination.

If no written notice or deferral of cancelation is given prior to the exam and the candidate fails to appear, (s)he is classified as a no-show, and a penalty fee of $70 will be deducted from fees paid. Any remainder will be held in the candidate's account pending further instructions. Monies left in the account after a candidate's eligibility period expires are subject to forfeiture.

CIA Exam Administration

About three weeks before the exam, candidates will receive an authorization letter with a candidate number, the exam site number and address, the date and time to report to the site, and the time the exam will begin and end (see example below). Any errors in the authorization letter should be reported to The IIA's Certification Department at (407) 937-1327, or e-mail: certification@theiia.org. When contacting The IIA, have the candidate ID number available. If you have not received your authorization letter within two weeks before the exam or you have lost your letter, then you should contact The IIA immediately.

The following items are **required** to be admitted to the exam site:

1. Authorization letter
2. Valid photo identification

CIA Candidate
«Address»
«CityStateZip»
«Country»

                                                                   Candidate/ID#

Dear Candidate:

This letter is your authorization to sit for the November 2004 CIA examination. You must present it along with a photo identification to gain admittance to the exam room. Arrive 30 minutes prior to start time.

Your requested language is: _____.

Your exam site is:

    «SiteNo» - «SiteName»
    «SiteAddr1»
    «SiteAddr2»
    «SiteAddr3»
    «SiteCityStateZip»
    «SiteCountry»

You are scheduled to take part(s):

For additional directions, contact (name and phone number of local contact).

The IIA Instructions to Candidates

The IIA instructions to candidates from a recent exam are reproduced below and on the next page to give you further insight into actual exam procedures.

Instructions to CIA Candidates

EXAMINATION SUPERVISORS ARE TO READ THESE INSTRUCTIONS VERBATIM TO THE CANDIDATES APPROXIMATELY FIVE MINUTES BEFORE START OF THE EXAMINATION. DO NOT EXTEMPORIZE.

(Extra copies for late arrivals, per IV.F of the "instructions.")

Do **not** open your booklet or write on the accompanying materials until instructed to do so.

As a courtesy to others, please turn off all cellular phones, beepers, etc., for the duration of the exam.

A No. 2 soft lead pencil must be used to complete the multiple-choice answer sheet. Darken only the appropriate blocks, as shown in the instructions on the multiple-choice answer sheet. **Marks outside the blocks could adversely affect the score you receive.**

At this time, please remove the white multiple-choice answer sheet and the colored control sheet from inside the exam booklet, and close the exam booklet.

On the multiple-choice answer sheet, write the exam language code (the language of your exam), exam site number and your candidate identification number in the blanks provided, and darken the appropriate boxes below each number. If your identification or ID number has fewer than 7 digits, please add any necessary zeroes to the **left** of your ID number so that the last digit of your ID number is in the space to the far right.

Locate the exam serial number on the upper left-hand corner of your exam booklet's cover, and copy this number in the space provided on the multiple-choice answer sheet.

Next, complete the control sheet, **making sure to read and sign the nondisclosure agreement.**

The specific restrictive rules that will be in effect during the examination are:

1. No reference material, templates, or other aids may be used, except for battery- or solar-powered, nonprinting, nonprogrammable, six-function calculators with only addition, subtraction, multiplication, division, square root, and percentage functions.

2. All answers submitted must be your own.

3. If you must be excused from the room, notify a monitor. You will be on the honor system during your absence. Only **one** candidate may leave the room at a time.

4. You may not talk during the examination.

5. You may not walk about the room during the examination.

6. No other act that appears to violate examination ethics will be permitted.

Breaking any of these rules could result in losing the privilege of sitting for this (or a future) CIA examination under Article 1 of The Institute of Internal Auditors' Code of Ethics.

You will have three and one-half hours in which to complete the examination. If you finish before the full time has elapsed, please turn in your materials and leave the room quietly.

Your <u>examination booklet, all scratch paper and notes</u> are to be turned in with your answers. You are not to discuss the examination with anyone.

I will announce when 30 minutes remain, when five minutes remain, and when time has expired. Please do **not** ask me or the other proctors to interpret any questions, as we are not permitted to discuss the content of the examination.

-- (continued) --

CANDIDATES WHO HAVE CONCERNS REGARDING EXAM QUESTIONS or the testing experience should submit their comments by fax (+1-407-937-1313) or by e-mail to certification@theiia.org. These comments must be received within 96 hours of completion of the exam so that they will be available to the Board of Regents for review before grading begins. Comments on exam questions must identify the general content of the question and briefly outline any perceived flaw. Candidate input will be gratefully acknowledged and considered in the evaluation of the exam and the testing program. If you prefer, I can collect specific comments and forward them to The IIA Certification Department.

Before beginning work on the exam, read carefully all the instructions on the exam booklet's cover and opening page.

Upon opening your exam booklet, check the page numbers to ensure no pages are missing. After the last question (Question #80), the phrase "End of Part" should appear.

Are there any questions?

You may now open your exam booklet and begin work.

Grading the CIA Exam and Grade Reporting

The examination proctors return the CIA examinations to The IIA offices by registered mail, Federal Express, or other means to guarantee the safety and security of the examination. The week following the examination, the exams are received and checked against shipping control lists prepared by the proctors. Individual candidate numbers are checked on each answer sheet of every candidate's exam. The highest priority is given to assuring that no candidate papers are misplaced or lost.

The grading process includes both a review of the suggested responses before the exam is given and a post-exam review of all questions that perform poorly in terms of difficulty and reliability. After this review, the Board may choose to accept more than one response as correct on certain questions that did not perform as well as expected.

The multiple-choice question answer sheets are graded using an optical scanner, and all irregularities are researched. If the difficulty of an exam part is higher than expected, a difficulty adjustment may be added to all candidates' scores before exam results are finalized. Statistical information from pre-tested questions is used to maintain comparable difficulty from one CIA exam to the next. Because the exact number of questions required to pass the exam may be slightly different from one exam to another, all raw scores are converted onto a reporting scale of 250 to 750 points, in order to ensure a common standard. A scaled score of 600 points or higher is required to pass the CIA exam. (A scaled score of 600 would be the equivalent of achieving 75 percent correct on an exam of appropriate difficulty.)

Examination results are mailed by July 15 for May exams and January 15 for November exams. If you earn a passing score, you are notified of passing and no specific grade is released. If you earn a score below the passing mark, it is reported to you along with a brief analysis of your exam performance by topic so you can see how much additional effort is required (see sample grade release letter on the next page). Plan on receiving good news soon!

DATE

CIA CANDIDATE
ADDRESS
CITYSTATEZIP
COUNTRY

Dear NAME: I.D. No. #####

Thank you for taking the November 2003 Certified Internal Auditor examination. Your results are listed below. CIA exam scores are now reported on a scale of 250 to 750 points (see insert), and a scaled score of 600 points or higher is required for successful completion of each part of the exam. No scores are released for parts passed.

PART I	PART II	PART III	PART IV*
PREVIOUSLY PASSED	PREVIOUSLY PASSED	485	PASSED

*If you have now passed Parts I, II, and III and plan to apply for Professional Recognition Credit for Part IV, please provide the necessary documents and payment by DATE in order to ensure prompt processing of your request. Instructions and a list of approved certifications are available on The IIA's website (www.theiia.org) under Certifications/CIA.

All scores are considered final. In order to help guide your future study, an analysis of the strengths and weaknesses of your exam performance is provided below for any part on which you received a non-passing score. The analysis includes (1) the main topic areas for the exam part (see IIA website for detailed outline), (2) the percentage of questions tested in each topic area, and (3) an assessment of improvement needed based on your performance on the November 2003 exam.

Performance Assessment For Part III

Business Processes (15-25%): You need a moderate amount of improvement in this area.

Financial Accounting and Finance (15-25%): You performed competently in this area but should review it during study.

Managerial Accounting (10-20%): You performed competently in this area but should review it during study.

Regulatory, Legal, and Economics (5-15%): You performed competently in this area but should review it during study.

Information Technology (IT) (30-40%): You need a large amount of improvement in this area.

We wish you the best in your pursuit of the Certified Internal Auditor designation.

The IIA Certification Department

Maintaining Your CIA Designation

After certification, CIAs are required to maintain and update their knowledge and skills. Practicing CIAs must complete and report 80 hours of Continuing Professional Education (CPE) every two years. Every February, CIAs who are required to report in the current year will receive reporting forms and instructions from The IIA. Completed forms should be filed with The IIA by May 31 of the required reporting year. Each July, participants in the current year's CPE program will receive a status report acknowledging acceptance of the number of hours reported. Even-numbered certificates report in even years and odd-numbered certificates in odd years.

PREPARING TO PASS THE CIA EXAM

Control: How To

You have to be in control to be successful during exam preparation and execution. Control can also contribute greatly to your personal and other professional goals. The objective is to be confident that the best possible performance is being generated. Control is a process whereby you

1. Develop expectations, standards, budgets, and plans.
2. Undertake activity, production, study, and learning.
3. Measure the activity, production, output, and knowledge.
4. Compare actual activity with expected and budgeted activity.
5. Modify the activity, behavior, or study to better achieve the desired outcome.
6. Revise expectations and standards in light of actual experience.
7. Continue the process or restart the process in the future.

Every day you rely on control systems implicitly. For example, when you groom your hair, you use a control system. You have expectations about the desired appearance of your hair and the time required to style it. You monitor your progress and make adjustments as appropriate. The control process, however, is applicable to all of your endeavors, both professional and personal. You should refine your personal control processes specifically toward passing the CIA exam.

In this book, we suggest explicit control systems for

1. Preparing to take the CIA exam
2. Studying an individual Gleim study unit
3. Answering individual multiple-choice questions

Most endeavors will improve with explicit control. This is particularly true of the CIA examination.

1. Develop an explicit control system over your study process.
2. Practice your question answering techniques (and develop control) as you prepare solutions to recent CIA questions during your study program.
3. Prepare a detailed plan of steps you will take at the CIA exam.

How Many Parts to Take

The CIA examination consists of four parts; however, according to The IIA, you may choose to take only one part at each sitting.

Our recommendation is to take and pass all four parts the first time. Some candidates, however, will not be able to follow this approach for a variety of reasons. Parts I and II cover internal auditing subject matter, whereas Part III, Business Analysis and Information Technology, and Part IV, Business Management Skills, cover a wide variety of material. Thus, most candidates planning to sit for only two parts of the initial exam will choose Parts I and II because of the efficiencies involved. Part III is the least related to traditional accounting. Part IV tests material more familiar to accounting majors.

Candidates have an initial eligibility period of 2 years from the first exam after their registration is approved. In addition, each time a candidate sits for an exam part, the candidate's eligibility period is extended 2 years from the date of the last exam part taken. A candidate's eligibility expires only if the candidate does not take a single exam part within any 2-year period. If a candidate's eligibility expires, the candidate loses credit for any part or parts passed and must submit a new CIA Exam Application Form and appropriate fees in order to take future examinations.

Study Plan, Time Budget, and Calendar

Complete one *CIA Review* study unit at a time. Initially, budget 3 to 4 hours per study unit (1 to 2 hours studying the outline and 1 to 2 minutes each on all the multiple-choice questions). Depending on your background, you may need significantly more time to prepare.

This Introduction	2
10 study units at 3.5 hours each	35
General review	3
Total Hours	40

Each week you should evaluate your progress and review your preparation plans for the time remaining prior to the exam. Use a calendar to note the exam dates and the weeks to go before the exam. Marking a calendar will facilitate your planning. Review your commitments, e.g., out-of-town assignments, personal responsibilities, etc., and note them on your calendar to assist you in keeping to your schedule.

How to Study a Study Unit (books only*)

1. Gain an overview of the study unit -- familiarity with the topic, number of pages of outline, number of multiple-choice questions -- and estimate the time you will invest.

2. Answer five to ten multiple-choice questions. Choose one or two questions from each subunit.

3. The purpose of answering multiple-choice questions before working through the study outline is to understand the standards to which you will be held. This will motivate you to concentrate on the study outline.

4. Work through the study outline. Learn and understand the concepts. Remember, you are aiming toward the analysis, synthesis, and evaluation levels of knowledge, not rote memorization. Study the outlines with the objective of being able to explain the subject matter to third parties.

* We recommend using *CIA Test Prep* software as discussed on the next page. It will give you a definite advantage.

5. After you are comfortable with the study outlines, apply your multiple-choice question answering technique (see page 17) to answer all of the multiple-choice questions by marking the correct answer before consulting the answer and answer explanation. It is essential to mark your answer choice before looking at the answer. Use the bookmark at the back of each Gleim *CIA Review* book to cover the answers.

6. Develop a 75%+ proficiency level within each study unit. You will achieve this proficiency level by studying the outlines and answering multiple-choice questions.

Learning from questions you answer incorrectly is very important. Each question you answer incorrectly is an opportunity to avoid missing actual test questions on your CIA exam. Thus, you should carefully study the answer explanations provided until you understand why the original answer you chose is wrong, as well as why the correct answer indicated is correct. This study technique may prove to be the difference between passing and failing for many CIA candidates.

You **must** determine why you answered questions incorrectly and learn how to avoid the same error in the future. Reasons for missing questions include:

    a.   Misreading the requirement (stem)
    b.   Failing to understand what is required
    c.   Making a math error
    d.   Applying the wrong rule or concept
    e.   Being distracted by one or more of the answers
    f.   Incorrectly eliminating answers from consideration
    g.   Lacking any knowledge of the topic tested
    h.   Employing bad intuition (Why?) when guessing

7.   Gleim **CIA Test Prep** software will significantly benefit your study efforts, especially when using the 20-question test routine discussed next.

Adding CIA Test Prep Software

Using *CIA Test Prep* really works! The software forces you to commit to your answer choice before looking at answer explanations. It also keeps track of your time and the results of your effort. Each study session and each test session are kept in the performance history and are viewable in either a table or a graphical format.

Each Test Prep disk covers a different part of the CIA exam, includes over 1,000 questions, and contains a Windows™ version of the program. All questions have been updated to reflect the current subject matter.

Read and study the following six steps regarding how to use the software with the books. Using *CIA Test Prep* will greatly facilitate your study and success on the CIA exam! DO NOT neglect diagnosing the reasons for answering questions incorrectly; i.e., learn from your mistakes while studying so you avoid making mistakes on the CIA exam.

> Avoid studying Gleim questions to learn the correct answers. Use Gleim questions to help you learn how to answer CIA questions under exam conditions. Expect the unexpected and be prepared to deal with the unexpected. Always take one 20-question test in test mode *before* studying the material in each study unit. These test sessions will allow you to practice answering questions you have not seen before. Become an educated guesser when you encounter questions in doubt; you will outperform the inexperienced exam taker.

The best way to prepare to PASS:

1 In test mode, answer a 20-question test from each study unit before studying the study unit.

2 Study the knowledge transfer outline for the study unit in your Gleim book.

3 Take two or three 20-question tests in test mode after studying knowledge transfer outlines.

4 After EACH test session, immediately switch to study mode and select questions "missed on last session" so you can reanswer these questions AND analyze why you answered each question incorrectly.

5 Continue the process until you approach a 75% proficiency level.

6 Modify the process to suit your individual learning process.

It is imperative that you complete at least one or two study units a week so you can review your progress and realize how attainable a comprehensive CIA review program is when using Gleim books and software. Remember to get ahead of your schedule to give yourself confidence.

> After you complete each 20-question test, ALWAYS do a study session of questions you missed. FOCUS on why you selected the incorrect answer, NOT the correct answer. You want to learn from your mistakes during study so you avoid mistakes on the exam.

If You Failed One or More Parts

The pass rate on each part of the CIA exam averages about 45%. Thus, you may not pass all parts attempted. If you failed one or more parts, you should retake them the next time the CIA exam is offered.

1. Once you have put the reaction to the bad news behind you, you should regroup and begin implementing the suggestions in this introduction. The Gleim system really works! Avoid thinking "I knew that" or "I don't have to study that again." What you knew and how you took the exam last time did NOT work. Develop new and improved perspectives.

2. Avoid failure on the next exam by **identifying**, **correcting**, and **understanding** your mistakes as you practice answering multiple-choice questions during your study sessions. Use *CIA Test Prep* software as described above. This methodology applies to all CIA candidates. Understand your mistakes while you study so you can avoid mistakes on the exam.

As you practice answering multiple-choice questions under exam conditions, it is imperative that you restudy each question you answer incorrectly.

Multiple-Choice Question Answering Technique

　　The following suggestions are to assist you in maximizing your score on each part of the CIA exam. Remember, knowing how to take the exam and how to answer individual questions is as important as studying/reviewing the subject matter tested on the exam.

1. **Budget your time**. We make this point with emphasis. Just as you would fill up your gas tank prior to reaching empty, so too should you finish your exam before time expires.

   a. You will have 210 minutes to answer 125 multiple-choice questions.

   b. As you work through individual multiple-choice items, monitor your time. Your goal is to answer all of the items and achieve the maximum score possible.

2. **Answer the items in numerical order**.

   a. Do **not** agonize over any one item. Stay within your time budget.

   b. Mark any items you are unsure of with a big "?" and return to them later if time allows.

   c. Plan on going back to all questions marked with a "?."

   d. Never leave a multiple-choice item unanswered on your answer sheet. Your score is based on the number of correct responses. You will not be penalized for guessing incorrectly.

3. **For each multiple-choice item:**

   a. **Cover up the answer choices** with your hand or a piece of scratch paper. Do not allow the answer choices to affect your reading of the item stem.

      1) If four answer choices are presented, three of them are incorrect. These incorrect answers are called **distractors**. Often, distractors are written to appear correct at first glance until further analysis.

      2) In computational items, distractors are often the result of making common mistakes.

   b. **Read the item** stem carefully (the part of the question that precedes the answer choices) to determine the precise requirement.

      1) You may wish to underline or circle key language or data used in the stem.

      2) Focusing on what is required enables you to ignore extraneous information and to proceed directly to determining the correct answer.

         a) Be especially careful to note when the requirement is an **exception**; e.g., "Which of the following is **not** an indication of fraud?"

   c. **Determine the correct answer** before looking at the answer choices.

      1) By adhering to these steps, you know what is required and which are the relevant facts.

      2) However, some multiple-choice items are structured so that the answer cannot be determined from the stem alone.

    d.   **Read the answer choices** carefully.

        1)   Even if answer (A) appears to be the correct choice, review the remaining answer choices. You may discover that answer (B), (C), or (D) is a better choice.

        2)   Treat each answer choice as a true-false question. Consider marking a "T" or an "F" next to each answer choice as you analyze it.

    e.   **Select the best answer.** Circle the most likely or best answer choice on the question booklet. If you are uncertain, guess intelligently to improve on your 25% chance of getting the correct answer.

        1)   For many of the multiple-choice questions, two answer choices can be eliminated with minimal effort. Eliminating them can reduce the risk of random guessing and increase your chances of success.

4.   After completing your first pass through all 125 questions, return to the questions that you marked with a "?."

5.   While answering questions, make sure you are within your time budget so you will have enough time to transfer your answers in an unhurried manner. Do not wait until the very end of the exam session to transfer answers because you may run out of time.

6.   After you have answered all 125 questions, **transfer your answers to the objective answer sheet**.

    a.   Double-check that you have transferred the answers correctly; e.g., recheck every fifth or tenth answer from your question booklet to your answer sheet to ensure that you have not fallen out of sequence.

If You Don't Know the Answer

Guess, but make it an educated guess, which means select the best possible answer. First, rule out answers that you feel are obviously incorrect. Second, speculate on The IIA's purpose and/or the rationale behind the question. These steps may lead you to the correct answer. Third, select the best answer, or guess between equally appealing answers. Mark the question with a "?" in case you have time to return to it for further analysis. However, unless you made an obvious mistake or computational error, try to avoid changing answers at the last minute. Your first guess is usually the most intuitive.

If you cannot make an educated guess, read the item and each answer and pick the best or most intuitive answer. Never leave a question unanswered.

Do **not** look at the previous answer to try to detect an answer. The answers are random, but it is possible to have four or more consecutive questions with the same answer letter, e.g., answer B.

NOTE: Do not waste time beyond the amount budgeted. Move ahead and stay on or ahead of schedule.

TAKING THE CIA EXAM

CIA Examination Preparation Checklist

1. **Register** for the exam program (see pages 6 and 7) by March 31 for the May exam dates or September 30 for the November exam dates.

2. **Apply** to take the desired parts on the same application form (for the initial registration and application), or file the reapplication form.

    a. As soon as your examination location is confirmed by The IIA, make travel and lodging reservations.

3. Acquire your study materials. Rely on *CIA Review* and *CIA Test Prep* as your primary study source.

4. Plan your study program.

5. Locate a suitable place to study.

6. Implement your study program.

7. Periodically review, reassess, and revise your study program as needed.

8. Recognize that an orderly, controlled study program builds confidence, reduces anxiety, and produces success!

9. **Pass the examination!**

Exam Psychology

Plan ahead for the exam and systematically prepare for it. Go to the exam and give it your best. Neither you nor anyone else can expect more. If you have undertaken a systematic preparation program, you will do well.

Maintain a positive attitude and do not become depressed if you encounter difficulties before or during the exam. An optimist will usually do better than an equally well-prepared pessimist. Remember, you are not in a position to be objective about your results during the exam. Many well-prepared examination candidates have been pleasantly surprised by their scores. Indeed, you should be confident because you are competing with many less-qualified persons who have not prepared as well as you. Optimism and a fighting spirit are worth points on every exam, and fear or depression tends to impair performance.

Logistical and Health Concerns

As soon as The IIA notifies you of your examination site, find suitable quarters at a hotel within walking distance of both the exam site and restaurants, if possible. Try to avoid being dependent on a car, parking spaces, etc., during the exam.

Some CIA examination sites are on university campuses. Begin by calling the student union to inquire about accommodations. Call the university's general number and ask for room reservations at the student union. If rooms are not available at the student union, ask for the office in charge of meetings, which should be able to recommend a convenient hotel.

Even if the exam is being given within driving distance of your home, consider staying by yourself at a hotel on Tuesday and Wednesday evenings to be assured of avoiding distractions. The hotel should be quiet and have a comfortable bed and desk suitable for study. If possible, stay at a hotel with recreational facilities that you normally use, e.g., a pool, exercise room, etc.

Plan to arrive at your hotel early Tuesday. To avoid any surprises, visit the examination site Tuesday afternoon or evening (remember, starting time is 8:30 a.m. Wednesday). Make sure you know where it is and how to get there. Decide where you want to sit so you have everything settled before Wednesday morning. You should locate the restroom to avoid confusion if you need to use it during the exam. Also, check on the availability of vending machines close to the exam room (for a quick soda, coffee, snack, etc., during the exam).

On Tuesday and Wednesday evenings, confine your study to a brief review of the major points covered in the next day's exam sessions. Concentrate on the sideheadings and key terms in *CIA Review*. For most CIA candidates, the best advice is to relax the evening before and to get a good night's rest. Sleep disturbance is less likely if you follow your normal routines. However, individual tastes vary, and you should do what you know has led to exam success in the past.

Proper exercise, diet, and rest during the weeks before the exam are very important. High energy levels, reduced tension, and a positive attitude are among the benefits. A good aerobic fitness program, a nutritious and well-balanced diet, and a regular sleep pattern will promote your long-term emotional and physical well-being as well as contribute significantly to a favorable exam result. Of course, the use of health-undermining substances should be avoided.

Pencils, Calculators, and Other Materials

The IIA specifically requires a No. 2 or soft-lead pencil for the multiple-choice answer sheet because it has a machine-gradable format. Nonprinting, nonprogrammable, battery- or solar-powered, six-function hand-held calculators are permitted during the CIA exam. You must supply your own pencils and calculator.

Although the instructions to proctors indicate that no food or beverages are allowed in the exam room, you should probably bring a thermos that you can take outside (if the proctors do not relent) to have a quick cup of tea, coffee, etc. Alternatively, there may be vending machines near the examination room.

Examination Tactics

1. Arrive at the site in time to have a margin of safety. Remember to bring your authorization letter and photo ID. Check in and select a seat. One advantage of being early is that you will have your choice of seats.

2. Dressing for exam success means emphasizing comfort, not appearance. Be prepared to adjust for changes in temperature, e.g., remove a sweater or put on a coat. Do not bring notes, this text, other books, etc., to the exam. You will only make yourself nervous and confused by trying to cram during the last 5 minutes before the exam. Books are not allowed in the exam room anyway. You should, however, bring an adequate supply of authorized items, e.g., pencils, erasers, a timepiece, and an appropriate calculator (nonprinting, nonprogrammable, battery- or solar-powered, six-function hand-held).

3. Use a clear plastic bag to carry your exam supplies. A larger size is more appropriate for storing pencils, an eraser, a calculator, breath mints, chewing gum, candy, etc.

4. Read the exam instructions carefully.

5. Answer the 125 questions in chronological order, circle the correct (or best guess) answer to each question. You can and should write in your exam booklet. Mark questions that you are leaving for later or you wish to review with big question marks.

6. You have 210 minutes (3.5 hours) to answer 125 questions. If you allocate 1.4 minutes per question, you will use only 175 minutes, leaving 35 minutes to review your answers and transfer your answers to the machine readable answer sheet. If you pace yourself during the exam, you will have adequate time to complete each part.

7. After you worked through all 125 questions, you should return to the questions you have marked with question marks and select the best answer.

8. After you have answered all 125 questions, review each question carefully. If you made an obvious mistake, e.g., misread the question, make the correction. DO NOT, however, begin changing answers and second guessing yourself. Your first answer to each question should be based on the systematic question answering technique that you have practiced throughout your preparation program.

9. As a final step, transfer all of your answers from your exam booklet to your machine readable answer sheet carefully and deliberately. Darken the correct answer with a number 2 pencil. Recheck your sequence; the question number in your exam booklet should correspond with the question number on your answer sheet (a sure way to fail is to transfer your answers incorrectly).

10. Do not discuss the examination and your solutions with other candidates at the noon breaks or on Wednesday evening. This will only make you nervous and reduce your confidence. Obviously such discussions cannot affect your grade. Remember that you are as competent as other candidates and were well-prepared for the exam.

11. As soon as you complete the exam, we would like you to e-mail, fax, or write to us with your comments on our books and software. We are particularly interested in which topics need to be added or expanded. We are NOT asking about specific CIA questions. Rather, we are asking for feedback on our books and software. Use the last two pages in each Gleim book to send us your comments. This approach is approved by The IIA.

22

GLEIM's
CIA Test Prep Software

- After completing each study unit, create customized tests with questions not appearing in the book.

- Each software part includes hundreds of additional questions and detailed explanations, not found in the book.

- Improve your chances by testing yourself in an interactive environment with past CIA exam questions.

- Another powerful tool in the GLEIM Knowledge Transfer System.

ORDER NOW!

$49⁹⁵

per part

GLEIM
KNOWLEDGE
TRANSFER
SYSTEMS.

www.gleim.com/cia
(800) 87-**GLEIM**

Ensure Your Success!

STUDY UNIT ONE
STRUCTURAL ANALYSIS AND STRATEGIES

(12 pages of outline)

This study unit commences with an overview of the strategic management process, including development of a grand strategy, planning, implementation, and control. The next two subunits address Porter's model for analyzing the structure of industries and competition. This model is based on five competitive forces and four generic competitive strategies. The final subunit considers an alternative model of competitive strategies that, like Porter's, has a marketing perspective.

1.1 STRATEGIC MANAGEMENT

1. Strategic management has a **long-term planning horizon**. Thus, a strategic orientation is traditionally associated with senior management. However, this orientation should pervade the organization because it encourages farsightedness by all employees. Strategic thinking also helps employees understand and implement managerial decisions. Moreover, it is consistent with the modern trend toward cooperation and teamwork and away from authoritarian managerial styles.

2. Strategic management is a process that includes

   a. Development of a **grand strategy** that describes how the organization's mission is to be achieved. This strategy is based on a **situational analysis** that considers organizational strengths and weaknesses (a capability profile) and their interactions with environmental opportunities and threats. Such an evaluation is also called a **SWOT analysis**.

      1) Strengths and weaknesses (the **internal environment**) are usually identified by considering the firm's capabilities and resources. What the firm does particularly well or has in greater abundance are known as **core competencies**.

         a) Core competencies are the source of competitive advantages that in turn are the basis for an overall strategy.

      2) Opportunities and threats (the **external environment**) are identified by considering **macroenvironment factors** (economic, demographic, political, legal, social, cultural, and technical) and **microenvironment factors** (suppliers, customers, distributors, competitors, and other competitive factors in the industry).

      3) For example, speed in reacting to environmental changes, introducing new products, etc., is an important competitive advantage. To achieve it, the organization may have to reengineer its processes.

b. **Strategic planning** to formulate specific and measurable objectives, plans, policies, and budgets. Thus, strategic planning involves **portfolio management** of the organization's businesses, determining the strength of each business with respect to the potential of markets and the position of businesses in their markets, and creating a strategy for each business.

1) At the highest level, a firm's strategic planning function involves formulating its **mission** (ultimate firm purposes and directions), determining its **strategic business units (SBUs)**, allocating resources to SBUs, planning to start new businesses, and downsizing or divesting old businesses.

   a) A mission statement should address reasonably limited **objectives**, define the firm's major **policies and values**, and state the firm's primary **competitive scopes** (e.g., industries, products and services, applications, core competencies, market segments, degree of vertical integration, and geographic markets).

   b) Businesses should be defined in market terms, that is, in terms of needs and customer groups. Moreover, a distinction should be made between a **target market definition** and a **strategic market definition**. For example, a target market for a railroad might be freight hauling, but a strategic market might be transportation of any goods and people.

   c) A business also may be defined with respect to customer groups and their needs and the technology required to satisfy those needs.

   d) A large firm has multiple businesses. Thus, the concept of the **strategic business unit** is useful for strategic planning by large firms. An SBU is a business (or a group) for which separate planning is possible. An SBU also has its own competitors and a manager who engages in strategic planning and is responsible for the major determinants of profit.

c. **Implementation**. Strategic plans must be filtered down the organizational structure through development of plans at each lower level. This process is most likely to succeed if the structure is compatible with strategic planning, personnel have the necessary abilities, the organizational culture is favorable or can be changed, and controls exist to facilitate implementation.

d. **Control**. Strategic controls should be established to monitor progress, isolate problems, identify invalid assumptions, and take prompt corrective action.

1) As plans are executed at each organizational level, control measurements are made to determine whether objectives have been achieved. Thus, objectives flow down the organizational hierarchy, and control measures flow up.

2) One category of strategic control measures relates to external effectiveness.

   a) At the business-unit level, these measures concern performance in the marketplace (market share, etc.).

   b) At the business-operating-system level, these measures concern customer satisfaction and flexibility.

   c) At the departmental or work-center level, these measures concern quality and delivery.

3) A second category of strategic control measures relates to internal efficiency.

   a) At the business-unit level, these measures concern financial results.

   b) At the business-operating-system level, these measures concern flexibility (both an external effectiveness and internal efficiency issue).

   c) At the departmental or work-center level, these measures concern cycle time (time to change raw materials into a finished product) and waste.

3. Strategic management is dependent on **forecasts** of outcomes of events, their timing, and their future values.

4. Strategic management is facilitated when managers think synergistically. **Synergy** occurs when the combination of formerly separate elements has a greater effect than the sum of their individual effects. The following are types of synergy observed in business:

   a. **Market synergy** arises when products or services have positive complementary effects. Shopping malls reflect this type of synergy.

   b. **Cost synergy** results in cost reduction. It manifests itself in many ways, for example, in recycling of by-products or in the design, production, marketing, and sales of a line of products by the same enterprise.

   c. **Technological synergy** is the transfer of technology among applications. For example, technology developed for military purposes often has civilian uses.

   d. **Management synergy** also entails knowledge transfer. For example, a firm may hire a manager with skills that it lacks.

5. An **operations strategy** formulates a long-term plan for using enterprise resources to reach strategic objectives. The following are five operations strategies:

   a. A **cost** strategy is successful when the enterprise is the low-cost producer. However, the product (e.g., a commodity) tends to be undifferentiated in these cases, the market is often very large, and the competition tends to be intense because of the possibility of high-volume sales.

   b. A **quality** strategy involves competition based on product quality or process quality. Product quality relates to design, for example, the difference between a luxury car and a subcompact car. Process quality concerns the degree of freedom from defects.

   c. A **delivery** strategy may permit an enterprise to charge a higher price when the product is consistently delivered rapidly and on time. An example firm is UPS.

   d. A **flexibility** strategy entails offering many different products. This strategy also may reflect an ability to shift rapidly from one product line to another. An example firm is a publisher that can write, edit, print, and distribute a book within days to exploit the public's short-term interest in a sensational event.

   e. A **service** strategy seeks to gain a competitive advantage and maximize customer value by providing services, especially post-purchase services such as warranties on automobiles and home appliances.

6. Stop and review! You have completed the outline for this subunit. Study multiple-choice questions 1 through 3 beginning on page 34.

1.2 STRUCTURAL ANALYSIS OF INDUSTRIES

1. **Michael E. Porter**, a leader in the field of strategic management, has developed a comprehensive model of the structure of industries and competition. One feature is his analysis of the **five competitive forces** that determine long-term profitability as measured by long-term return on investment. This analysis includes an evaluation of the underlying, basic economic and technical characteristics that determine the strength of each force and the attractiveness of the industry.

2.   **Rivalry** among existing firms will be intense when an industry contains many strong competitors. Price-cutting, large advertising budgets, and frequent introduction of new products are typical of intense competitive rivalry. The intensity of rivalry and the threat of entry vary with the following factors:

   a.   The stage of the **industry life cycle**, e.g., rapid growth, growth, maturity, decline, or rapid decline. Thus, growth is preferable to decline. In a declining or even a stable industry, a firm's growth must come from winning other firms' customers, thereby strengthening competition.

   b.   The degree of **product differentiation** and the **costs of switching** from one competitor's product to another. Less differentiation tends to heighten competition based on price, with price cutting leading to lower profits. On the other hand, high costs of switching suppliers weakens competition.

   c.   Whether **fixed costs** are high in relation to variable costs. High fixed costs indicate that rivalry will be intense. The greater the cost to generate a given amount of sales revenues, the greater the **investment intensity** and the greater the need to operate at or near capacity. Hence, price cutting to sustain demand is typical of such firms.

   d.   **Capacity expansion**. If it must be made in **large increments**, competition will be more intense. The need for large-scale expansion to achieve production efficiency may result in an excess of industry capacity over demand.

   e.   **Concentration and balance**, e.g., when no firm is dominant. If an industry has a few equal competitors, the situation tends to be unstable and the rivalry intense.

   f.   The extent of **exit barriers**. Low exit costs make an industry more attractive.

   g.   **Competitors' incentives** to remain in the industry. When incentives are low, competitors are less likely to incur the costs and risks of intense rivalry.

3.   **Threats of, and barriers to, entry.** The prospects of long-term profitability are contingent upon the industry's exit and entry barriers.

   a.   Factors that **increase the threat of entry** are the following:

      1)   **Economies of scale** (and learning curve effects) are not significant.
      2)   **Brand identity** of existing products is weak.
      3)   Costs of switching suppliers are low.
      4)   Existing firms do not enjoy the cost advantages of vertical integration.
      5)   Proprietary product differences are few.
      6)   Access to existing suppliers is not blocked, and distribution channels are willing to accept new products.
      7)   Capital requirements are low.
      8)   Existing firms are unlikely to retaliate against a new firm.
      9)   The government's policy is to encourage new entrants.

   b.   The most favorable industry condition is one in which entry barriers are high and exit barriers are low. The following grid reflects Porter's view of the relationship of **returns, entry barriers, and exit barriers**:

		Exit Barriers	
		Low	High
Entry Barriers:	Low	Low, stable returns	Low, risky returns
	High	High, stable returns	High, risky returns

      1)   When the threat of new entrants is minimal and exit is not difficult, returns are high, and risk is reduced in the event of poor performance.
      2)   Low entry barriers keep long-term profitability low because new firms can enter the industry, increasing competition and lowering prices and the market shares of existing firms.

3) **Exit barriers** are reasons for a firm to remain in an industry despite poor (or negative) profits. They include

a) Assets with a low residual value because of obsolescence or specialization.

b) Legal or ethical duties to stakeholders, such as employees, creditors, suppliers, or customers.

c) Governmental regulations.

d) Lack of favorable alternative investments.

e) Substantial vertical integration.

f) Emotional factors, such as history and tradition.

4. The **threat of substitutes** limits price increases and profit margins. The greater the threat, the less the attractiveness of the industry to potential entrants. **Substitutes** are types (not brands) of goods and services that have the same purposes, for example, plastic and metal or minivans and SUVs. Hence, a change in the price of one such product (service) causes a change in the demand for its substitutes.

a. The **price elasticity of demand** is a measure of the threat posed by substitutes. It is the ratio of the percentage change in the quantity of a product (service) demanded to the percentage change in the price causing the change in the quantity.

1) Demand is **elastic** when the ratio exceeds 1.0 (ignoring the minus sign that results because the price and demand changes are in opposite directions). If demand is elastic, the effect of a price change on a firm's **total revenue** will be in the opposite direction of the change.

a) If demand is **inelastic** (the ratio is less than 1.0), the price effect on total revenue is greater than the quantity effect. Thus, a firm could increase total revenue by raising its prices.

2) The better the substitutes for a product (service), the more likely that demand is elastic and the greater the threat of substitutes.

b. **Structural considerations** affecting the threat of substitutes are

1) Relative prices,

2) Costs of switching to a substitute, and

3) Customers' inclination to substitute.

5. As the **threat of buyers' bargaining power** increases, the appeal of an industry to potential entrants decreases. Buyers seek lower prices, better quality, and more services. Moreover, they use their purchasing power to obtain better terms, possibly through a bidding process. Thus, buyers affect competition.

a. **Buyers' bargaining power** varies with the following factors:

1) When purchasing power is **concentrated** in a few buyers, or when buyers are well organized, their bargaining power is greater. This effect is reinforced when sellers are in a capital-intensive industry.

2) High (low) **switching costs** decrease (increase) buyers' bargaining power.

3) The threat of **backward (upstream) vertical integration**, that is, the acquisition of a supply capacity, increases buyers' bargaining power.

4) Buyers are most likely to bargain aggressively when their profit margins are low and a supplier's product accounts for a substantial amount of their costs.

5) Buyers are in a stronger position when the supplier's product is **undifferentiated**.

6) The more important the supplier's product is to buyers, the less bargaining power they have.

    b.   The foregoing analysis applies whether buyers are end users or intermediaries (e.g., distributors).

    c.   A supplier may seek to limit buyers' power by choosing those with the least ability to bargain or switch to other suppliers. However, a preferable response is to make offers that are difficult to reject.

6.   As the **threat of suppliers' bargaining power** increases, the appeal of an industry to potential entrants decreases. Accordingly, suppliers affect competition through pricing and the manipulation of the quantity supplied.

    a.   **Suppliers' bargaining power** is greater when

        1)   Switching costs are substantial.

        2)   Prices of substitutes are high.

        3)   They can threaten forward (downstream) vertical integration.

        4)   They provide something that is a significant input to the value added by the buyer.

        5)   Their industry is concentrated, or they are organized.

    b.   Buyers' best responses are to develop favorable, mutually beneficial relationships with suppliers or to diversify their sources of supply.

7.   Stop and review! You have completed the outline for this subunit. Study multiple-choice questions 4 through 14 beginning on page 35.

1.3 GENERIC COMPETITIVE STRATEGIES

1.   Although profitability is substantially determined by the industry in which the firm functions, its relative position in the industry is also important. That position is influenced by its choice of competitive strategy.

2.   Michael E. Porter's **generic strategies model** is well known. It is based on the concept that each of a firm's **competitive advantages** ultimately may be categorized as either a **cost** advantage or a **differentiation** advantage.

    a.   The firm's advantages should be used within the firm's **competitive (target) scope** to achieve its objectives. This scope may be **broad** (e.g., industry wide) or **narrow** (e.g., a market segment).

3.   Using the variables of **competitive advantage** (cost and differentiation) and **competitive scope** (broad and narrow), Porter described four generic strategies to be applied by business units.

    a.   **Cost leadership** is the generic strategy favored by a firm that seeks competitive advantage through **lower costs**. This strategy has a **broad competitive scope**. Such a firm can earn higher profits than its competitors at the industry average price or charge a lower price to increase market share.

        1)   A firm may **acquire a cost advantage** over its competitors by

            a)   Vertical integration.

            b)   Exclusive access to low-cost materials.

            c)   Economies of scale or other production efficiencies resulting in low unit cost.

            d)   Outsourcing.

        2)   **Strengths of cost leaders.** The typical firm that follows a cost leadership strategy has low profit margins, a high volume of sales, and a substantial market share. Such a firm

            a)   Has efficient supply and distribution channels.

            b)   Is capable of large capital investment.

       c)   If it is a manufacturer, has strengths in product design and process engineering.

       d)   Closely supervises its labor force.

3)   The **risks** of this strategy include the possibility that advances in technology or successful imitation may allow other firms to erase the cost leader's advantage.

       a)   Furthermore, multiple firms following a strategy with a **narrow focus on cost** may achieve advantages in their market segments.

       b)   Still another risk is that the emphasis on cost may cause managers to overlook product and marketing changes. For example, the cost advantage must suffice to outweigh the differentiation advantages held by others.

4)   **Organization**. A cost leader is ordinarily highly structured to achieve close control of costs. Detailed reports are provided with great frequency, and benefits are tied to numerical goals.

b.   **Differentiation** is the generic strategy favored by a firm that seeks competitive advantage through providing a **unique product or service**. This strategy has a **broad competitive scope**. Such a firm may earn higher profits because consumers are willing to pay a price higher than that charged by competitors. However, that price difference must exceed the additional cost of the differentiated product or service.

1)   A successful differentiation strategy creates a buyer perception that few, if any, **substitutes** are available. Thus, the firm may have the additional advantage of being able to pass supplier **cost increases** to buyers.

       a)   Uniqueness may be based on, for example, massive promotion, excellence of design, superior service, technical leadership, or brand identification.

       b)   A differentiation strategy does not signify a disregard for cost control, but simply a greater emphasis on creating a perception of the uniqueness of the product or service.

2)   Typical **strengths** of successful broad-scope differentiators are

       a)   An effective R & D function.

       b)   Creative product development.

       c)   A strong marketing function that communicates (or helps to create) the uniqueness of the product or service that is perceived by the mass audience.

       d)   A reputation for quality or technical leadership.

       e)   A tradition reaching back for decades.

       f)   Effective coordination with suppliers and distributors.

       g)   An ability to apply the expertise of other enterprises.

3)   The **risks** of a differentiation strategy include the following:

       a)   The maturing of the industry produces successful imitation by competitors.

       b)   Consumer tastes evolve as they become more sophisticated buyers or as they have less need for the differentiating factor.

       c)   Multiple firms following a strategy with a narrow focus on differentiation can achieve advantages in their market segments.

       d)   The differentiating factor may no longer justify its premium price. Brand loyalty may erode as lower-cost competitors improve the quality and image of their products or services.

4) An **organization** adopting a differentiation strategy usually has close cooperation among its research, development, and marketing functions. Incentive compensation is often based on relatively subjective performance measures, and the firm must succeed in attracting highly skilled or creative individuals.

c. **Cost focus** in the generic strategy favored by a firm that seeks competitive advantage through **lower costs** but with a **narrow competitive scope** (e.g., a regional market or a specialized product line). The rationale for a cost-focus strategy is that the narrower market can be better served because the firm knows it well.

1) Firms that successfully adopt a cost-focus strategy achieve very strong **customer loyalty**, a disincentive to potential competitors.

2) The **strengths** of successful firms employing a cost-focus strategy are similar to those of broad-target firms.

3) The **risks** of a cost-focus strategy include the following:

a) A narrow focus means lower purchasing volume and therefore a weaker position relative to suppliers.

b) The cost (or differentiation) advantage of servicing a narrow target may be more than offset by the cost advantage achieved by broad-target competitors through economies of scale and other factors.

c) Even more narrowly focused competitors may serve their niches better.

d) A firm following a broad-target strategy may, by imitation or otherwise, change its product or service to compete more effectively in the narrower market.

e) The narrower market itself may change.

4) The **organizational attributes** of firms employing a cost-focus strategy are similar to those of broad-target firms.

d. **Focused differentiation** is the generic strategy favored by a firm that seeks competitive advantage through providing a **unique product or service** but with a **narrow competitive scope**, e.g., a regional market or a specialized product line.

1) The analysis of these firms is similar to that for cost-focus firms.

4. According to Porter, using a **combination of generic strategies** may leave the firm "**stuck in the middle**," i.e., unable to create or sustain a competitive advantage. The danger is that attempting to follow more than one generic strategy will prevent the firm from achieving a competitive advantage. Thus, pursuit of, for example, both cost leadership and differentiation may interfere with reaching either objective. Furthermore, even if the firm could succeed by following multiple generic strategies, the result might be an ambiguous public image.

a. In Porter's view, a firm that pursues multiple generic strategies may be more likely to succeed if it creates a separate **strategic business unit** to implement each strategy.

1) However, some writers disagree with Porter's advice not to pursue a combination of strategies. They argue that following a single strategy may not serve the needs of customers who want the best combination of product attributes, e.g., price, service, and quality.

b. A firm also may become **stuck in the middle** as a result of the changes that occur as the firm, its products or services, and the industry proceed through their **life cycles**.

1) For example, an appropriate and successful focus strategy may need to be changed to a cost leadership strategy as the firm matures.

5. **Porter's generic strategies** are responses to the **five competitive forces**.

    a. **Rivalry Among Existing Firms**

        1) **Cost leadership** permits a firm to compete by charging lower prices.
        2) **Differentiation** strengthens brand loyalty.
        3) **Focus strategies** provide superior attention to customer needs, whether for quality, price, or other product attributes.

    b. **Threats of, and Barriers to, Entry**

        1) **Cost leadership** permits a firm to reduce prices as a deterrent to potential entrants.
        2) **Differentiation** creates brand loyalty that a new entrant may not be able to overcome.
        3) **Focus strategies** develop core competencies in a narrow market that potential entrants may not be able to match.

    c. **Threat of Substitutes**

        1) **Cost leadership** may result in low prices that substitutes cannot match.
        2) **Differentiation** may create unique product (service) attributes not found in substitutes.
        3) **Focus strategies** are efforts to develop core competencies or unique product attributes that may protect against substitutes as well as potential entrants.

    d. **Buyers' Bargaining Power**

        1) **Cost leadership** may enable a firm to remain profitable while charging the lower prices required by strong buyers.
        2) **Differentiation** may reduce the leverage enjoyed by strong buyers because of the uniqueness of the product and the resulting lack of close substitutes.
        3) **Focus strategies** also may reduce buyers' ability to negotiate in a narrow market. Substitutes may not be able to compete on price, quality, etc.

    e. **Threat of Suppliers' Bargaining Power**

        1) **Cost leadership** provides protection from strong suppliers.
        2) **Differentiation** may permit a firm to increase its price in response to suppliers' price increases.
        3) **Focus strategies** must allow for the superior bargaining power of suppliers when sellers operate in a narrow, low-volume market. For example, focused differentiation may permit the firm to pass along suppliers' price increases.

6. Stop and review! You have completed the outline for this subunit. Study multiple-choice question 15 on page 38.

1.4 MARKET-BASED COMPETITIVE STRATEGIES

1. The dominant firm in a market pursues a **market-leader strategy**.

    a. The leader should attempt to **increase total demand** in the market because the market leader will gain the most. Demand will increase if the firm

        1) Attracts **new users**.

            a) A **market-penetration strategy** focuses on customers who might use the product or service.
            b) A **new-market segment strategy** pursues customers who have never used the product or service.
            c) A **geographical expansion strategy** targets users in previously unserved localities.

2)   Encourages **new uses** of the product or service.

3)   Promotes **increased use**, for example, by planned obsolescence.

b.   The leader must **defend market share** through offensive and defensive actions.

1)   Constant innovation to improve products and services, control costs, and increase distribution effectiveness is the basis for a good **offensive strategy**. The leader must continuously improve the value offered to customers.

2)   Kotler and Singh have identified six **defense strategies**.

a)   A **position defense** strengthens the firm's **brand power.**

b)   A **flank defense** creates outposts that protect the leader's position. For example, a firm might respond to a competitor's price attack on one of its major products by introducing new brands. One of these might be sold at the same price as the attacker's brand and a second at a lower price, in effect outflanking the attacker.

c)   A **preemptive defense** anticipates an attack, such as by targeting particular competitors before they can launch assaults, flooding the market with products for every segment and niche, or by sending **market signals** indicating ways in which the leader intends to anticipate attacks.

d)   A **counteroffensive defense** is a counterattack. For example, the leader may meet an attacker's price cuts in one market by slashing prices in another market that is more important to the attacker.

e)   A **mobile defense** may involve **market broadening**, a reorientation from a specific product to the underlying need. An example is the repositioning of oil companies as energy companies. An alternative is **market diversification**, an effect of conglomerate mergers of firms in wholly different industries.

f)   A **contraction defense** is planned contraction or strategic withdrawal. This defense involves concentrating resources in the areas of greatest strength rather than defending all of the firm's positions.

c.   The leader may attempt to obtain a **greater market share**. In general, a firm that increases its market share in its **served (target) market**, as opposed to the total market, will increase profits if it adopts an appropriate strategy.

1)   This strategy must avoid the risk of **antitrust** suits.

2)   The **economic cost** of the strategy must be acceptable. Beyond a certain **optimal market share**, profits may decline. The incremental market share may not provide economies of scale and experience, costs borne by the market leader (e.g., legal and lobbying costs) may increase, and customers may want more than one supplier.

3)   The leader must adopt the right **marketing mix** (the marketing methods used). For example, market share should be earned, not bought by lower profit margins.

a)   Most firms that gain market share ordinarily are leaders in introducing new products, product quality, and marketing outlays.

2.   Trailing (runner-up) firms may choose a **market challenger strategy**.

a.   A challenger must determine its strategic objective (such as leadership or a larger market share) and specific targets.

1)   The challenger may attack the leader, for example, by across-the-board innovation or by better serving the market.

2)   The attack may be directed at firms of similar size that are not serving the market, e.g., by failing to introduce new products or by overpricing.

3) The challenger may seek to grow by absorbing small firms.

b. Kotler suggests five general **attack strategies** by a challenger.

1) A **frontal attack** directly pits the firm's products, prices, promotions, and methods of distribution against the target's.

a) An example of a modified frontal attack is price cutting, a strategy that may succeed if there is no retaliation and the perception is that the product's quality equals that of the target.

2) A **flank attack** may be directed at a geographic or segmental weakness of the target (an underserved market) or an unmet need (such as the desire for more healthful fast food).

a) A flank attack succeeds when market segments shift. The result is a gap in need fulfillment that the attacker can convert into a strong position in a profitable segment.

3) An **encirclement attack** is used by a challenger with an advantage in resources. It is an assault on multiple marketing fronts.

4) The **bypass attack** directs the assault against markets other than those where the competitive target is strong. It may involve diversification of products or geographic markets. It may also entail developing next-generation technology so as to move the competition to an arena where the challenger is in a stronger position.

5) **Guerilla warfare** consists of numerous small attacks designed to reduce the strength of the target, e.g., by ad campaigns, carefully chosen price decreases, and lawsuits. Such warfare ordinarily must be followed by a different (and stronger) type of attack if the challenge is to succeed.

c. The market challenger also must devise combinations of strategies that are more specific than the general strategies.

1) **Price discounting** tends to succeed if buyers are price sensitive, the product and service are similar to the market leaders, and the discounts are not matched.

2) **Lower-price goods** of average quality may substantially outsell higher quality goods if the price is much lower.

3) **Prestige goods** are high-quality items sold at a high price.

4) **Product proliferation** is a strategy based on better product variety.

5) Other specific strategies emphasize improved service, development of a new distribution channel, increased marketing expenditures, or manufacturing efficiencies.

3. **Market-follower strategies** are adopted by firms that do not wish to challenge the leader.

a. These firms may adhere to the view that **product imitation** may be preferable to **product innovation**. Because the innovator has already incurred the expenses of bringing the new product to market, the imitator that introduces a similar product may be profitable without being the leader.

b. Some industries are characterized by **conscious parallelism**. These industries (e.g., fertilizers and chemicals) tend to have high fixed costs and little product and image differentiation. Market followers tend to imitate the leader because competing for a greater market share provokes painful retaliation.

   c.   A market follower requires a strategy to maintain its share of current and new customers, fend off challengers, protect its advantages (e.g., service or location), lower its costs, and improve the quality of its products and services.

      1)   A **counterfeiter** operates illegally by selling copies on the black market.

      2)   A **cloner** sells cheap variations of a product with sufficient differentiation to avoid liability for counterfeiting.

      3)   An **imitator** sells a product that is significantly differentiated, e.g., with respect to price, promotion, location, and packaging.

      4)   An **adapter** improves products and may operate in different markets or evolve into a market challenger.

   d.   Market followers ordinarily have lower percentage returns than market leaders.

4.   **Market-nicher strategies** are followed by small or mid-size firms that compete in small (niche) markets that may be overlooked by large firms.

   a.   Successful niche marketers often have higher rates of return than firms in large markets. They often sell high quality products at premium prices and have low manufacturing costs.

      1)   These firms excel in need satisfaction because they know their markets well.

   b.   Successful niche marketers have high profit margins. By contrast, mass marketers sell in high volume.

   c.   Niche marketers must create, expand, and protect their niches. The risk is that a niche may evaporate or be entered by a large firm.

   d.   The essence of niche marketing is **specialization**. However, success often depends on **multiple niching**. Creating new niches diversifies risk and increases the firms's probability of survival.

5.   Choosing and implementing an effective market-based competitive strategy should never be at the expense of maintaining a **customer orientation**. Firms with this orientation are more likely to be alert to customer-related needs, threats, and opportunities than firms that are competitor oriented.

6.   Stop and review! You have completed the outline for this subunit. Study multiple-choice questions 16 and 17 beginning on page 38.

QUESTIONS

1.1 Strategic Management

1. Which of the following is not an example of synergy?

   A.   A shopping mall with several businesses providing different products and performing different services.

   B.   A store provides warranties on automobile parts in order to maximize customer value.

   C.   A manufacturing company hires a new manager with technological experience lacking in the company.

   D.   Military humvees are converted into sports utility vehicles for sale to civilians.

Answer (B) is correct. *(Publisher)*
   REQUIRED: The arrangement that does not exhibit synergy.
   DISCUSSION: Synergy occurs when the combination of formerly separate elements has a greater effect than the sum of their individual effects. It is unclear here whether the store is a car dealership or a parts shop. Therefore, this is seen more as an operational service strategy that seeks to gain a competitive advantage and maximize customer value by providing services such as warranties, rather than market synergy. Market synergy arises when products or services have positive complementary effects (i.e. a parts shop and a service warranty on parts).
   Answer (A) is incorrect because it is an example of market synergy. Answer (C) is incorrect because it is an example of management synergy. Answer (D) is incorrect because it is an example of technological synergy.

2. Which of the following best describes a market synergy?

- A. Technology transfer from one product to another.
- B. Bundling of products distributed through the same channels.
- C. Production of multiple products at one facility.
- D. Use of complementary management skills to achieve entry into a new market.

Answer (B) is correct. *(IIA, adapted)*
REQUIRED: The item representative of market synergy.
DISCUSSION: Market synergy arises when products or services have positive complementary effects. Shopping malls reflect this type of synergy. Also, bundling of products, distribution through the same distribution channels, and usage of the same sales force are other examples of market synergies.
Answer (A) is incorrect because technology transfer constitutes technology synergy. Answer (C) is incorrect because the production of multiple products at one production facility is an example of cost synergy. Answer (D) is incorrect because using complementary management skills is an example of management synergy.

3. Which of the following is a market-oriented definition of a business versus a product-oriented definition of a business?

- A. We make air conditions and furnaces.
- B. We supply energy.
- C. We produce movies.
- D. We sell men's shirts and pants.

Answer (B) is correct. *(IIA, adapted)*
REQUIRED: The market-oriented business definition.
DISCUSSION: Businesses should be defined in market terms, that is, in terms of needs and customer groups. Moreover, a distinction should be made between a target market definition and a strategic market definition. For example, a target market for a railroad might be freight hauling, but a strategic market might be transportation of any goods and people. Accordingly, stating that a business supplies energy is a market-oriented definition as opposed to the product-oriented definition. Moreover, it is also a strategic market definition.
Answer (A) is incorrect because air conditioners and furnaces are products, not customer needs. Answer (C) is incorrect because movies are products, not a customer need (e.g., entertainment). Answer (D) is incorrect because shirts and pants are products, not an underlying need.

1.2 Structural Analysis of Industries

4. Which of the following factors is not typical of an industry that faces intense competitive rivalry?

- A. Price-cutting.
- B. Large advertising budgets.
- C. Frequent introduction of new products.
- D. Inelastic demand.

Answer (D) is correct. *(Publisher)*
REQUIRED: The situation not typical in an industry facing intense rivalry.
DISCUSSION: Rivalry among existing firms will be intense when an industry has many strong competitors. Inelastic demand exists when quantity purchased is not greatly affected by price changes. Thus, price cutting does not increase sales for the industry, and is therefore atypical of an intensely competitive industry.
Answer (A) is incorrect because price-cutting is typical for a firm in an industry with intense competitive rivalry. Answer (B) is incorrect because a large advertising budget is typical for a firm in an industry with intense competitive rivalry. Answer (C) is incorrect because frequent introduction of new products is typical for a firm in an industry with intense competitive rivalry.

5. Intensity of rivalry among firms in an industry increases when there is

I. A low degree of product differentiation
II. Low consumer switching costs

- A. I only.
- B. II only.
- C. Both I and II.
- D. Neither I nor II.

Answer (C) is correct. *(Publisher)*
REQUIRED: The situation(s), if any, that increase the intensity of rivalry in an industry.
DISCUSSION: The degree of product differentiation and the costs of switching from one competitor's product to another increase the intensity of rivalry and competition in an industry. Less differentiation tends to heighten competition based on price, with price cutting leading to lower profits. Low costs of switching products also increase competition.
Answer (A) is incorrect because low consumer switching costs also increase rivalry. Answer (B) is incorrect because a low degree of product differentiation also increases rivalry. Answer (D) is incorrect because both low consumer switching costs and a low degree of product differentiation increase rivalry.

6. The prospect for the long-term profitability of an existing firm is greater when

A. The firm operates in an industry with a steep learning curve in its production process.

B. The costs of switching suppliers is low.

C. New entrants are encouraged by government policy.

D. Distribution channels are willing to accept new products.

Answer (A) is correct. *(Publisher)*
REQUIRED: The circumstance improving the prospect of long-term profitability.
DISCUSSION: The prospects of long-term profitability are contingent upon the industry's exit and entry barriers. The entry of new firms in a market decreases the prospect for long-term profitability. When a firm operates in an industry that has a steep learning curve, it is more difficult for new firms to enter the market. Thus, the prospects of long-term profitability are greater for an existing firm.
Answer (B) is incorrect because, when the costs of switching suppliers is low, the threat of entry by new firms is increased. Answer (C) is incorrect because, when new entrants are encouraged by government policy, the threat of entry by new firms is increased. Answer (D) is incorrect because, when distribution channels are willing to accept new products, the threat of entry by new firms is increased.

7. Structural considerations affecting the threat of substitutes include all of the following except

A. Relative prices.

B. Brand identity.

C. Cost of switching to substitutes.

D. Customers' inclination to use a substitute.

Answer (B) is correct. *(Publisher)*
REQUIRED: The structural consideration that does not affect the threat of substitutes.
DISCUSSION: Substitutes are types of goods and services that serve the same purpose. All products that can replace a good or service should be considered substitutes. For example, bicycles and cars are substitutes for public transportation. Structural considerations determine the effect substitutes have on one another. However, because substitutes are types (not brands) of goods and services that have the same purposes, brand identity is not a structural consideration affecting the threat of substitutes.
Answer (A) is incorrect because relative price is a structural consideration affecting the threat of substitutes. Answer (C) is incorrect because the cost of switching is a structural consideration affecting the threat of substitutes. Answer (D) is incorrect because a customers' inclination to use a substitute is a structural consideration affecting the threat of substitutes.

8. Logistics Corp. is performing research to determine the feasibility of entering the truck rental industry. The decision to enter the market is most likely to be deterred if

A. Buyer switching costs are high.

B. Buyers view the product as differentiated.

C. The market is dominated by a small consortium of buyers.

D. Buyers enjoy large profit margins.

Answer (C) is correct. *(Publisher)*
REQUIRED: The deterrent to market entry.
DISCUSSION: When purchasing power is concentrated in a few buyers, or when buyers are well organized, their bargaining power is greater. This effect is reinforced when sellers are in a capital-intensive industry, such as trucking.
Answer (A) is incorrect because high switching costs decrease buyers' bargaining power. Answer (B) is incorrect because buyers are in a weaker position when the supplier's product is differentiated. Answer (D) is incorrect because buyers are most likely to bargain aggressively when their profit margins are low, especially if the supplier's product accounts for a substantial amount of their costs.

9. Which industry factor does not contribute to competitive rivalry?

A. Price-cutting, large advertising budgets, and frequent introduction of new products.

B. A firm's growth must come from winning other firms' customers.

C. High costs of switching suppliers.

D. High fixed costs.

Answer (C) is correct. *(Publisher)*
REQUIRED: The industry factor that does not contribute to competitive rivalry.
DISCUSSION: If it is expensive to switch suppliers, customers will be less motivated to respond to competitor advances.
Answer (A) is incorrect because price-cutting, large advertising budgets, and frequent introduction of new products are characteristic of intense competitive rivalry. Answer (B) is incorrect because winning other firms' customers is essential to a firm's growth and strengthens competition. Answer (D) is incorrect because, the greater the fixed cost to generate a given amount of sales revenues, the greater the incentive to compete on price, service, etc., to maintain and increase sales levels.

10. Which condition does not increase the threat of new competitor entry into the industry?

A. Strong brand identity.

B. Existing firms do not enjoy the cost advantages of vertical integration.

C. Few proprietary product differences.

D. Low capital requirements.

Answer (A) is correct. *(Publisher)*
REQUIRED: The condition that decreases the threat of new competition.
DISCUSSION: Strong brand identity decreases the threat that new competitors will enter an industry. New competitors have difficulty because potential customers are loyal to established firms in the industry.
Answer (B) is incorrect because cost advantages of existing firms make entry difficult for new competitors. Answer (C) is incorrect because proprietary product differences make entry more difficult. Answer (D) is incorrect because high capital requirements make entry more difficult.

11. The concurrent action of basic competitive forces as defined by Porter's model determines

A. The long-term profitability and the competitive intensity of the industry.

B. The entrance barriers that potential players must face to get into the industry.

C. The rivalry inside the industry.

D. The strategy that a firm should follow to achieve its objectives.

Answer (A) is correct. *(IIA, adapted)*
REQUIRED: The industry factors determined by the basic competitive forces in Porter's model.
DISCUSSION: Michael E. Porter, a leader in the field of strategic management, has developed a comprehensive model of the structure of industries and competition. One feature is his analysis of the five competitive forces that determine long-term profitability measured by long-term return on investment. This analysis determines the attractiveness of an industry.
Answer (B) is incorrect because entry barriers constitute one of the five forces that define competitive intensity and potential profitability. Answer (C) is incorrect because rivalry is one of the five forces that define competitive intensity and potential profitability. Answer (D) is incorrect because the analysis of the effects of the five forces is only the first step in the development of the definition of a strategy.

12. Which factor most likely encourages entry into an existing market?

A. Governmental subsidies for new investors.

B. High product differentiation, principally produced by trademarks.

C. Knowledge of the industry, with high investments in development.

D. Low fixed exit costs.

Answer (A) is correct. *(IIA, adapted)*
REQUIRED: Factors likely to encourage market entry.
DISCUSSION: Subsidies for new firms lower entry barriers. Thus, new firms may enter the industry and intensify competition. Government policy also may affect competition via regulations that encourage or discourage substitutes or affect costs, that govern competitive behavior, or that limit growth. Government also may be a buyer or supplier.
Answer (B) is incorrect because product differentiation is an entry barrier. New firms may be incapable of offering a comparable product, so the industry's profitability is protected. Answer (C) is incorrect because the learning period of the industry is an asset that new firms must acquire. This cost in some cases becomes extremely high and may discourage new firms from entering the industry. Answer (D) is incorrect because low fixed exit costs facilitate exit when firms decide to leave the industry. They mildly encourage entry because they make investment less risky. Exit costs would not particularly encourage entry of new firms.

13. Which of the following is a favorable condition for a firm competing in a profitable, expanding industry?

A. The firm does not have a strong customer base.

B. A few suppliers who can restrict supply.

C. Competitors find it difficult to acquire the firm's customers.

D. The firm has high costs relative to other firms in the industry.

Answer (C) is correct. *(IIA, adapted)*
REQUIRED: The favorable conditions for a firm competing in a profitable, expanding industry.
DISCUSSION: A firm that has successfully differentiated its products through developing a desirable image, better services, cost leadership, the features of the product, or other means is in a favorable competitive position. Competitors find it difficult to acquire the firm's customers, for example, by price cutting. The reason is that the firm's products are perceived to have few substitutes, and brand loyalty is high. Furthermore, barriers to entry are favorable to the firm. These barriers deter competitors from entering the market. Existing firms can increase market share and emphasize cutting costs and increasing value.
Answer (A) is incorrect because, without brand loyalty, growth or even survival is difficult. Answer (B) is incorrect because these few suppliers can bid up the prices at the expense of the firm. Answer (D) is incorrect because the firm will not be able to reap economies of scale and lower their production costs.

14. Which basic force(s) drive(s) industry competition and the ultimate profit potential of the industry?

I.   Threat of new entrants.
II. Bargaining power of suppliers.
III. Favorable access to raw materials and labor.
IV. Product differentiation.

   A. I only.

   B. I and II only.

   C. III and IV.

   D. I, II, III, and IV.

Answer (B) is correct. (IIA, adapted)
REQUIRED: The factor(s) driving industry competition and the profit potential in the industry.
DISCUSSION: Threat of new entrants and bargaining power of suppliers are among the five basic forces that drive industry competition and the ultimate profit potential in the industry. This potential is measured in terms of long-term return on invested capital. The other three forces are rivalry among existing firms, threat of substitutes, and threat of buyers' bargaining power.
Answer (A) is incorrect because the bargaining power of suppliers also drives industry competition and ultimate profit potential. Answer (C) is incorrect because labor unrest and material shortages are short run factors that may affect competition and profitability but are not among the five basic forces driving competition. Answer (D) is incorrect because product differentiation is a competitive strategy, not one of the five basic forces.

1.3 Generic Competitive Strategies

15. A manufacturing company produces plastic utensils for a particular segment at the lowest possible cost. The company is pursuing a cost

   A. Leadership strategy.

   B. Focus strategy.

   C. Differentiation strategy.

   D. Containment strategy.

Answer (B) is correct. (IIA, adapted)
REQUIRED: The cost strategy pursued by the manufacturing company.
DISCUSSION: A cost focus strategy aims at cost leadership in a particular segment, such as a regional market or a specialty product line. The rationale for a focus strategy is that the narrower market can be better served.
Answer (A) is incorrect because a cost leader is the lowest cost producer in the industry as a whole. Answer (C) is incorrect because cost differentiation aims at providing a product at different costs in different market segments. Answer (D) is incorrect because cost containment aims at controlling costs related to a particular product/market but not necessarily producing at the lowest possible cost.

1.4 Market-Based Competitive Strategies

16. A runner-up firm in a market may choose a market-challenger strategy. Which general attack strategy adopted by a market challenger is directed at a gap in customer need fulfillment?

   A. Guerilla warfare.

   B. Bypass attack.

   C. Frontal attack.

   D. Flank attack.

Answer (D) is correct. (Publisher)
REQUIRED: The general attack strategy adopted by a market challenger to exploit a need-fulfillment gap.
DISCUSSION: A flank attack may be directed at a geographic or segmental weakness of the target (an underserved market) or an unmet need (such as the desire for more healthful fast food). A flank attack succeeds when market segments shift. The result is a gap in need fulfillment that the attacker can convert into a strong position in a profitable segment.
Answer (A) is incorrect because guerilla warfare consists of numerous small attacks designed to reduce the strength of the target, e.g., by ad campaigns, carefully chosen price decreases, and lawsuits. Such warfare ordinarily must be followed by a different (and stronger) type of attack if the challenge is to succeed. Answer (B) is incorrect because the bypass attack directs the assault against markets other than those where the competitive target is strong. It may involve diversification of products or geographic markets. It may also entail developing next-generation technology so as to move the competition to an arena where the challenger is in a stronger position. Answer (C) is incorrect because a frontal attack directly pits the firm's products, prices, promotions, and methods of distribution against the target's.

17. The dominant firm in a market pursues a market-leader strategy. This strategy may involve

   A. Holding the market stable to avoid attracting new competitors.

   B. A flank defense to strengthen the firm's brand.

   C. Sending market signals as a mobile defense.

   D. Innovations as an offensive strategy.

Answer (D) is correct. *(Publisher)*
   REQUIRED: The action taken by a market leader.
   DISCUSSION: Constant innovation to improve products and services, control costs, and increase distribution effectiveness is the basis for a good offensive strategy. The leader must continuously improve the value offered to customers.
   Answer (A) is incorrect because, as the firm most likely to gain, the leader should attempt to increase total demand, for example, by attracting new users, encouraging new uses, and promoting increased use. Answer (B) is incorrect because a position defense strengthens the firm's brand power. Answer (C) is incorrect because a preemptive defense anticipates an attack, such as by targeting particular competitors before they can launch assaults, flooding the market with products for every segment and niche, or by sending market signals indicating ways in which the leader intends to anticipate attacks.

Use Gleim's **CIA Test Prep** for interactive testing with over 2,000 additional multiple-choice questions!

STUDY UNIT TWO
INDUSTRY AND MARKET ANALYSIS

(16 pages of outline)

This study unit begins with the broad subject of competitive intelligence, including customer value analysis. Without accurate intelligence, effective competitive analysis is not feasible. The next subunit addresses methods for determining how diversification should be used to achieve the firm's objectives. These methods include the growth-share matrix and General Electric's multifactor portfolio matrix. The third subunit covers the evaluation of competitors' indirect market communications, or market signals. The following subunit extends the analysis of an industry as a whole in Study Unit 1. It considers strategic groups in an industry and competitor analysis. The final subunit builds on the concepts of competitive forces and the product life cycle. The outline shows how evolutionary processes move an industry from its initial structure to its potential structure.

2.1 COMPETITIVE INTELLIGENCE

1. Leonard Fuld defines competitor intelligence as "highly specific and timely information about a corporation" (Competitor Intelligence, Wiley, 1985).

2. A **competitive intelligence system** should be established to identify competitor strategies, monitor their new-product introductions, analyze markets for the firm's own new-product introductions and acquisitions, obtain information about nonpublic firms, evaluate competitor R & D activity, learn about competitors' senior executives, and perform other necessary information gathering tasks.

   a. **Setting up the system** involves determining the kinds of information to be collected, sources, and persons responsible.

   b. **Data collection** should be a continuous process. Field sources include the firm's own sales agents, distributors, and suppliers. Trade associations and market researchers are also useful sources.

      1) Other information may come from competitors' customers and suppliers and observation of competitors.

      2) An enormous amount of published information is publicly available from various services (Dun & Bradstreet, Moody's, Standard & Poor's, and others), newspapers, general business periodicals, special business publications, government data, reports submitted to government regulators, and much more.

      3) The Internet, e.g., websites of competitors, trade associations, and governments, is a fertile source of business intelligence. Patent applications, help wanted ads, licensing agreements, and many other activities may be revealing.

   c. **Data analysis** entails validating and processing the intelligence gathered.

   d. **Information dissemination** to decision makers is the final step in the establishment of an intelligence system. The system should be able to transmit timely information and to respond to queries.

3. Competitive intelligence permits a firm to create effective competitive strategies that target the appropriate competitors.

    a. A starting point is **customer value analysis (CVA)**. The premise of CVA is that customers choose from competitors' products or services the brands that provide the greatest customer value. It equals **customer benefits** (product, service, personnel, and image benefits) minus **customer costs** (price and the costs of acquisition, use, maintenance, ownership, and disposal). The **steps in a CVA** are to

        1) Determine what customers value.

        2) Assign quantitative amounts to the elements of customer value and have customers rank their relative significance.

        3) Evaluate how well the firm and its competitors perform relative to each element.

        4) Focus on performance with respect to each element compared with an important competitor in a given market segment. For example, if the firm outperforms the competitor in every way, it may be able to raise its price.

        5) Repeat the foregoing steps as circumstances change.

4. Using the results of the CVA, the firm may then target a given **class of competitors**.

    a. Targeting **weak competitors** may be the cheapest way to gain market share. However, targeting **strong competitors** also may be appropriate because this strategy forces the firm to improve. Moreover, a strong competitor may have an exploitable weakness.

    b. **Close competitors**, that is, firms that are similar, are the usual targets. Nevertheless, **distant competitors** are also threats. For example, any beverage may be a competitor of soft drink makers.

    c. **Bad competitors** should be targeted rather than **good competitors**. The former disturb the competitive equilibrium, e.g., by excessive expansion of capacity or overly risky behavior. The latter make sound business decisions that promote the long-term health of the industry, e.g., about prices, entry into new segments, and pursuit of market share.

5. Stop and review! You have completed the outline for this subunit. Study multiple-choice questions 1 through 3 beginning on page 56.

2.2 PORTFOLIO TECHNIQUES OF COMPETITIVE ANALYSIS

1. Firms use **diversification** to grow, improve profitability, and manage risk.

    a. **Vertical integration** occurs upstream (backward) by acquiring suppliers or downstream (forward) by acquiring wholesalers and retailers.

    b. **Horizontal integration** is the acquisition of competitors.

    c. **Concentric diversification** results from developing or acquiring related businesses that do not have products, services, or customers in common with current businesses, but that offer **internal synergies**, e.g., through common use of brands, R & D, plant facilities, or marketing expertise.

    d. **Horizontal diversification** is the acquisition of businesses making products unrelated to current offerings but that might be demanded by the firm's current customers.

    e. **Conglomerate diversification** is the acquisition of wholly unrelated businesses. The objectives of such an acquisition are financial, not operational, because of the absence of common products, customers, facilities, expertise, or other synergies.

2. A large firm may be viewed as a portfolio of investments in the form of strategic business units (SBUs). Hence, **techniques of portfolio analysis** have been developed to aid management in making decisions about resource allocation, new business startups and acquisitions, downsizing, and divestitures.

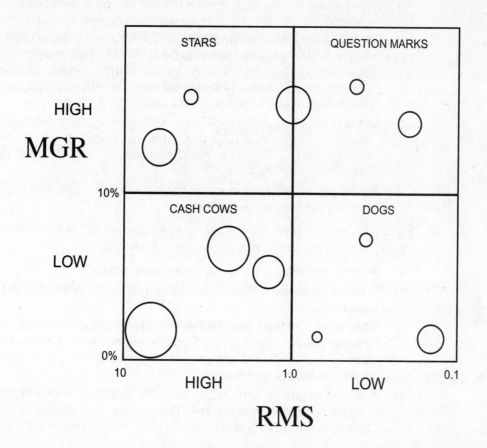

a. One of the two portfolio models most frequently used for competitive analysis was
    created by the **Boston Consulting Group (BCG)**. This model, the **growth-share
    matrix**, has two variables. The **market growth rate** (MGR) is on the vertical axis,
    and the firm's **relative market share** (RMS) is on the horizontal axis.

    1) The annual MGR is stated in constant units of the currency used in the
        measurement. It reflects the maturity and attractiveness of the market and the
        relative need for cash to finance expansion.

        a) An MGR of **10% or more** is generally regarded as high.

    2) The RMS reflects the SBU's competitive position in the market segment. It
        equals the SBU's absolute market share divided by that of its leading
        competitor.

        a) An RMS of **1.0 or more** signifies that the SBU has a strong competitive
            position.

    3) The growth-share matrix has four quadrants. The firm's SBUs are commonly
        represented in their appropriate quadrants by circles. The size of a circle is
        directly proportional to the SBU's sales volume.

        a) **Dogs** (low RMS, low MGR) are weak competitors in low-growth markets.
            Their net cash flow (plus/minus) is modest.

        b) **Question marks** (low RMS, high MGR) are weak competitors in
            high-growth markets. They need large amounts of cash not only to
            finance growth and keep pace with the market but also to increase RMS,
            but do poorly in cash generation. If RMS increases significantly, a
            question mark may become a star. If not, it becomes a dog.

    c)   **Cash cows** (high RMS, low MGR) are strong competitors and cash generators. An SBU that is a cash cow ordinarily enjoys high profit margins and economies of scale. Financing for expansion is not needed, so the SBU's excess cash can be used for investments in other SBUs. However, marketing and R & D expenditures should not necessarily be slashed excessively. Maximizing net cash inflow might precipitate a premature decline from cash cow to dog.

    d)   **Stars** (high RMS, high MGR) are strong competitors in high growth markets. Such an SBU is profitable, but needs large amounts of cash for expansion, R & D, and to meet competitors' attacks. Net cash flow (plus/minus) is modest.

    e)   A portfolio of SBUs should not have too many dogs and question marks or too few cash cows and stars.

4)   Each SBU should have objectives, a strategy should be formulated to achieve those objectives, and a budget should be allocated.

    a)   A **hold strategy** is used for strong cash cows.

    b)   A **build strategy** is necessary for a question mark with the potential to be a star.

    c)   A **harvest strategy** maximizes short-term net cash inflow. Harvesting means zero-budgeting R & D, reducing marketing costs, not replacing facilities, etc. This strategy is used for weak cash cows and possibly question marks and dogs.

    d)   A **divest strategy** is normally used for question marks and dogs that reduce the firm's profitability. The proceeds of sale or liquidation are then invested more favorably.

        i)   A harvest strategy may undermine a future divestiture by decreasing the fair value of the SBU.

5)   The **life cycle of a successful SBU** is reflected by its movement within the growth-share matrix. The progression is from question mark to star, cash cow, and dog. Accordingly, a firm should consider an SBU's current status and its probable progression when formulating a strategy.

6)   A serious **mistake** is not to tailor objectives (e.g., rates of return or growth) to the circumstances of each SBU.

    a)   Cash cows should not be underfunded. The risk is premature decline. However, overfunding cash cows means less investment in SBUs with greater growth prospects.

    b)   A large investment in a dog with little likelihood of a turnaround is also a typical mistake.

    c)   A firm also should not have too many question marks. Results are excess risk and underfunded SBUs.

b.   The other most frequently used (and more detailed) portfolio model for competitive analysis was developed by **General Electric**. Shell, McKinsey and Company, and Arthur D. Little have also developed portfolio models. The GE model is a multifactor portfolio matrix with two variables. **Business strength or competitive position** (BUS) is on one axis, and **market attractiveness** (MAT) is on the other.

	ZONE 1	ZONE 1	ZONE 2
STRONG			
	ZONE 1	ZONE 2	ZONE 3
MEDIUM			
	ZONE 2	ZONE 3	ZONE 3
WEAK			
	HIGH	MEDIUM	LOW

BUS

MAT

1) BUS is classified as strong, medium, or weak, and MAT is classified as high, medium, or low. Thus, the matrix in this model is 3 × 3 and has **nine cells**.

2) SBUs are shown in the matrix as **circles** (omitted from the diagram above). Circle size is directly proportional to the size of the related market, with a shaded portion in the circle that represents the SBU's market share.

3) To **measure BUS and MAT**, the firm must isolate the multiple factors affecting each, quantify them, and create an index. Factors will vary with each business. The measurements will provide the values on the axes of the matrix.

    a) Typical **BUS factors** are the SBU's size, market share, growth rate, customer loyalty, profit margins, distribution network, technology position, and marketing skills.

    b) Typical **MAT factors** are market size, growth rate, competitive intensity, price levels, profit margins, technology requirements, and degree of regulation.

    c) One approach to the computation of BUS or MAT is to rate each factor on a scale from 1 to 5 (the highest ranking), weight each ranking by the factor's relative significance (0 to 1.0 each for a total of 1.0), and add the results.

4) The nine cells in the matrix may be classified into **three zones**.

    a) **Zone 1 (strong BUS and high MAT, medium BUS and high MAT, strong BUS and medium MAT).** The SBUs in the three cells in the upper left corner have strong overall attractiveness. Investment and growth are indicated.

    b) **Zone 2 (strong BUS and low MAT, medium BUS and MAT, weak BUS and high MAT).** The SBUs in the three cells on the diagonal from the lower left to the upper right of the matrix have medium overall attractiveness. Selective investment and management for earnings are indicated.

    c) **Zone 3 (medium BUS and low MAT, weak BUS and medium MAT, weak BUS and low MAT).** The SBUs in the three cells in the lower right corner have low overall attractiveness. A harvest or divest strategy is indicated.

5) Forecasts for the next 3-5 years should be made to estimate each SBU's position given the current strategy, the stage of the product life cycle, competitor actions, and other events. These forecasts may be indicated by arrows drawn on the matrix.

  c. Portfolio models should be used with care. They may over-emphasize entry into high growth markets and increasing market share and may lead to inadequate attention to current SBUs.

    1) Moreover, because averages and weights are used in many models, they are subject to manipulation. Also, businesses in the same cell may have very different ratings for the multiple analytical factors.

    2) Strategies for SBUs in the middle positions may be hard to determine.

    3) Synergies among SBUs are ignored. Thus, divesting a low-rated SBU may be a mistake because of benefits it offers to other SBUs, such as a vital core competency.

3. Stop and review! You have completed the outline for this subunit. Study multiple-choice questions 4 through 7 on page 57.

2.3 MARKET SIGNALS

1. Michael E. Porter defines a **market signal** as "any action by a competitor that provides a direct or indirect indication of its intentions, motives, goals, or internal situation." These indirect market communications are helpful in **competitive analysis** and the design of **competitive strategies**.

  a. The firm must be aware, however, that signals may be sent to warn or mislead rather than to indicate a genuine intention to execute a planned action. Accordingly, the firm must understand competitors so as not to ignore, or be deceived by, their signals.

2. The major types of market signals may be classified as **true signals** or **bluffs**. The types of signals vary with the nature of the competitor's signaling behavior and the media used.

  a. **Prior announcements of moves**, that is, to do or not do something, have value as signals in part because an announced move need not actually occur. A competitive battle may be fought entirely with announcements, thus avoiding the negative effects of, for example, a price war.

    1) Prior announcements of moves may

      a) Preempt competition, such as by inducing customers to wait for the introduction of the firm's new product.

b) Threaten action, for example, by declaring that the firm will substantially undercut a competitor's intended price reduction.

c) Test competitor sentiment, as when the firm floats a proposal for a new customer warranty program. The reaction then determines whether the firm continues with, modifies, or withdraws the program.

d) Express pleasure or displeasure with a competitor's action. Announcement of a move has greater force than simply communicating pleasure or displeasure in an interview or speech.

e) Minimize the provocation caused by a future strategic adjustment, e.g., a price cut. Such a move may be a genuine attempt to realign prices with changes in costs, not an aggressive grab for market share. However, the move may also be an attempt to mislead.

f) Avoid costly simultaneous moves, such as capacity expansions that might result in overcapacity.

g) Be intended to influence the financial community. The firm may wish to raise its share price or improve its reputation, but such announcements may be misread by competitors.

h) Be a means of ending internal debate.

2) A firm must examine the competitor's possible motives for a prior announcement to determine whether it is preemptive or conciliatory. The latter is more likely if preemptive benefits are few, the announced action is less damaging than it could have been, or the announcement is made far in advance.

3) A **bluff** is an announcement of an action not intended to be executed. For example, a firm may issue a threat in an effort to prevent a competitor action even though following through would not be beneficial.

a) Bluffs may cause loss of credibility for future announcements.

4) Prior announcements may be in many media. Examples are interviews with journalists, news conferences, meetings with securities analysts, updates of website content, and regulatory disclosures.

a) The medium and the breadth of the audience chosen have signaling value. Thus, an announcement that is widely disseminated may represent a greater commitment.

b. **Announcements of results or actions after the fact**, especially of information difficult to obtain or that is surprising, ensure competitor awareness. Misleading announcements of this kind may be intended to preempt action or affirm commitment.

1) However, a firm's discovery that an announcement is misleading (or wrong) may be a source of useful inferences about the competitor's purposes and strengths.

c. **Competitors' public discussions of the industry** address such matters as cost increases and forecasts of demand, prices, and capacity. These discussions may signal, perhaps unintentionally, the firm's assumptions underlying its strategy. Thus, they may be sincere efforts to clarify motives, prevent conflict, and promote cooperation.

1) The discussions also may be ways for the firm to seek an advantage, for example, to portray competitors' prices as excessive. Hence, other firms must evaluate the firm's true intent by determining whether and how the firm's position may be improved by its interpretation of industry conditions.

2) Direct commentary on a competitor's moves likewise may be subject to different interpretations of its motives.

d.   **Competitors' discussions of their own moves** may be in public or private forums (e.g., with customers or suppliers) with the intent of signaling to competitors. One motive is to persuade others that a move is appropriate and not provocative. A second motive is preemption. A third motive is to express commitment.

e.   **Competitors' tactics** may have signaling content if they differ from the feasible alternative conduct. A(n) conciliatory (aggressive) signal is conveyed by a move within the range of options that is the least (most) harmful to competitors.

f.   The **manner of initially implementing a strategic change** may signal aggressive intent or a cooperative attitude, or it may be a bluff. For example, initial price cutting on a competitor's key products rather than in secondary markets, introducing a new product targeted to a competitor's most important customers, or undertaking a move at an unusual time during the year may signal aggressive if not punitive intent.

g.   A firm's **divergence from prior strategic objectives** suggests that other firms should be alert to profound changes in its objectives and assumptions.

h.   A firm's **divergence from industry precedent**, e.g., discounting of never-before-discounted items, implies aggressive intent.

i.   The **cross-parry** is a response to a competitor's move in one area with a move in another. For example, firm X, which is well entrenched in region A, may move to compete with firm Y in its stronghold in region B. Firm Y's cross-parry is to enter the market in region A.

   1)   A cross-parry is an indirect response by the defending firm that potentially avoids destructive conflict in the newly penetrated market. However, it also signals the possibility of retaliation, especially if it occurs in one of the initiating firm's key markets. For example, price cutting as a cross-parry may be very effective against a firm with a large share of the market where the parry is made. This firm has more to lose in a price war in that market. Consequently, maintenance of a presence in a cross market deters the large-share firm from attacking elsewhere.

j.   Introduction of a **fighting brand** by a firm threatened or potentially threatened by a competitor is a tactic similar to the cross-parry. The brand may threaten or deter the rival, or it may bear the burden of competition. Thus, a competitor's product that is gaining market share could be countered by introduction of a very similar product in the competitor's key markets.

k.   A **private antitrust suit**, which can be dismissed by the plaintiff at any time, may simply indicate displeasure without incurring the risks of a more serious signal, e.g., a price cut. Suits also may be harassing or delaying tactics.

   1)   A suit by a large firm against a small firm is a way to punish the defendant regardless of the outcome. The legal costs of the small firm may be high, and the suit may prove a distraction over a long period.

3.   One aspect of competitor analysis is the study of the relationship between a firm's signals and later moves or other events. This study may reveal unconscious signals (what poker players call "tells") that help to interpret and react to the firm's actions.

   a.   The danger is that the past may not be prologue. Consequently, an effective competitor analysis should discover any economic and organizational factors that might cause a firm to behave in a manner inconsistent with its prior patterns.

4.   Stop and review! You have completed the outline for this subunit. Study multiple-choice questions 8 and 9 on page 59.

2.4 STRUCTURAL ANALYSIS WITHIN AN INDUSTRY

1. An **industry** consists of firms selling products or services that are substitutes.

   a. One way to describe an industry considers the number of sellers and the extent of differentiation of products and services, an approach used in microeconomics.

      1) A **monopoly** consists of a single seller of a product or service in an area, such as a utility. A monopoly may be regulated so as to compel better service and a lower price.

      2) An **oligopoly** consists of a few large firms. If products are standardized, competition may be based solely on price. If products are partially differentiated, each firm may attempt to lead the industry regarding a given attribute, e.g., price, quality, service, or features.

      3) In **monopolistic competition**, an industry has numerous sellers who offer differentiated products and services.

      4) In **pure competition**, differentiation is absent, and the same prices are charged by all sellers.

   b. Another way to characterize an industry is by reference to its **entry, exit, or mobility barriers**.

      1) **Entry barriers** may be high or low. Industries vary as to the necessary capital investment, economies of scale, intellectual property, materials, locations, distribution channels, and other factors.

      2) **Exit barriers** may consist of legal and moral obligations, regulatory requirements, lack of alternative investments, vertical integration, low residual value of assets, and tradition.

      3) **Mobility barriers** restrict movement within an industry's segments. They are similar to industry entry barriers.

      4) In general, high entry and mobility barriers and low exit barriers promote profitability.

   c. The **cost structure** of an industry affects its competitive strategy. For example, the physical plant and distribution costs of oil refineries are much greater than those of restaurants. Other industries may have especially high R & D costs (pharmaceutical industry) or marketing costs (the brewery industry).

   d. The degree of backward or forward **vertical integration** along the value chain varies with the industry. For example, a manufacturer that has acquired suppliers is **backward integrated**, and a movie producer that has acquired a chain of theaters is **forward integrated**.

      1) Integration may reduce costs, and a firm may be able to choose where in the value chain to earn profits and pay the lowest taxes.

      2) However, an integrated firm may be inflexible and face high exit barriers.

   e. The extent of **globalization** varies with the industry. For example, restaurants are in a local industry, and manufacturers of large passenger aircraft are in a global industry, one that requires large R & D outlays and economies of scale.

2. To analyze competition within an industry, its **strategic groups** should be evaluated. Hence, a potential entrant into an industry must consider which strategic group to target. The choice of strategic group and a firm's ability to implement its competitive strategy will determine profitability.

a. A strategic group consists of firms in an industry that have adopted **similar competitive strategies**. The analysis of strategic groups addresses such issues as

1) Their composition, number, and size.
2) Mobility barriers, i.e., barriers to movement among groups. The ability to move depends on the firm's current strategic group and its targeted group.
3) The bargaining power of a group.
4) The degree of the threat of substitutes.
5) Intergroup competition.

    a) The level of competition primarily depends on

       i) **Market interdependence**, i.e., the extent to which groups pursue the same customers. The greater the interdependence, the stronger the competition.

       ii) Product differentiation or substitutability. Lower substitutability means less competition.

       iii) Number and size of groups. The greater the number and the more equal their size, the greater the competition.

b. The **dimensions of the competitive strategies** adopted by the firms in a strategic group include specialization, brand identification (e.g., within the distribution channels or with ultimate consumers), selection of channels, product or service quality, technical leadership, cost, service, price, degree of integration, degree of leverage, relationship with regulators, and relationship with the parent firm.

c. An **overall industry analysis** considers

1) The characteristics of the industry (growth, demand, technology, strength of suppliers and buyers, and other factors)
2) The industry's strategic groups in relation to the five competitive forces
3) How the firm compares with the competitors within the chosen strategic group, e.g., on the basis of its scale of operations, the intensity of group rivalry, and the differences in the ability of the group members to implement their strategies

d. A **strategic group analysis**

1) Determines what mobility barriers exist
2) Determines which groups are weak
3) Forecasts future group actions and trends
4) Predicts reaction patterns to events such as competitive attacks
5) Addresses the risks confronting the firms in the group. These risks include those that lower mobility barriers, those that arise from the investments needed to raise protective mobility barriers, and those resulting from entering a new strategic group
6) Helps the firm to make competitive choices, such as whether to move to another strategic group, improve the strategic group's structural position or the firm's relative position within the group, or to establish its own strategic group

3. **Analysis of competitors** begins with determining the firm's actual and potential competitors. Accordingly, a firm must consider which other firms attempt to satisfy the same **customer needs** (a market approach to competitive analysis). Moreover, a firm may be more threatened by new entrants or the evolution of technology (notably, the Internet) than by existing competition.

a. Each **competitor's characteristics** should be considered, e.g., revenues, profits, market share, financial position, and relations with its parent firm. Moreover, the SBU and product-market entry sales and market share are especially interesting. They are measures of the effectiveness of a competitor's strategy.

    b.   Each **competitor's objectives** also should be considered.

        1)   The organizational structure suggests the significance of given functions, where decisions are made, and the status of the competitor within a larger entity.

        2)   Tradeoffs may be made among financial and market position goals, in particular in the short run. For example, some firms emphasize short-run profits, but others may concentrate on market-share growth and long-run profits.

        3)   The competitor may believe itself to be the overall market leader or a leader in price or technology. An issue is what the competitor will do to remain in that position. The competitor's assumptions about its products, its position, and other firms in its strategic group may reveal probable objectives and possible blindspots.

        4)   The incentive and control systems of the competitor affect its ability to react to competitive pressures.

        5)   The experience, background, and attitudes of senior managers and directors may be clues to the competitor's objectives. Such factors may also be indicative of the nature of the corporate culture.

        6)   Various commitments (e.g., debt or joint ventures) may limit a competitor's flexibility.

        7)   Regulatory restraints, e.g., on price, may also limit a competitor's options.

        8)   Recent setbacks or successes are often predictors of future behavior.

        9)   The analysis of the parent of a competitor may provide many insights, for example, the reasons for the parent's entry into the competitor firm's business, its significance to the parent, the parent's use of generic strategies with other businesses it controls, the parent's corporate strategies, and the parent's results.

      10) The competitor's portfolio of businesses should be assessed to determine which are successful.

      11) A crucial question about a competitor's objectives is whether it plans to expand.

    c.   The **competitor's history** may be revealing. Its current and past performance, record in relevant markets, successful and unsuccessful actions, and past reactions to strategic moves by rivals are factors identifying past and current **competitor strategies**.

    d.   A competitor's **strengths and weaknesses** indicate whether and how it may be attacked.

        1)   Areas to be addressed are **innovation** (ability to develop new products and technologies), **manufacturing** (capacity, efficiency, workforce, access to materials, degree of integration), access to **financing** at low cost, **product** quality and availability, **marketing and selling** (brands, distribution, advertising, customer orientation, diversity of products, relations with retailers), **service**, **management** skills at all levels (quality of decisions, loyalty), the firm's **portfolio** (investments, degree of diversification), and the **organizational structure**.

        2)   A firm should identify a competitor's **core competencies** and assess its growth potential, ability to respond quickly to threats and opportunities, and staying power in the industry.

        3)   Evaluating a competitor's market position is necessary to judge how and whether to challenge it. According to Arthur D. Little, an organization of consultants, a competitor firm may hold one of the following **competitive positions**:

           a)   A **dominant firm** has a choice of strategies. It controls other firm's actions.

           b)   A **strong firm** can act independently and sustain its long-term status irrespective of the behavior of others.

        c)   A firm in a **favorable position** has strengths to use that give it a better-than-average chance to improve its status.

        d)   The performance of a firm in a **tenable position** justifies continuation of the business, but its chance for improvement is below average.

        e)   The performance of a firm in a **weak position** must change, or it must withdraw from the business.

        f)   A **nonviable firm** is a poor performer with no chance of improvement.

   4)   Arthur D. Little also suggests a three-factor model for assessing a competitor's current and future market share.

        a)   **Market share** is the share of the target market.

        b)   **Mind share** is the percentage of customers who name the firm as the first "that comes to mind" in the industry.

        c)   **Heart share** is the percentage of customers who name the firm as the one from which they "would prefer to buy."

        d)   A competitor that improves its mind share and heart share will ultimately increase its market share and profits.

   5)   Bruce Henderson has analyzed firms' **reaction patterns** when confronted with competitive attacks. A key to the analysis is **competitive equilibrium**.

        a)   Almost **identical competitors** have an unstable equilibrium because differentiation cannot be sustained. Price wars are common.

        b)   When one major factor is the **critical factor**, the equilibrium is unstable. A cost advantage obtained through economies of scale, technology gains, or experience allows a firm to gain market share.

        c)   Given **multiple critical factors** (quality, service, price, convenience, etc.), differentiation is more likely. More competitors can secure an advantage with respect to a critical factor in a market segment or niche.

        d)   The **number of competitors** is directly related to the number of critical factors.

        e)   When one competitor has approximately twice the **market share** of a second competitor, equilibrium exists. The costs of gaining market share outweigh the benefits to either party.

4.   A competitor analysis may be used to assess a firm's best strategy for countering a competitor.

   a.   The **offensive ability** of a firm to make a competitive move depends on

      1)   Its satisfaction with the status quo.
      2)   Its probable competitive moves.
      3)   The strength and seriousness of its competitive moves.

   b.   A firm's **defensive ability** to respond to a competitive move depends on

      1)   Its vulnerability to environmental threats.
      2)   The extent of the provocation, that is, the moves that cause a reaction.
      3)   The effectiveness of retaliation.

        a)   A competitor may be unable to respond quickly to some events.

5.   Stop and review! You have completed the outline for this subunit. Study multiple-choice questions 10 through 15 beginning on page 59.

2.5 INDUSTRY EVOLUTION

1. The **five competitive forces** within an industry or market identified by Porter are a basis for analyzing its structure. However, that structure and the firm's competitive strategies appropriate to it will evolve. Early recognition of change and prompt adjustment of strategies are essential to maintaining a competitive advantage. The costs of adjustments will be lower and their benefits greater the sooner they are made.

   a. The analysis of industry evolution should begin with how it affects each competitive force (see 1.2, Structural Analysis of Industries).

2. Another concept useful in analysis of industry evolution is the **product life cycle**. It has the following stages:

   a. **Precommercialization** (product development). The strategy in this stage is to innovate by conducting R & D, marketing research, and production tests. During product development, the firm has no sales, but it has high investment costs.

   b. The **introduction stage** is characterized by slow sales growth and lack of profits because of the high expenses of promotion and selective distribution to generate awareness of the product and encourage customers to try it. Thus, the per-customer cost is high. Competitors are few, basic versions of the product are produced, and higher-income customers (innovators) are usually targeted. Cost-plus prices are charged. They may initially be high to permit cost recovery when unit sales are low. The strategy is to infiltrate the market, plan for financing to cope with losses, build supplier relations, increase production and marketing efforts, and plan for competition.

   c. In the **growth stage**, sales and profits increase rapidly, cost per customer decreases, customers are early adopters, new competitors enter an expanding market, new product models and features are introduced, and promotion spending declines or remains stable. The firm enters new market segments and distribution channels and attempts to build brand loyalty and achieve the maximum share of the market. Thus, prices are set to penetrate the market, distribution channels are extended, and the mass market is targeted through advertising. The strategy is to advance by these means and by achieving economies of productive scale.

   d. In the **maturity stage**, sales peak but growth declines, competitors are most numerous but may begin to decline in number, and per-customer cost is low. Profits are high for large market-share firms. For others, profits may fall because of competitive price-cutting and increased R & D spending to develop improved versions of the product. The strategy is to defend market share and maximize profits through diversification of brands and models to enter new market segments, still more intensive distribution, cost cutting, advertising and promotions to encourage brand switching, and emphasizing customer service.

      1) Some writers identify a separate stage between growth and maturity. During the **shakeout period**, the overall growth rate falls, price cutting occurs, and weaker firms leave the market.

   e. During the **decline stage**, sales and profits drop as prices are cut, and some firms leave the market. Customers include late adopters (laggards), and per-customer cost is low. Weak products and unprofitable distribution media are eliminated, and advertising budgets are pared to the level needed to retain the most loyal customers. The strategy is to withdraw by reducing production, promotion, and inventory.

   f. **Criticisms** of the PLC concept are that some stages may be hard to distinguish, and their length may vary substantially among industries. Moreover, sales growth may not follow the pattern described above, partly because the firm's strategies affect growth. Still another consideration is that industry characteristics (degree of concentration, R & D costs, advertising costs, price competition, etc.) differ among industries. Accordingly, the PLC model is not by itself adequate to analyze industry evolution.

3. According to Porter, **evolutionary processes** are the "incentives or pressures" that cause structural change in an industry. These processes operate to move an industry from its **initial structure** (technology, entry and exit barriers, power of suppliers and buyers, product traits, beginning size constraints, etc.) to its **potential structure**. The nature of that structure and the speed at which it will be achieved are unlikely to be known. They depend on numerous factors that are hard to predict, such as innovations in technology and marketing, resources and skills of firms, favorable or unfavorable random events, and judgments about investments (e.g., which marketing or technology approaches to follow). The major evolutionary processes described by Porter are interacting and dynamic factors common to all industries, although their speed and direction vary.

    a. **Long-run changes in the industry growth rate** affect rivalry, entry, expansion, and supply. These changes occur because of changes in five external factors: demographic traits (such as consumer ages and income levels), trends in needs of buyers (caused by changes in regulation, tastes, lifestyles), relative positions of substitute products, relative positions of complementary products, and sales to new customers (market penetration).

        1) Product innovation, an internal factor, alters the industry's position regarding the external factors.

    b. **Changes in buyer segments served** occur when new segments are created (e.g., sale of computers to scientists, then to business, and finally to consumers), existing segments are subdivided, and old segments are no longer served. Consequently, industry structure evolves to meet the requirements of new customers.

    c. **Learning by buyers** who become more sophisticated and better informed causes a decrease in product differentiation. These buyers tend increasingly to demand similar product characteristics (quality, service, etc.). Thus, products may become more akin to commodities.

        1) This effect may be offset by changes in the product or its marketing and by attracting new, inexperienced customers.

    d. **Reduction of uncertainty** about such factors as the potential market size, resolution of technical problems, possible buyers, and marketing methods occurs as a result of experimentation. Successful strategies will be imitated and unsuccessful strategies will be discarded. Moreover, the reduction in risk will attract new and often larger competitors, especially if the potential market is large.

    e. **Proprietary knowledge** may become more available to potential competitors as the industry evolves. This diffusion may result from reverse engineering (a form of imitation) or another form of competitive intelligence (e.g., that obtained from suppliers, distributors, or customers), expiration of patents, purchase, migration of personnel to new firms, and spinoffs of operating segments.

        1) Thus, because barriers created by proprietary knowledge and specialized personnel tend to disappear, new competitors may emerge, and vertical integration becomes more likely. However, if further technological advances are feasible, economies of scale in R & D may create a protective barrier against new competition. The problem of diffusion may be met by creation of a substantial capacity to develop new proprietary knowledge.

    f. **Accumulation of experience** (the learning curve effect) permits unit costs of manufacturers to decrease. This lead may not be sustainable because of diffusion of proprietary knowledge. A one-time leader may then be at a disadvantage because it has incurred costs not borne by its competitor-imitators.

    g. **Expansion** of industry scale and firm scale permits a broader group of strategies to be implemented, with potentially greater economies of scale, capital needs, and desirability and feasibility of vertical integration. Also, suppliers and customers in an expanding industry will gain bargaining power. All these factors raise entry barriers.

1) An increase in the scale of the industry may attract new, large firms once the scale has reached a level that provides sufficient opportunity to justify the necessary investment.

2) Contraction of an industry has effects opposite to those of expansion.

h. **Changes in input costs** (of labor, materials, capital, communication, and transportation) most directly affect the cost and price of the product and the demand for it. These changes also affect the existence of economies of scale and may promote substitution of inputs, reorganization of production, and use of different marketing media. Distribution channels and geographic market boundaries also may be altered.

1) Exchange rate changes have similar effects on competition.

i. **Product innovation** may broaden markets or increase product differentiation. Furthermore, barriers are affected because innovation may involve high costs to market new products. It may also change marketing, distribution, and manufacturing methods and the related economies of scale.

1) Innovation cancels buyer experience and therefore changes purchasing behavior.

2) Product innovation may come from external sources and from suppliers and buyers.

j. **Marketing innovation** (e.g., in media, channels, or themes) may increase demand by differentiating the product, appealing to new buyers, or lowering costs. Indirect effects may include changes in economies of scale, e.g., as a result of changing to a wider-scope but more expensive medium.

k. **Process innovation** in manufacturing may affect the degree to which it is more or less capital intensive, economies of scale, vertical integration, the proportions of fixed and variable costs, and the gaining of experience, among other things.

1) Technology changes may occur outside the industry, so a firm must extend its awareness of such developments.

l. **Structural changes in suppliers' and customers' industries** affect their bargaining power. For example, as concentration of customers' industries increases, the tendency is for sellers' industries to become more concentrated so as to counter their greater power.

m. **Government policies** affect industry evolution by explicit regulation of entry, competitive practices, licensing, and pricing. Moreover, strong government regulation has profound effects on foreign trade and global competition.

1) Governments also regulate such matters as product quality and safety, worker safety and compensation, environmental quality, and investor protection. The social benefits must be weighed against the costs of regulation, which increase capital requirements and entry barriers and lessen competition.

n. **Entry** changes industry structure, especially when strong outsiders with special skills and large resources are the entrants. Entry occurs when outside firms believe that potential growth and profits justify the costs of entry.

o. **Exit** is motivated by diminished returns on investment. It is impeded by exit barriers. Exit improves the position of the remaining firms, but exit barriers weaken those firms.

p. Firms should consider how each evolutionary process may affect industry structure, their strategic position, and the ways of coping with the resulting change. Thus, firms must monitor the environment for the **strategic signals** relative to each evolutionary process. Moreover, firms must be aware that some processes (e.g., learning) may be operating without the occurrence of obvious external events.

4.   **Key Relationships**

a.   An industry is a **system**. Hence, a change in one subsystem (e.g., marketing) tends to trigger cascading changes elsewhere (e.g., in manufacturing methods leading to greater economies of scale and backward vertical integration that reduces suppliers' power).

b.   **Industry concentration and mobility barriers** are directly correlated. Thus, increasing barriers normally predict increasing concentration.

c.   **Low or decreasing barriers** generally signify an absence of concentration because unsuccessful exiting firms will likely be replaced.

d.   **Exit barriers** keep unsuccessful firms in the industry and therefore limit concentration to the detriment of successful firms.

e.   **Potential for above-average long-term profits** for the remaining firms depends on an industry's structure in its maturity stage, i.e., the presence of high mobility barriers.

f.   **Industry boundaries** change, for example, when refrigeration and genetic engineering allowed perishables to be transported long distances.

g.   Firms may **influence industry structure** by initiating changes (e.g., product, marketing, or process innovation) or responding to changes (e.g., by influencing regulation or licensing externally developed technology to control its diffusion).

5.   Stop and review! You have completed the outline for this subunit. Study multiple-choice questions 16 through 22 beginning on page 61.

QUESTIONS

2.1 Competitive Intelligence

1. Which of the following is not a step in the establishment of a competitive intelligence system?

    A. Data analysis.

    B. Data collection.

    C. Information dissemination.

    D. Classification of competitors.

Answer (D) is correct. *(Publisher)*
REQUIRED: The choice that is not a step in the setup of a competitive intelligence system.
DISCUSSION: A competitive intelligence system is established to identify competitor strategies, monitor their new-product introductions, analyze markets for the firm's own new-product introductions and acquisitions, obtain information about nonpublic firms, evaluate competitor R & D activity, learn about competitors' senior executives, and perform other necessary information gathering tasks. Its establishment consists of setting up the system, collecting data, analyzing the data, and disseminating the information. Classification of competitors, however, is not a step in this process. Competitors are classified, and targeted by a firm based on that classification, following the results of a customer value analysis (CVA).
Answer (A) is incorrect because the data analysis phase of the establishment of a competitive intelligence system follows the data collection phase. Answer (B) is incorrect because the data collection phase of the establishment of a competitive intelligence system follows the system setup phase. Answer (C) is incorrect because the information dissemination phase of the establishment of a competitive intelligence system follows the data analysis phase.

2. Which of the following are steps in a customer value analysis (CVA)?

I.   Determining what customers value.

II. Having customers rank the relative significance of the elements of customer value.

III. Evaluating how well the firm and its competitors perform relative to the elements of customer value.

IV. Focusing on performance with respect to each element of customer value.

A. I, III, and IV only.

B. I, II, and III only.

C. I, II, and IV only.

D. I, II, III, and IV.

Answer (D) is correct.   *(Publisher)*
REQUIRED: The steps that are part of a customer value analysis (CVA).
DISCUSSION: The steps in a CVA are to:

- Determine what customers value.
- Assign quantitative amounts to the elements of customer value and have customers rank their relative significance.
- Evaluate how well the firm and its competitors perform relative to each element.
- Focus on performance with respect to each element, vis-à-vis an important competitor in a given market segment.
- Repeat the foregoing steps as circumstances change.

3. Usually, the cheapest way to gain market share is by targeting what class of competitors?

A. Close competitors.

B. Distant competitors.

C. Weak competitors.

D. Bad competitors.

Answer (C) is correct.   *(Publisher)*
REQUIRED: The class of competitors to target in order to gain market share cheaply.
DISCUSSION: Using the results of a customer value analysis, a firm may target a given class of competitors in order to gain market share. Although there are various methods, targeting weak competitors is usually the cheapest way to gain market share because weak competitors generally do not offer much resistance.
Answer (A) is incorrect because close competitors are firms that are similar and are the usual targets, but it is not necessarily easy or cheap to take away market share from them. Answer (B) is incorrect because distant competitors are not direct competitors. They are indirect competitors that pose a "distant" threat. Thus, taking away market share from them may not necessarily guarantee your firm the entire share taken. Moreover, such a taking may be costly. Answer (D) is incorrect because bad competitors are ones that disturb the competitive equilibrium by engaging in such activities as excessive expansion of capacity or overly risky behavior. Although targeting a bad competitor would be a good move by the firm because it would be the healthiest thing for the industry, it may not necessarily be cheap to topple such an erratic foe.

2.2 Portfolio Techniques of Competitive Analysis

4. Lemon & Lime Corporation, an up-and-comer in the soda industry, acquires market leader, Fizz Corporation, in an effort to increase its market share. This diversification strategy is known as

A. Vertical integration.

B. Horizontal integration.

C. Concentric diversification.

D. Conglomerate diversification.

Answer (B) is correct.   *(Publisher)*
REQUIRED: The diversification strategy that involves the acquisition of a competitor.
DISCUSSION: Firms use diversification to grow, improve profitability, and manage risk. The diversification strategy involving the acquisition of competitors is known as horizontal integration.
Answer (A) is incorrect because vertical integration occurs when suppliers, wholesalers, or retailers are acquired.
Answer (C) is incorrect because concentric diversification results from developing or acquiring related businesses that do not have products, services, or customers in common with current businesses. Answer (D) is incorrect because conglomerate diversification is the acquisition of wholly unrelated businesses.

5. A strategic business unit (SBU) has a relative market share (RMS) of 2.0 and a market growth rate (MGR) of 9.5%. According to the portfolio model for competitive analysis created by the Boston Consulting Group, such an SBU is considered a

   A. Star.

   B. Question mark.

   C. Cash cow.

   D. Dog.

Answer (C) is correct. *(Publisher)*
REQUIRED: The appropriate quadrant of the growth-share matrix for an SBU that is a strong competitor in a low-growth market.
DISCUSSION: The annual MGR reflects the maturity and attractiveness of the market and the relative need for cash to finance expansion. An MGR of 10% or more is generally regarded as high. The RMS reflects an SBU's competitive position in the market segment. An RMS of 1.0 or more signifies that the SBU has a strong competitive position. Cash cows have high RMS and low MGR. They are strong competitors and cash generators in low-growth markets.
Answer (A) is incorrect because stars have both high RMS and high MGR because they are strong competitors in high growth markets. Answer (B) is incorrect because question marks are weak competitors in high-growth markets, meaning they have a low RMS and a high MGR. Answer (D) is incorrect because dogs have both low RMS and low MGR, meaning they are weak competitors in low-growth markets.

6. Which of the following is not a potential benefit of vertical integration?

   A. Improved logistics in the supply chain.

   B. Increased entry barriers to new competition.

   C. Access to new distribution channels.

   D. Economies of scale.

Answer (D) is correct. *(Publisher)*
REQUIRED: The statement that is not a benefit of vertical integration.
DISCUSSION: Economies of scale are derived from selling more of the same product and represent a benefit achieved through horizontal integration. This could result from internal growth or acquisition that expands the firm into a new geographic region.
Answer (A) is incorrect because improved coordination in the supply chain is a potential benefit of vertical integration. Answer (B) is incorrect because, if the firm could gain control of a limited resource, it would increase the entry barrier for potential customers. Answer (C) is incorrect because, if a firm expands through forward integration, it may gain access to previously inaccessible downstream distribution channels.

7. When firms compete in different geographical locations or have multiple product lines that do not necessarily overlap, the most effective way of responding to an aggressive move by a competitor without directly triggering destructive moves and countermoves is to

   A. Mislead the competitor into taking or not taking an action.

   B. Make a prior announcement of intended moves.

   C. Initiate a move in the market where the competitor is strong.

   D. Initiate direct aggressive moves.

Answer (C) is correct. *(IIA, adapted)*
REQUIRED: The most effective response to an aggressive move by a competitor.
DISCUSSION: Initiating a move in the market where the competitor is strong is a cross-parry. A cross-parry is an effective way to signal displeasure and raise the threat of more serious retribution without directly triggering destructive moves and countermoves.
Answer (A) is incorrect because misleading other firms into taking or not taking an action to benefit the firm is a bluff. A bluff is a form of market signal that is not intended to be carried out. Answer (B) is incorrect because a market signal by a competitor that provides a direct or indirect indication of its intentions, motives, goals, or internal situation is a means of communicating in the market place and an essential input in competitor analysis. A prior announcement may therefore incite countermoves. Answer (D) is incorrect because direct aggressive moves are aimed at reducing the performance of significant competitors or threaten their goals. They are likely to cause a countermove.

2.3 Market Signals

8. Prior announcements of moves have value as market signals in part because an announced move need not actually occur. Which of the following is true regarding the effects of prior announcements of moves on the market?

I. They may preempt competition.

II. They may express pleasure or displeasure with a competitor's action.

III. They may be a means of ending all external debate.

IV. They may test competitor sentiment.

    A. I, II, and III only.

    B. I, II, and IV only.

    C. II, III, and IV only.

    D. I, II, III, and IV.

Answer (B) is correct. *(Publisher)*
REQUIRED: The true statements about the effects of prior announcements of moves.
DISCUSSION: Among other things, prior announcements of moves may preempt competition, threaten action, test competitor sentiment, express pleasure or displeasure with a competitor's action, and act as a means of ending internal debate. Moreover, prior announcements of moves may be a means of ending some external debate (i.e., if the announcement was aimed at the financial community in order to answer questions about the firm's liquidity). However, all external debate would be impossible to end, even by means of prior announcements of moves.
Answer (A) is incorrect because all external debate would be impossible to end, even by means of prior announcements of moves. Moreover, prior announcements of moves may be used to test competitor sentiment regarding a new firm proposal. Answer (C) is incorrect because all external debate would be impossible to end, even by means of prior announcements of moves. Furthermore, prior announcements of moves may preempt competition, such as by inducing customers to wait for the introduction of the firm's new product. Answer (D) is incorrect because all external debate would be impossible to end, even by means of prior announcements of moves.

9. A firm discounts never-before-discounted items. This is an example of a firm's

    A. Divergence from industry precedent.

    B. Cross-parry.

    C. Divergence from prior strategic objectives.

    D. Bluff.

Answer (A) is correct. *(Publisher)*
REQUIRED: The nature of a firm's discounting of never-before-discounted items.
DISCUSSION: The discounting of never-before-discounted items implies aggressive intent. It is an example of a firm's divergence from industry precedent.
Answer (B) is incorrect because the cross-parry is a firm's response to a competitor's move in one area with a move in another. Answer (C) is incorrect because a firm's divergence from prior strategic objectives suggests that other firms should be alert to profound changes in its objectives and assumptions. Answer (D) is incorrect because a firm's bluff is an announcement of an action not intended to be executed. The discounts have already been executed; thus, they are considered true signals, not bluffs.

2.4 Structural Analysis Within an Industry

10. In which industry characterization is differentiation absent, and all sellers charge the same price?

    A. Monopoly.

    B. Monopolistic competition.

    C. Oligopoly.

    D. Pure competition.

Answer (D) is correct. *(Publisher)*
REQUIRED: The industry characterization where differentiation is absent and the same prices are charged by all sellers.
DISCUSSION: An industry consists of firms selling products or services that are substitutes. One way to describe an industry considers the number of sellers and the extent of differentiation of products and services. In pure competition, differentiation is absent and the same prices are charged by all sellers.
Answer (A) is incorrect because a monopoly consists of a single seller of a product or service in an area. Answer (B) is incorrect because, in monopolistic competition, an industry has numerous sellers who offer differentiated products and services. Answer (C) is incorrect because an oligopoly consists of a few large firms whose products may be standardized, in which case, competition may be based solely on price, or differentiated.

11. Which of the following statements is true with regard to a vertically integrated acquisition?

    A. A grocery store chain that purchases a dairy and begins to make milk-based products under its own brand is forward integrated.

    B. A movie producer that acquires a chain of theaters is backward integrated.

    C. A clothing manufacturer that acquires a chain of clothing stores is forward integrated.

    D. A soda maker that purchases its leading competitor is backward integrated.

Answer (C) is correct. *(Publisher)*
    REQUIRED: The true statement regarding a vertically integrated acquisition.
    DISCUSSION: Vertical integration occurs upstream (backward) by acquiring suppliers or downstream (forward) by acquiring wholesalers and retailers. An example of forward integration is a clothing manufacturer's acquisition of a chain of clothing stores, in which to sell its products.
    Answer (A) is incorrect because a grocery store chain that begins to make its own brand of dairy products is backward integrated. It acquired a supplier. Answer (B) is incorrect because a movie producer that acquires a chain of theaters is forward integrated. Answer (D) is incorrect because the acquisition of a leading competitor is horizontal integration.

12. A strategic group analysis does all but which of the following?

    A. Determines what mobility barriers exist.

    B. Forecasts future group actions and trends.

    C. Considers how the firm compares with the competitors within the chosen strategic group.

    D. Predicts reaction patterns to events such as competitive attacks.

Answer (C) is correct. *(Publisher)*
    REQUIRED: The false statement regarding a strategic group analysis.
    DISCUSSION: An overall industry analysis, not a strategic group analysis, considers how the firm compares with the competitors within the chosen strategic group, e.g., on the basis of its scale of operations, the intensity of group rivalry, and the differences in the ability of the group members to implement their strategies.
    Answer (A) is incorrect because it is a true statement regarding a strategic group analysis. Answer (B) is incorrect because it is a true statement regarding a strategic group analysis. Answer (D) is incorrect because it is a true statement regarding a strategic group analysis.

13. According to Arthur D. Little, a competitor firm that can act independently and sustain its long-term status irrespective of the behavior of others holds which of the following competitive positions?

    A. A dominant position.

    B. A strong position.

    C. A favorable position.

    D. A tenable position.

Answer (B) is correct. *(Publisher)*
    REQUIRED: The competitive position held by a competitor firm that can act independently and sustain its long-term status irrespective of the behavior of others.
    DISCUSSION: Evaluating a competitor's market position is necessary to judge how and whether to challenge it. As such, a firm that is in a strong competitive position can act independently and sustain its long-term status irrespective of the behavior of others.
    Answer (A) is incorrect because a competitor firm in a dominant position has a choice of strategies, and it controls other firm's actions. Answer (C) is incorrect because a firm in a favorable position has strengths to use that give it a better-than-average chance to improve its status. Answer (D) is incorrect because the performance of a firm in a tenable position justifies continuation of the business, but its chance for improvement is below average.

14. The retail petroleum industry consists of a few large firms that sell a standardized product. Which of the following best describes this industry?

    A. Monopoly.

    B. Oligopoly.

    C. Monopolistic competition.

    D. Pure competition.

Answer (B) is correct. *(Publisher)*
    REQUIRED: The type of industry that describes the retail petroleum industry.
    DISCUSSION: An oligopoly consists of a few large firms. If products are standardized, competition may be based solely on price. If products are partially differentiated, each firm may attempt to lead the industry regarding a given attribute, e.g., price, quality, service, or features. The retail petroleum industry is dominated by a small number of firms that control a vast majority of the market. Furthermore, this is an example of an industry that sells a standardized product where competition is based primarily on price.
    Answer (A) is incorrect because a monopoly consists of a single seller of a product or service in an area, such as a utility. Answer (C) is incorrect because monopolistic competition has numerous sellers that offer differentiated products and services. Answer (D) is incorrect because pure competition has numerous sellers that offer undifferentiated products.

15. UniCorp produces uniforms that it sells and rents to businesses. It recently acquired a textile mill that produces synthetic cloth. This acquisition is an example of

	List A	List B
A.	Horizontal integration	Forward integration
B.	Horizontal integration	Backward integration
C.	Vertical integration	Forward integration
D.	Vertical integration	Backward integration

Answer (D) is correct. *(Publisher)*
REQUIRED: The type of integration.
DISCUSSION: The degree of backward and forward vertical integration along the value chain varies with the industry. Unicorp acquired one of its suppliers, which is on a different level of the value chain. Thus, the combination involved vertical integration. Moreover, the acquisition of a supplier is characteristic of backward integration.
Answer (A) is incorrect because horizontal integration occurs between two firms on the same level of the value chain. Forward horizontal integration does not exist. Answer (B) is incorrect because horizontal integration occurs between two firms on the same level of the value chain. Backward horizontal integration does not exist. Answer (C) is incorrect because forward vertical integration occurs when a firm acquires one of its customers.

2.5 Industry Evolution

16. Of the major processes affecting the evolution of an industry, which one affects rivalry, entry, expansion, and supply?

A. Long-run changes in the industry growth rate.

B. Changes in input costs.

C. Structural changes in suppliers' and customers' industries.

D. Government policies.

Answer (A) is correct. *(Publisher)*
REQUIRED: The evolutionary process that affects rivalry, entry, expansion, and supply.
DISCUSSION: Long-run changes in the industry growth rate affect rivalry, entry, expansion, and supply. These changes occur because of changes in five external factors: demographic traits (such as consumer ages and income levels), trends in needs of buyers (caused by changes in regulation, tastes, lifestyles), relative positions of substitute and complementary products, sales to new customers (market penetration), and product innovation–an internal factor–alters the industry's position regarding the external factors.
Answer (B) is incorrect because changes in input costs most directly affect the cost and price of the product and the demand for it. Answer (C) is incorrect because structural changes in suppliers' and customers' industries affect their bargaining power. Answer (D) is incorrect because government policies affect industry evolution by explicit regulation of entry, competitive practices, licensing, and pricing.

17. During the growth stage of a product's life cycle:

A. The quality of products is poor.

B. New product models and features are introduced.

C. There is little difference between competing products.

D. The quality of the products becomes more variable and products are less differentiated.

Answer (B) is correct. *(IIA, adapted)*
REQUIRED: The true statement regarding the growth stage of a product's life cycle.
DISCUSSION: In the growth stage, sales and profits increase rapidly, cost per customer decreases, customers are early adopters, new competitors enter an expanding market, new product models and features are introduced, and promotion spending declines or remains stable. The firm enters new market segments and distribution channels and attempts to build brand loyalty and achieve the maximum share of the market. Thus, prices are set to penetrate the market, distribution channels are extended, and the mass market is targeted through advertising. The strategy is to advance by these means and by achieving economies of productive scale.
Answer (A) is incorrect because poor product quality is evident during the introduction stage of the product life cycle. Answer (C) is incorrect because competitors are most numerous and products become less differentiated during the maturity stage of the product life cycle. In this stage, imitators have entered the market and competitors have learned which technologies and features are successful. Answer (D) is incorrect because the quality of the products becomes more variable and products are less differentiated during the decline stage of the product life cycle.

18. In a product's life cycle, the first symptom of the decline stage is a decline in the

    A. Firm's inventory levels.

    B. Product's sales.

    C. Product's production cost.

    D. Product's prices.

Answer (B) is correct. *(IIA, adapted)*
    REQUIRED: The initial symptom of the decline stage in a product's life cycle.
    DISCUSSION: The sales of most product types and brands eventually decrease permanently. This decline may be slow or rapid. This first symptom of the decline stage of a product's life cycle triggers such other effects as price cutting, narrowing of the product line, and reduction in promotion budgets.
    Answer (A) is incorrect because a decline in the firm's purchases–resulting in a decline in the firm's inventory levels–is not the first symptom. It will occur only when production declines as a result of a drop in sales. Answer (C) is incorrect because a decline in production costs may be due to many factors, e.g., new plant technology or the increased availability of raw materials. Moreover, production costs may decrease in any stage of a product's life cycle and not specifically in the decline stage. Answer (D) is incorrect because a change in prices is a marketing decision. It is an action that may be taken in the maturity stage to compete in the market. Moreover, a decrease in the product's prices is a response to a permanent decline in sales.

19. At the introduction stage of an innovative product, the profit growth is normally slow due to

    A. Expensive sales promotion.

    B. High competition.

    C. A mass market.

    D. Available alternatives.

Answer (A) is correct. *(IIA, adapted)*
    REQUIRED: The reason for slow profit growth during the introduction stage of an innovative product.
    DISCUSSION: The introduction stage is characterized by slow sales growth and lack of profits because of the high expenses of promotion and selective distribution to generate awareness of the product and encourage customers to try it. Thus, the per-customer cost is high. Competitors are few, basic versions of the product are produced, and higher-income customers (innovators) are usually targeted. Cost-plus prices are charged. They may initially be high to permit cost recovery when unit sales are low. The strategy is to infiltrate the market, plan for financing to cope with losses, build supplier relations, increase production and marketing efforts, and plan for competition.
    Answer (B) is incorrect because, during the introduction stage, little competition exists. Competitors tend not to enter the market until they have greater assurance of profits. Answer (C) is incorrect because no mass market is available during the introduction stage. Answer (D) is incorrect because, by definition, not many alternatives are available during the introduction stage of an innovative product.

20. While auditing a marketing department, the internal auditor discovered that the product life cycle model was used to structure the marketing mix. Under such a philosophy, the price charged on a consistent basis for a specific product would probably be lowest during which life cycle stage?

    A. Introduction stage.

    B. Growth stage.

    C. Maturity stage.

    D. Decline stage.

Answer (C) is correct. *(IIA, adapted)*
    REQUIRED: The product life cycle stage during which the price charged on a consistent basis for a specific product is likely to be the lowest.
    DISCUSSION: During the maturity stage, competition is at its greatest and costs are at their lowest. Moreover, firms are engaged in competitive price-cutting measures, resulting in some of the lowest prices seen during a product's life cycle.
    Answer (A) is incorrect because, during the introduction stage, pre-unit costs of production are high and little competition exists. Hence, prices are at their highest. Answer (B) is incorrect because, during the growth stage, prices will be lower than during the introduction stage, but not as low as during the maturity stage. In the growth stage, costs are dropping and competitors are being added, but costs are not at their minimum and competitors are not at their maximum. Answer (D) is incorrect because, during the decline stage, price-cutting predominates as firms struggle to maintain sales volume in the face of a permanent decrease in demand. However, late in the decline stage, there are few competitors, so prices can be raised. In addition, pre-unit costs are on the rise because volume is declining, resulting in higher prices.

21. While auditing a marketing department, the internal auditor discovered that the product life cycle model was used to structure the marketing mix. Under such a philosophy, the opportunity for cost reductions would be greatest in which stage of the life cycle?

- A. Introduction stage.
- B. Growth stage.
- C. Maturity stage.
- D. Decline stage.

Answer (B) is correct. *(IIA, adapted)*
REQUIRED: The product life cycle stage during which the opportunity for cost reductions is greatest.
DISCUSSION: During the growth stage, the opportunity for cost reductions is at its maximum because production volume is increasing at a high rate. Thus, fixed costs are being spread over more units of production, and the benefits of the learning curve are being realized.
Answer (A) is incorrect because production volume is low during the introduction stage. Although costs are also high during this period, low volume reduces the opportunities for cost reductions. Answer (C) is incorrect because production volume changes little during the maturity stage. The result is less opportunity for cost reductions. Answer (D) is incorrect because costs per unit typically rise during the decline stage as production volume declines.

22. While auditing a marketing department, the internal auditor discovered that the product life cycle model was used to structure the marketing mix. The manager has asked the auditor for advice about increasing advertising of various products. During which stage of the life cycle would it be appropriate to advertise that the company's product is the lowest price and best quality of all competitors?

- A. Introduction stage.
- B. Growth stage.
- C. Maturity stage.
- D. Decline stage.

Answer (C) is correct. *(IIA, adapted)*
REQUIRED: The product life cycle stage during which it is appropriate to advertise that the firm's product is lower-priced and of better quality than competing products.
DISCUSSION: The maturity stage is the ideal time for advertising lower prices and superior quality because this is the period during a product's life when competition is greatest. Due to the availability of many alternatives or substitutes, a firm has reasons to set itself apart. Because price and quality are both concerns of customers during the maturity stage, it is ideal for the firm to differentiate its product by advertising low prices and higher quality.
Answer (A) is incorrect because few competitors exist during the introduction stage, and quality is sometimes poor. Answer (B) is incorrect because buyers are less concerned with price and quality during the growth stage than in the maturity stage. Answer (D) is incorrect because few competitors exist during the decline stage. Moreover, prices may rise late in the decline stage for the remaining firms as per-unit costs increase.

Use Gleim's ***CIA Test Prep*** for interactive testing with over 2,000 additional multiple-choice questions!

STUDY UNIT THREE
ENVIRONMENTS AND STRATEGIC DECISIONS

(24 pages of outline)

This study unit addresses the content specification outline's coverage of competitive strategies in three stages of the industry life cycle: fragmentation, emergence, and decline. It continues with an analysis of the unique characteristics of competition in global industries. The final three subunits use the analytical methods applied in the previous material to discuss certain strategic decisions.

3.1 FRAGMENTED INDUSTRIES

1. According to Michael E. Porter, individual firms in a **fragmented industry** have insignificant market shares and little influence on industry outcomes. Examples are retailing, agriculture, and creative enterprises. Thus, the situation approximates what economists call **pure competition**. Moreover, the industry has many small- or medium-sized firms with no market leader, products may or may not be significantly differentiated, and the technology may or may not be sophisticated.

2. Although industries may be fragmented for purely historical reasons, **economic causes for fragmentation** exist in other situations.

   a. **Low entry barriers** constitute a necessary but not a sufficient condition for fragmentation.

   b. **Economies of scale and a learning curve (experience) effect** usually do not exist in fragmented industries, for example, because operations are simple or labor-intensive.

   c. **High transportation costs** may outweigh economies of scale, for example, when customers must come to a service provider or vice versa.

   d. **High inventory carrying costs or sharp and unpredictable changes in sales volume** also may affect a large producer's advantage in economies of scale. A smaller firm's greater flexibility in adapting to demand changes may be a decisive competitive advantage.

   e. **Buyers or suppliers** may have such strong bargaining power that size offers little additional advantage in dealing with them.

   f. **Important diseconomies of scale** may favor fragmentation. For example, small, flexible firms have an advantage when the following needs are important: quick responses to style changes, the maintenance of low overhead, customization of a diverse product line to the special requirements of particular customers, substantial creative content in the product, individualized personal service, and local contacts and image.

g. **Diverse market needs** resulting from fragmentation of buyers' tastes may prevent the product standardization needed to prevent fragmentation.

h. High product differentiation based on an **image of exclusivity** also promotes fragmentation. Buyers may wish to have their own brands, and suppliers (e.g., performing artists) may wish to deal with firms that create a unique image.

i. **Exit barriers** keep firms in the industry and minimize concentration.

j. **Local regulations** that vary from community to community impede concentration even when other conditions are not present.

k. **Government antitrust laws** may prohibit significant concentration.

l. **Newness** is a reason for fragmentation. New firms may not yet have the resources and abilities to achieve concentration.

3. **Overcoming fragmentation** has significant strategic payoffs given that entry is not costly and competitors are weak. If the factor(s) preventing consolidation can be eliminated, industry structure will change.

   a. One method is to use technology to create **economies of scale** in production, marketing, distribution, service, etc. For example, television marketing has led to consolidation of many industries.

   b. **Standardizing diverse market needs** may result from introducing a new product, e.g., one that appeals to most buyers in a market. Another possibility is developing a new product design, e.g., to facilitate mass production of modularized components that may be assembled in different ways.

   c. **Isolating factors responsible for fragmentation** has been achieved in, for example, the fast food industry. The need to have numerous local operations under tight control and near customers has been isolated or neutralized by franchising to local owners. The franchisor provides national advertising, centralized purchasing, and other services, which result in economies of scale and industry consolidation. In effect, the service or production function is separated from the rest of the business.

      1) Another approach when diverse market needs exist is for a firm to use multiple brands to appeal to the tastes of different customers.

   d. **Acquisitions** may enable a firm to expand when competing with local firms might be difficult because of their contacts and image.

   e. **Early recognition of trends** may permit a firm to exploit them. For example, if the fragmentation is the result of industry newness, the firm may recognize the early signs of industry evolution. Early awareness of external factors, such as technology changes, that negate the causes of fragmentation also provide an opportunity for the firm.

   f. Industries may be **"stuck" in a fragmented state** for reasons other than underlying economic factors.

      1) Firms in the industry lack the resources, skills, awareness, or ambition to make the strategic moves needed for consolidation.

      2) Outside firms do not recognize the opportunity offered by an industry "stuck" in a fragmented state, for example, because it is new, small, or obscure.

4. **Coping with fragmentation** requires strategic positioning.

   a. When local management, close control, and personal service are critical success factors, **tightly managed decentralization** may be the appropriate strategy. Local operations remain small scale and autonomous, but managers are held to high standards with performance-based compensation.

   b. Developing **formula facilities** for use in numerous localities reduces construction and operating costs via standardization.

c. When products or services cannot be significantly differentiated, the best strategy may be to **increase the value added**, for example, by adding services or by forward integration.

d. **Specialization by product type or segment** is a focus strategy. This focus may enhance bargaining power with suppliers. It may also increase differentiation because of the perceived expertise and image. The downside is reduced growth opportunities.

e. Specialization by customer type (e.g., small customers or those who are not price sensitive), type of order (e.g., small orders for quick delivery or custom orders), or geographic areas are other focus strategies.

f. A cost strategy is to adopt a **bare bones, no frills** approach by emphasizing tight control of costs, low overhead, and low payroll.

g. **Backward integration** is the selective acquisition of suppliers to reduce costs.

5. The following are **strategic traps** in a fragmented industry:

a. Barring basic change in the industry's structure, **seeking dominance** is usually a losing strategy.

b. **Lack of strategic discipline** means straying from a focus on an appropriate strategy for a fragmented industry (again, assuming that the structure can be altered).

c. **Overcentralization** of the organizational structure is often a mistake. In the intense competition of a fragmented industry, quick response times, local contacts, personal service, and tight operating control are essential.

d. Assuming that competitors have similar costs and objectives is frequently wrong. Small, privately held firms in the industry may be content with much lower rates of return, use family members in the business, and avoid some costs of regulation.

e. **Overreaction to new products** results when investments are made to respond to new product demand that are inconsistent with the industry structure. As the product enters maturity, price competition from many rivals will become intense, and the profit margins needed to pay for the investments will vanish.

6. The following is Porter's framework for developing a **competitive strategy in a fragmented industry**:

a. Determine the industry's structure and the circumstances of major competitors.

b. Create a full list of the reasons for (causes of) fragmentation, if any, and their connection with the industry's economics.

c. Analyze whether the causes of fragmentation can be overcome by innovation, strategic changes, additional resources, or a new perspective.

1) Determine the effects of trends.

d. Assuming fragmentation can be overcome, evaluate whether the new structure will yield acceptable returns and what position the firm should occupy to earn those returns. This step requires repeating the first step above given the new structural equilibrium.

e. If fragmentation cannot be overcome, select the best strategy for operating in a fragmented environment.

7. Stop and review! You have completed the outline for this subunit. Study multiple-choice questions 1 through 4 beginning on page 88.

3.2 EMERGING INDUSTRIES

1. An **emerging industry** is new or newly formed and is small in size initially. It results from innovation, changes in cost structures, new customer needs, or another factor that creates an attractive opportunity for selling a product or service.

   a. The competitive issues in emerging industries are also confronted by established firms that must cope with the foregoing changes in environmental factors.

   b. Porter observes that no rules exist for an emerging industry, a condition that creates risks and opportunities.

2. **Structural Characteristics**

   a. An emerging industry is characterized by **technological uncertainty** regarding products and production methods.

   b. **Strategic uncertainty** arises because effective strategies have not yet been identified. Hence, firms are experimenting with product features, production methods, marketing approaches, etc. Moreover, competitive intelligence is necessarily poor because competitors have not been identified and industry sales and other data are not available.

   c. **Initial costs** are high, but the **learning curve** is steep. When the efficiency gains from experience combine with economies of scale achieved by growth, cost decreases are dramatic.

   d. **Embryonic companies** (firms newly formed and not new units of established entities) are most numerous in the emerging phase of industry evolution. Entry is not discouraged by the presence of economies of scale or strategic certainty. **Spin-offs** from existing firms also are common. Given the uncertainties described above and the lure of equity interests, employees have incentives to create new firms. Their motive is often to exploit ideas that may not have received a favorable reception by their former employers.

   e. By definition, customers are **first-time buyers**. The marketing problem is to convince these customers that the benefits of substituting the product or service for something else exceed the risks.

   f. The **short time horizon** for product and customer development means that policies may evolve for reasons other than well-researched decision making.

   g. **Subsidy** of early entrants by government or others may occur when the technology is radically new or societal concern is strong. Subsidies create instability because they result from political decisions and interference in the market.

   h. **Early mobility barriers** tend to consist of willingness to accept risk, proprietary technology, access to resource supplies, and the lower costs of more experienced firms. Barriers tend not to be branding, economies of scale, or capital intensity.

3. **Limits on industry development** arise because it is new, depends on external entities for growth, and must persuade customers to substitute its product or service for another.

   a. **Raw materials and components** may be scarce because new suppliers must be found or existing suppliers must expand or modify their output.

   b. **Raw materials prices** may increase rapidly as suppliers struggle to keep pace with demand during the early phase of industry development.

   c. **Infrastructure** (e.g., distribution channels, service centers, skilled labor, and complementary products or services) may not be available.

   d. **Standardization** lags because of product and technology uncertainty.

   e. Customers' belief that product **obsolescence** will occur rapidly may cause slow growth.

f. **Customer confusion** is created by technological uncertainty, absence of standardization, and the proliferation of competing products. Confusion increases the risk of purchase.

g. **Product quality** may be uneven because of the presence of many new firms and technological uncertainty (and the consequent lack of agreed-upon technical standards).

h. Because of the foregoing factors, the industry's **image and financial credibility** may suffer. Thus, lenders may be unwilling to provide debt capital at favorable rates, and customers may have difficulty in securing credit.

i. **Regulatory approval** may be hard to obtain, especially if customer needs are already served by an established regulated industry. However, favorable government policy may jump-start an industry, for example, when use of a safety product becomes mandatory. Moreover, further growth of an industry may be stunted when it attracts first-time regulation.

j. Initially **high unit costs** may require below-cost pricing or slow industry growth.

k. **Threatened entities** (e.g., makers of substitutes, unions, or distributors with entrenched relationships with old suppliers) may respond. For example, the responses may be in the form of political pressure, lobbying of regulators, collective bargaining, lower prices, or greater investment designed to reduce costs.

   1) Entities threatened by substitution are more likely to adopt a price or investment strategy when **exit barriers** are high.

4. Forecasting **early and late markets** is necessary to shape product development and marketing efforts and to predict structural evolution. Markets, market segments, and customers within a segment may vary in how quickly they accept a new industry's product or service. The following are factors affecting acceptance:

a. The **nature of the benefit** is the most significant factor. At one extreme, the benefit may consist of a **performance advantage** unattainable by other methods. At the other extreme, the benefit may be a pure **cost advantage**. Ordinarily, early markets purchase a product because it offers a performance advantage. Early markets tend to be suspicious of a product offering a cost advantage.

   1) With respect to a performance advantage, the receptivity of the buyer depends on the magnitude of the advantage, how obvious it is, the buyer's need for it, whether it improves the buyer's competitiveness, the competitive pressures felt by the buyer, and the buyer's price or cost sensitivity.

   2) With respect to a cost advantage, the receptivity of the buyer depends on the magnitude of the advantage, how obvious it is, whether lowered cost will result in a lasting competitive benefit, the competitive pressure to effect a change, and the degree to which the buyer's strategy is cost-based.

b. Early adoption depends on the **technical performance** buyers require. To obtain significant benefits, different buyers may require different levels of product development.

c. A higher risk **cost of product failure** for a buyer leads to later adoption. For example, a buyer that will use the product as part of an integrated system or pay a high price for interrupted service has a high cost of failure.

d. Buyers vary in the **switching costs** they face, e.g., retraining, additional equipment purchases, disposal of old equipment, requirements for support services (repair, engineering, and R & D), capital needs, and modification of related processes or business elements.

e.   The **cost of obsolescence** will be less for emerging technology if an initial version will meet later buyer needs even though upgrades appear periodically.

f.   Different buyers face different **regulatory, governmental, or union** constraints.

g.   Buyer **resource availability** affects the decision to change.

h.   The **perception of technological change** will be less daunting to a technically sophisticated buyer. Moreover, change may be a threat to some but an opportunity to others.

i.   The greater the **personal risk to the decision maker**, the less the likelihood of early adoption.

5.   **Strategic Choices**

a.   The firm is best able to **shape the industry structure** when the industry is emerging. It is best able to influence to its advantage industry approaches on such matters as pricing, marketing, and product policy.

b.   A firm in an emerging industry needs to consider **externalities in industry development**. It should balance its self interest with the need to promote the image and credibility of the industry. Thus, to appeal to first-time buyers and encourage substitution, the firm's enlightened self-interest ordinarily requires **industry cooperation**, improved quality, and standardization. However, as the industry matures, the firm should be less industry-oriented.

1)   An initial industry orientation also may require the firm to follow a strategy and enter market segments on a temporary basis.

c.   A firm benefits by early awareness and exploitation of the **changing role of suppliers and distribution channels**, which may become more cooperative as the industry strengthens.

d.   **Early mobility barriers** may disappear as the industry grows and technology improves. Hence, the firm may no longer be able to rely on early advantages, such as proprietary technology. The necessary response may be a large capital investment.

e.   The **nature of entrants** may change to include larger firms attracted by the proven and less risky industry. Firms must predict when such entry is likely given existing and probable future barriers and the costs of surmounting them. Firms also need to predict how new entrants will compete, e.g., on the basis of marketing power or economies of scale. Furthermore, new entrants may emerge through vertical integration.

f.   **Timing of entry** is a critical choice. Pioneering firms face high risk but low barriers and may earn high returns.

1)   Factors favoring early entry: pioneering improves the firm's reputation, the learning curve (experience) advantage is important and will persist, customer loyalty will be high, and cost advantages (through early commitment to suppliers or distributors) can be secured.

2)   Factors not favoring early entry: the bases of competition and market segments will change significantly, costs of opening the market are high and the benefits cannot be retained by the firm, early competition will be expensive and larger and stronger competitors will emerge later, and early products and processes will become obsolete.

3)   **Tactical moves** that may be beneficial include early commitment to suppliers and taking advantage of lower capital costs if investors are attracted to the industry.

g. **Responding to competitors** during the emerging phase of industry development is often a poor strategic choice. A firm is frequently best served by reinforcing its strengths and by developing the industry, perhaps through encouraging new entrants (e.g., by licensing) who will sell the industry's products and expedite its technological evolution.

6. Stop and review! You have completed the outline for this subunit. Study multiple-choice questions 5 and 6 on page 89.

3.3 DECLINING INDUSTRIES

1. A **declining industry** is not simply at a low point in the business cycle but has sustained a permanent decrease in unit sales over the long run. Michael E. Porter's view is that this phase of the industry life cycle does not correspond exactly to the decline stage in the product life cycle. Moreover, he argues that the nature of the competition and the range of strategic choices in the decline phase are diverse and vary widely from industry to industry. The result is that some industries may be able to negotiate decline without intense rivalry, long-term overcapacity, and ruinous losses.

2. **Structure and competition** in the decline phase rest on the reality that unit sales are decreasing and more intense competition will decrease profits. However, various factors affect the degree of the damage suffered.

    a. The **conditions of demand** and the nature of market segments determine competition in this phase.

        1) **Perceived uncertainty about demand** by competitors is a major influence on the competitive intensity. Rivalry will likely be bitter if demand is expected to rebound. However, if all firms expect demand to decrease, the weaker firms may plan early withdrawal and a graceful reduction of capacity.

            a) The stronger the firm and the higher its exit barriers, the more likely that its demand perception will be optimistic.

        2) The **rate and pattern of decline** affect uncertainty, which stimulates competitive volatility. Thus, a slow decline creates uncertainty, but a rapid decline tends to reduce uncertainty and unjustified optimism. Moreover, the rapid decline makes wholesale decreases in capacity more probable.

            a) The pattern of decline may not be readily distinguishable from the normal seasonal or other variability of sales. In this case, uncertainty is heightened.

            b) The rate of decline in demand is influenced by the pattern of withdrawal. For example, the departure of some suppliers may encourage customers to switch to substitutes so as to guarantee the availability of inputs.

            c) The rate of decline also tends to increase as withdrawals decrease sales volume and increase costs and prices.

        3) The **structure of the remaining pockets of demand** determines whether the surviving firms can be profitable. Prospects are favorable if the pockets include price-insensitive buyers of highly differentiated products. Prospects also are favorable if buyers have little bargaining power because of high switching costs or other factors, such as the need to replace the equipment of the suppliers that have withdrawn from the industry.

            a) Furthermore, firms operating in remaining pockets may thrive if mobility barriers are high (preventing firms in other segments from competing) and if substitute products or strong suppliers are not threats.

4) The **causes of decline** in industry demand include innovation or shifts in costs or quality that make attractive substitutes available. Other causes are a reduction in the size of a demographic customer group and changes in the needs or tastes of customers. A firm should consider these causes when evaluating the uncertainty of future demand and potential profits from remaining in particular market segments.

b. High **exit barriers** may restrain firms from leaving the industry even though their returns are poor.

1) **Specialized assets** and inventory in a declining industry may have a low liquidation value. Few purchasers who wish to operate in the same industry may be available. **Durable assets** may have a carrying amount far greater than the liquidation value. Hence, liquidation may result in a loss that the firm may not wish to recognize. Furthermore, a low liquidation value means that the future discounted cash flows from remaining in the industry may exceed the **opportunity cost** of the capital invested in the declining industry. Thus, the returns from the proceeds of liquidation may be less than the returns from keeping those assets in the business.

2) Net liquidation value is reduced when the **fixed costs of exit** are high, e.g., the costs of labor settlements, payments to professionals involved in the divestiture (CPAs, attorneys, etc.), cancelation of contracts (with distributors, suppliers, managers, etc.), and resettlement or retraining. Moreover, announcement of exit may have such effects as reduced employee productivity, loss of customers, and a decline in supplier reliability. However, some required investments, such as in environmental safeguards, may be avoided.

3) One type of **strategic exit barrier** exists when a divested business is part of a group executing an overall strategy. Divesting the business may undermine the strategy. For example, it may be important to the parent's image, relations with distributors, or bargaining power with suppliers. Thus, the **interrelatedness** of the divested business with other components should always be considered.

a) Exit may harm the **financial standing** of a firm. For example, the financial markets may react by lowering the firm's share price and raising its cost of capital. Recognition of a simple large loss from liquidation may subsequently be worse than a succession of small losses from operating the business.

b) **Vertical integration** of a business may require exit from the entire chain when the reasons for decline affect all its parts. However, when only one part is affected, integration is an argument for exit. Divestiture prevents the weak link from harming the entire chain.

4) **Information barriers** exist when one business is closely related to others in the firm. Its actual performance may be obscured in these circumstances, and the information needed to identify the business as an exit candidate may be hard to isolate.

5) **Management and emotional barriers** to exit arise from human nature. Managers may be committed to the business because of their personal involvement in it or the role it played in the firm's history. Managers also may not wish to admit failure, and they may be concerned about their future employment.

6) **Government and social barriers** reflect opposition to the negative effects of exit: unemployment and harm to local communities.

7) High exit barriers tend to keep capacity in a declining industry, intensifying rivalry and harming even healthy firms.

    c.   The method of **asset disposition** affects the health of the declining industry. For example, sale of a firm's assets within the industry but at a discount provides the buyer with a lower investment base than the remaining firms. Hence, the buyer may be able to take financially rational actions (e.g., concerning prices) that damage those firms. Discounted sales of assets to employee groups and government subsidies to failing firms have similar negative effects.

    d.   Price wars are more likely in the decline phase. **Rivalry** is more volatile (intense) when the product is viewed as a commodity, fixed costs are high, exit barriers are high, firms have strategic reasons for remaining and the resources to do so, firms are relatively equally strong, and firms are tempted to take ill-advised competitive actions because of uncertainty about their positions.

        1)   The greater power of suppliers and distributors in the decline phase means higher prices and worse service for industry firms and more intense rivalry.

3.   **Strategies in Declining Industries**

    a.   A **leadership strategy** is pursued by a firm that believes it can achieve market share gains to become the dominant firm. An assumption is that additional investment can be recovered. A second assumption is that success will put the firm in a better position to hold its ground or subsequently to follow a harvest strategy.

        1)   This strategy may entail aggressive pricing, marketing, or other investments that raise the stakes for competitors; reducing competitors' exit barriers by acquisitions of their capacity or products, assuming their contracts, and producing spare parts and generic versions of goods for them; demonstrations of strength and resolve to remain in the industry; and publicizing accurate data about the reality of future decline so as to dispel competitors' uncertainty.

    b.   A **niche strategy** seeks a market segment (pocket of demand) with stable or slowly decreasing demand with the potential for above-average returns. Some of the moves undertaken when following a leadership strategy may be appropriate. The firm may eventually change to a harvest or divest strategy.

    c.   A **harvest strategy** is in effect a controlled, gradual liquidation. It maximizes cash flow by minimizing new investment, R & D, advertising, service, maintenance, etc., and by exploiting the firm's remaining strengths (e.g., goodwill) to increase prices or maintain sales volume.

        1)   To be successful, the strategy assumes that the firm has certain strengths and intense competition is absent. The strengths permit the firm to maintain sales for a time in the face of price increases, reduced advertising, etc. Absence of intense competition means that other firms will be less likely to seize market share or lower prices. Moreover, a firm must be capable of cost reductions that do not cause immediate failure.

        2)   Actions pursuant to a harvest strategy may be **visible** to customers (less advertising or higher prices) or **invisible**. A firm without strength may be confined to the latter.

    d.   A **quick divestment strategy** assumes that the highest net recovery is obtained by sale early in the decline phase. It is then that uncertainty about the industry's future is greatest and other markets for the assets are most favorable. Indeed, divestiture may be indicated during the maturity phase prior to decline. But the firm risks being wrong about the onset of the decline phase.

4.   **Choice of Strategy**

    a.   One factor in the choice is whether the declining industry is likely to yield profits to the firm, that is, whether **industry structure** is favorable (e.g., with regard to uncertainty, competitor exit barriers, conditions of demand, etc.).

b.   A second factor is the firm's relative position, or **strengths and weaknesses**.

c.   Given a **favorable industry structure**, a firm with strengths in the remaining pockets of demand is most likely to follow a leadership or niche strategy. Lacking such strengths, it will most likely pursue a harvest or quick divestment strategy.

d.   Given an **unfavorable industry structure**, a firm with strengths in the remaining pockets of demand is most likely to follow a niche or harvest strategy. Lacking such strengths, it will most likely pursue a quick divestment strategy.

e.   However, the firm's **strategic needs** may affect the choice. For example, a need for cash flow may override other considerations and prompt an early sale.

f.   A crucial element of a strategy in the decline phase is to discover methods for influencing competitors to exit.

g.   **Potential mistakes** made by firms in a declining industry are not recognizing the onset of decline, engaging in wars of attrition with competitors having high exit barriers, and adopting a harvest strategy in the absence of strengths.

h.   **Preparing for decline** during the maturity phase may be possible given accurate forecasts, e.g., by avoidance of actions creating exit barriers, focusing on market segments that will be profitable in the decline phase, and increasing the customers' costs of switching in those segments.

5.   Stop and review! You have completed the outline for this subunit. Study multiple-choice questions 7 through 9 beginning on page 90.

3.4 COMPETITION IN GLOBAL INDUSTRIES

1.   The analysis of a competition in an industry requires consideration of the economics of the industry and the characteristics of competitors. However, in a global industry, the analysis is not limited to one market, but extends to all markets (geographic or national) taken together. Michael E. Porter defines a **global industry** as "one in which the strategic positions of competitors in major geographic or national markets are fundamentally affected by their overall global positions." The rapid proliferation of global industries, also known as **globalization**, is a development of great significance. Competitive analysis must now often address issues of global competition.

a.   A true global industry is one that requires a firm to compete internationally. Accordingly, an **industry is not global** simply because some or all competitors are multinational. When nonmultinationals can compete in a geographic or national market, the industry is not global.

b.   Global competition obviously differs in important ways from national competition. For example, costs, market characteristics, and the roles of governments vary among countries. Available resources, competitive monitoring, and objectives also vary. Nevertheless, the **five competitive forces** and the basic, underlying **structural factors** are the same as in national competition. Of course, the structural analysis of the forces and factors must still address foreign competitors, a larger group of possible entrants, a wider range of substitute products, and an even higher probability that firms will vary in their strategic objectives and corporate cultures.

c.   The primary issues are whether a firm should compete and the extent of the threat to the firm from global competition.

2.   **Sources of Global Competitive Advantage**

a.   Participation in foreign markets is usually by **licensing**; **export**; or, after the firm has obtained experience, **direct investment**. A genuinely global industry will have significant export activity or direct investment. Nevertheless, direct investment does not necessarily signal the existence of global competition. Direct investment also may occur when purely national factors determine a subsidiary's competitive position.

    b.   An industry becomes global because it perceives a net strategic advantage to competing, as Porter says, "in a coordinated way in many national markets." Thus, the sources of competitive advantage must have greater weight than the impediments.

       1)   A firm should consider the materiality of the source of advantage to total cost. Moreover, it also should consider the element of the business where the firm has a global competitive advantage. Still another consideration is that the sources of advantage reflect the implied presence of **mobility barriers**.

    c.   The **competitive advantage** of a nation regarding the cost or quality of a product means that it will produce and export the product. Consequently, a global firm's position in that nation is vital.

    d.   **Economies of scale in centralized production** may yield a cost advantage achievable only when output exceeds the demand in one country and exports are feasible. Vertical integration may provide the necessary scale.

    e.   **Global experience** may result in more rapid movement along the learning curve when similar products are sold in multiple national markets. Thus, the global firm may be first to achieve the maximum cost advantage from experience. Its cumulative production volume grows more rapidly than that of a purely national firm.

    f.   **Logistical economies of scale** may be attained by a global firm that spreads its fixed costs by supplying multiple national markets. A logistical cost advantage also may result because a global firm uses specialized logistical systems.

    g.   **Marketing economies of scale** may exceed the volume achievable in a national market even though much marketing is necessarily local. For example, one sales force may be employed globally when buyers are few and technical considerations are complex. Furthermore, some brands require no incremental investment to have international strength. Also, some advertising campaigns may be effective across national borders.

    h.   **Purchasing economies of scale** may confer a cost advantage. A global firm will make larger purchases than a purely national firm. One result may be longer and therefore more economical production runs. Another result may be greater bargaining power versus suppliers.

    i.   **Product differentiation** through enhanced image and reputation may be achieved in national markets by operating globally.

    j.   **Proprietary technology** may be applicable in multiple national markets, thereby creating a global competitive advantage. Furthermore, achieving such an advantage may only be feasible in a global industry. Economies of scale for R & D may only be attainable when the market is global. Also, global operation may help a firm to stay in touch with new developments.

    k.   **Mobility of production** allows a global firm to more readily achieve economies of scale and share proprietary technology among operating activities in multiple national markets. For example, a construction firm may have a larger organization than would be feasible in a national market. The fixed costs of that organization and of developing its technology will be lower relative to revenues because the global market is greater. Global operation is more likely to be profitable when construction crews and equipment are mobile.

3. **Impediments to Global Competition**

    a.   Impediments may increase direct costs, make management more difficult, be imposed by governments or institutions, or consist of perceptual or resource limitations.

       1)   Impediments that do not block global competition may still create niches for national firms.

b.   **High transportation and storage costs** may require construction of plants in each market.

c.   **Product needs** may differ from country to country because of culture, climate, degree of economic development, income, legal requirements, technical standards, and other factors. This barrier limits global procurement and achievement of economies of scale and experience. The height of the barrier depends on the costs of product modifications. **Complex segmentation within geographic markets** has similar effects.

d.   Access to **established distribution channels** may be difficult, especially when large volumes of low-cost items are sold. Concessions required to persuade a channel to substitute the product for a domestic producer's may be too great. Chances are better if channels are not established or are few and high-volume.

e.   The need for a **direct sales force** creates a barrier based on a diseconomy of scale, especially if local competitors' sales agents market wide product lines. The need for **local repair** is similar.

f.   **Sensitivity to lead times** means that global firms may not respond with the necessary rapidity to changes in fashion, technology, etc., in a national market. Centralized functions may be at too great a distance from that market to meet quickly evolving customer needs, especially when local needs vary. The relevant lead times include those for physical transportation at an economically acceptable cost.

g.   **Lack of world demand** may derive from the product's lack of appeal except in a few markets or its early position in the **product life cycle of world trade**. Initial introduction of the product is in a few markets where the product has the greatest appeal. Demand then builds elsewhere by product imitation and technology diffusion, resulting in exports and foreign investment by the pioneer firms. Greater demand and diffusion may also result in production in other markets by foreign firms. During the maturity stage, the product is standardized, price competition increases, and local firms enter the market. Thus, global competition may require some industry maturity, but the level of maturity is lower when experienced global competitors can rapidly spread the product to new markets.

h.   **Differing marketing tasks** are required in different national markets. Hence, local firms with superior marketing experience in their countries may have the advantage. A possible solution is to have a local marketing function.

i.   Local firms tend to be more responsive than global firms when **intensive local services** or other customer contacts are necessary. Hence, the local firm's advantages in marketing and other services could outweigh the global firm's advantages.

j.   **Rapid changes in technology** that require product and process modifications for a local market also favor the local firm.

k.   **Governmental impediments** are generally imposed for the announced purpose of protecting local firms and jobs. They consist of tariffs; duties; quotas; domestic content rules; preferences for local firms regarding procurement, taxes, R & D, labor regulations, and other operating rules; and laws (e.g., bribery or tax) enacted by a national government that impedes national firms from competing globally. These impediments are most likely when industries are viewed as crucial.

l.   **Perceptual impediments** arise because the complexities of global competition may impair the firm's ability to identify (visualize) global opportunities.

m.   **Resource impediments** consist of information and search costs, the costs of large-scale facilities construction, and the investments needed to penetrate new markets.

4. **Evolution of Global Markets**

   a. The **triggers** of this evolution establish or exploit the **sources** of global competitive advantage. In the alternative, if resources are adequate, they negate the **impediments** to global competition. Moreover, a **strategic innovation** is always necessary for the industry to become global.

   b. **Environmental triggers** include an increase in any of the types of economies of scale, lower transportation or storage costs, changes in distribution channels that facilitate access by foreign firms, changes in the costs of the factors of production, increased similarity of economic and social conditions in other nations, and reduction of governmental limitations.

   c. **Strategic innovations** may begin globalization even if environmental triggers are not present.

      1) **Product redefinition** may take the form of a reduction in national product differences resulting from industry maturity and product standardization. However, a marketing innovation that redefines the product's concept or image may make it more acceptable in global markets.

      2) **Identification of common market segments** among countries that are badly served by national firms is possible even if national product differences persist.

      3) Despite national product differences, **reducing the costs of adapting the product**, for example, by modularization or increasing the product's range of compatibility, may permit global competition. **Design changes** may have the same impact when they result in standardization of components.

      4) Combining centralized production with local assembly (disintegration of production) may satisfy governmental requirements while creating sufficient economies of scale to trigger global competition.

      5) **Elimination of resource or perceptual constraints** may result from entry of new firms with greater resources or with a fresher perspective that is helpful in developing new strategies and identifying new opportunities.

      6) **Access to the largest markets** may be critical to successful globalization of an industry.

5. **Strategic Alternatives in Global Industries**

   a. **Broad line global competition** is competition over the full product line of the firm based on differentiation or low cost. The firm needs large resources for this long-term strategy. Governmental relations should emphasize impediment reduction.

   b. A **global focus strategy** is limited to an industry segment with low impediments where the firm can defend its position against broad line firms. The focus of competition is low cost or product differentiation.

   c. A **national focus strategy** is limited to a national market or the segments with the greatest impediments to global competitors. Low cost or product differentiation is the focus of competition.

   d. A **protected niche strategy** is applied in nations where global competitors are discouraged by governmental impediments. The strategy is designed to be effective in markets with governmental constraints and requires close attention to the national government.

   e. **Transnational coalitions** may be created to help the firms overcome impediments to executing the broader strategies, for example, market access or technology barriers.

6. **Trends in Global Competition**

   a. **Economic differences** among developed and newly developed countries have narrowed.

b.   Some countries are pursuing more **aggressive industrial policies** by providing resources to stimulate industries to achieve global status.

c.   **Governmental protection of distinctive national assets**, such as natural assets, is reflected in direct ownership or joint ventures with private firms. A large labor pool is another asset increasingly recognized by some governments.

d.   The **freer flow of technology** allows many firms, including those in newly developed countries, invest in world-class facilities.

e.   **New large scale markets** are emerging, e.g., China, Russia, and India.

f.   **Newly developed countries**, e.g., Brazil, Taiwan, and South Korea, have emerged as global competitors because of their greater ability to make large investments, acquire new technology, and accept high risks.

7.   Stop and review! You have completed the outline for this subunit. Study multiple-choice questions 10 through 14 beginning on page 91.

3.5 INTEGRATION STRATEGIES

1.   **Vertical integration** combines within a firm production, distribution, selling, or other separate economic processes needed to deliver a product or service to a customer. All such processes could in principle be performed through market transactions with outside firms. However, vertical integration uses internal or administrative transactions for these purposes in the expectation they will increase efficiency or decrease costs and risks.

a.   The **decision to integrate** should consider not only direct economic issues (needed investment and effects on costs), but also broader strategic issues and the potential difficulties of administering a vertically integrated firm. Thus, the extent of integration depends on the balance of economic and administrative benefits and costs. This balance varies with the industry, the firm's position, and whether the firm engages in full integration, **tapered (partial) integration**, or **quasi-integration** (use of alliances, not ownership, to achieve the effects of integration).

2.   **Generic Strategic Benefits**

a.   **Upstream** (backward) or **downstream** (forward) integration is the acquisition of a capability that otherwise would be performed by external parties that are suppliers or customers, respectively, of the firm. Whether integration should occur depends on the firm's volume of transactions with the external parties (**throughput**) and the magnitude of the capability required to achieve necessary **economies of scale**.

1)   If the integrating firm's need is for a capability less than the efficient scale, one of its options is to acquire a capability with a cost inefficient scale. The other option is to acquire an efficient capability that provides excess output (in the upstream case) or creates excess demand (from, for example, a distribution capability in the downstream case). This option will require the integrated firm to sell or buy in the open market. Thus, the second option carries the risk of having to deal with competitors.

b.   **Economies of vertical integration** occur when throughput is great enough to achieve economies of scale. For example, economies of integration are available when the firm builds a supply facility that is large enough to be cost efficient, and the firm can use all of its output.

1)   **Economies of combined operations** may reduce production steps, handling and transportation, and slack time. For example, facilities for technologically different processes might be located near each other, or the same machines may be used for different steps.

2) **Economies of control and coordination** result from better delivery scheduling, common oversight of functions, increased reliability of supply by a related entity, internal redesign or new product introductions, and a leaner control structure.

3) **Economies of information** are achieved by an integrated firm because some information may no longer be needed, the fixed costs of competitive intelligence and forecasting are borne by additional subunits of the firm, and information may flow more rapidly between related than unrelated entities.

4) Economies result from **avoiding some market transactions**. Transaction costs of dealing with outside parties are greater than those of dealing with inside parties.

5) **Stable relationships** between internal sellers and buyers create economies because they need not fear loss of the related buyers and sellers. They also need not fear undue economic pressure from each other. Furthermore, because the relationship is locked in, more efficient procedures for their relationship (e.g., dedicated controls and records) may be implemented. Another advantage is the internal sellers and buyers may more fully adapt to each other's needs than they would or could when dealing with outsiders.

c. A **tap into technology** of upstream or downstream firms is an integration benefit that is a vital economy of information. However, integration to obtain a better understanding of technology is usually tapered so as to manage risk.

d. Providing **assurance of supply or demand** is an integration benefit because it reduces some of the uncertainty caused by market fluctuations. Thus, the firm has less risk of interruptions, changes in customers and suppliers, or payment of excessive prices in emergencies. However, demand in the absolute sense is not affected. For example, when a downstream subunit faces lower external demand, its internal supplier will also face lower demand.

1) To promote overall firm efficiency, **transfer prices** most likely should be market-based.

e. Integration benefits include **offsetting the bargaining power** of strong suppliers and customers. If such parties have returns greater than the opportunity cost of capital, the firm benefits even if no other advantages accrue from integration. Thus, upstream integration eliminates **input cost distortion** caused by the supplier's power, and downstream integration eliminates the customer's power to obtain an unjustifiably low price. Moreover, the special costs of dealing with powerful parties will also be eliminated.

1) Upstream integration also has the advantage of disclosing the true cost of the input provided by the powerful supplier. This information helps the firm to adjust its input mix and prices.

f. An integrated firm may have a better **ability to differentiate** itself because it has greater opportunities to offer value to customers, such as by improved service through integrated distribution channels.

g. Integration that generates any of the foregoing benefits will also raise **entry and mobility barriers**. Integration may confer a competitive advantage not matched by a nonintegrated firm, especially if it requires large capital investment or economies of scale.

h. Integration may increase the firm's **overall** return on investment after considering any costs of overcoming barriers to integration.

i. Integration may be a **defense against foreclosure of access** to suppliers or customers. It is a response to integration by competitors who threaten to secure the low-cost or high-quality suppliers, favorable distribution channels, or largest customers. Defensive integration also increases mobility when investment or economies of scale are large.

3. **Generic Strategic Costs**

   a. Integration is a special case of entry into a new business. Thus, the firm must incur **costs to overcome mobility barriers** to enter the adjacent business: economies of scale, proprietary technology, capital investment, sources of materials, etc.

   b. Integration **increases fixed costs and operating leverage**, which is in itself a cause of increased business risk. Thus, an integrated firm is exposed to fluctuations affecting any of its components. For example, sales of an upstream component depend on sales of downstream components.

   c. Integration **reduces the flexibility to change business partners** because it increases the costs of switching to different suppliers or customers. For example, a supplier component may ultimately be providing an obsolete, overpriced, or poorly designed product. A customer component may lose market share.

   d. Integration may increase any of the **exit barriers** described in the preceding subunit.

   e. Integration **requires investment capital**. The return must at least equal the firm's opportunity cost of capital (after considering all strategic analytical factors. Furthermore, the integration decision is in part dependent on the **appetite for capital** of the adjacent business to be entered. The danger is that it may continually require capital that could be more profitably invested elsewhere in the firm. This loss of flexibility of capital allocation may prevent profitable diversification.

   f. Integration may **foreclose access to supplier or customer technology**. The integrated firm may have to create its own technology rather than taking advantage of supplier/customer expertise.

   g. Integration requires **maintaining a balance** among the operations of the firm's subunits. Excess output or demand of a subunit may necessitate selling to, or buying from, competitors unless the needs can be satisfied by sales or purchases on the open market. Imbalance may result because of unequal changes in capacity caused by technological change or alterations in the product mix or quality.

   h. Integration may **reduce incentives**. For example, a buyer may not bargain as aggressively with an in-house seller, and a seller may not compete as aggressively because it is assured of a customer. Thus, internal projects may not be as strictly scrutinized as external transactions. The response is for management to require that internal relationships be treated as if they are genuinely at arms'-length. Furthermore, subunit managers must resist the natural temptation to assist a failing subunit, thereby damaging the successful subunits.

   i. A significant cost and risk of integration is that subunits have **differing managerial requirements**. It is a mistake to apply the same methods used in the core business to other parts of the integrated firm.

4. **Strategic Issues – Forward Integration**

   a. **Enhanced product differentiation** may follow forward integration because of better control of production, marketing, retailing, or service that adds value.

   b. Forward integration may secure **access to distribution channels**.

   c. **Access to market information** is improved. A forward subunit (the **demand leading stage**) controls the amount and mix of demand to be satisfied upstream. At the very least, forward integration improves the timeliness of demand information, production planning, inventory control, and the costs of being under- or over-stocked. It may also provide information about changing tastes, competitors' moves, and the ideal mix of products.

      1) Whether forward integration is indicated depends on the relative instability of demand and the effect on information reliability of the number of customers.

    d.   Forward integration may permit **higher price realization**, for example, by moving into businesses in which the price elasticity of demand is relatively high and lower prices must be set. When demand is elastic, raising prices decreases revenue. Thus, the firm may benefit by acquiring customers with high elasticities while selling to customers with low elasticities.

5.   **Strategic Issues – Backward Integration**

    a.   Backward integration allows the firm to protect its **proprietary knowledge** from suppliers.

    b.   Controlling inputs may permit the firm to **differentiate its product** more effectively, or at least to argue persuasively that it does so.

6.   **Contracts and Economies of Integration**

    a.   Some of the economies of integration may be secured by contracts (long- or short-term) with independent parties, for example, through a long-term agreement with a supplier to provide all of the firm's needs for an input. However, such arrangements may be difficult to create because of the parties' dissimilar interests and the risks involved.

    b.   **Tapered (partial) integration** implies that the firm can fully support an efficient subunit but has additional needs to be met in the market. If the in-house subunit will not be efficient, that inefficiency must be weighed against the benefits of tapering.

        1)   Tapering results in **lower fixed costs** than full integration. Furthermore, the strategy may allow the firm's subunit(s) to maintain constant production rates while external parties bear the **risk of fluctuations**. Another use of tapering is to protect against operational **imbalances** among the subunits.

        2)   A risk of tapering is selling to, or buying from, competitors. Another is greater coordination cost.

        3)   Advantages of tapering are avoidance of locked-in relationships, some access to external expertise, increased managerial incentives, offering a credible threat of full integration to suppliers or customers, and obtaining knowledge of the adjacent business and an emergency supply source.

    c.   **Quasi-integration** is something more than a long-term contract and less than full ownership. It may be achieved by a minority common stock interest, debt guarantees, cooperation in R & D, an exclusive dealing arrangement, etc.

        1)   Buyer and seller may, as a result, have a special community of interest leading to lower costs, smoothing of supply/demand fluctuations, or mitigating against bargaining power. Quasi-integration may avoid commitment to an adjacent business with its investment and management requirements. But many benefits of full integration may not be achievable in this way.

7.   **Common Illusions of Integration**

    a.   Strength in one part of the chain necessarily carries over to the other parts.
    b.   Doing something internally is cheaper.
    c.   Integrating into a highly competitive business is often wise.
    d.   Integration may save a strategically sick firm.
    e.   Experience in one part of the chain always carries over to other parts.

8.   Stop and review! You have completed the outline for this subunit. Study multiple-choice questions 15 through 19 beginning on page 93.

3.6 CAPACITY EXPANSION

1. Whether to expand capacity is a major **strategic decision** because of the capital required, the difficulty of forming accurate expectations, and the long time frame of the lead times and the commitment. The key forecasting problems are **long-term demand** and **behavior of competitors**. The key strategic issue is **avoidance of industry overcapacity**. Capacity expansion is also referred to as market penetration.

   a. Undercapacity in a profitable industry tends to be a short-term issue. Profits ordinarily lure additional investors. Overcapacity tends to be a long-term problem because firms are more likely to compete intensely rather than reverse their expansion.

2. The formal **capital budgeting** process entails predicting future cash flows related to the expansion project, discounting them at an appropriate interest rate, and determining whether the **net present value** is positive. This process permits comparison with other uses of the firm's resources.

   a. The apparent simplicity of this process is deceptive because it depends upon, among many other things, which expansion method is chosen, developments in technology, and profitability. The latter factor in turn depends on such uncertainties as total long-term demand and the expansion plans of rival firms.

3. Michael E. Porter's **model of the decision process for capacity expansion** has the following interrelated steps:

   a. The firm must **identify the options** in relation to their size, type, degree of vertical integration (if any), and possible response by competitors.

   b. The second step is to **forecast demand, input costs, and technology developments**. The firm must be aware that its technology may become obsolete or that future design changes to allow expansion may or may not be possible. Moreover, the expansion itself may put upward pressure on input prices.

   c. The next step is **analysis of competitors** to determine when each will expand. The difficulty is that forecasting their behavior depends on knowing their expectations. Another difficulty is that each competitor's actions potentially affect all other competitors' actions, with the industry leader being most influential.

   d. Using the foregoing information, the firm predicts **total industry capacity and firms' market shares**. These estimates, together with the expected demand, permit the firm to predict **prices and cash flows**.

   e. The final step is **testing for inconsistencies**.

4. The **extent of uncertainty about future demand** is a crucial variable in determining the nature of industry expansion. For example, if uncertainty is great, firms willing to take greater risks because of their large cash resources or strategic stake in the industry will act first. Other firms will await events.

   a. When demand uncertainty is low, firms will tend to adopt a strategy of **preemption**, usually with strong market signals, to forestall competitors' expansion plans. Excess preemption leads to excess industry capacity because firms overestimate their competitive strengths, misunderstand market signals, or fail to accurately assess competitors' intentions.

5. **Causes of overbuilding** extend beyond poorly played games of preemption.

 a. Overbuilding is most frequent in firms that produce **commodities**. One reason is that such firms are usually **cyclical** so that capacity is always excessive at low points in the cycle. Moreover, many tend to overestimate the strength of upturns. A second reason is that commodities tend to be **undifferentiated**. Thus, competition is based on price, cost efficiency is crucial, and sales depend on capacity.

 b. The following are **technological factors** that may lead to overbuilding:

 1) Capacity may need to be added in **large increments**.
 2) The presence of **economies of scale** or a **steep learning curve** encourages preemption.
 3) **Long lead times** increase the risk of competitive inferiority if a firm does not act quickly to begin raising its capacity.
 4) When the **minimum efficient scale** increases, large plants are becoming more efficient. Unless demand is growing, the number of plants must decline to avoid overbuilding.
 5) **Changes in production technology** result in new construction while old plants remain in operation, particularly when exit barriers are high.

 c. The following are **structural factors** that may lead to overbuilding:

 1) **Exit barriers** are high. Thus, the period of overcapacity is extended.
 2) **Suppliers** of capital, equipment, materials, etc., face their own competitive pressures. Thus, lower supplier prices, government subsidies, favorable interest rates, and similar incentives may promote expansion by customer industries.
 3) **Credibility** of new products is promoted by capacity expansion that gives assurance to large buyers. Such customers need to know that capacity will exist to meet their long-term needs and that a few suppliers will not have excessive bargaining power.
 4) When **competitors are integrated**, the pressure to build in the face of uncertain demand intensifies. Each firm wants to ensure that it can supply the downstream component of the firm.
 5) **Capacity leadership** is important in some industries as a means of increasing market share. Customers may be more likely to seek out the capacity leader. The **age and type of capacity** may also be competitive advantages.

 d. The following are **competitive factors** that may lead to overbuilding:

 1) **Many firms** with the ability to add capacity are seeking to improve market share.
 2) The **lack of a credible market leader(s)** makes for a less orderly expansion. A stronger leader can retaliate effectively against inappropriate expansion by others.
 3) **New entrants**, possibly encouraged by low entry barriers and favorable economic conditions, may cause or intensify overcapacity.
 4) **First mover advantages** may be significant. Thus, shorter lead times, lower costs, and the ability to exploit an excess of demand over supply may encourage too many firms to expand.

e.   The following are **information flow factors** that may lead to overbuilding:

1)   **Future expectations** may be inflated because of industry buzz.

2)   Firms' **assumptions or perceptions** about competitors' strengths, weaknesses, and plans may be inaccurate.

3)   **Market signaling** may be ineffective because it is no longer regarded as credible. Firms' signals may no longer be trusted on indicators of planned moves, such as expansion, because of new entrants, a period of bitter rivalry, or other reasons.

4)   **Changes in industry structure** may lead directly to new investment or create uncertainties leading to faulty decisions.

5)   The **financial community** plays a role in overbuilding when analysts criticize firms that have not expanded. Also, management's optimistic comments to the financial community may be taken as aggressive signals by competitors.

f.   The following are **managerial factors** that may lead to overbuilding:

1)   Management that is **production-oriented** may be more likely to overbuild than marketing- or finance-oriented management.

2)   A manager's career **risk is asymmetric** when the consequences of overcapacity appear to be less grave than those of undercapacity.

g.   The following are **governmental factors** that may lead to overbuilding:

1)   **Tax incentives** may promote excess capacity, for example, by permitting foreign subsidiaries to pay no tax of earnings retained in the business.

2)   A nation may wish to create an **indigenous industry**. When the minimum efficient scale is great in relation to worldwide demand, the excess production in the country may contribute to global overcapacity.

3)   **Governmental employment pressures** may result in overbuilding to create jobs or avoid job loss.

h.   The following are **limits on capacity expansion**:

1)   Most firms have great **uncertainty** about future conditions.

2)   The firm faces **financial constraints**.

3)   The firm is **diversified**. As a result, the opportunity cost of capital is greater, and management's perspective is broader.

4)   Senior managers have **finance backgrounds**.

5)   **Expansion is costly**, e.g., because of environmental regulations.

6)   The firm experienced distress during a **prior period of overbuilding**.

7)   A firm's behavior sends **signals** to competitors that building is unwise, for example, by announcing an expansion project or by indicating in some way that forecasts of demand are unfavorable or that current technology will soon be obsolete.

6.   **Preemptive Strategies**

a.   Preemption requires investments in plant facilities and the ability to accept short-term unfavorable results. The strategy is risky because it anticipates demand and often sets prices in the expectation of future cost efficiencies. Moreover, a failed preemption strategy may provoke intense, industry-damaging conflict. The following conditions must be met for the strategy to succeed:

1)   The expansion must be **large relative to the market**, and competitors must believe that the move is preemptive. Hence, the firm should know competitors' expectations about the market or be able to influence them favorably. A move that is too small is by definition not preemptive.

2) **Economies of scale** should be large in relation to demand, or the **learning-curve effect** will give an initial large investor a permanent cost advantage. For example, the preemptive firm may be able to secure too much of the market to allow a subsequent firm to invest at the efficient scale. That is, the residual demand available to be met by the later firm is less than the efficient scale of production. The later firm therefore must choose between intense competition at the efficient scale or a cost disadvantage.

3) The preempting firm must have **credibility** to support its statements and moves, such as resources, technology, and a history of credibility.

4) The firm must provide **credible signals before action by competitors**.

5) The **competitors** of the firm should be willing not to act. This condition may not be met if competitors have noneconomic objectives, the business is strategically vital to them, or they have greater ability or willingness to compete.

7. Stop and review! You have completed the outline for this subunit. Study multiple-choice questions 20 through 22 beginning on page 94.

3.7 ENTRY INTO NEW BUSINESSES

1. **Entry through internal development** ordinarily entails creation of a full-fledged new business entity. This **internal entrant** must cope with structural barriers and retaliation by existing firms.

   a. Thus, costs include initial investments to overcome **entry barriers** (facilities, inventory, branding, technology, distribution channels, sources of materials, etc.), operating losses in the start-up phase, and the effects of **retaliation** (e.g., higher marketing costs, capacity expansion, or lower prices). Other costs include the price increases for factors of production that may result because of the new entry. Also, the **capacity** added to the industry by the entrant may affect the equilibrium level of supply and demand. The result may be additional competitive costs as firms with excess capacity cut prices.

   b. An internal entrant is most likely to cause industry disruption and **retaliation**, with a consequent negative effect on future results, in the following industries:

      1) In a **slow-growth** industry, existing firms cannot compensate for the loss in market share, and the added capacity will depress prices.

      2) If the product is a commodity or is commodity-like, brand identification and market segmentation do not exist to protect existing firms. Price cuts are probable.

      3) **High fixed costs** signify that existing firms will retaliate if their capacity usage decreases materially.

      4) In a **highly concentrated industry**, the internal entrant is more likely to have a significant and noticeable effect on particular firms with the ability to retaliate. In a fragmented industry, many firms might be affected but not significantly. These firms also might have no ability to retaliate.

      5) Existing firms view the industry as **strategically important**, e.g., as a source of cash flow or growth or because of integration.

      6) **Management attitudes** of well-established firms, especially if engaged in a single business, may provide psychological rationale for retaliation. An internal entrant should consider the prior behavior of such firms when they were faced with new entrants or with existing firms attempting to move to a new strategic group.

c.   The internal entrant should undertake a **structural analysis**, including consideration of profitability as a function of the **five competitive forces**, to **identify target industries**.

1)   If the industry is **in equilibrium**, the internal entrant should expect normal (average) profits even if entrenched firms earn above-average profits. The reason is that the internal entrant's costs exceed those of existing firms. It must pay the costs of hurdling entry barriers and coping with retaliation. If the entry costs did not negate above-average profits, other firms would previously have entered the industry and lowered the available profits. Consequently, unless the firm has special advantages, it should most likely not target an industry in equilibrium.

2)   However, a firm may be able to achieve **above-average profits** by choosing appropriate targets.

a)   An industry may be in **disequilibrium**.

i)   In a **new industry**, the structure is not established, entry barriers are low, retaliation is unlikely, resource supplies have not been locked up, and brands are not well developed. However, initial firms may have greater costs than later entrants, who may face low entry barriers.

ii)   **Rising entry barriers** favor an early entrant whose subsequent competitors will face higher costs. The early entrant also may have an edge in product differentiation.

iii) **Poor information** may perpetuate disequilibrium because firms that might enter the industry may not be aware of its potential.

iv)   An internal entrant must understand that the indicators of disequilibrium may be apparent to other firms. Hence, the firm's decision to enter should be based on some advantage that will enable it to earn above-average profits.

b)   The tradeoff between expected profits and entry costs also may be favorable when existing firms in an industry do not or cannot **retaliate against the internal entrant swiftly and effectively**. Industries of this kind do not have the attributes discussed earlier (see 1.b.). Also, the following factors may be in play:

i)   The internal entrant may be able to calculate that the **costs to existing firms of retaliation exceed the benefits**. The new firm also may be able to persuade existing firms that the costs are excessive.

ii)   The industry may have a **dominant firm or a long-time leadership group** that acts to protect the industry rather than maximize its own standing, e.g., by retaliating against a new entrant.

iii) Existing firms' **costs of retaliation are high** in relation to the need to protect their business. For example, a response might alienate distributors, reduce sales of key products, or be at odds with the retaliating firm's image.

iv)   **Conventional wisdom** about industy operating practices may impair the ability of existing firms to retaliate. A new firm may perceive circumstances in which the conventional wisdom does not apply.

        c)   **Lower industry entry costs** may be incurred by a firm with special advantages, such as a well-known brand, proprietary technology, or a strong distribution network. Such a powerful competitor might also command great respect and therefore be less likely to endure retaliation.

        d)   A **distinctive ability to influence industry structure** is another basis for earning above-average profits. Thus, an ability to raise mobility barriers after the firm has entered the industry is a reason to target that industry. Moreover, a firm may be able to recognize that entering a fragmented industry will start a process of consolidation and increased entry barriers.

        e)   Internal entry having a **positive effect on the firm's existing businesses** is justified even if above-average profits cannot be earned in the new industry.

    d.   The following **generic entry concepts** are methods of cheaply surmounting entry barriers:

        1)   **Product costs** may be reduced by use of new process technology, economies of scale, a modern plant, or sharing functions with existing businesses.

        2)   A **low initial price** that sacrifices profits for market share may succeed if competitors do not retaliate.

        3)   A **better product or service** overcomes the product differentiation barrier.

        4)   Barriers can be overcome by finding an **unserved niche market**.

        5)   A **marketing innovation** overcomes product differentiation and distribution barriers.

        6)   Use of an **established distribution network** is another way to overcome entry barriers.

2.   **Entry Through Acquisition**

    a.   The analysis differs from that for entry by internal development. A key point is that prices are set in the **market for acquisitions**. In the industrialized countries, this market is active and well organized, indicating that it is also efficient and therefore tends to eliminate above-average profits.

        1)   One factor contributing to **efficiency** (and the elimination of above-average profits for a buyer) is that a seller normally can choose to continue running the business. Accordingly, a bidder ordinarily must pay the seller a premium in excess of the expected present value to the seller of continuing operations. The price minus that **floor** value equals the premium.

    b.   Acquisitions are most likely to be profitable when

        1)   The **floor is low**, e.g., because the seller perceives that it needs funds, has management weaknesses, or cannot grow or compete because of capital limits.

        2)   The **market for acquisitions is imperfect**.

            a)   The buyer may have better information.
            b)   There are few bidders.
            c)   The economy is weak.
            d)   The seller is weak.
            e)   The seller has reasons to sell other than profit maximization.

   3) The **buyer may have a unique ability to operate the seller**.

      a) The buyer may be uniquely able to improve operations.

      b) The buyer purchases a firm in an industry that meets one of the conditions for internal development.

      c) The purchase may improve the buyer's position in its current businesses.

   4) A pitfall to avoid is competition from **irrational bidders**. An acquisition may be a genuine or perceived value to the irrational bidder, which exceeds the value to the firm.

   c. **Sequential entry** may be the best entry strategy. It involves entering one **strategic group** in the industry with subsequent mobility to another group(s).

3. Stop and review! You have completed the outline for this subunit. Study multiple-choice questions 23 and 24 beginning on page 95.

QUESTIONS
3.1 Fragmented Industries

1. Firms in a fragmented industry have insignificant market shares and little influence on such matters as market price and total output. A likely economic cause of this fragmentation is the existence of

   A. A learning curve effect.

   B. Diseconomies of scale.

   C. High entry barriers.

   D. Low exit barriers.

Answer (B) is correct. *(Publisher)*
   REQUIRED: The likely economic cause of fragmentation.
   DISCUSSION: Important diseconomies of scale may favor fragmentation. For example, small, flexible firms have an advantage when the following needs are important: quick responses to style changes, the maintenance of low overhead, customization of a diverse product line to the special requirements of particular customers, substantial creative content in the product, individualized personal service, and local contacts and image.
   Answer (A) is incorrect because economies of scale or a learning curve effect provide cost advantages to larger or older firms, respectively. However, economies of scale and a learning curve (experience) effect usually do not exist in fragmented industries, for example, because operations are simple or labor-intensive. Answer (C) is incorrect because low entry barriers, not high entry barriers, constitute a necessary but not a sufficient condition for fragmentation. Answer (D) is incorrect because high exit barriers, not low exit barriers, keep firms in the industry and minimize concentration.

2. In which of the following industry environments would an internal auditor be most likely to recommend strategies such as franchising and horizontal mergers?

   A. Emerging industries.

   B. Declining industries.

   C. Fragmented industries.

   D. Mature industries.

Answer (C) is correct. *(IIA, adapted)*
   REQUIRED: The use of franchising and horizontal mergers.
   DISCUSSION: Strategies such as chaining, franchising, and horizontal mergers are commonly used in fragmented industries. Emerging industries have low barriers to entry. Economies of scale and a learning curve do not exist because operations are simple.
   Answer (A) is incorrect because emerging industries are new and initially small in size. Answer (B) is incorrect because declining industries have high exit barriers and are not looking to expand and take over competitors. Answer (D) is incorrect because mature industries have consistent sales and do not need to take over competitors and franchise to gain market share.

3. The opportunity for franchising comes from the ability to

   A. Develop products.

   B. Differentiate products.

   C. Standardize products.

   D. Diversify products.

Answer (C) is correct. *(IIA, adapted)*
   REQUIRED: The opportunities for franchising.
   DISCUSSION: Standardizing products means to maintain the same product or to standardize the production, operations, and facilities in different locations or markets. Franchises all use standardized products to reduce costs.
   Answer (A) is incorrect because developing products means adding more value or features to the existing product. Answer (B) is incorrect because differentiating products implies that the products are to be different in different markets. Answer (D) is incorrect because diversifying products means to deal in different products, although they may be related (part of the same line).

4. A firm in a fragmented industry must position itself by adopting a competitive strategy appropriate to the industry. Which of the following is most clearly a focus strategy?

   A. Specialization by product type.

   B. Backward integration.

   C. An emphasis on low overhead and low payroll.

   D. Development of formula facilities.

Answer (A) is correct. *(Publisher)*
   REQUIRED: The focus strategy.
   DISCUSSION: A focus strategy is directed at a buyer group, segment of the product line, or geographic area. Thus, the strategic target is narrow compared with an industrywide strategy designed to achieve cost leadership or product differentiation. Specialization by product type or segment is a focus strategy. This focus may enhance bargaining power with suppliers. It may also increase differentiation because of the perceived expertise and image. The downside is reduced growth opportunities.
   Answer (B) is incorrect because backward integration is the selective acquisition of suppliers to reduce costs. Answer (C) is incorrect because a cost strategy is to adopt a bare bones, no frills approach by emphasizing tight control of costs, low overhead, and low payroll. Answer (D) is incorrect because developing formula facilities for use in numerous localities reduces construction and operating costs via standardization.

3.2 Emerging Industries

5. An emerging industry is new or newly formed and is small in size initially. It results from innovation, changes in cost structures, new customer needs, or another factor that creates an attractive opportunity for selling a product or service. Which of the following is a structural characteristic of an emerging industry?

   A. A long time horizon for product development.

   B. Low initial costs and a shallow learning curve.

   C. Mobility barriers include economies of scale and brand identification.

   D. The presence of embryonic companies and spinoffs.

Answer (D) is correct. *(Publisher)*
   REQUIRED: Characteristics of an emerging industry.
   DISCUSSION: Embryonic companies (firms newly formed and not new units of established entities) are numerous in the emerging phase of industry evolution. Entry is not discouraged by the presence of economies of scale or strategic certainty. Spin-offs from existing firms also are common. Given the strategic uncertainties and the lure of equity interests, employees of these firms may have the incentive, and be well-placed, to create new firms. Their motive is to exploit ideas that may not have received a favorable reception by their former employers.
   Answer (A) is incorrect because the time horizon for product and customer development is short. Thus, policies may evolve for reasons other than well-researched decision making. Answer (B) is incorrect because initial costs are high, but the learning curve is steep. When the efficiency gains from experience combine with economies of scale achieved by growth, cost decreases are dramatic. Answer (C) is incorrect because early mobility barriers tend to consist of willingness to accept risk, proprietary technology, access to resource supplies, and the lower costs of experienced firms. Branding, economies of scale, and the need for capital tend not to be barriers.

6. Strategic choices in an emerging industry are inherently subject to great uncertainty and risk with regard to competitors, industry structure, and competitive rules. Accordingly, a firm considering entry into an emerging industry

   A. Has little need to be concerned with industry cooperation.

   B. Is least likely to be able to shape the industry structure at this stage.

   C. May enjoy such benefits of pioneering as experience advantages and early commitment to suppliers.

   D. Must be prepared for responding vigorously to competitors' moves.

Answer (C) is correct. *(Publisher)*
   REQUIRED: The true statement about strategic considerations by a potential entrant into an emerging industry.
   DISCUSSION: Timing of entry is a critical choice. Pioneering firms face high risk but low barriers and may earn high returns. The following are factors favoring early entry: pioneering improves the firm's reputation, the learning curve (experience) advantage is important and will persist, customer loyalty will be high, and cost advantages (through early commitment to suppliers or distributors) can be secured.
   Answer (A) is incorrect because a firm in an emerging industry needs to consider externalities in industry development. It should balance its self interest with the need to promote the image and credibility of the industry. Thus, to appeal to first-time buyers and encourage substitution, the firm's enlightened self-interest ordinarily resides in industry cooperation, improved quality, and standardization. However, as the industry matures, the firm should be less industry-oriented. Answer (B) is incorrect because the firm is best able to shape the industry structure when the industry is emerging. It is best able to influence to its advantage industry approaches on such matters as pricing, marketing, and product policy. Answer (D) is incorrect because responding to competitors during the emerging phase of industry development is often a poor strategic choice. A firm is frequently best served by reinforcing its strengths and by developing the industry, perhaps through encouraging new entrants (e.g., by licensing) who will sell the industry's product and expedite its technological evolution.

3.3 Declining Industries

7. Industry structure and competition during the decline phase may result in intense and destructive competition. Which factor is most likely to contribute to this condition?

- A. Firms do not expect demand to rebound.
- B. The decline is rapid.
- C. Attractive substitutes are not available.
- D. Exit barriers are high.

Answer (D) is correct. *(Publisher)*
REQUIRED: The factor most likely to contribute to destructive competition in a declining industry.
DISCUSSION: High exit barriers may restrain firms from leaving the industry even though their returns are poor. For example, specialized assets and inventory in a declining industry may have a low liquidation value. Few purchasers who wish to operate in the same industry may be available. Durable assets may have a carrying amount far greater than the liquidation value. Hence, liquidation may result in a loss that the firm may not wish to recognize. Furthermore, a low liquidation value means that the future discounted cash flows from remaining in the industry may exceed the opportunity cost of the capital invested in the declining industry. Thus, the returns from the proceeds of liquidation may be less than the returns from keeping those assets in the business, the fixed costs of exit (such as contract cancelation) may be high, the firm is part of a group executing a larger strategy, a government discourages exit to preserve employment, or managers have an emotional tie to the business.

Answer (A) is incorrect because perceived uncertainty about demand by competitors is a major influence on the competitive intensity. Rivalry will likely be bitter if demand is expected to rebound. However, if all firms expect demand to decrease, the weaker firms may plan early withdrawal and a graceful reduction of capacity. Answer (B) is incorrect because the rate and pattern of decline affect uncertainty, which stimulates competitive volatility. Thus, a slow decline creates uncertainty, but a rapid decline tends to reduce uncertainty and unjustified optimism. Moreover, the latter makes wholesale decreases in capacity more probable. Answer (C) is incorrect because the causes of decline in industry demand include innovation or shifts in costs or quality that make attractive substitutes available. Other causes are a reduction in the size of a demographic customer group and changes in the needs or tastes of customers. A firm should consider these causes when evaluating the uncertainty of future demand and potential profits from remaining in particular market segments.

8. A firm in a declining industry ordinarily adopts one of four strategies. A firm that follows a

- A. Quick divestment strategy should have divested during the maturity phase.
- B. Leadership strategy may assume that success will enable it to subsequently pursue a harvest strategy.
- C. Harvest strategy seeks a pocket of stable demand.
- D. Niche strategy is engaged in a gradual liquidation.

Answer (B) is correct. *(Publisher)*
REQUIRED: The true statement about a strategy followed by a firm in a declining industry.
DISCUSSION: A leadership strategy is pursued by a firm that believes it can achieve market share gains to become the dominant firm. An assumption is that additional investment can be recovered. A second assumption is that success will put the firm in a better position to hold its ground or subsequently to follow a harvest strategy. This strategy may entail aggressive pricing, marketing, or other investments that raise the stakes for competitors; reducing competitors' exit barriers by acquisitions of their capacity or products, assuming their contracts, and producing spare parts and generic versions of goods for them; demonstrations of strength and resolve to remain in the industry; and publicizing accurate data about the reality of future decline so as to dispel competitors' uncertainty.

Answer (A) is incorrect because a quick divestment strategy assumes that the highest net recovery is obtained by sale early in the decline phase. It is then that uncertainty about the industry's future is greatest and other markets for the assets are most favorable. Indeed, divestiture may be indicated. Answer (C) is incorrect because a niche strategy seeks a market segment (pocket of demand) with stable or slowly decreasing demand with the potential for above-average returns. Some of the moves undertaken when following a leadership strategy may be appropriate. The firm may eventually change to a harvest or divest strategy. Answer (D) is incorrect because is incorrect because a harvest strategy is in effect a controlled, gradual liquidation. It maximizes cash flow by minimizing new investment, R&D, advertising, service, maintenance, etc., and by exploiting the firm's remaining strengths (e.g., goodwill) to increase prices or maintain sales volume.

9. Which of the following is not characteristic of a mature industry environment?

    A. Consolidation.

    B. Competitive interdependence.

    C. Falling demand.

    D. Strategic focus on deterring entry of new competitors into the marketplace.

Answer (C) is correct. *(IIA, adapted)*
    REQUIRED: The characteristics of a mature industry environment.
    DISCUSSION: Falling demand is characteristic of declining industries. These industries have sustained a permanent decrease in unit sales over the long run.
    Answer (A) is incorrect because consolidation is characteristic of a mature industry environment. Answer (B) is incorrect because competitive interdependence is characteristic of a mature environment. Answer (D) is incorrect because strategic focus on deterring entry of new competitors into the marketplace is competitive of a mature industry environment.

3.4 Competition in Global Industries

10. A global industry is one that

    A. Contains competitors that are multinationals.

    B. Has secured a competitive advantage based on economies of scale in centralized production.

    C. Has a strategic advantage by establishing coordinated competition in many national markets.

    D. Has made large direct investments abroad.

Answer (C) is correct. *(Publisher)*
    REQUIRED: The nature of a global industry.
    DISCUSSION: The analysis of a competition in an industry requires consideration of the economics of the industry and the characteristics of competitors. However, in a global industry, the analysis is not limited to one market, but extends to all markets (geographic or national) taken together. Michael E. Porter defines a global industry as "one in which the strategic positions of competitors in major geographic or national markets are fundamentally affected by their overall global positions." Thus, an industry becomes global because it perceives a net strategic advantage to competing, as Porter says, "in a coordinated way in many national markets."
    Answer (A) is incorrect because a true global industry is one that requires a firm to compete internationally. Accordingly, an industry is not global simply because some or all competitors are multinational. When nonmultinationals can compete in a geographic or national market, the industry is not global. Answer (B) is incorrect because economies of scale in centralized production may yield a cost advantage achievable only when output exceeds the demand in one country and exports are feasible. Vertical integration may provide the necessary scale. However, a global competitive advantage may be based on other factors, such as other economies of scale (purchasing, marketing, or logistical), proprietary technology, product differentiation, or mobility of production. Answer (D) is incorrect because participation in foreign markets is usually by licensing; export; or, after the firm has obtained experience, direct investment. A genuinely global industry will have significant export activity or direct investment, but the presence of the latter does not necessarily signal the existence of global competition. Direct investment also may occur when national factors only determine a subsidiary's competitive position.

11. Which strategy in a global industry is most likely to be facilitated by a transnational coalition?

    A. A protected niche strategy.

    B. A national focus strategy.

    C. A national segment strategy.

    D. Broad line global competition.

Answer (D) is correct. *(Publisher)*
    REQUIRED: The strategy in a global industry most likely to be facilitated by a transnational coalition.
    DISCUSSION: Broad line global competition is competition over the full product line of the firm based on differentiation or low cost. The firm needs large resources for this long-term strategy. Governmental relations should emphasize impediment reduction. Transnational coalitions may be created to help the firms overcome impediments to executing the broader strategies, for example, market access or technology barriers.
    Answer (A) is incorrect because a protected niche strategy is applied in nations where global competitors are discouraged by governmental impediments. The strategy is designed to be effective in markets with governmental constraints and requires close attention to the national government. Answer (B) is incorrect because a national focus strategy is limited to a national market or the segments with the greatest impediments to global competitors. Low cost or differentiation is sought. Answer (C) is incorrect because a national focus strategy is limited to a national market or the segments with the greatest impediments to global competitors. Low cost or differentiation is sought.

12. Which of the following would be a source of global competitive advantage?

A. Low fixed costs.

B. Production economies of scale.

C. Weak copyright protection.

D. Intensive local service requirements.

Answer (B) is correct.   *(IIA, adapted)*

REQUIRED: The source of global competitive advantage.

DISCUSSION: To the extent that n+1st unit is cheaper than the nth, large concentrated producers on a global scale have an advantage. (The archetypal example is oil refining). In other words, economies of scale in centralized production may yield a cost advantage achievable only when output exceeds the demand in one country and exports are feasible.

Answer (A) is incorrect because low fixed costs generally imply weak barriers to entry, and consequent ability of local competitors to effectively engage against a larger global firm. Answer (C) is incorrect because weak intellectual property rights enforcement would enable small local competitors to produce efficiently, if illicitly, in the short term. Answer (D) is incorrect because, to the extent that a product needs local support, this dilutes the advantage of being a large and efficient global competitor.

13. Governments restrict trade in order to

I.   Help foster new industries.
II. Protect declining industries.
III. Increase tax revenues.

A. I only.

B. I and II only.

C. II and III only.

D. I, II, and III.

Answer (D) is correct.   *(IIA, adapted)*

REQUIRED: The reason governments restrict trade.

DISCUSSION: The government normally restricts trade to develop new industries, protect declining industries, and to increase tax revenues.

Answer (A) is incorrect because developing new industries is only one reason the government restricts trade. Answer (B) is incorrect because the government also restricts trade to increase tax revenues. Answer (C) is incorrect because the government also restricts trade to protect declining industries.

14. Which one of the following is a social trend affecting the organization?

A. Changes in the labor markets.

B. Tougher legislation to protect the environment.

C. Rising inflation.

D. Replacements for steel in cars and appliances.

Answer (A) is correct.   *(IIA, adapted)*

REQUIRED: The types of social trends that affect organizations.

DISCUSSION: Social trends are changes that occur in society, such as changes in labor markets, that would also have an impact on an organization.

Answer (B) is incorrect because this is a political trend where the government is involved. Answer (C) is incorrect because inflation is connected with the economy, hence this is an economic trend. Answer (D) is incorrect because this represents a technological trend.

3.5 Integration Strategies

15. The decision to engage in the vertical integration of a firm is in large part a function of an analysis of throughput and economies of scale. If throughput is less than the efficient scale, the firm

    A. Should acquire a capability equal to its throughput.

    B. Must sell or buy in the open market if it vertically integrates at the efficient scale.

    C. Should engage in quasi-integration.

    D. Should not vertically integrate.

Answer (B) is correct. *(Publisher)*
REQUIRED: The effect of the analysis of throughput and economies of scale in a vertical integration decision.
DISCUSSION: Upstream (backward) or downstream (forward) integration is the acquisition of a capability that otherwise would be performed by external parties that are suppliers or customers, respectively, of the firm. Whether integration should occur depends on the firm's volume of transactions with the external parties (throughput) and the magnitude of the capability required to achieve necessary economies of scale. If the integrating firm's need is for a capability less than the efficient scale, one of its options is to acquire a capability with a cost inefficient scale. The other option is to acquire an efficient capability that provides excess output (in the upstream case) or creates excess demand (from, for example, a distribution capability in the downstream case). This option will require the integrated firm to sell or buy in the open market. Thus, the second option carries the risk of having to deal with competitors.
Answer (A) is incorrect because a full analysis of strategic benefits and costs may indicate that acquiring a capability with a cost inefficient scale may be best. The cost disadvantage may be offset by many other factors. Answer (C) is incorrect because a full analysis of strategic benefits and costs may indicate that acquiring a capability with a cost inefficient scale may be best. The cost disadvantage may be offset by many other factors. Quasi-integration (use of alliances, not ownership) may not provide many benefits of full integration. Answer (D) is incorrect because the best strategic decision may be to integrate either at the efficient or inefficient scale.

16. Which of the following is an arrangement that involves partial integration and implies the ability to fully support an efficient subunit?

    A. Quasi-integration.

    B. Tapered integration.

    C. Upstream integration.

    D. Contract integration.

Answer (B) is correct. *(Publisher)*
REQUIRED: The arrangement that involves partial integration and implies the ability to support fully an efficient subunit.
DISCUSSION: Tapered (partial) integration implies that the firm can fully support an efficient subunit but has additional needs to be met in the market. If the in-house subunit will not be efficient, that inefficiency must be weighed against the benefits of tapering. Tapering results in lower fixed costs than full integration. Furthermore, the strategy may allow the firm's subunit(s) to maintain constant production rates while external parties bear the risk of fluctuations. Another use of tapering is to protect against operational imbalances among the subunits. A risk of tapering is selling to, or buying from, competitors. Another is greater coordination cost. Advantages of tapering are avoidance of locked-in relationships, some access to external expertise, increased managerial incentives, offering a credible threat of full integration to suppliers or customers, and obtaining knowledge of the adjacent business and an emergency supply source.
Answer (A) is incorrect because quasi-integration is something more than a long-term contract and less than full ownership. It may be achieved by a minority common stock interest, debt guarantees, cooperation in R&D, an exclusive dealing arrangement, etc. Answer (C) is incorrect because upstream integration is backward integration by acquiring or building a supply capability. Answer (D) is incorrect because some of the economies of integration may be secured by contracts (long- or short-term) with independent parties, for example, through a long-term agreement with a supplier to provide all of the firm's needs for an input. However, such arrangements may be difficult to create because of the parties' dissimilar interests and the risks involved.

17. The effect of just-in-time production approaches

- A. Reduces the dependency on suppliers.
- B. Reduces the cost of implementing strategies.
- C. Decreases production facility flexibility.
- D. Increases the need for a dependable workforce.

Answer (B) is correct. *(IIA, adapted)*
   REQUIRED: The effect of just-in-time production approaches.
   DISCUSSION: Just-in-time (JIT) production approaches can reduce the cost of production. It lowers or eliminates inventory costs and requires production improvements to eliminate product defects.
   Answer (A) is incorrect because just-in-time (JIT) production approaches increase the need for reliable suppliers. When inventories are at low or nonexistent levels, supplier performance is critical. Answer (C) is incorrect because just-in-time (JIT) production increases flexibility. Production is pulled by demand. Answer (D) is incorrect because JIT requires workers to be multiskilled and independent. Such traits are needed in a pull system.

18. Backward integration strategy is most appropriate when the firm's current suppliers are

- A. Highly reliable.
- B. Not reliable.
- C. Geographically dispersed.
- D. Geographically concentrated.

Answer (B) is correct. *(IIA, adapted)*
   REQUIRED: The use of backward integration.
   DISCUSSION: Backward integration is appropriate when the firm's current suppliers are unreliable. It allows the firm to protect its proprietary knowledge from suppliers.
   Answer (A) is incorrect because backward integration is less likely if the firm's current suppliers are highly reliable. Answer (C) is incorrect because the reliability of suppliers is more important than whether they are geographically dispersed. Answer (D) is incorrect because the reliability of suppliers is more important than whether they are geographically concentrated.

19. A milk producer company acquires its own dairy farms to supply milk. The growth strategy adopted by the company can be identified as

- A. Horizontal integration.
- B. Vertical integration.
- C. Concentric diversification.
- D. Conglomerate diversification.

Answer (B) is correct. *(IIA, adapted)*
   REQUIRED: The correct type of growth strategy.
   DISCUSSION: Vertical integration occurs when a company becomes its own supplier or distributor. It combines within a firm production, distribution, selling, or other separate economic processes needed to deliver a product of service to a customer.
   Answer (A) is incorrect because horizontal integration may be described as adding new products to existing markets or new markets to existing products. Answer (C) is incorrect because concentric diversification occurs when a company adds new products which have technological synergies with the existing products. Answer (D) is incorrect because conglomerate diversification means making new products for an entirely new class of customers.

3.6 Capacity Expansion

20. What is the key strategic issue when a firm is considering capacity expansion?

- A. Forecasting long-term demand.
- B. Analyzing the behavior of competitors.
- C. Identifying options.
- D. Avoiding industry overcapacity.

Answer (D) is correct. *(Publisher)*
   REQUIRED: The key strategic issue when a firm is considering capacity expansion.
   DISCUSSION: Whether to expand capacity is a major strategic decision because of the capital required, the difficulty of forming accurate expectations, and the long time frame of the lead times and the commitment. The key forecasting problems are long-term demand and behavior of competitors. The key strategic issue is avoidance of industry overcapacity. Undercapacity in a profitable industry tends to be a short-term issue. Profits ordinarily lure additional investors. Overcapacity tends to be a long-term problem because firms are more likely to compete intensely rather than reverse their expansion.
   Answer (A) is incorrect because forecasting long-term demand, input costs, and technology developments is a step preliminary to predicting total industry capacity and firms' market shares. Answer (B) is incorrect because analyzing the behavior of competitors is a step preliminary to predicting total industry capacity and firms' market shares. Answer (C) is incorrect because identifying options is a step preliminary to predicting total industry capacity and firms' market shares.

21. When demand uncertainty is low, firms tend to adopt a strategy of preemptive expansion. The conditions for successful preemption expansion include which of the following?

    A. The firm should avoid market signals that alert competitors to the firm's plans.

    B. The expansion should be small relative to the market to minimize risk.

    C. Economies of scale should be large relative to demand.

    D. The business should be strategically vital to competitors.

Answer (C) is correct. *(Publisher)*
    REQUIRED: The condition for successful preemption.
    DISCUSSION: Economies of scale should be large in relation to demand, or the learning-curve effect should give an initial large investor a permanent cost advantage. For example, the preemptive firm may be able to secure too much of the market to allow a subsequent firm to invest at the efficient scale. That is, the residual demand available to be met by the later firm is less than the efficient scale of production. The later firm therefore must choose between intense competition at the efficient scale or a cost disadvantage.
    Answer (A) is incorrect because the firm must provide credible signals before action by competitors. Answer (B) is incorrect because the expansion must be large relative to the market, and competitors must believe that the move is preemptive. Hence, the firm should know competitors' expectations about the market or be able to influence them favorably. A move that is too small is by definition not preemptive. Answer (D) is incorrect because the competitors of the firm should be willing not to act. This condition may not be met if competitors have noneconomic objectives, the business is strategically vital to them, or they have greater ability or willingness to compete.

22. Capacity expansion is also referred to as

    A. Market penetration.

    B. Market development.

    C. Product development.

    D. Diversification.

Answer (A) is correct. *(IIA, adapted)*
    REQUIRED: The term used for capacity expansion.
    DISCUSSION: Market penetration is growth of existing products or development of existing markets. It occurs in mature firms within an industry.
    Answer (B) is incorrect because market development seeks new markets for current products. Answer (C) is incorrect because product development is launching new products in existing markets. Answer (D) is incorrect because diversification is launching new products for new markets.

3.7 Entry into New Businesses

23. Entry into a new business may be made by internal development or acquisition. Entry through internal development usually involves creation of a full-fledged new business entity. The costs likely to be incurred by an internal entrant include

I. Investments to overcome entry barriers.

II. Change in the equilibrium level of supply and demand.

III. Lower prices charged by competitors.

IV. Higher marketing costs.

    A. I and II only.

    B. I and IV only.

    C. II, III, and IV only.

    D. I, II, III, and IV.

Answer (D) is correct. *(Publisher)*
    REQUIRED: The costs likely to be incurred by an internal entrant.
    DISCUSSION: An internal entrant must cope with structural barriers and retaliation by existing firms. Costs incurred by the internal entrant include initial investments to overcome entry barriers (facilities, inventory, branding, technology, distribution channels, sources of materials, etc.), operating losses in the start-up phase, and the effects of retaliation (e.g., higher marketing costs, capacity expansion, or lower prices). Other costs include the price increases for factors of production that may result because of the new entry. Also, the capacity added to the industry by the entrant may affect the equilibrium level of supply and demand. The result may be additional competitive costs as firms with excess capacity cut prices.

24. Entry into a new business may be made by acquisition. The analysis differs from that for entry by internal development. A key point is that prices are set in the market for acquisitions. Accordingly, a buyer should most likely expect to make above-average profits when

    A. The market is active and well organized.

    B. The seller can choose to continue operating the business.

    C. The market for acquisitions is imperfect.

    D. It adopts a sequential entry strategy.

Answer (C) is correct. *(Publisher)*
REQUIRED: The circumstances in which entry through acquisition is most likely to result in above-average profits.
DISCUSSION: Acquisitions are more likely to earn above-average profits when the expected present value to the seller of continuing operations is low, e.g., because the seller needs funds, has capital limits, or has management weaknesses. Above-average profits are also more likely when the market for acquisitions is imperfect. For example, a) the buyer may have better information, b) there are few bidders, c) the economy is weak, d) the seller is weak, or d) the seller has reasons to sell other than profit maximization. Moreover, the buyer may have a unique ability to operate the seller.
Answer (A) is incorrect because, when the market is active and well organized, it is also efficient and therefore tends to eliminate above-average profits. Answer (B) is incorrect because one factor contributing to efficiency (and the elimination of above-average profits for a buyer) is that a seller normally can choose to continue running the business. Accordingly, a bidder ordinarily must pay the seller a premium in excess of the expected present value to the seller of continuing operations. The price minus that floor value equals the premium. Answer (D) is incorrect because sequential entry may be the best entry strategy. It involves entering one strategic group in the industry with subsequent mobility to another group(s). However, sequential entry is less likely to result in above-average profits than the existence of market imperfections.

Use Gleim's *CIA Test Prep* for interactive testing with over 2,000 additional multiple-choice questions!

STUDY UNIT FOUR
GLOBAL BUSINESS ISSUES

(10 pages of outline)

Globalization has progressed rapidly because of advances in communication, travel, transportation, and free trade agreements. Accordingly, The IIA has added the global environment to the CIA exam content specification outline.

4.1 OVERVIEW OF GLOBAL BUSINESS DEVELOPMENT

1. **Methods of Expanding into International Markets**

   a. **Licensing** gives firms in foreign countries the right to produce or market products or services within a geographical area for a fee.

      1) Licensing a process, patent, trade secret, etc., is a way to gain a foothold in a foreign market with little immediate risk. However, the licensor may have insufficient control over the licensee's operations, profits are lost if the arrangement succeeds, and the licensee ultimately may become a competitor.

   b. **Exporting** is the sale of goods manufactured in one country and then sold in other countries.

   c. In a **local storage and sale arrangement**, products manufactured in one country are then shipped to a marketing facility located in another country.

   d. **Local component assembly** involves shipping individual parts from one country to an assembly facility in a second country. They are then turned into a salable product and sold in the second country or exported to other countries.

   e. In **multiple or joint ventures**, several firms, even competitors, work together to create products that are sold under one or more brand names in different countries. They share responsibility, ownership, costs, and profits.

   f. An **indirect export strategy** operates through intermediaries, such as home-country merchants who buy and resell the product, home-country agents who negotiate transactions with foreign buyers for a commission, cooperatives that represent groups of sellers, and export-management firms that receive fees for administering the firm's export efforts. **Indirect export** requires lower investment than direct export and is less risky because of the intermediaries' expertise.

   g. **Direct investment** has many advantages: (1) cheaper materials or labor, (2) receipt of investment incentives from the host government, (3) a strong relationship with interested parties in the host country, (4) control of the investment, (5) a better image in the host country, and (6) market access when domestic contest rules are in effect. However, direct investment is risky because of exposure to currency fluctuations, expropriation, potentially high exit barriers, and restraints on sending profits out of the country.

h. The **internationalization process** is of crucial interest to nations that wish to encourage local firms to grow and to operate globally. According to Swedish researchers, it involves the following steps:

1) Lack of regular exports;
2) Export via independent agents to a few markets, with later expansion to more countries;
3) Creation of sales subsidiaries in larger markets; and
4) Establishment of plants in foreign countries.

i. **Attractiveness** of a foreign market is a function of such factors as geography, income, climate, population, and the product. Another major factor is the unmet needs of a developing nation, for example, China or India.

1) Entry into a market abroad may be based on many factors, for example, **psychic proximity**. Thus, a first-time venture abroad might be in a market with a related culture, language, or laws.

2. **Limited Entry.** According to Ayal and Zif, the following are factors indicating that few national markets should be entered:

a. Entry costs are high;
b. Market control costs are high;
c. Product adaptation costs are high;
d. Communication adaptation costs are high;
e. The first countries selected have large populations, high income, and a high rate of growth; and
f. A dominant firm can erect high entry barriers.

3. **Organizational Progression of Marketing in the International Environment**

a. **Export Division.** This is the first step for an organization when it begins selling products beyond its own borders. Generally, a firm's initial entry is in other markets that share a common language or similar cultural norms.

b. **International Division.** Large corporations make this step before becoming true global organizations. They generally focus their efforts in certain geographical regions that are led either from a central structure or are locally run and managed. Moreover, operating units report to the head of the division, not to a CEO or executive committee. Operating units may be geographical units, world product groups, or subsidiaries.

c. **Global Organization.** All elements of the organization are geared toward creating and selling products to a worldwide market. Thus, all elements of the firm can be made to be more efficient in the global arena. These elements include management, production facilities, and the procurement of raw materials and components.

1) **Glocalization** of a global organization localizes some of its elements but standardizes other elements.

4. **Comparative and Competitive Advantage – Porter**

a. A country has a **comparative advantage** when it can achieve a lower cost of production due to a focus on, and a cooperative specialization in, a particular product.

b. A firm has a **competitive advantage** when it can achieve a lower cost of production on particular items compared with firms in another country because of factors that are indigenous to its country.

c. Sources of competitive advantage include

1) A lower cost of production through natural resources or geography,
2) Quality or market factor differences, and
3) Supplementary supply patterns that enhance production advantages.

d. **Competitive Advantage in Global Industries**

1) **Cost Drivers**

a) Location of raw materials and other resources
b) Differences in costs between countries
c) Economy of scale potential in certain industries
d) Transportation costs

2) **Customer Drivers**

a) Common customer needs give an advantage to globalization.
b) Global customers.
c) Global channels are inhibited when strong local channels are in place.
d) Universal marketing enjoys an advantage when little change is required to market goods in a variety of nations.

3) **Competitive Drivers**

a) The existence of global competitors may indicate that the market is ripe for global expansion.
b) An industry may be a good target when the existing firms are enjoying product cross-subsidization.

4) **Government Drivers**

a) Trade policies may either be an advantage or disadvantage for a particular industry.
b) Technical standards may be lower in one country, giving producers a competitive edge in that arena.
c) Regulations may lead to lower costs of production in certain nations.

5. **Factors of National Advantage – Porter's Diamond Model**

a. The following are Porter's four determinants of why firms in some countries are more successful than others. The diamond model for determining factors of national advantage can be used by firms to identify their home-country advantages. It can also be used by governments to develop policies to create national advantages industries can exploit.

1) **Factor conditions** are specific production factors that include skilled labor, infrastructure, etc. Firms in each country will naturally select those industries that will give them an advantage due to their unique factor conditions.

2) **Home demand conditions** determine the inherent demand for goods or services that originate within the home country. Porter believes that home markets exert a much higher influence on a firm's ability to recognize consumer trends than those in a foreign market.

3) **Related and supporting industries** determine whether industries within the home country provide support for a given industry. Firms in countries that have a close-knit group of industries that support each other will enjoy an advantage over firms in other nations that do not.

4) **Firm strategy, structure, and rivalry.** How much firms work together or compete with each other can determine the advantage firms in a particular nation may enjoy over others. Also, organizational structure, how firms are established, and how they are managed will contribute to effectiveness in the global business environment.

6. **Strategies for Global Marketing Organization**

 a. A **multinational strategy** adopts a portfolio approach. Its emphasis is on national markets because the need for global integration is not strong.

  1) The product is customized for each market and therefore incurs higher production costs.
  2) Decision making is primarily local with a minimum of central control.
  3) This strategy is most effective given large differences between countries.
  4) Also, exchange rate risk is reduced when conducting business in this manner.

 b. A **global strategy** regards the world as one market.

  1) The product is essentially the same in all countries.
  2) Central control of the production process is relatively strong.
  3) Faster product development and lower production cost are typical.

 c. A **glocal strategy** combines some elements of local responsiveness or adaptation with some elements of global integration.

  1) Successful telecommunications firms are examples of balancing these elements.
  2) **Local responsiveness** is indicated when local product tastes and preferences, regulations, and barriers are significant.
  3) **Global integration** is indicated when demand is homogeneous and economies of productive scale are large.

7. **Global vs. Transnational Firms**

 a. **Global firms** are primarily managed from one central country. Even though their products may be sold throughout the globe, their headquarters and most of their policy decisions are set from a central base of operations.

 b. **Transnational firms** lack a national identity. These organizations rely on a decentralized structure for management and decision-making. They tend to be more attuned to local customs and market forces because they take much more of their input from a local or regional management team.

8. **Regional Free Trade Zones**

 a. The international **Triad Market** is considered to be the U.S., Western Europe, and Japan.

 b. The **European Union (EU)** is a collection of 15 European nations that have lowered trade barriers among member states and share a common currency and trade policy.

 c. The **North American Free Trade Agreement (NAFTA)** was created among the U.S., Mexico, and Canada. NAFTA will likely be expanded into South American countries.

 d. **MERCOSUL** is a free-trade agreement among South American nations. They include Argentina, Brazil, Uruguay, and Paraguay. Chile and Bolivia are associate members.

 e. **APEC** (the Asian Pacific Economic Cooperation forum) is a collection of 21 Pacific-rim nations, including the NAFTA countries, China, and Japan, dedicated to fostering increased trade with each other and the rest of the world.

9. **Cartels**. A cartel is an organization of sellers (e.g., the oil cartel OPEC) who undertake joint action to maximize members' profits by controlling the supply, and therefore the price, of their product. Under the laws of many nations, such collusive conduct is illegal when engaged in by firms subject to those laws. The reason is that, as a result of the monopolistic and anticompetitive practices of cartels, supply is lower, prices are high, competition is restrained, and the relevant industry is less efficient.

10. **Dumping**. Dumping is an unfair trade practice that violates international agreements. It occurs when a firm charges a price (1) lower than that in its home market or (2) less than the cost to make the product. Dumping may be done to penetrate a market or as a result of export subsidies.

11. Stop and review! You have completed the outline for this subunit. Study multiple-choice questions 1 through 11 beginning on page 107.

4.2 GLOBAL MARKETING ISSUES

1. **International Marketing Programs**

   a. Firms that operate globally must choose a marketing program after considering the need for adaptation to local circumstances. The possibilities lie on a continuum from a purely standardized marketing mix to a purely adapted marketing mix. The former chooses to standardize products, promotion, and distribution. The latter adapts the elements of the mix to each local market. Worldwide standardization of all elements should be the lowest cost marketing strategy. However, even well established global brands ordinarily undergo some adaptation to local markets.

   b. **Product and Promotion**

      1) Using a **straight extension** strategy, a higher profit potential exists because virtually no changes are made in the product or its promotion. There is a downside potential if foreign consumers are not familiar with this type of product or do not readily accept it.

      2) Using a **product adaptation** strategy, a firm makes changes in the product for each market but not in its promotion. This strategy can reduce profit potential but may also provide a marketing advantage by considering local wants and needs.

      3) Using a **product invention** strategy, a new product is created specifically for a certain country or regional market. A product may either include advancements for developed countries or have certain elements removed in places where a lower cost is a key selling point. **Backward invention** is the reintroduction of an earlier version of the product to meet local needs. This variant of the invention strategy reflects the possibility that different countries may be in different stages of the international product life cycle. **Forward invention** requires developing a new product for the unique needs of a foreign market.

      4) **Communication adaptation** is a strategy that does not change the products, but advertising and marketing campaigns are changed to reflect the local culture and beliefs.

      5) A **dual adaptation** strategy changes both the product and the promotion to provide the best chance of acceptance in a foreign market.

c.   **Price**

    1)   The gray market poses difficulties for a firm that sells products at different prices in different countries. In a **gray market**, products imported from one country to another are sold in a third country, or even in the original exporters country, by persons trying to make a profit from differences in retail prices.

    2)   The **price escalation** problem requires setting different prices in different countries. Price escalation is caused by an accumulation of additional costs, e.g., currency fluctuations; transportation expenses; profits earned by importers, wholesalers, and retailers; and import duties. Three strategies address this issue:

        a)   A firm may set a **standard price** globally. However, this strategy may result in prices being unprofitable in some markets and too high in others.

        b)   A firm may set a **market-based price** in each market. The drawback of this strategy is that it ignores cost differences. It also may create a gray market situation between certain regions.

        c)   A firm may set a **cost-based price** in each market with a standard markup. In a region or country where costs are high, this strategy may result in prices that are too high to be competitive within the local market.

    3)   A **transfer price** is the price charged by one subunit of a firm to another. When the subsidiary-buyer is in a foreign country, the higher the transfer price, the higher the potential tariffs. However, the tax levied on a subsequent sale by the subsidiary will be lower because of its higher acquisition cost.

d.   **Distribution channels** are a necessity to ensure goods are successfully transferred from the production facility to end users. These channels include three distinct links that must work smoothly together.

    1)   The **international marketing headquarters** (export department or international division) is where decisions are made with regard to the subsequent channels and other aspects of the marketing mix.

    2)   **Channels between nations** carry goods to foreign borders. They include air, land, sea, or rail transportation channels. At this stage, in addition to transportation methods, intermediaries are selected (e.g., agents or trading companies), and financing and risk management decisions are reached.

    3)   **Channels within nations** take the goods from the border or entry point to the ultimate users of the products. Among nations, the number of the levels of distribution, the types of channels, and the size of retailers vary substantially.

2.   **Steps to Brand Globally**

a.   These steps must be followed to try to avoid the risks of expanding into foreign markets and to maximize growth potential.

    1)   A firm must understand how diverse markets tie together to form a global branding landscape. Individual countries vary in their historical acceptance of products and services. However, firms may also capitalize on similarities that are found in certain areas and regions.

    2)   Branding and brand-building must be a process. New markets must be developed from the "ground up." Global firms must build awareness of the product and then create sources of brand equity.

    3)   Establishing a **marketing infrastructure** is crucial. To create a successful marketing structure, the firm either must merge with the local marketing channels or create a completely new method of distribution.

      4) **Integrated marketing communications** should be developed. Markets must be approached with a broad range of messages. Sole reliance on advertising should be avoided. Other marketing communications include merchandising, promotions, and sponsorship.

      5) The firm may create **branding partnerships**. Global firms often form alliances with local distribution channels to increase their profitability while decreasing their marketing costs.

      6) The firm should determine the **ratio of standardization and customization**. Products that can be sold virtually unchanged throughout several markets provide a greater profit opportunity for a global firm. However, cultural differences may require extensive customization to appeal to markets in different countries.

      7) The firm should determine the **ratio of local to global control**. Local managers may understand the wants and needs of their market, but the global firm must still retain control of certain elements of the marketing process and strategy.

      8) The firm should establish local guidelines so the local sales and profit goals are met.

      9) The firm should create a **global brand equity tracking system**. This equity system is a set of research processes that provide the marketers with pertinent information. The marketers can use this tracking system to create both long- and short-term strategies for expanding product sales and reach.

      10) The firm should maximize brand elements. Large global firms can achieve much greater expansion rates when the brand elements are successfully employed at the launch of a product or service.

3. Stop and review! You have completed the outline for this subunit. Study multiple-choice questions 12 through 25 beginning on page 110.

4.3 LEADERSHIP IN GLOBAL OPERATIONS

1. The most important characteristic of a successful leader has been determined to be the ability to develop additional leaders within his/her own team. The following are other **common characteristics of successful leaders in global organizations**:

    a. Extensive international travel during childhood prior to entering the working world.

    b. Influence and encouragement by family.

    c. A series of events that shaped their belief systems to include a foundation of honesty and trustworthiness.

    d. Key learning experiences that instilled the ability to be flexible and adaptable in a variety of situations.

    e. Strong role models who emphasized the importance of being fair, consistent, and true to inner principles and beliefs.

    f. Effective interpersonal skills and the ability to communicate successfully with a wide variety of individuals.

    g. Ability to speak one or more additional languages and extensive exposure to nonnative cultures.

    h. Effective problem-solving skills that draw from a multidisciplinary approach. The best candidates have varied backgrounds and can draw on a multitude of life experiences.

2. Research has been conducted on the success of different **leadership styles** in various countries.

    a. These leadership styles are based on the **path-goal** approach.

        1) A **directive style** establishes specific expectations, guidelines, schedules, rules, and standards.

        2) A **supportive style** regards employees as equals and attempts to improve their circumstances.

        3) A **participative style** entails consultation with employees and serious attention to their ideas.

        4) An **achievement-oriented style** sets high goals, emphasizes continuous improvement, and maintains confidence that employees will perform.

    b. The participative style, although not always the best, is the most widely accepted internationally.

    c. The directive style is the least accepted internationally. It was not deemed appropriate in the U.S., U.K., Canada, Australia, Germany, and Sweden.

    d. The achievement-oriented style was found unacceptable in such countries as Brazil, France, Italy, and Japan.

    e. The supportive style was not accepted in such countries as Brazil, France, India, and Sweden.

3. **Attitudes Toward Global Operations**

    a. An **ethnocentric attitude** assumes that the home country's people, practices, and ideas are superior to all others. Thus, the firm's identification is with the owner's nationality. Authority and decision making are centralized, so communication is likely to involve a high volume of information flow in the form of orders and advice to subsidiaries. Moreover, home-country standards are apt to be used for performance evaluation of entities and individuals. Also, this ethnocentric attitude is perpetuated by recruiting and developing home-country individuals for key posts throughout the firm. The advantages of an ethnocentric attitude are simplicity and close control. The disadvantages are social and political problems in foreign countries, poor feedback, ineffective planning, lack of flexibility and innovative thinking, and high turnover of managers in foreign subsidiaries.

    b. A **polycentric attitude** assumes that cultural differences require local managers to make most decisions because they are more knowledgeable about local conditions than are central administrators. Thus, development of local managerial talent is crucial. Another result is that foreign operating performance is primarily evaluated based on results. As a consequence, methods, training, and incentives vary significantly among subsidiaries. Furthermore, control is predominantly local, the firm is identified with the nationality of the host nation, and relatively little communication occurs with central administration or among subsidiaries. One disadvantage is that local operations may have inefficiencies because of duplication of activities. Another disadvantage is that the goals of local entities may not be consistent with those of the firm as a whole. Advantages are more capable and motivated local managers, better results in local markets, local development of new product ideas, and stronger support by host governments.

    c. A **geocentric attitude** is truly internationally oriented while absorbing the best that various cultures offer. It is a completely balanced approach with full collaboration between central administrators and subsidiaries, control and evaluation methods that harmonize local and overall firm standards, and frequent communication in all directions (i.e., between central administrators and subsidiaries and among subsidiaries). Moreover, talent, not nationality, determines personnel decisions throughout the firm.

4. Stop and review! You have completed the outline for this subunit. Study multiple-choice questions 26 through 31 beginning on page 115.

4.4 HUMAN RESOURCES ISSUES IN GLOBAL OPERATIONS

1. **Cross-cultural differences** are critical issues for global firms. Edward T. Hall defined **culture** as "a population's taken-for-granted assumptions, values, beliefs, and symbols that foster patterned behavior" (see Kreitner, *Management*, 9th ed.). Thus, in international business, misunderstanding and conflict arise because people from different cultures have fundamentally different assumptions, values, etc.

2. Hall drew a distinction between high-context and low-context cultures. In **high-context cultures** (e.g., Japanese, Chinese, Arabic, and Korean), much meaning is transmitted by nonverbal cues and situational circumstances. Thus, a person's status in a firm, rank in society, and reputation convey the primary message. In **low-context cultures** (e.g., Northern Europe and North America), primary messages are transmitted verbally. Hence, precise written contractual agreements are highly valued in a low-context culture. In contrast, social events are more valued in a high-context culture.

3. **Other Causes of Cultural Diversity**

   a. **Individualistic cultures** are societies that place a higher value on the rights and accomplishments of individual persons within the society. Examples are the U.S., U.K., Canada, and Australia. **Collectivist cultures** focus much more on the goals of family, friends, country, and the organization. Examples are China, India, Mexico, Japan, and Egypt.

   b. The perception of time as it relates to business and social life varies with the culture. **Polychronic time** is based on a perception that time is nonlinear, flexible, and multidimensional. This perception is typical of Mediterranean, Latin American, and Arabic cultures. **Monochronic time** is based on a perception that time is the same for everyone and is measurable in standard units. This perception is common in Northern Europe and the U.S. These western cultures believe in punctuality and that time is money and should not be wasted.

   c. **Interpersonal space** varies from only a few inches to several feet. Managers must be aware of these distances because they may be dramatically different from culture to culture. For example, Northern Europeans and North Americans tend to prefer holding conversations at arm's length. In Arabic and Asian cultures, however, the preferred conversational distance may be only six inches.

   d. Because of the **differences in language** even within the same country, special care must be taken not to make mistakes or offend others in a foreign land. It is nearly impossible for someone who has studied a foreign language only briefly to understand its subtleties.

   e. Global firms must respect local **religious beliefs and customs** to be successful. For example, local religious holidays, days off from work, and food restrictions should be understood.

4. **How American Management Theories Work in Other Countries**

   a. Dutch researcher Geert Hofstede has compared and contrasted the management characteristics of American managers with prevailing styles in 40 other countries.

      1) The following are the four cultural dimensions Hofstede used to categorize his results:

         a) **Power distance** is the degree of acceptance of unequal distribution of power in an organization.

         b) **Uncertainty avoidance** concerns the extent of the threat posed by ambiguous circumstances, the significance of rules, and the pressure for conformity.

          c)   The **individualism-collectivism** dimension addresses whether the organization protects its members in return for their loyalty or the individual must meet his/her own security needs.

          d)   The **masculinity versus feminity** dimension is the balance of masculine traits (aggressiveness, acquisitions, and performance) compared with the traditionally female traits (concern for others and the quality of life).

       2)   The U.S. received a low ranking on uncertainty avoidance, a less low ranking on power distance, a high ranking on masculinity, and the highest ranking on individualism. The conclusion, given the wide variance of these results with those for many other countries, is that American management theories need to be altered when applied in other countries.

    b.   Americans experience a high rate of failure when living and working abroad primarily as a result of not being adequately prepared to succeed within the new culture. Failure does not usually stem from technical incompetence.

       1)   American firms will probably enjoy greater success with expatriate managers if they better prepare their executives for cultural differences.

5.   **Training for Working in a Foreign Culture**

    a.   **Documentary programs** provide text-based or videotape preview of the history, culture, institutions, beliefs, and economy of the foreign country.

    b.   **Cultural assimilation practice** is similar to role-play techniques that are frequently used to train salespeople. Problem scenarios are presented to managers and workers, and they are coached on how to respond to them.

    c.   **Language instruction** is provided by various means to senior executives and mid-level managers who are now expected to learn the language of the country where they will be working. Some languages take years, not months, to master, but multilingual ability is a necessity.

    d.   **Sensitivity training** is focused mainly on educating workers about the beliefs and mores of the foreign country. Special care is given to topics that might bring embarrassment to a manager or offend his/her hosts.

    e.   **Experience in the field** involves actually traveling to the foreign country and interacting with its people. Usually, one or more guides are on hand to answer questions and provide feedback.

    f.   A firm's **management training** for work in a foreign country should be part of a planned career path that includes selection, orientation and training, and repatriation (professional and cultural readjustment). The last step includes a commitment from the firm that the expatriate will not be at a professional disadvantage because of his/her work abroad. Moreover, the process should also address the needs of families.

6.   Stop and review! You have completed the outline for this subunit. Study multiple-choice questions 32 through 35 beginning on page 117.

QUESTIONS

4.1 Overview of Global Business Development

1. Which of the following is the most significant reason that domestic governments and international organizations seek to eliminate cartels?

A. The increased sales price reduces the amount of corporate tax revenues payable to the government.

B. True competition keeps prices as low as possible, thus increasing efficiency in the marketplace.

C. Small businesses cannot survive or grow without government protection.

D. The economic stability of developing countries depends on a global free market.

Answer (B) is correct. *(IIA, adapted)*

REQUIRED: The best reason to eliminate cartels.

DISCUSSION: A cartel is an organization of sellers (e.g., the oil cartel OPEC) who undertake joint action to maximize members' profits by controlling the supply, and therefore the price, of their product. Under the laws of many nations, such collusive conduct is illegal when engaged in by firms subject to those laws. The reason is that, as a result of the monopolistic and anticompetitive practices of cartels, supply is lower, prices are high, competition is restrained, and the relevant industry is less efficient. Accordingly, governmental and international organizations seek to protect consumers and the health of the domestic and global economy through anti-cartel efforts.

Answer (A) is incorrect because an increased sales price would raise corporate profits. Thus, the tax revenue lost through eliminating cartel activity would serve as a disincentive to government anti-cartel efforts. Answer (C) is incorrect because, although the effect of cartel activities may be harmful to small businesses, the greatest impact is on the overall economy. Macroeconomic effects are the primary reasons for anti-cartel efforts by governments and international organizations. Answer (D) is incorrect because the contribution of a free market to the stability of developing countries' economies does not provide a compelling reason for domestic anti-cartel efforts in industrialized countries.

2. When a multinational firm decides to sell its products abroad, one of the risks it faces is that the government of the foreign market charges the firm with dumping. Dumping occurs when

A. The same product sells at different prices in different countries.

B. A firm charges less than it costs to make the product to enter or win a market.

C. Lower quality versions of the product are sold abroad so as to be affordable.

D. Transfer prices are set artificially high so as to minimize tax payments.

Answer (B) is correct. *(IIA, adapted)*

REQUIRED: The nature of dumping.

DISCUSSION: Dumping is an unfair trade practice that violates international agreements. It occurs when a firm charges a price (1) lower than that in its home market or (2) less than the cost to make the product. Dumping may be done to penetrate a market or as a result of export subsidies.

Answer (A) is incorrect because, in a gray market, the same product sells at different prices in different countries. The effect differs from that of dumping. A seller in a low-price market tries to sell the goods in a higher-price market. Products are not dumped to penetrate a market. Instead, a dealer seeks to resell at a favorable price. Answer (C) is incorrect because selling a lower quality product at a fair price is a perfectly acceptable strategy. Answer (D) is incorrect because a transfer price is a price charged to a subunit of an enterprise. Setting a high price to avoid an unfavorable tax rate has the opposite effect of dumping, assuming the subunit passes the cost on to its customers.

3. A global firm

A. Has achieved economies of scale in its domestic market.

B. Plans, operates, and coordinates business globally.

C. Relies on indirect export.

D. Tends to rely more on one product market.

Answer (B) is correct. *(Publisher)*

REQUIRED: The nature of a global firm.

DISCUSSION: According to Kotler, "Global firms plan, operate, and coordinate their activities on a worldwide basis." Thus, a global firm secures cost or product differentiation advantages not available to domestic firms.

Answer (A) is incorrect because one reason to go abroad is that economies of scale are so great that they cannot be achieved in a domestic market. Answer (C) is incorrect because global firms do not rely only on indirect export. They also rely on direct export, which is potentially more profitable. Answer (D) is incorrect because a global firm may be a small firm that sells one product or class of products, or it may be a large firm with a multiproduct line.

4. A firm expands into international markets

    A. To be in foreign markets.

    B. To eliminate foreign competition

    C. To pursue new, higher-profit opportunities.

    D. To preclude piracy of its products.

Answer (C) is correct. *(Publisher)*
REQUIRED: The reason to expand globally.
DISCUSSION: A firm may decide to go abroad for many reasons, for example, to respond to a competitive challenge in its home country by another global firm, to pursue opportunities yielding greater profits, to achieve economies of scale, to diversify, or to follow customers who need international service.
    Answer (A) is incorrect because a firm should enter international markets for well-defined purposes, not for some vague reason such as establishing a presence. Answer (B) is incorrect because a firm's counterattack in a foreign market is not likely to eliminate the competitor. However, it may serve as a market signal that will influence the foreign competitor's behavior in a way favorable to the firm. Answer (D) is incorrect because expansion does not prevent piracy.

5. A firm wishing to become global must consider how many national markets to enter. A firm should enter fewer national markets when

    A. Communication adaptation costs are low.

    B. The product need not be adapted.

    C. Entry costs are low.

    D. The first countries chosen are heavily populated and have high incomes.

Answer (D) is correct. *(Publisher)*
REQUIRED: The reason for a global firm to enter fewer national markets.
DISCUSSION: According to Ayal and Zif, the following are factors indicating that few national markets should be entered: (1) entry costs are high; (2) market control costs are high; (3) product adaptation costs are high; (4) communication adaptation costs are high; (5) the first countries selected have large populations, high incomes, and high income growth; and (6) a dominant firm can erect high entry barriers.
    Answer (A) is incorrect because low communication adaptation costs argue operations in many countries. Answer (B) is incorrect because low product adaptation costs argue for operations in many countries. Answer (C) is incorrect because low entry costs argue for operations in many countries.

6. The least risky method of entering a market in a foreign country is by

    A. Indirect exports.

    B. Licensing.

    C. Direct exports.

    D. Direct investments.

Answer (A) is correct. *(Publisher)*
REQUIRED: The least risky method of entering a market in a foreign country.
DISCUSSION: An indirect export strategy operates through intermediaries, such as home-country merchants who buy and resell the product, home-country agents who negotiate transactions with foreign buyers for a commission, cooperatives that represent groups of sellers, and export-management firms that receive fees for administering the firm's export efforts. Indirect export requires lower investment than direct export and is less risky because of the intermediaries' expertise.
    Answer (B) is incorrect because licensing a process, patent, trade secret, etc., is a way to gain a foothold in a foreign market with little immediate risk. However, the licensor may have insufficient control over the licensee's operations, profits are lost if the arrangement succeeds, and the licensee ultimately may become a competitor. Answer (C) is incorrect because direct export involves higher risk and investment but may yield higher returns. Answer (D) is incorrect because direct investment has many advantages: (1) cheaper materials or labor, (2) receipt of investment incentives from the host government, (3) a strong relationship with interested parties in the host country, (4) control of the investment, (5) a better image in the host country, and (6) market access when domestic contest rules are in effect. However, direct investment is risky because of exposure to currency fluctuations, expropriation, potentially high exit barriers, and restraints on sending profits out of the country.

7. An advantage of a direct investment strategy when entering a foreign market is

A. Reduction in the capital at risk.

B. Shared control and responsibility.

C. Assurance of access when the foreign country imposes domestic content rules.

D. Avoidance of interaction with the local bureaucracy.

Answer (C) is correct. *(Publisher)*
REQUIRED: The advantage of direct investment.
DISCUSSION: Direct investment has many advantages: (1) cheaper materials or labor, (2) receipt of investment incentives from the host government, (3) a strong relationship with interested parties in the host country, (4) control of the investment, (5) a better image in the host country, and (6) market access when domestic contest rules are in effect. However, direct investment is risky because of exposure to currency fluctuations, expropriation, potentially high exit barriers, and restraints on sending profits out of the country.
Answer (A) is incorrect because direct investment maximizes capital at risk. Answer (B) is incorrect because direct investment avoids shared control and responsibility. Answer (D) is incorrect because direct investment means a closer relationship with governmental entities in the host country.

8. A firm that moves from not exporting on a regular basis to establishing plants in foreign countries has

A. Globalized.

B. Nationalized.

C. Glocalized.

D. Internationalized.

Answer (D) is correct. *(Publisher)*
REQUIRED: The process of moving from not exporting on a regular basis to establishing plants in foreign countries.
DISCUSSION: The internationalization process is of crucial interest to nations that wish to encourage local firms to grow and to operate globally. According to Swedish researchers, it involves the following steps: (1) Lack of regular exports; (2) export via independent agents with a few markets, with later expansion to more countries; (3) creation of sales subsidiaries in larger markets; and (4) establishment of plants in foreign countries.
Answer (A) is incorrect because all elements of a global organization are geared toward selling in a worldwide market. Answer (B) is incorrect because nationalization is the takeover of an industry by a national government. Answer (C) is incorrect because glocalization of a global organization localizes some of its elements but standardizes other elements.

9. Which strategy for a global marketing organization is based on a portfolio of national markets?

A. Creation of a division to manage international marketing.

B. A multinational strategy.

C. A glocal strategy.

D. Creation of an export department.

Answer (B) is correct. *(Publisher)*
REQUIRED: The global organization strategy based on a portfolio of national markets.
DISCUSSION: International marketing efforts take three basic forms: creation of an export department, creation of a division to manage international marketing, or global organization. The latter encompasses genuinely worldwide functions, e.g., manufacturing, marketing, finance, and logistics. Thus, worldwide operations are the organization's focus, not merely that of a department or division of a national firm. A global organization may follow a multinational, global, or glocal strategy. A multinational strategy adopts a portfolio approach. Its emphasis is on national markets because the need for global integration is not strong. The product is customized for each market and therefore incurs higher production costs. Decision making is primarily local with a minimum of central control. This strategy is most effective given large differences between countries. Also, exchange rate risk is reduced when conducting business in this manner.
Answer (A) is incorrect because export departments and international divisions are organizational arrangements that precede the firm's evolution into a global organization. Answer (C) is incorrect because glocal strategy balances local responsiveness and global integration. Answer (D) is incorrect because export departments and international divisions are organizational arrangements that precede the firm's evolution into a global organization.

10. Which strategy for a global marketing organization balances local responsiveness and global integration?

   A. Global.

   B. Multinational.

   C. Glocal.

   D. Transnational.

Answer (C) is correct. *(Publisher)*
   REQUIRED: The strategy for a global marketing organization that balances local responsiveness and global integration.
   DISCUSSION: A glocal strategy combines some elements of local responsiveness or adaptation with some elements of global integration. Successful telecommunications firms are examples of balancing these elements. Local responsiveness is indicated when local product tastes and preferences, regulations, and barriers are significant. Global integration is indicated when demand is homogeneous and economies of productive scale are large.
   Answer (A) is incorrect because a global strategy is weighted toward global integration. Answer (B) is incorrect because a multinational strategy is weighted toward local responsiveness. Answer (D) is incorrect because the term "transnational" is sometimes applied to firms that operate internationally but with a decentralized overall structure.

11. The creation of regional free trade zones is a global phenomenon. Trade barriers are lowered in these areas, and other steps are taken to promote economic cooperation. For example, a common currency has been adopted by the nations of

   A. NAFTA.

   B. MERCOSUL.

   C. APEC.

   D. The European Union.

Answer (D) is correct. *(Publisher)*
   REQUIRED: The nations that have adopted a common currency.
   DISCUSSION: The European Union (EU) is a collection of 15 European nations that have lowered trade barriers among member states and share a common currency and trade policy. The euro is the common currency of the European Union.
   Answer (A) is incorrect because the North American Free Trade Agreement (NAFTA) was created by the U.S., Mexico, and Canada. It will likely be expanded to South American countries. However, NAFTA does not provide for a common currency. Answer (B) is incorrect because MERCOSUL is a free-trade agreement of South American nations, which includes Argentina, Brazil, Uruguay, and Paraguay, with Chile and Bolivia as associate members. However, these nations have no common currency. Answer (C) is incorrect because APEC (the Asian Pacific Economic Cooperation forum) is a collection of 21 Pacific-rim nations dedicated to foster increased trade with each other and the rest of the world. However, these nations have no common currency.

4.2 Global Marketing Issues

12. Firms that sell products worldwide are most likely to have the lowest costs with a marketing mix that is

   A. Adapted to each market.

   B. Standardized for all markets.

   C. A combination of new and adapted products in each market.

   D. A combination of standardized products and adapted promotions.

Answer (B) is correct. *(Publisher)*
   REQUIRED: The marketing mix most likely to have the lowest costs.
   DISCUSSION: Firms that operate globally must choose a marketing program after considering the need for adaptation to local circumstances. The possibilities lie on a continuum from a purely standardized marketing mix to a purely adapted marketing mix. The former chooses to standardize products, promotion, and distribution. The latter adapts the elements of the mix to each local market. Worldwide standardization of all elements should be the lowest cost marketing strategy. However, even well established global brands ordinarily undergo some adaptation to local markets.
   Answer (A) is incorrect because adaptation to each market incurs greater costs. Some economies of scale are lost. Answer (C) is incorrect because pure standardization of products, promotion, and distribution is likely to be the lowest-cost, but not necessarily highest-revenue, strategy. Answer (D) is incorrect because pure standardization of products, promotion, and distribution is likely to be the lowest-cost, but not necessarily highest-revenue, strategy.

13. A firm sells the same product in different countries and uses the same promotion methods. According to Keegan's model of adaptation strategies, this firm has adopted a strategy of

    A. Straight extension.

    B. Product adaptation.

    C. Product invention.

    D. Dual adaptation.

Answer (A) is correct. *(Publisher)*
    REQUIRED: The adaptation strategy followed.
    DISCUSSION: Using a straight extension strategy, a higher profit potential exists because virtually no changes are made in the products or its promotion. There is a downside potential if foreign consumers are not familiar with this type of product or do not readily accept it.
    Answer (B) is incorrect because, using a product adaptation strategy, a firm makes changes to the product for each market but not its promotion. This can reduce profit potential but may also provide a marketing advantage by taking into account local wants and needs. Answer (C) is incorrect because, using a product invention strategy, a new product is created specifically for a certain country or regional market. A product may either include advancements for developed countries or have certain elements removed in places where a lower cost is a key selling point. Backward invention is the reintroduction of an earlier version of the product to meet local needs. This variant of the invention strategy reflects the possibility that different countries may be in different stages of the international product life cycle. Forward invention requires developing a new product for the unique needs of a foreign market. Answer (D) is incorrect because a dual adaptation strategy changes both the product and promotion to provide the best chance of acceptance in a foreign market.

14. A firm wishing to sell its well-known brand of men's clothing in a certain foreign country redesigned the products because of the greater average size of consumers in that country. However, the firm retained the same basic advertising campaign. According to Keegan's model of adaptation strategies, this firm has adopted a strategy of

    A. Straight extension.

    B. Product adaptation.

    C. Forward invention.

    D. Backward invention.

Answer (B) is correct. *(Publisher)*
    REQUIRED: The adaptation strategy followed.
    DISCUSSION: Using a product adaptation strategy, a firm makes changes to the product for each market but not its promotion. This can reduce profit potential but may also provide a marketing advantage by taking into account local wants and needs.
    Answer (A) is incorrect because the product was adapted. Answer (C) is incorrect because no new product was created. Answer (D) is incorrect because no older product was reintroduced.

15. A firm that manufactures refrigerators sold ice boxes in urban areas of less developed countries. Many residents lacked electricity to power refrigerators but could purchase blocks of ice from local vendors for use in ice boxes. According to Keegan's model of adaptation strategies, this firm adopted a strategy of

    A. Product adaptation.

    B. Dual adaptation.

    C. Backward invention.

    D. Forward invention.

Answer (C) is correct. *(Publisher)*
    REQUIRED: The adaptation strategy followed.
    DISCUSSION: Using a product invention strategy, a new product is created specifically for a certain country or regional market. A product may either include advancements for developed countries or have certain elements removed in places where a lower cost is a key selling point. Thus, an ice box, a precursor of the modern refrigerator, is a backward invention.
    Answer (A) is incorrect because the refrigerator was not adapted. An older precursor product was reintroduced. Answer (B) is incorrect because dual adaptation involves product adaptation, not invention. Answer (D) is incorrect because forward invention is the development of a new product.

16. Gray market activity is in essence a form of arbitrage. To prevent this activity by their distributors, multinational firms

I.   Raise prices charged to lower-cost distributors.
II. Police their distributors.
III. Change the product.

    A. I only.

    B. I and II only.

    C. II and III only.

    D. I, II, and III.

Answer (D) is correct. *(Publisher)*
REQUIRED: The reaction to gray market activities.
DISCUSSION: In a gray market, products imported from one country to another are sold by persons trying to make a profit from the difference in retail prices between the two countries. These activities clearly lower the profits in some markets of the multinational firm that was the initial seller. One response is to monitor the practices of distributors and retaliate if necessary. A second response is to charge higher prices to the low-cost distributors to reduce their incentives to participate in a gray market. A third response is to differentiate products sold in different countries, e.g., by adapting the product or offering distinct service features.

17. A firm buys like-new computer equipment from bankrupt companies and resells it in foreign markets at prices significantly below those charged by competitors. The firm is

    A. Engaged in dumping.

    B. Engaged in price discrimination.

    C. Operating in a gray market.

    D. Operating in a black market.

Answer (C) is correct. *(Publisher)*
REQUIRED: The term for sale in a higher-price market of goods acquired cheaply in another market.
DISCUSSION: In a gray market, products imported from one country to another are sold by persons trying to make a profit from the difference in retail prices between the two countries. In essence, the seller firm in this case was exploiting a price difference between markets.
Answer (A) is incorrect because dumping is sale below cost or at less than the price charged in the home market. Answer (B) is incorrect because price discrimination involves illegally selling the same products at different prices to different customers. Answer (D) is incorrect because black market operations are illegal.

18. A firm ships its product to a foreign subsidiary and charges a price that may increase import duties but lower the income taxes paid by the subsidiary. The most likely reason for these effects is that the

    A. Price is an arm's-length price.

    B. Price is a cost-plus price.

    C. Transfer price is too low.

    D. Transfer price is too high.

Answer (D) is correct. *(Publisher)*
REQUIRED: The reason that sale to a subsidiary results in high import duties.
DISCUSSION: A transfer price is the price charged by one subunit of a firm to another. When the subsidiary-buyer is in a foreign country, the higher the transfer, the higher the potential tariffs. However, the tax levied on a subsequent sale by the subsidiary will be lower because of its higher acquisition cost.
Answer (A) is incorrect because an arm's-length price is what a competitor would charge in that market. Answer (B) is incorrect because a cost-plus price does not necessarily trigger higher import duties. Answer (C) is incorrect because, if the transfer price is too low, import duties would be lower and taxes would be higher.

19. A global firm establishes a cost-based price for its product in each country. The most likely negative outcome is that this pricing strategy will

    A. Set too high a price in countries where the firm's costs are high.

    B. Overprice the product in some markets and underprice it in others.

    C. Create a gray market.

    D. Result in dumping.

Answer (A) is correct. *(Publisher)*
REQUIRED: The most likely negative result of a cost-based pricing strategy.
DISCUSSION: A firm may set a cost-based price in each market with a standard markup. In a region or country where costs are high, this strategy may result in prices that are too high to be competitive within the local market.
Answer (B) is incorrect because a uniform pricing policy may overprice the product in some markets and underprice it in others. Answer (C) is incorrect because charging what consumers can afford in each country may create a gray market. Answer (D) is incorrect because dumping often entails charging a below-cost price.

20. A firm sells its product in a foreign market for a much higher price than in its home market. The reason is most likely

A. Price elasticity of demand.

B. Dumping.

C. Gray market activity.

D. Price escalation.

Answer (D) is correct. *(Publisher)*
REQUIRED: The most likely reason for disparate prices in different national markets.
DISCUSSION: Price escalation is caused by an accumulation of additional costs, e.g., currency fluctuations; transportation expenses; profits earned by importers, wholesalers, and retailers; and import duties.
Answer (A) is incorrect because price elasticity of demand is the relationship of total revenue to a change in price. If demand is price elastic, a price increase results in lower revenue. Answer (B) is incorrect because dumping is sale at a price below cost or below the price in the home country. Answer (C) is incorrect because In a gray market, products imported from one country to another are sold by persons trying to make a profit from the difference in retail prices between the two countries.

21. A firm sold the same product in many foreign countries but changed the ad copy to allow for language and cultural differences. According to Keegan's model of adaptation strategies, the firm adopted a strategy of

A. Product adaptation.

B. Communication adaptation.

C. Dual adaptation.

D. Straight extension.

Answer (B) is correct. *(Publisher)*
REQUIRED: The adaptation strategy followed.
DISCUSSION: Communication adaptation is a strategy that does not change the products, but advertising and marketing campaigns are changed to reflect the local culture and beliefs. For example, a firm may use one message but with changes in language, name, and colors. It may use a consistent theme but change the ad copy in each market. Another option is for a firm to devise a group of ads from which each market may choose the most effective. Still another option is to develop promotion campaigns locally.
Answer (A) is incorrect because the firm did not change the product. Answer (C) is incorrect because a dual adaptation strategy changes both the product and promotion to provide the best chance of acceptance in a foreign market. Answer (D) is incorrect because the firm did not change the product.

22. A firm that sells in foreign markets should consider all aspects of how products move from the firm to ultimate users. Where in the whole channel are marketing mix decisions most likely made?

A. Export department of the seller firm.

B. Import department of the buyer firm.

C. Channels within nations.

D. Channels between nations.

Answer (A) is correct. *(Publisher)*
REQUIRED: The place in an international marketing channel where marketing mix decisions are most likely made.
DISCUSSION: Distribution channels are a necessity to ensure that goods are successfully transferred from the production facility to end users. These channels include three distinct links that must work smoothly together.

1) The international marketing headquarters (export department of international division) is where decisions are made with regard to the subsequent channels and other aspects of the marketing mix.

2) Channels between nations carry goods to foreign borders. They include air, land, sea, or rail transportation channels. At this stage, in addition to transportation methods, intermediaries are selected (e.g., agents or trading companies) and financing and risk management decisions are reached.

3) Channels within nations take the goods from the border or entry point to the ultimate users of the products. Among nations, the number of levels of distribution, the types of channels, and the size of retailers vary substantially.

Answer (B) is incorrect because the seller makes these decisions. Answer (C) is incorrect because the seller's export department makes these decisions. Answer (D) is incorrect because the seller's export department makes these decisions.

23. The inherent attractiveness of a national market is most likely increased by which factor?

A. The firm's strategic position.

B. The market's exclusion from a regional free trade zone.

C. Unmet needs of a developing nation.

D. Product adaptation is costly.

Answer (C) is correct. *(Publisher)*
REQUIRED: The factor most likely increasing market attractiveness.
DISCUSSION: Attractiveness is a function of such factors as geography, income, climate, population, and the product. Another major factor is the unmet needs of a developing nation, for example, China or India.
Answer (A) is incorrect because the inherent attractiveness of a national market is primarily determined by its characteristics. Answer (B) is incorrect because, given the emergence of regional free trade blocs (e.g., the European Union, APEC, or MERCOSUL), a firm is more likely to enter a regional rather than a purely national market. Answer (D) is incorrect because low adaptation costs are attractive.

24. A firm considering entry into a market abroad may make its selection based on many criteria. For example, a Portuguese firm applying a psychic proximity criterion will most likely choose to enter which market?

A. Poland.

B. China.

C. India.

D. Brazil.

Answer (D) is correct. *(Publisher)*
REQUIRED: The market chosen on the basis of psychic proximity.
DISCUSSION: Psychic proximity means the nearness of the market's culture, language, and laws to those of the firm's home country. For example, Portuguese is spoken in Brazil.

25. Developing brand equity in a foreign market may be desirable but is subject to considerable risk. A global firm launching a new product in a new market most likely should

A. Initially place most of its emphasis on advertising geared to the local culture.

B. Fully decentralize control of the marketing process.

C. Avoid creating partnerships with local distribution channels to avoid dilution of the brand.

D. Balance standardization and customization of the product.

Answer (D) is correct. *(Publisher)*
REQUIRED: The most likely step taken by a global firm launching a new product in a new market.
DISCUSSION: The firm should determine the ratio of standardization and customization. Products that can be sold virtually unchanged throughout several markets provide a greater profit opportunity for a global firm. However, cultural differences may require extensive customization to appeal to markets in different countries.
Answer (A) is incorrect because integrated marketing communications should be developed. Markets must be approached with a broad range of messages. Sole reliance on advertising should be avoided. Other marketing communications include merchandising, promotions, and sponsorship.
Answer (B) is incorrect because the firm should determine the ratio of local to global control. Local managers may understand the wants and needs of their market, but the global firm must still retain control of certain elements of the marketing process and strategy. Answer (C) is incorrect because the firm may create branding partnerships. Global firms often form alliances with local distribution channels to increase their profitability while decreasing their marketing costs.

4.3 Leadership in Global Operations

26. Managerial attitudes toward global operations are viewed by researcher Howard Perlmutter as a key to understanding multinational firms. An ethnocentric attitude is indicated by

- A. An identification with the nationality of the host country.
- B. Collaboration between the firm's subsidiaries and its central administration.
- C. A high volume of information glow in the form of orders and advice to subsidiaries.
- D. A staffing emphasis on finding and developing the best people in the world for key positions anywhere in the firm.

Answer (C) is correct. *(Publisher)*
REQUIRED: The indicator of an ethnocentric attitude.
DISCUSSION: An ethnocentric attitude assumes that the home country's people, practices, and ideas are superior to all others. Thus, the firm's identification is with the owner's nationality. Authority and decision making are centralized, so communication is likely to involve a high volume of information flow in the form of orders and advice to subsidiaries. Moreover, home-country standards are apt to be used for performance evaluation of entities and individuals. Also, this ethnocentric attitude is perpetuated by recruiting and developing home-country individuals for key posts throughout the firm. The advantages of an ethnocentric attitude are simplicity and close control. The disadvantages are social and political problems in foreign countries, poor feedback, ineffective planning, lack of flexibility and innovative thinking, and higher turnover of managers in foreign subsidiaries.
Answer (A) is incorrect because a polycentric attitude is indicated by an identification with the nationality of the host country. An ethnocentric attitude is indicated by an identification with the nationality of the owner. Answer (B) is incorrect because a geocentric attitude is indicated by collaboration between the firm's subsidiaries and its central administration. Answer (D) is incorrect because a geocentric attitude is indicated by a staffing emphasis on finding and developing the best people in the world for key positions anywhere in the firm.

27. Managerial attitudes toward global operations are viewed by researcher Howard Perlmutter as a key to understanding multinational firms. A polycentric attitude is indicated by

- A. An identification with the nationality of the owner.
- B. Evaluation and control standards that are both local and global.
- C. High information flow in multiple directions.
- D. Relatively little decision making by the central administrative authority.

Answer (D) is correct. *(Publisher)*
REQUIRED: The indicator of a polycentric attitude.
DISCUSSION: A polycentric attitude assumes that cultural differences require local managers to make most decisions because they are more knowledgeable about local conditions than are central administrators. Thus, development of local managerial talent is crucial. Another result is that foreign operating performance is primarily evaluated based on results. As a consequence, methods, training, and incentives vary significantly among subsidiaries. Furthermore, control is predominantly local, the firm is identified with the nationality of the host nation, and relatively little communication occurs with central administration or among subsidiaries. One disadvantage is that local operations may have inefficiencies because of duplication of activities. Another disadvantage is loss of goal congruence between local entities and the firm as a whole. Advantages are more capable and motivated local managers, better results in local markets, local development of new product ideas, and stronger support by host governments.
Answer (A) is incorrect because an identification with the nationality of the owner is an indicator of an ethnocentric attitude. Answer (B) is incorrect because evaluation and control standards that are both local and global is an indicator of a geocentric attitude. Answer (C) is incorrect because high information flow in multiple directions is an indicator of a geocentric attitude.

28. Managerial attitudes toward global operations are viewed by researcher Howard Perlmutter as a key to understanding multinational firms. A geocentric attitude is indicated by

    A. An identification with national perspectives even though the firm is genuinely international.

    B. Control and evaluation methods that are locally determined.

    C. Decision making concentrated in the central administrative authority.

    D. Little communication among subsidiaries.

Answer (A) is correct. *(Publisher)*
    REQUIRED: The indicator of a geocentric attitude.
    DISCUSSION: A geocentric attitude is truly internationally oriented while absorbing the best that various cultures offer. It is a completely balanced approach with full collaboration between central administrators and subsidiaries, control and evaluation methods that harmonize local and overall firm standards, and frequent communication in all directions (i.e., between central administrators and subsidiaries and among subsidiaries). Moreover, talent, not nationality, determines personnel decisions throughout the firm.
    Answer (B) is incorrect because control and evaluation methods that are locally determined is an indicator of a polycentric attitude. Answer (C) is incorrect because decision making concentrated in the central administrative authority is an indicator of an ethnocentric attitude. Answer (D) is incorrect because little communication among subsidiaries is an indicator of an ethnocentric attitude.

29. According to research on the international contingency model of leadership, which path-goal leadership style is most likely to be accepted around the world as culturally appropriate?

    A. Directive.

    B. Participative.

    C. Supportive.

    D. Achievement-oriented.

Answer (B) is correct. *(Publisher)*
    REQUIRED: The path-goal leadership style most likely to be accepted around the world.
    DISCUSSION: A participative style entails consultation with employees and serious attention to their ideas. The participative style, although not always the best, is the most widely accepted internationally. Every country surveyed found it to be culturally acceptable.
    Answer (A) is incorrect because the directive style is the least accepted internationally. It was not deemed appropriate in the U.S., U.K., Canada, Australia, Germany, and Sweden. Answer (C) is incorrect because the supportive style was not accepted in such countries as Brazil, France, India, and Sweden. Answer (D) is incorrect because the achievement-oriented style was found unacceptable in such countries as Brazil, France, Italy, and Japan.

30. Research on the common characteristics of leaders of global firms found that

    A. Ambition and relentless drive were more significant than honesty and trustworthiness.

    B. They tended to have multidisciplinary problem solving ability.

    C. Being multilingual was unimportant.

    D. Having traveled extensively before entering the working world was relatively uncommon.

Answer (B) is correct. *(Publisher)*
    REQUIRED: The common characteristic of leaders of global firms.
    DISCUSSION: A common characteristic of successful leaders of global firms is that they have effective problem-solving skills that draw from a multidisciplinary approach. The best candidates have varied backgrounds and can draw on a multitude of life experiences. They also tend to be flexible and adaptable, have good interpersonal skills, and communicate successfully.
    Answer (A) is incorrect because these leaders were found to have been exposed to a series of events that shaped their belief systems to include a foundation of honesty and trustworthiness. They also had strong role models who emphasized the importance of being fair, consistent, and true to inner principles and beliefs. Answer (C) is incorrect because these leaders had the ability to speak one or more additional languages. In addition, they had extensive exposure to cultures that were nonnative. Answer (D) is incorrect because these leaders had engaged in extensive international travel during childhood prior to entering the working world.

31. For a multinational firm, which of the following is a disadvantage of an ethnocentric staffing policy in which all key management positions are filled by parent-company nationals?

A. It significantly raises compensation, training, and staffing costs.

B. It produces resentment among the firm's employees in host countries.

C. It limits career mobility for parent-country nationals.

D. It isolates headquarters from foreign subsidiaries.

Answer (B) is correct. *(IIA, adapted)*
REQUIRED: The disadvantage of ethnocentric staffing of key positions.
DISCUSSION: An ethnocentric staffing policy has the advantage that expatriates may understand the objectives, policies, and procedures of the parent firm better than local employees do. However, ethnocentrism in hiring has the following disadvantages, among others: (1) Expatriate managers have difficulty in adapting to a new culture, language, and physical environment; (2) training and relocation costs may be high; (3) host-country governments prefer local control; and (4) the morale and performance of host-country employees will suffer.
Answer (A) is incorrect because the key disadvantages of a geocentric staffing policy are that it significantly raises compensation, training, and staffing costs. Although an ethnocentric strategy involves relocation costs and higher compensation for expatriate managers, it allows the overall compensation structure to follow national levels in each country. Answer (C) is incorrect because this strategy limits career mobility of host country employees, not parent company employees. Answer (D) is incorrect because a polycentric staffing policy isolates headquarters from foreign subsidiaries.

4.4 Human Resources Issues in Global Operations

32. Cultures have been described as low-context or high-context. Which culture is high-context?

A. Germany.

B. Saudi Arabia.

C. Great Britain.

D. Switzerland.

Answer (B) is correct. *(Publisher)*
REQUIRED: The high-context culture.
DISCUSSION: Hall drew a distinction between high-context and low-context cultures. In high-context cultures (e.g., Japanese, Chinese, Arabic, and Korean), much meaning is transmitted by nonverbal cues and situational circumstances. Thus, a person's status in a firm, rank in society, and reputation convey the primary message. In low-context cultures (e.g., Northern Europe and North America), primary messages are transmitted verbally. Hence, precise written contractual agreements are highly values. In contrast, social events are more highly valued in a high-context culture.
Answer (A) is incorrect because Northern European cultures are low-context. Answer (C) is incorrect because Northern European cultures are low-context. Answer (D) is incorrect because Northern European cultures are low-context.

33. Which country is best described as having an individualistic culture?

A. India.

B. Japan.

C. Canada.

D. China.

Answer (C) is correct. *(Publisher)*
REQUIRED: The individualistic culture.
DISCUSSION: Individualistic cultures are societies that place a higher value on the rights and accomplishments of individual persons within the society. Examples are the U.S., U.K., Canada, and Australia. Collectivist cultures focus much more on the goals of family, friends, country, and the organization. Examples are China, India, Mexico, Japan, and Egypt.
Answer (A) is incorrect because India is an example of a collectivist culture. Answer (B) is incorrect because Japan is an example of a collectivist culture. Answer (D) is incorrect because China is an example of a collectivist culture.

34. According to Edward T. Hall, the perception of time is monochronic or polychronic. Which cultures perceive time as monochronic?

    A. Northern European.

    B. Latin American.

    C. Arabic.

    D. Mediterranean.

Answer (A) is correct. *(Publisher)*
REQUIRED: The cultures that perceive time as monochronic.
DISCUSSION: The perception of time as it relates to business and social life varies with the culture. Polychronic time is based on a perception that time is nonlinear, flexible, and multidimensional. This perception is typical of Mediterranean, Latin American, and Arabic cultures. Monochronic time is based on a perception that time is the same for everyone and is measurable in standard units. This perception is common in Northern Europe and the U.S. These western cultures believe in punctuality and that time is money and should not be wasted.
    Answer (B) is incorrect because, in a Latin American culture, time tends to be perceived as polychronic. Answer (C) is incorrect because, in an Arabic culture, time tends to be perceived as polychronic. Answer (D) is incorrect because, in a Mediterranean culture, time tends to be perceived as polychronic.

35. Dutch researcher Geert Hofstede has examined the cultural dimensions of organizational behavior in 40 countries. The United States ranked the highest in which dimension?

    A. Power distance.

    B. Uncertainty avoidance.

    C. Individualism.

    D. Masculinity.

Answer (C) is correct. *(Publisher)*
REQUIRED: The cultural dimension in which the United States ranked the highest.
DISCUSSION: The individualism-collectivism dimension addresses whether the organization or individual must meet his/her own security needs.
    Answer (A) is incorrect because the U.S. had a moderately low ranking on power distance. Answer (B) is incorrect because the U.S. had a low ranking on uncertainty avoidance. Answer (D) is incorrect because the U.S. had a high, but not the highest, ranking on masculinity.

Use Gleim's **CIA Test Prep** for interactive testing with over 2,000 additional multiple-choice questions!

STUDY UNIT FIVE
MOTIVATION AND COMMUNICATIONS

(17 pages of outline)

This study unit begins with a discussion of the individual needs that serve as a basis for motivation. It continues with a review of the various theories concerning the motivation of employees in an organization. The remaining subunits address the closely related subject of communication, including its nature and forms and the obstacles it encounters.

5.1 INDIVIDUAL DYNAMICS

1. Individual dynamics is fundamental to an understanding of motivation. It is concerned with the psychological model of a single personality. In contrast, group dynamics attempts to explain the behavior of people in groups.

   a. **Abraham Maslow** (1940s and 1950s) presented one of the most widely cited theories of motivation. He saw human needs as a hierarchy, from lowest to highest. Lower-level needs must be satisfied before higher-level needs can influence the individual. He concluded that as the set of needs on each level was satisfied, those needs ceased to be a motivator.

   b. Maslow's **hierarchy of needs** is listed below, from lowest to highest:

      1) **Physiological needs** are the basic requirements for sustaining human life, such as water, food, shelter, and sleep. Maslow believed that, until these needs are satisfied to the degree needed to maintain life, higher-level needs will not serve as motivators.

      2) **Security or safety needs** include freedom from physical or emotional harm, the loss of a job, and other threats.

      3) **Affiliation or acceptance needs** are the needs of people as social beings for love, affection, friendship, and belonging.

      4) **Esteem** is the need to be valued by both one's self and others. These needs are satisfied by power, prestige, status, and self-confidence.

      5) **Self-actualization** is the highest need in the hierarchy. It is the need to realize one's own potential for growth and continued development. Thus, the job itself is an **intrinsic** motivation; no **extrinsic** motivation (such as rewards or reinforcements) is needed. Intrinsic motivation provides the worker with psychological utility.

c. Research does not support the concept of a strict hierarchy in all situations, except for the requirement that biological needs be satisfied before other needs begin to serve as motivators.

1) Physiological and safety needs tend to decrease in importance for fully-employed people. Needs for acceptance, esteem, and self-actualization tend to increase.

2) Higher-level needs, esteem and self-actualization, are variable in their motivational effects, depending upon the individual.

d. Maslow's hierarchy does not apply equally to all situations. It is dependent on the social, cultural, and psychological backgrounds of the people involved.

1) People of different cultures respond differently.
2) Professional workers, skilled workers, and unskilled workers react differently.
3) Other social, ethnic, and cultural factors make people react differently.
4) The hierarchy is not a smooth, step-by-step path; it is a complicated, intermingled, and interdependent set of relationships.

a) However, the tendency to move upward as lower needs are satisfied does exist.

e. According to **David McClelland**, motivation is based on the **needs** for achievement, power, and affiliation.

1) The need for **achievement** is the drive to succeed in relation to a set of standards. Thus, high achievers wish to do something better than it has been done before. They thrive when the job provides personal responsibility, feedback, and moderate risks. They avoid very easy or very difficult tasks, and they do not like to succeed by chance.

2) The need for **power** is a desire to compel others to behave in certain ways, to influence or control others. Individuals with a high need for power are concerned with prestige and status and prefer to be in charge.

3) The need for **affiliation** is the need for close, amicable interpersonal relationships. Individuals with a high need for affiliation seek friendship, cooperative rather than competitive situations, and mutual understanding.

f. The **ERG theory** developed by Clayton Alderfer states that the core needs are existence (physiological and security needs), relatedness (affiliation and external esteem needs), and growth (self-actualization and internal esteem needs).

1) ERG theory argues that multiple needs may serve as motivators at the same time.

2) Frustration of a higher need may lead to regression to a lower need. For example, frustration of growth needs through inability to find more fulfilling work may result in a heightened need to make money.

g. **Individual values**

1) Values are specific to each individual person and involve moral and personal issues.
2) Values are learned from family, friends, school, and life experience in general.
3) Values can be modified throughout life but ordinarily tend to stay the same.
4) It is important to reward good values in a corporation to prevent fraud, theft, and deception and improve worker morale.

a) The value structure is an important part of the corporate culture.

5) Personal beliefs, such as those on religious and political matters, cannot be the basis of personnel actions. Discrimination on the basis of personal beliefs could expose the organization to legal action.

h.   **Human defense mechanisms**

1)   Defense mechanisms come into play when an employee feels jeopardized or threatened. Some of the most common methods of defense are listed below.

a)   Rationalization entails giving more acceptable reasons for behavior than the actual ones.

b)   Regression involves reversion to child-like behavior.

c)   Repression eliminates stressful items from working memory.

d)   Projection is the attribution of one's own ideas, feelings, or attitudes to others, especially the externalization of blame, guilt, or responsibility as a defense against anxiety.

e)   Compensation attempts to offset bad qualities with good qualities.

f)   Withdrawal is simply avoidance.

g)   Aggression involves a direct attack on the perceived causes of the problem.

2.   Stop and review! You have completed the outline for this subunit. Study multiple-choice questions 1 through 6 beginning on page 135.

5.2 MOTIVATION

1.   Motivation describes an entire class of drives, desires, needs, fears, and similar forces that cause behavior.

a.   The ideal management action motivates subordinates by structuring situations and requiring behaviors that will simultaneously satisfy the needs of subordinates and the organization.

b.   The organization's needs and those of the individual **need not conflict**.

c.   The **level of motivation** is determined by individuals' opportunity to satisfy their needs within the organizational setting. The greater the ability to satisfy these needs, the greater the motivational level.

1)   The inducements that an organization offers an individual should be matched with the contributions expected from that individual. Thus, each side should be willing to give up something to receive a desired benefit.

2)   The task of a **leader** is to make available the kinds and amounts of inducements an individual requires in exchange for the kinds and amounts of contributions the organization requires.

2.   **Classical views** stress fear and economics as motivators, i.e., the carrot-and-stick approach. For example,

a.   Economic incentive programs or bonuses (carrots).

b.   Losing one's job or being demoted (sticks).

c.   According to **Frederick Taylor's** scientific school of management, motivation in the business organization was simple. His concept of motivation began and ended with monetary incentives. He felt that money was the common ground between workers and management. Prosperity for the company must be accompanied by prosperity for the worker, and vice versa.

3.   **Behavioralists** believe that these motivational strategies are effective only for the short run or for people who don't have job alternatives. This approach focuses on participation and personal involvement in the work situation as motivational factors.

4. **Chris Argyris** (1964) proposed a theory of motivation that involves integrating the needs of the individual with those of the organization.

    a. Conflict arises when a mature, independent adult who seeks self-actualization joins a highly structured, demanding, and limiting organization.

        1) EXAMPLE: A highly competent aeronautical engineer who takes a job with the federal government may find his/her attempts to pursue technical excellence through intellectual effort stifled by the rules and procedures that are characteristic of a bureaucracy.

        2) Self-actualization is the process of accomplishing goals to the limit of one's ability because of the personal need to excel.

        3) Challenging new job assignments are a means of satisfying an employee's self-actualization needs.

5. **Douglas McGregor's Theory X and Theory Y** (1960s) are simplified models that define the extremes of managers' views on employee conduct. They permit a manager to evaluate his/her own tendencies.

    a. **Theory X** is the viewpoint of the autocratic manager. It is thought to be very common.

        1) "Average human beings have an inherent dislike of work and will avoid it if possible."

        2) "Because of this dislike for work, most people must be coerced, controlled, directed, and threatened with punishment to get them to put forth adequate effort toward the achievement of organizational objectives."

        3) "Average human beings prefer to be directed, have relatively little ambition, and want security above all."

    b. **Theory Y** is the extreme opposite of Theory X. The permissive manager assumes that

        1) "The expenditure of physical and mental effort in work is as natural as play or rest -- to average human beings,"

        2) "External control and the threat of punishment are not the only means for bringing about individual effort toward organizational objectives. Employees will exercise self-direction and self-control in their efforts to accomplish goals thought to be worthwhile,"

        3) "Commitment to objectives is proportional to the rewards associated with their achievement,"

        4) "Average human beings learn, under proper conditions, not only to accept responsibility, but to seek it,"

        5) "The capacity to exercise a relatively high degree of imagination, ingenuity, and creativity in the solution of organizational problems is widely, not narrowly, distributed in the population," and

        6) "Under the conditions of modern industrial life, the intellectual potentialities of the average human being are only partially realized."

    c. McGregor did not suggest that Theory Y was the only correct managerial behavior. He suggested these theories as starting points from which a manager can examine his/her own views about human nature.

6. **Theory Z**.

    a. William Ouchi (*Theory Z: How American Management Can Meet the Japanese Challenge*, Addison-Wesley, 1981) analyzed the characteristics of **Japanese companies** that produce high employee commitment, motivation, and productivity. At many of these companies, employees are guaranteed a position for life, increasing their loyalty to the organization. Careful evaluation occurs over a long period, and the responsibility for success or failure is shared among employees and management. Most employees do not specialize in one skill area. Their career paths are **cross-functional**; that is, they work at several different tasks, learning more about the company as they develop. The Japanese companies also are often concerned about all aspects of their employees' lives, on and off the job.

    b. Ouchi also analyzed successful American companies and identified those that had Japanese and American characteristics. These **hybrid or Theory Z organizations** tended to have stable employment, high productivity, and high employee satisfaction. Such outcomes are those sought by Theory Y managers. The following are traits of Theory Z organizations:

        1) The **goal** of Theory Z is to achieve a long-range orientation among workers.

        2) The promise of long-term employment creates intense **job loyalty**. This opportunity is the foundation of Theory Z.

        3) **Teamwork** is a key requirement of a Theory Z organization. Collective (participative) decision making occurs in all activities.

            a) This approach is a bottom-up process. It is slower than a top-down approach.

        4) **Promotion and performance evaluation** occur more slowly than is typical in American companies.

            a) The result is that a long-range orientation is rewarded and less emphasis is put on short-term successes.

            b) However, because most workers in Western companies are accustomed to more frequent promotions, performance must be recognized in other ways.

        5) Despite the focus on group decision making, Theory Z still emphasizes **individual responsibility**. Because sole reliance on a group decision is hard for Western businesses to accept, Theory Z recommends that an individual be assigned responsibility for carrying out the group's decision.

        6) Theory Z requires **trust** among employees and between employees and management.

            a) The concept of egalitarianism stresses that each person can work autonomously and without supervision because (s)he is to be trusted.

        7) The **holistic orientation** of Theory Z organizations includes employees and their families in all decisions. Work and social life are integrated.

        8) Theory Z balances the concept of **self-control** with the external control methods favored by most American organizations.

        9) Criticisms of Theory Z include:

            a) Japanese success is due to their work ethic, not their management style. Adopting this style will not alter the basic values of the American worker.

            b) Theory Z creates a work atmosphere that is resistant to change, crushes individual expression through conformity, and lacks the ability to make quick decisions.

            c) Theory Z is just a new name for practices that have existed for many years.

7. **Frederick Herzberg's two-factor theory of motivation** (late 1950s) is based on satisfaction. He argued that two classes of motivational factors exist in the job situation.

    a. **Dissatisfiers (maintenance or hygiene factors).** These factors are found in the **job context**. Their presence will not especially motivate people, but their absence will lead to diminished performance. They include organizational policy and administration, supervision, working conditions, interpersonal relations, salary, status, and job security.

    b. **Satisfiers (motivational factors).** These factors relate to **job content**. Their absence will not diminish performance, but their addition or availability will motivate employees. They include achievement, recognition, challenging work, advancement, growth in the job, and responsibility.

    c. Satisfaction and dissatisfaction are on a continuum. In the middle of this continuum is the point at which an employee experiences neither job satisfaction nor dissatisfaction. At this point, (s)he is not dissatisfied with the job context but also is not positively motivated.

    d. If Herzberg is correct, considerable attention should be given to upgrading job content through the use of job enrichment strategies.

    e. Herzberg's work has not gone unchallenged. Other researchers have found hygiene factors to be potent in yielding both satisfaction and dissatisfaction and therefore motivation. Nevertheless, Herzberg's ideas have been well received by practicing managers because many of them hold similar beliefs about motivation.

        1) Based on Herzberg's analysis, some jobs obviously do not contain many motivators, but others have more than are being fully used by management. For example,

            a) Routine, low-status work such as mail sorting has few motivators.

            b) A company that may be paying above the industry average (maintenance factor) could also increase satisfaction by openly acknowledging sales or other efforts by initiating a salesperson of the week recognition program.

8. **Job Design**

    a. **Job design** is the process of linking tasks to particular jobs in a way consistent with the organization's strategies, structure, and resources (including technology). One approach is to **adapt people to the jobs**. The following are techniques for avoiding job dissatisfaction when this approach is used:

        1) A **realistic job preview** is a full explanation of what the job involves, including its negative aspects. The purpose is to reduce or eliminate false expectations. Written previews should be provided before hiring, and verbal previews should be provided after hiring.

        2) **Job rotation** may introduce a welcome element of change in boring, highly specialized jobs. It may also have such benefits as cross-functional training and avoidance of repetitive stress injuries.

        3) **Contingent time off** is an award earned by early completion of a fair performance quota for a day's work without loss of pay.

    b. Another approach to job design is to **adapt the job to the people** performing them. The following are common methods:

        1) **Job enlargement** is primarily a technique for combating boredom at repetitive or highly paced jobs through the assignment of a variety of simple tasks as part of one job. Such jobs are horizontally loaded.

2) **Job enrichment** attempts to structure the job so that each worker participates in planning and controlling. The purpose is to maximize the satisfaction of both social and ego needs and to avoid the disadvantages of routine, highly specialized work. Job enrichment should improve motivation by **vertically loading** the job, that is, increasing its complexity and challenge.

    a) According to the **job characteristics model** developed by J.R. Hackman and G.R. Oldham, jobs are enriched by improving the following basic aspects of a job:

        i) **Skill variety**, or the diversity of talents required;

        ii) **Task identity**, or the performance of a job from start to finish of an identifiable, entire work product;

        iii) **Task significance**, or the effect on other people within or outside the firm;

        iv) **Autonomy**, or greater discretion over methods, sequence, and pace of work; and

        v) **Feedback**, or receipt of information about performance.

    b) Enrichment should produce three critical psychological states: meaningfulness, responsibility, and knowledge of results. The first three core characteristics determine the meaningfulness of work. Autonomy results in responsibility for work outcomes, and clear feedback provides knowledge of actual outcomes. These states should produce high motivation, performance, and satisfaction; low turnover; and low absenteeism.

    c) The model computes a **motivating potential score** (MPS) as follows:

$$\left(\frac{Skill\ Variety \times Task\ Identity \times Task\ Significance}{3} \right) \times Autonomy \times Feedback$$

9. **Expectancy theory** (Victor Vroom, 1960s) is based on the commonsense idea that people have subjective expectations of rewards derived from their unique personal motive structures (achievement, affiliation, power, etc.), beliefs as to what is valuable (a trip to Acapulco, a gold watch, a pat on the back), and expectations of receiving these rewards if they exert effort (probability assessments, such as, "If I do this, will I get that reward?").

    a. High effort expended, ability, and accurate role assessment will lead to a high performance level (i.e., putting appropriate effort into the right task and having the right amount of ability to do it will lead to high performance).

        1) Insufficient ability will impede performance despite effort.

        2) Executing a task that is not desired or is improperly performed according to role definition will impede performance despite effort or ability.

    b. Expectancy theory is based on **individual perception** of

        1) The value of rewards,

        2) The probability the required effort will result in the required performance, and

        3) The probability that the required performance will result in receipt of the desired rewards.

    c. **Expectancy** results from past experiences and measures the strength of belief (the probability assessments) that a particular act will be followed by a specific outcome.

        1) **Management** is more able to control the expectancy factor than the individual perception of the value of rewards because expectations are based on past experiences. A consistent management policy will reinforce employee expectations.

    d.   **Performance** leads to rewards.

        1)   Individuals evaluate rewards on the basis of equity ("Did I get what I deserved for what I did?") compared with others in similar jobs.

        2)   If inequity exists, individuals react, usually negatively.

    e.   Perception of the equity of rewards leads to **satisfaction** ("I got what I earned.")

        1)   The level of satisfaction or dissatisfaction feeds back into the next cycle's estimates of reward values, individual abilities, and role perceptions.

10.   **Goal-setting theory** is another attempt to explain motivation. According to Edwin Locke's goal-setting theory, specific, difficult goals to which the employee is committed provide the best motivation tool.

    a.   Performance improves when goals are **specific** rather than general, **difficult** rather than easy, and **participative** (self-set) rather than imposed by others.

    b.   Furthermore, **specific feedback**, especially self-generated feedback, also improves performance compared with lack of feedback.

    c.   Goals serve as motivators because they

        1)   Focus **attention** on specific objectives,
        2)   Require **effort** to achieve,
        3)   Necessitate continued actions (**persistence**), and
        4)   Create an incentive for developing **strategies and action plans**.

11.   **Equity theory** states that employee motivation is affected significantly by relative as well as absolute rewards. An employee compares the ratio of what (s)he receives from a job (outcomes such as pay or recognition) to what (s)he gives to the job (inputs such as effort, experience, ability, or education) with the ratios of relevant others.

    a.   If the ratios are equal, equity exists, but if they are unequal, equity tension exists, and the employee will be motivated to eliminate the tension.

    b.   The referent chosen (the employee's experience inside or outside the organization or the experiences of others inside or outside the organization) tends to be affected by the employee's job tenure, education, and salary level. For example, better-educated employees are more likely to make comparisons with outsiders, and longer-tenured employees may rely on coworkers.

    c.   Equity tension leads to changes in inputs or outcomes, distorted perceptions of one's effort or of the referent, choice of a different referent, or abandonment of the job.

12.   **Cognitive evaluation theory** holds that intrinsic rewards (such as competence, responsibility, and achievement) tend to be reduced when extrinsic rewards (such as higher pay, promotion, and better working conditions) are provided for superior performance.

    a.   The reason may be that the individual perceives a loss of control over his/her behavior. However, research suggests that the negative effects of extrinsic rewards on motivation do not apply when a job provides either a very high or a very low level of intrinsic rewards. In the latter case, extrinsic rewards may actually increase intrinsic motivation.

13.   **Rewards** are the benefits, psychological and otherwise, of work to employees. Proper management of reward systems should improve job satisfaction and performance.

    a.   **Extrinsic rewards** are received from others. They range from pay to praise.

        1)   **Intrinsic rewards** are the internal psychological payoffs that an employee gives to him/herself. The higher levels of Maslow's hierarchy consist of such rewards.

    b.   **Employee compensation** accounts for a high proportion of the organization's total costs. It also involves many complex legal and taxation questions.

1) **Nonincentive plans** include payment of hourly wages or annual salaries. These plans are easy to manage but provide no performance incentives.

2) **Incentive plans** include **piece rate** (a fixed amount for each unit of physical output) and **sales commission** compensation. **Merit pay** provides bonuses for excellent performance. **Sharing** of profits, productivity gains, or cost savings gives employees a vested interest in the organization's success. However, performance may be affected by factors that employees cannot control. **Stock-based employee compensation** has advantages and disadvantages similar to those of profit sharing. **Knowledge-based** plans pay employees for skills learned or completion of degree requirements.

3) A **cafeteria-plan** (life-cycle benefits plan) provides for employee choices that suit their personal circumstances. For example, age or marital status may determine whether an employee desires health insurance, pension benefits, or family leave.

4) A compensation plan should be perceived by employees as fair. It meets the **personal equity** test if rewards are proportional to effort. (But overpaid employees also may perceive inequity.) It meets the **social equity** test if an employee believes that his/her effort-to-reward ratio is proportionate to that of others in similar circumstances.

5) In accordance with **expectancy theory**, an effective plan should be administered so that employees believe that their efforts will be rewarded.

6) A plan also should provide additional rewards for excellent **performance**. Hourly and annual compensation plans may not be effective in this respect.

7) Other types of employee compensation include

   a) **Flextime** (flexible working hours). Granting reasonable scheduling flexibility tends to improve manager-employee relations, promote better performance, and minimize absenteeism. Disadvantages are higher administrative costs and ensuring that job duties are performed.

   b) **Job-sharing**, a practice favored by many parents.

   c) Permanent part-time work.

   d) Compressed work weeks (e.g., 40 hours over 4 days).

   e) **Wellness programs**, such as those promoting physical fitness, smoking cessation, weight loss, or stress reduction.

   f) **Family support**, such as paid or unpaid parental leave, family sickness leave, on-site daycare, emergency childcare, and eldercare.

8) Family support may be required by law. In the U.S., the Family and Medical Leave Act (FMLA) mandates the availability of unpaid leave for child care and other family and personal needs. However, most businesses and 43% of employees are not covered.

   a) The law applies to the federal, state, and local governments and to companies with 50 or more employees living within 75 miles of work. Eligible employees must have worked for the employer for an average of 25 hours a week for one year (1,250 hours over 12 months).

   b) The law provides up to 12 weeks of unpaid leave after the birth or adoption of a child. Both parents are eligible.

   c) Leave may also be taken to care for a sick spouse, child, or parent, or when an employee is too sick to work.

   d) Employees must give 30 days' notice if feasible.

   e) Employers must provide **health benefits** during the leave period and give returning workers the **same or an equivalent job** in terms of pay, responsibilities, and other working conditions.

f) Employers may exclude the highest-paid 10% of employees. They also may require that employees use other leave time (vacation or sick days) first.

g) If a state parental or family law provides better benefits, employees may choose that option.

h) In many companies, employees may substitute paid "sick leave" for unpaid leave, but this is not a requirement of the law.

14. For outlines of subjects closely related to this subunit, see Study Unit 8, Influence and Leadership.

15. Stop and review! You have completed the outline for this subunit. Study multiple-choice questions 7 through 24 beginning on page 137.

5.3 NATURE OF COMMUNICATION

1. **Communication** is the process of conveying and understanding information between one person and another. It affects all organizational activities and moves in many directions.

2. The **communication process** has five elements (the mnemonic is SSMRF).

   a. **Sender**, the person who originates the message
   b. **Symbols**, in which the message is **encoded**
   c. **Medium**, the channel through which the message flows
   d. **Receiver**, the person who decodes the message and interprets the sender's meaning
   e. **Feedback**, acknowledging to the sender that the message was correctly understood

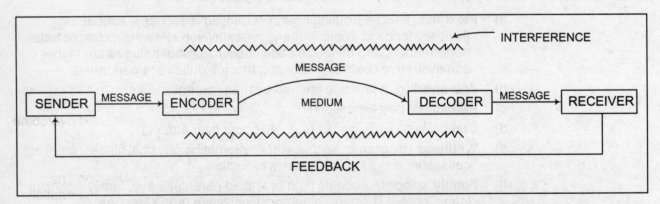

3. Because all managerial functions require communication, it is the secret to the success of any manager. A manager's ability to understand other people and their ability to understand the manager are crucial to accomplishing organizational objectives. Communication is the link that ties an organization together and transforms a diverse group of people into a cohesive whole.

   a. An organization's internal communications network is designed to facilitate decision making among managers, promote goal congruence among employees, integrate the efforts of all employees, and build high morale and mutual trust.

   b. **Formal communication** is conducted through the formal structure of the organization, e.g., budgets, bonus programs, memoranda, or technical manuals.

   c. Informal communication (the **grapevine**) operates outside of formal structural media.

      1) The grapevine exists wherever there are people.

      2) Grapevines can exist in several **patterns**. For example, one person may tell one other person who tells one other person, etc. (a **single strand** pattern); one person may tell all people in a group (**gossip**); individuals may tell selected others (a **cluster** pattern, the most common); or individuals may tell others at random (a **probability** pattern).

3) The grapevine is usually accurate, but it can carry gossip and rumor, and it serves as an emotional outlet for employees. It also satisfies employees' innate desire to know what is actually happening. The emergence of electronic media in the workplace has made the grapevine even more pervasive and important.

4) Managers can minimize the damage that a grapevine can cause by transmitting accurate and timely information and maintaining open media of communication. The effective manager stays tuned in to the grapevine and uses it constructively.

d. **Written communication** provides a permanent record of the message and tends to be accurate but can be time consuming to prepare. An inherent weakness of written communication is that it inhibits feedback because the sender and the receiver are not in simultaneous communication.

e. **Oral communication** is less formal and less accurate than written communication but permits immediate feedback. It also permits messages to be transmitted rapidly. Most managers spend more of their time in oral communication than in written communication.

f. **Electronic communication**. Modern technology (e.g., voice mail, fax, and e-mail) blurs the distinction between written and oral communications. The benefits of electronic communication include better control of information, more timely information, elimination of tedious tasks, improvement of competitiveness due to improved technology, standardization of procedures by computer programs, assistance for strategic planning, and optimization of organizational resources to improve productivity.

g. **Directions of Communication**

1) **Downward communication** (from superior to subordinate) is vertical communication consisting of orders, instructions, notices, memos, bulletins, newsletters, handbooks, loudspeakers, and the chain of command.

2) **Upward communication** (from subordinate to superior) is vertical communication consisting of morale surveys, traditional grievance procedures, peer review of grievances, suggestion systems, informal meetings, Internet chat, exit interviews, and conferences. Upward communication must overcome more barriers and is slower than downward communication.

3) **Horizontal (lateral) communication** is from one peer to another.

h. Lengel and Daft have proposed a **contingency model for media selection**. Its fundamental concept is **media richness**, which is the ability "to convey information and promote learning."

1) Media richness may be high, e.g., in a face-to-face meeting or in another interactive framework. A rich medium is characterized by many cues (content, tone of voice, body language, its personal emphasis, and immediate feedback).

2) Media richness may be lean (low), e.g., company memos or general e-mail that may be viewed as impersonal static. A lean medium is essentially the opposite of a rich medium.

3) The **management problem** is to choose the appropriate medium with the degree of richness appropriate to the circumstances. For example, rich (lean) media should be used for nonroutine (routine) problems.

4.   The **effectiveness of communication** can be determined only when the sender seeks feedback and observes the impact of the communication on the receiver.

   a.   The sender is obligated to solicit feedback to ensure the communication process is complete.

   b.   The receiver is obligated to give feedback to the sender.

   c.   The importance of feedback to verify the effectiveness of the communication process indicates the limitations of one-way communications (e.g., memos).

5.   Managers must consider the **nature of the message receiver**. Receivers vary in their perception of messages because of language, education, culture, attitudes toward the sender and job, etc. This variance may result in communication distortion.

   a.   EXAMPLES:

      1)   In some cultures, to move toward a person while speaking is expected. In others, it is considered an act of aggression.

      2)   In some cultures, consistently being late to appointments means laxness, lack of concern, discourtesy, and disinterest. In others, it is normal, expected, and carries no particular meaning.

6.   **Organizational structure** is a determinant of how communication is transmitted.

   a.   **Traditional or classical management** stresses the sending of one-way communications from top management down to the subordinates. This military model of organization (command and control) is autocratic or mechanistic and ignores the need for feedback.

   b.   **Participative management** stresses multidirectional communication. All parts of the organization are allowed and expected to communicate with each other, not merely along lines of authority.

   c.   **Systems theory** stresses the importance of feedback in determining the effectiveness of communications. Without a channel from the receiver back to the sender, the sender has no idea how the information has affected the performance or actions of the receiver, if at all.

7.   **Nonverbal Communication**

   a.   **Nonverbal signals** occur in clusters, whether or not accompanied by verbal communication. They include such nonverbal nuances as

      1)   Vocal characteristics such as tone of voice
      2)   Facial expressions and eye contact
      3)   Hand and body gestures and other movements
      4)   Breathing, sighs, and other noises that are not words
      5)   Physical distance between the sender and the receiver
      6)   Posture and other aspects of physical appearance
      7)   Touch
      8)   Mode of attire
      9)   Decoration and layout of rooms

   b.   Nonverbal communication is easily misunderstood because

      1)   Different cultures and languages employ different nonverbal signals, and
      2)   Clarifying the ambiguities inherent in nonverbal communication is difficult.

   c.   Interpreting nonverbal communication requires the establishment of the norms in a particular person's nonverbal repertoire.

      1)   For example, folded arms may signify resistance or inflexibility, or may simply be a habit.

      2)   People should not be judged solely on established or learned norms of nonverbal communication but instead on an individual basis.

    d. For any communication to be effective, both verbal and nonverbal messages should complement each other.

8. **Organizational communication strategy continuum**. Clampitt, DeKoch, and Cashman have devised a model with two dimensions. **Communication effectiveness** (the vertical dimension) is the degree to which meaning is fully and precisely transmitted. The **amount of information** (the horizontal dimension) may be large or small.

    a. The **spray-and-pray strategy** ineffectively conveys too great an amount of information using one-way, impersonal methods, such as corporate e-mail, that require receivers to determine the central issues.

    b. The **tell-and-sell strategy** conveys less information and indicates what is important. It is often used by senior managers attempting to gain support for major corporate changes. The result is greater effectiveness. A weakness is that refining the presentation may be done at the expense of not addressing the needs of the receiver.

    c. The **underscore-and-explore strategy** is interactive. It states priorities and reasons for action and allows employees to give feedback "in a disciplined way." Its success depends on communicating the appropriate amount of information, effective listening, resolution of misunderstandings, and striving for consensus.

    d. The **identify-and-reply strategy** is reactive, and the emphasis is on listening. Employees are presumed to understand the central issues. Moreover, they effectively "set the agenda." Managers may use this strategy to reply to leaks or rumors.

    e. The **withhold-and-uphold strategy** is characterized by stringent control of information and a Theory X view of management. Managers view secrecy as promoting (upholding) their power. Communication effectiveness is low because too little information is shared and both rumors and resentment abound.

    f. The optimal strategy is underscore and explore. Tell-and-sell and identify-and-reply strategies should be used infrequently. The other, low-effectiveness strategies should not be used.

    g. Within cost limits, managers should adopt the **richest medium** to implement a communications strategy.

9. Stop and review! You have completed the outline for this subunit. Study multiple-choice questions 25 through 43 beginning on page 142.

5.4 PROBLEMS IN COMMUNICATION

1. **Encoding** is the way that meaning is transmitted in communication. **Decoding** is the way a recipient of a message applies meaning to what is received. **Poorly encoded messages** result from

    a. Inappropriate choice of words or phrases.

        1) An example is using technical language (jargon) in speaking with a lay person. The skill levels of both the sender and the recipient are pertinent to the manner in which a message should be encoded.

    b. Careless omissions of key ideas.

    c. Lack of coherence in forming the message.

    d. Inconsistency between verbal and nonverbal messages.

    e. Incomplete ideas or ideas out of the receiver's context.

    f. **Projection**, which is the tendency of the sender to attribute his/her traits, values, and emotions to the receiver, and vice versa.

    g. **Filtering** the message so that it reflects more favorably on the sender, a typical problem in upward communication.

2. **Faulty Medium Selection**

   a. Trying to speak while a loud airplane flies overhead

   b. Gesturing to someone who cannot see the gesture

3. **Noise in the communications medium** is an outside disruption that impedes the flow of a message, for example,

   a. Asking for a raise during discussion of an operational problem,

   b. Random events that cause a breakdown in communication (lost mail, phone service disruption, etc.), or

   c. Use of technical language by the sender that is unlikely to be understood by the receiver.

4. **Perceptual problems** can be minimized with feedback from the receiver concerning his/her perceptions and interpretations of the message, understanding of the sender's perspective by the receiver, the sender's sensitivity to the receiver's problems, and implementation of an organization-wide training program to improve communication skills. These perceptual errors may arise from

   a. The sender's dislike of the receiver, or vice versa;

   b. Distortion created by personal enthusiasm for embellishing good news and downplaying the bad, or vice versa;

   c. Status differences among people that impede free and open communication;

      1) Few people are secure enough to tell a superior that what was just said was not understood.

   d. **Selective perception** caused by the receiver's needs, motives, projections, experiences, and expectations; or

      1) People tend to interpret what they see and hear in the light of their own needs, etc., and to regard that interpretation as reality.

      2) Moreover, people necessarily must narrow their perception to avoid sensory overload. Such screening is required to organize and interpret experience.

   e. **Stereotyping** or attributing to another person traits that are commonly associated with a category or group to which that person belongs.

5. **Use of Communication Media for Enhancement of Personal Status**

   a. Some lower-level employees who have the ear of management become influential among their peers. These individuals are, in effect, **gatekeepers** because they can determine which messages will be communicated. For example, an editor of a newspaper is a gatekeeper. (S)he can control what is communicated through the newspaper.

   b. **Opinion leaders** can be used to enhance the reception that a message obtains. Celebrities may or may not be good opinion leaders. For example, the opinion of a local mechanic about a new car might carry greater weight than would a celebrity endorsement of the same car.

   c. A **media liaison** is an individual in an organization who has been formally charged with the job of facilitating communication. An example is a public relations director.

6. **Loss in Transmission and Poor Retention**

   a. As much as 30% of the information in oral communication is lost in each transmission. Even written communications are subject to some loss. After passing through a chain of command, little of the message may have been retained.

   b. Poor retention. One study found that as little as 50% of communicated information was retained by employees.

7. **Nonreception**. The receiver commonly fails to receive any communication.

   a. Inattention or disinterest in the message--Messages are sometimes screened and those in which the recipient has no interest are ignored.

   b. Information overload--The receiver is already receiving so many messages that (s)he cannot process what (s)he is hearing.

   c. Confusing messages--The sender is not sending enough information to fully communicate thoughts, and the receiver must allocate too much time to interpreting what the sender is saying.

8. **Formal Breakdowns of Communications Media**

   a. EXAMPLE: Omissions from mailing lists

9. **Solutions to Communications Problems**

   a. The message should be in the context of the receiver's perceptions.

      1) Explaining an accounting concept to a nonaccountant will require terms different from those used with someone who has an accounting background.

   b. The sender must monitor media to ensure they are free from distortion or breakdown.

   c. The sender must actively solicit feedback to ensure reception and understanding.

   d. The organizational climate should encourage the elimination of interpersonal barriers to communication.

   e. The sender should look for nonverbal cues or feedback (such as body language).

   f. The sender must remember that it is his/her responsibility to deliver the communication with appropriate symbols through appropriate media and never to make assumptions about the receiver's reaction.

   g. Two-way (interactive) communication should be used whenever possible to permit ease of feedback.

   h. Communication can be improved through redundancy, that is, by repeating the message in several different formats and in several media.

10. Stop and review! You have completed the outline for this subunit. Study multiple-choice questions 44 through 61 beginning on page 147.

5.5 LISTENING AND ELECTRONIC COMMUNICATION

1. **Listening** is the responsibility of both the speaker (sender) and the listener (receiver). Listening is one of the problems in communication that can be improved by the manager. The art of listening must be exercised effectively to

   a. Gain more information about the work situation, and

   b. Have a positive effect on both superiors and subordinates through showing concern for their views.

2. **Problems in Listening**

   a. People can listen several times faster than words can be spoken, which may result in inattention and mind-wandering.

   b. Evaluating, or prejudgment of the message, before or during the communication process, may reduce the ability to listen objectively. In other words, the recipient could be biased and fail to give the message adequate consideration.

   c. Concentration may be focused on the words used to the exclusion of the ideas. In other words, there is a decoding problem.

3. **Guides to More Effective Listening**

    a. **Empathy** is the process of mentally putting oneself in another person's position to better understand his/her feelings, attitudes, and thoughts. Empathy

    1) Enables the sender and the receiver to take into account each other's backgrounds, biases, beliefs, and values,

    2) Aids in anticipating others' reactions to messages, and

    3) Aids in effective communication by guiding the choice of

        a) Words used and their meanings,
        b) Word inflection and emphasis, and
        c) Tone of voice and gestures.

    b. **Sensitivity training** gives managers a greater awareness of, or sensitivity to, their own attitudes, feelings, and beliefs. This understanding helps them perceive how their behavior affects the people with whom they communicate.

    1) Such training is designed to result in better listening skills, tolerance for individual differences, and an awareness of the impact of one's personality on other people.

    2) The disadvantage is that some managers may spend a disproportionate amount of time focusing on relationships rather than on the day-to-day problems of the job.

    c. **Interpersonal communications training**. Supervisors and their subordinates receive formal training in how to give and receive both written and oral communication. The advantage is that everyone has the same training and can practice working together using specific problems.

    d. Effective listening tools include paraphrasing what has been heard, being attentive physically and mentally, asking relevant questions, avoiding premature judgments, and summarizing after the speaker has finished.

4. **Electronic Communication**

    a. **Telecommuting**. People who are computer literate have in recent years begun working from outside the office. They correspond with their offices by means of telecommunication.

    1) Advantages are savings of travel time and expenses, reduced cost of office space, access to larger pool of employees, avoidance of office distractions, and potentially greater productivity.

    2) Problems associated with these employees include a tendency to fall behind in their fields of specialization, a lack of strong working relationships with other employees, a loss of career opportunities, and inadequate organizational socialization.

    3) The primary strength of these individuals, however, has been their communication skills.

    4) Many corporations have taken advantage of fax machines, e-mail, file transfer protocol (ftp), high-speed modems, the Internet, and various network configurations to make telecommuting more practical and useful.

    b. **E-mail** is part of a global communications revolution. To avoid its excessive, inefficient, or offensive use, an organization should adopt an e-mail **policy**.

    1) Employees should understand that the organization has the legal right to monitor their use of the e-mail system.

    2) The policy should stress that the system is not for private use.

    3) Filters should be installed to protect against spam. If it eludes the filters, it should be promptly deleted.

        4)   The principles of good writing apply to e-mail messages, especially the need for conciseness.

        5)   The policy should provide guidelines for transmission, receipt, and retention of e-mail.

  c. **Cell phones** provide mobile communications at reasonable cost. Because they provide a means of performing work outside a traditional work place, business communications may be more timely, flexible, and convenient.

        1)   The disadvantage of cell phones is the increased **risk of security**. Thus, critical information might be revealed to eavesdroppers.

        2)   Cell phone use should be consistent with the principles of good manners, including consideration for people nearby.

  d. **Videoconferencing** permits people at distant locations to meet without the cost and expenditure of time required for travel.

        1)   Videoconferencing via live television or the **Internet** may enhance productivity. Its expense has decreased, and its availability (e.g., through rental of a videoconferencing facility) has increased.

5.   Stop and review! You have completed the outline for this subunit. Study multiple-choice questions 62 through 67 beginning on page 152.

QUESTIONS

5.1 Individual Dynamics

1. Maslow's theory of motivation is based on a hierarchy of human needs. The need satisfied by greater income is

  A. Self-actualization.

  B. Safety.

  C. Participation.

  D. Authority.

Answer (B) is correct. *(Publisher)*
  REQUIRED: The need satisfied by greater income.
  DISCUSSION: Maslow saw human needs as a hierarchy and held that lower-level needs (physiological and safety needs) must be satisfied before higher-level needs (acceptance by peers, esteem, self-actualization) can influence the individual. Safety needs involve protection not only from physical harm but also from economic insecurity. Job and income security help to satisfy the need for safety.
  Answer (A) is incorrect because, according to Maslow, the highest need in the hierarchy is self-actualization. It is the desire to become what one is capable of becoming, to realize one's potential, and to accomplish to the limit of one's ability. Challenging work helps to satisfy this need. Answer (C) is incorrect because participation is not part of Maslow's hierarchy. Answer (D) is incorrect because authority is not part of Maslow's hierarchy.

2. Connections Inc., the largest provider of mental health services in its area, was encountering personnel problems. Their facilities housed many clients, but funding never seemed adequate to hire quality, live-in staff. A new administrator is determined to facilitate long-term employment of the best possible care-giving staff. Besides paying better wages, she feels it is important that the staff be strongly motivated by the work itself. According to Maslow's hierarchy of needs, the best employees would have a need for

  A. Esteem.

  B. Belonging.

  C. Self-actualization.

  D. Safety and security.

Answer (C) is correct. *(CMA, adapted)*
  REQUIRED: The aspect of Maslow's hierarchy of needs that refers to the motivation by the work itself.
  DISCUSSION: Self-actualization is the highest level need in Maslow's hierarchy. Self-actualization refers to the desire to become what one is capable of becoming, to realize one's potential and accomplish to the limit of one's ability. It becomes important only after the lower level needs have been met. The work itself becomes the motivator after all lower level needs are satisfied.
  Answer (A) is incorrect because esteem is the need to be valued, which is satisfied by power, prestige, status, and self-confidence. Answer (B) is incorrect because belonging is the need to be accepted by others, which would not be applicable when the desire is to have people motivated by the work itself. Answer (D) is incorrect because safety and security are met by higher wages. The question asks about something above and beyond higher wages.

3. A manager has a small team of employees, but each individual is self-motivated and could be termed a "high achiever." The manager has been given a particularly difficult assignment. Even for a high achiever, the probability that this job can be completed by one individual by the required deadline is low. Select the best course for the audit manager.

    A. Assign one individual since high achievers thrive on high risks.

    B. Assign two employees to moderate the risk of failure.

    C. Assign all employees to ensure the risk of failure is low.

    D. Ask company management to cancel the job.

Answer (B) is correct.   *(CIA, adapted)*
    REQUIRED: The best course of action for a manager whose team consists of high achievers.
    DISCUSSION: High achievers wish to do something better than it has been done before. According to McClelland's theory of needs, high achievers thrive when the job provides for personal responsibility, feedback, and moderate risks. They avoid very easy or very difficult tasks, and they do not like to succeed by chance. Accordingly, one high achiever should not be assigned a job when the probability of its successful completion is very low.

4. Which of the following statements is true with respect to a change in values?

    A. Values are neither stable nor enduring.

    B. The process of questioning values will result in a change.

    C. Values are not fixed, and when they change, they change quickly.

    D. Values are established in early years and are unlikely to change.

Answer (D) is correct.   *(CIA, adapted)*
    REQUIRED: The true statement about values.
    DISCUSSION: Values are specific to each individual and involve moral and personal issues. They tend to be learned in childhood from parents, friends, and others. Values can be modified throughout life but ordinarily tend to stay the same.
    Answer (A) is incorrect because values are stable and enduring. Answer (B) is incorrect because questioning values may result in their reinforcement. Answer (C) is incorrect because values are relatively fixed and change only slowly.

5. Which of the following is not an advantage of teamwork compared with work performed by individuals?

    A. Teams provide support to the team members.

    B. Teams make decisions that are more easily accepted.

    C. Teams provide a clear link between effort and outcome.

    D. Teams control and discipline members.

Answer (C) is correct.   *(CIA, adapted)*
    REQUIRED: The item that is not an advantage of teamwork.
    DISCUSSION: In a culture that strongly emphasizes individual identity and competition, the preference tends to be for a clear link between effort and outcome. However, teams tend to submerge individual identity and responsibility and therefore to blur the link between individual effort and its results.

6. There has been an increased emphasis on group decision making in organizations. Which of the following statements has been found to hold true in studies of individual decision making as compared to group decision making? Individual decision making tends to

    A. Be more conservative.

    B. Evaluate more complete information.

    C. Generate more alternatives.

    D. Increase the perceived legitimacy of the decision.

Answer (A) is correct.   *(CIA, adapted)*
    REQUIRED: The true comparison between individual and group decision making.
    DISCUSSION: Group decision making is often characterized by greater acceptance of risk because of the dispersal of accountability. Individual decision making tends to be more conservative because accountability can be specifically assigned.
    Answer (B) is incorrect because a group has greater resources of knowledge and experience than an individual. Answer (C) is incorrect because a group has a wider diversity of views and should be able to offer a wider range of solutions. Answer (D) is incorrect because group decisions are more likely to be accepted by those affected.

5.2 Motivation

7. Frederick Herzberg postulated a two-factor theory of human behavior that included satisfiers and dissatisfiers. Which of the following is a dissatisfier?

   A. Promotion to another position.

   B. Salary.

   C. Challenging work.

   D. Responsibility.

Answer (B) is correct. *(CIA, adapted)*
   REQUIRED: The item that is a dissatisfier.
   DISCUSSION: Frederick Herzberg's two-factor theory of human behavior postulates that there are two classes of factors in the job situation. Maintenance of hygiene factors (dissatisfiers) are those the presence of which will not especially motivate people but the absence of which will diminish performance. These factors are extrinsic to the work itself. They include supervision, working conditions, interpersonal relations, salary, and status. Motivational factors (satisfiers) are those the absence of which will not diminish performance but the addition or availability of which will motivate employees. Intrinsic to the work itself, these include achievement, recognition, challenging work, advancement, growth in the job, and responsibility.
   Answer (A) is incorrect because recognition and status are satisfiers. Answer (C) is incorrect because challenging work is a satisfier. Answer (D) is incorrect because responsibility is a satisfier.

8. Which of the following motivational theories are most alike in that they assume employees want to work and can do so unsupervised?

   A. Theory X and Theory Y.

   B. Theory X and Theory Z.

   C. Theory Y and Theory Z.

   D. Theory Y and Herzberg's two-factor theory.

Answer (C) is correct. *(Publisher)*
   REQUIRED: The two motivational theories that are alike in assuming that employees like to work and can do so unsupervised.
   DISCUSSION: Ouchi's Theory Z is based on the Japanese practice of providing long-term employment to workers. Decisions are made on a team basis, and trust is an important aspect of the theory, including the issue of trusting employees to complete their work satisfactorily and unsupervised. Theory Y assumes that employees like to work and will do so unsupervised.
   Answer (A) is incorrect because Theory X assumes that employees have an inherent dislike of work and will avoid it if possible. Answer (B) is incorrect because Theory X assumes that employees have an inherent dislike of work and will avoid it if possible. Answer (D) is incorrect because Herzberg's theory looks at what motivates workers rather than on how workers feel about work itself.

9. Alternative work schedules for employees are said to increase the efficiency of business operations. They are consistent with the underlying concepts of which theory?

   A. Motivation-Hygiene theory.

   B. Theory X.

   C. Equity theory.

   D. Cognitive evaluation theory.

Answer (A) is correct. *(CIA, adapted)*
   REQUIRED: The theory that supports alternative work schedules.
   DISCUSSION: Herzberg's two-factor theory of human behavior postulates two classes of factors: motivational and hygiene. Hygiene factors (dissatisfiers) include those factors whose presence will not especially motivate people but whose absence will lead to diminished motivation. These factors are extrinsic to the work itself. They include status, interpersonal relations, and alternative work schedules. Hygiene factors such as work schedules need to be adequate so that workers will have little dissatisfaction. The absence of motivational factors (satisfiers) will not diminish performance, but their addition or availability will motivate employees. Intrinsic to the work itself, they include achievement, advancement, and recognition.
   Answer (B) is incorrect because Theory X assumes that workers have to be coerced, controlled, or threatened to achieve goals. Answer (C) is incorrect because, according to equity theory, individuals compare their inputs and outputs with those of others. Answer (D) is incorrect because, according to cognitive evaluation theory, allocating extrinsic rewards for behavior that had been previously intrinsically rewarded tends to decrease the overall level of motivation.

10. An employee's self-actualization need would be met by

A. Attractive pension provisions.

B. Challenging new job assignments.

C. Good working conditions.

D. Regular positive feedback.

Answer (B) is correct.   *(IIA, adapted)*
REQUIRED: The item that meets an employee's self-actualization need.
DISCUSSION: Self-actualization is the highest human need. It is the desire to become what one is capable of becoming, to realize one's potential and accomplish to the limit of one's ability. In other words, the job itself is an intrinsic motivation; no extrinsic motivation (such as rewards or reinforcements) is needed. Intrinsic motivation provides the worker with psychological income. Thus, challenging new job assignments meet an employee's self actualization needs.
Answer (A) is incorrect because attractive pension provisions meet an employee's physiological needs. Answer (C) is incorrect because good working conditions meet an employee's physiological needs. Answer (D) is incorrect because regular positive feedback meets an employee's esteem needs.

11. Both Maslow and Herzberg have developed popular motivational theories. Which statement best distinguishes Herzberg's theory?

A. Job performance improves as job satisfaction increases.

B. Job performance improves as physiological needs are met.

C. Job esteem improves as physiological needs are met.

D. Job esteem improves as job satisfaction increases.

Answer (A) is correct.   *(CIA, adapted)*
REQUIRED: The statement that best distinguishes Herzberg's theory.
DISCUSSION: Frederick Herzberg's two-factor theory of human behavior postulates that there are two classes of factors in the job situation. Maintenance or hygiene factors are those whose presence will not especially motivate people but whose absence will diminish performance. These factors are extrinsic to the work itself. They include supervision, working conditions, interpersonal relations, salary, and status. Motivational factors are those the absence of which will not diminish performance but the addition or availability of which will motivate employees. Intrinsic to the work itself, these include achievement, recognition, challenging work, advancement, growth in the job, and responsibility.
Answer (B) is incorrect because physiological needs are at the base of Maslow's hierarchy of needs. Answer (C) is incorrect because Maslow's theory is that higher needs emerge as lower needs are met. Answer (D) is incorrect because esteem and satisfaction are almost synonymous.

12. Some behavioral models stress employee participation as a key to motivation. A limitation of the participative approach is

A. Workers are intrinsically lazy and must be driven.

B. A number of dissatisfiers must be present in order for the approach to work.

C. It is difficult to elicit the participation of all employees.

D. Unresolvable conflicts arise when a mature, capable, creative person joins a structured, demanding, and limiting organization.

Answer (C) is correct.   *(CIA, adapted)*
REQUIRED: The limitation of the participative approach.
DISCUSSION: For a participative management approach to succeed, the parties must have sufficient time, the issues must be relevant to employees' interests, employees must have the abilities (training and communication skills) to participate, and the company culture should support participation. Accordingly, a limitation of the participative approach is that it is unlikely that all employees are willing to participate in decision making.
Answer (A) is incorrect because the participative approach assumes that workers are positively motivated. Answer (B) is incorrect because the presence of dissatisfiers is not consistent with the participative approach. Answer (D) is incorrect because such conflicts arise when the needs of individuals are not integrated with the needs of the organization.

13. Motivation is

A. The extent to which goal-specific performance is recognized by supervisors.

B. The extent to which individuals have the authority to make decisions.

C. The extent of the attempt to accomplish a specific goal.

D. The desire and the commitment to achieve a specific goal.

Answer (D) is correct.   *(Publisher)*
REQUIRED: The definition of motivation.
DISCUSSION: Motivation is the desire to attain a specific goal (goal congruence) and the commitment to accomplish the goal (managerial effort). Managerial motivation is therefore a combination of managerial effort and goal congruence.
Answer (A) is incorrect because recognition of goal-specific performance is characteristic of a reward system. Answer (B) is incorrect because goal congruence is the sharing of goals by supervisors and subordinates. Answer (C) is incorrect because autonomy is the extent to which individuals have the authority to make decisions.

14. Which of the following is false concerning job motivation?

- A. Increased planning and decision making in a job is a positive motivator only if accompanied by a salary increase.
- B. Recognition of achievement motivates performance.
- C. Poor working conditions create dissatisfaction with the job.
- D. Poor interpersonal relations create dissatisfaction with the job.

Answer (A) is correct. *(CIA, adapted)*
REQUIRED: The false statement about job motivation.
DISCUSSION: Frederick Herzberg's two-factor theory of human behavior postulates that there are two classes of factors in the job situation. Maintenance of hygiene factors (dissatisfiers) are those the presence of which will not especially motivate people but the absence of which will diminish performance. These factors are extrinsic to the work itself. They include supervision, working conditions, interpersonal relations, salary, and status. Motivational factors (satisfiers) are those the absence of which will not diminish performance but the addition or availability of which will motivate employees. Intrinsic to the work itself, these include achievement, recognition, challenging work, advancement, growth in the job, and responsibility. Thus, increased planning and decision making enrich the job and serve to increase satisfaction and motivation. A pay increase is not necessary to achieve this positive effect, but a perceived inadequacy of compensation would act as a dissatisfier.
Answer (B) is incorrect because public recognition is a satisfier. Answer (C) is incorrect because poor working conditions are a dissatisfier. Answer (D) is incorrect because poor interpersonal relations are a dissatisfier.

15. A production manager is working on a plan to increase employee motivation at a local plant by comparing results of employee interviews to those from employees at a higher performing plant. The manager is puzzled about the results of two sets of employee interviews. The employees interviewed performed identical jobs. Local employees thought their jobs were boring and unfulfilling while the other plant's employees were very satisfied. Even new employees at the local plant indicated they quickly lost enthusiasm. Identify the primary element the manager must overcome to enhance performance.

- A. Negative job perception.
- B. Inadequate job autonomy.
- C. Lack of skill variety.
- D. Low task significance.

Answer (A) is correct. *(CIA, adapted)*
REQUIRED: The element to be overcome to enhance performance.
DISCUSSION: The tasks and environment for both sets of employees are the same. Thus, the individuals' perceptions are the key to the problem.
Answer (B) is incorrect because both sets of employees have the same degree of autonomy. Answer (C) is incorrect because both sets of employees exhibit the same skill variety. Answer (D) is incorrect because both sets of employees perform the same tasks.

16. In many jobs, excessive specialization can eventually lead to poor motivation, boredom, and alienation. In order to cope with the potential problems in such a situation, managers should

- A. Focus on their employees' higher-level needs in order to help them achieve self-actualization.
- B. Remove dissatisfiers such as low salary, bad supervision, lack of job security, and poor working conditions.
- C. Implement an optimal organizational rewards system and provide all needed training to keep employees up to date on technology.
- D. Change the jobs to fit the employees' needs or rotate employees to jobs that satisfy their needs.

Answer (D) is correct. *(CIA, adapted)*
REQUIRED: The approach to cope with employee boredom, poor motivation, and alienation.
DISCUSSION: Job design theories of motivation specifically address the issue of overspecialization. These theories focus on the match between the person and the job as the key to motivation. The recommendation for dealing with the potential problems of overspecialization and boredom is either to enrich the job or to move the employee to a job that provides the appropriate level of challenge.
Answer (A) is incorrect because focusing on employees' higher-level needs in order to help them achieve self-actualization is a recommendation based on Maslow's hierarchy of needs that does not address the job itself as a source of motivation. Answer (B) is incorrect because removing dissatisfiers does not address the issue of overspecialization, although it may remove some of the obstacles to motivation. Answer (C) is incorrect because implementing an optimal organizational rewards systems and providing extensive training to keep employees up to date do not address the job and the issue of overspecialization.

17. As a manager, you should be striving for a high level of job satisfaction for your staff for all the following reasons except

   A. A happy, satisfied worker is always a more productive worker.

   B. High job satisfaction usually results in lower turnover.

   C. Dissatisfied employees are often less healthy.

   D. Many people feel job satisfaction is as important as remuneration.

Answer (A) is correct. *(CIA, adapted)*
   REQUIRED: The item that is not a reason to strive for high employee job satisfaction.
   DISCUSSION: Studies have shown that worker satisfaction does not necessarily lead to improved productivity. In fact, studies indicate that it is more likely that a productive worker is a happy worker.
   Answer (B) is incorrect because satisfaction is negatively correlated with turnover. However, level of performance is a moderating factor on the relationship. Superior performers have lower turnover in part because management makes stronger efforts to retain them. Answer (C) is incorrect because job satisfaction is directly correlated with good health and longevity. Answer (D) is incorrect because a happy worker is not necessarily a more productive worker.

18. According to the behavioral theory of management,

   A. Employees are motivated to fulfill needs.

   B. Morale problems are not goal related.

   C. Compensation is a universal motivator.

   D. Productivity is not correlated with job satisfaction.

Answer (A) is correct. *(Publisher)*
   REQUIRED: The behavioral theory of management.
   DISCUSSION: The behavioral theory of management holds that all people (including employees) have complex needs, desires, and attitudes. The fulfillment of needs is the goal toward which employees are motivated. Effective leadership matches need-fulfillment rewards with desired behavior (tasks) that accomplishes organizational goals.
   Answer (B) is incorrect because management's role in the directing process is to motivate people to contribute toward accomplishment of organizational goals. Answer (C) is incorrect because, although management theories differ as to the motivational value of wages, compensation is not a motivator for all persons at all times. Answer (D) is incorrect because, while research has indicated that satisfaction and productivity are not directly related, behavioral theorists believe that they must have some relationship.

19. Two managers were discussing the merits of goal setting to improve employee performance. One manager felt that specific goals should not be established and that, to provide for flexibility, only generalized goals should be used. The other manager felt that specific, difficult goals produce the best results. As the discussion continued, other methods of goal setting were identified. Select the best method for setting goals.

   A. The manager should provide generalized goals.

   B. The manager should select specific, difficult goals.

   C. The employee should develop generalized goals and obtain management concurrence.

   D. The employee should develop specific, difficult goals and obtain management concurrence.

Answer (D) is correct. *(CIA, adapted)*
   REQUIRED: The best method for setting goals.
   DISCUSSION: According to Edwin Locke's goal-setting theory, specific, difficult goals to which the employee is committed provide the best motivation tool. Performance improves when goals are specific rather than general, difficult rather than easy, and self-set rather than imposed by others. Feedback, especially self-generated feedback, also improves performance compared with lack of feedback. Commitment to goals, that is, a determination not to reduce or abandon them, and self-efficacy, that is, a belief in one's ability to accomplish the task, are additional qualities that result in better performance.
   Answer (A) is incorrect because specific, difficult goals provide more motivation than generalized goals. Answer (B) is incorrect because employee involvement in goal setting provides better assurance that employees will be committed to the goals. Answer (C) is incorrect because specific, difficult goals provide more motivation than generalized goals.

20. According to management literature, worker absenteeism, turnover, and error rates are likely to be greatest

   A. When workers alternate in performing different jobs.

   B. In simplified assembly-line jobs.

   C. In job sharing situations.

   D. When flexible working hours are provided.

Answer (B) is correct. *(Publisher)*
   REQUIRED: The instance in which worker turnover, absenteeism, etc., are greatest.
   DISCUSSION: The literature tends to support the theory that, while job satisfaction has an economic importance only indirectly related to productivity, satisfied workers exhibit lower rates of absenteeism, turnover, tardiness, apathy, and sabotage. Organizations with more organic or flexible organization structures may use more of the worker's skills and present a greater variety of work challenges, thus improving morale. Mass production technology usually involves repetitive, boring tasks.

21. Job enrichment is a motivational approach used by management that

A. Emphasizes the need for close supervision.

B. Is based on Maslow's analysis of survival needs.

C. Is based on Herzberg's analysis of factors extrinsic to the work.

D. Applies the principle of worker participation.

Answer (D) is correct. *(Publisher)*
REQUIRED: The true statement about job enrichment.
DISCUSSION: Job enrichment increases the scope of boring, repetitive tasks by using more of the employee's skills and allowing the employee more power to make decisions concerning the job, such as order of tasks, etc. Thus, it encourages worker participation in decisions previously made by management.
Answer (A) is incorrect because job enrichment is based on the assumption that employees who have qualitatively improved jobs need less supervision. Answer (B) is incorrect because survival needs are at the bottom of Maslow's hierarchy. Job enrichment seeks to meet the higher-level needs (affiliation, esteem, self-actualization). Answer (C) is incorrect because the intrinsic factors (challenge, growth, responsibility, etc.) are relevant to job enrichment.

22. Job enlargement is typified by

A. Horizontal loading of the job.

B. Vertical loading of the job.

C. Increased worker control of tasks.

D. More rapid performance feedback.

Answer (A) is correct. *(Publisher)*
REQUIRED: The characteristic of job enlargement.
DISCUSSION: Job enlargement is a quantitative (horizontal) extension of the job. It does not necessarily involve any greater worker control, responsibility, or challenge. An example is job rotation through assignment to duties requiring similar skills.
Answer (B) is incorrect because vertical loading is a term used in management literature to describe qualitative job enhancement (enrichment). It entails greater control and responsibility and increased chances for growth. Answer (C) is incorrect because it is typical of job enrichment. Answer (D) is incorrect because it is typical of job enrichment.

23. The punishing of employees is made less effective by

A. Stating the offending behavior specifically.

B. Postponing the start of disciplinary procedures.

C. Permitting employees to challenge their culpability.

D. Focusing the discussion on the offending behavior instead of the offender.

Answer (B) is correct. *(CIA, adapted)*
REQUIRED: The action that renders the discipline process less effective.
DISCUSSION: Effective discipline requires immediate corrective action to eliminate the negative effects of the undesirable employee conduct and to establish and reinforce appropriate behavior. Delay merely invites more serious consequences. Moreover, the punishment should be commensurate with the offense, and the employee should clearly perceive the relationship between the punishment and the behavior.
Answer (A) is incorrect because stating the undesirable behavior clarifies for the employee the link between conduct and consequences. Answer (C) is incorrect because, in U.S. legal culture, the accused has the right to be heard in his/her defense. Answer (D) is incorrect because focusing on the offense rather than the offender is less likely to engender fear and resentment on the part of the employee.

24. When supervising employees, the behavior most likely to attain long-term positive results for a manager would be to

A. Discipline employees immediately for undesirable behaviors, using oral reprimands, written warnings, and temporary suspensions.

B. Hold weekly meetings during which employees are reminded of work procedures and are praised for the week's accomplishments.

C. Praise employees on a random schedule and link rewards to performance.

D. Tell employees that working overtime now will result in a better performance review in 6 months.

Answer (C) is correct. *(CIA, adapted)*
REQUIRED: The supervisory behavior most likely to have long-term positive results.
DISCUSSION: Variable-interval schedules of reinforcement lead to higher performance. Employees are more alert because of the uncertainty involved, and performance and reward are connected.
Answer (A) is incorrect because punishment only leads to short-term suppression of the behavior and may cause the employee to avoid the manager, who is seen as punishing rather than helpful. Answer (B) is incorrect because fixed-interval reinforcement schedules do not clearly link performance and rewards. Answer (D) is incorrect because 6 months is too long an interval for linking performance and reward.

5.3 Nature of Communication

25. The basic purposes of an organization's internal communications network include all of the following except

    A. Obtaining a common focus among employees.

    B. Informing potential investors about company operations and financial results.

    C. Aiding high-quality decision making.

    D. Integrating the efforts of specialists.

Answer (B) is correct. *(CMA, adapted)*
    REQUIRED: The item not one of the basic purposes of an organization's internal communications network.
    DISCUSSION: Because all managerial functions require communication, it is the secret to the success of any manager. A manager's ability to understand other people, and their ability to understand the manager, are crucial to accomplishing organizational objectives. Communication is the link that ties an organization together and transforms a diverse group of people into a cohesive whole. An organization's internal communications network is designed to facilitate decision making among managers, to promote goal congruence among employees, integrate the efforts of all employees, and build high morale and mutual trust. Informing potential investors about company operations is a purpose of the external, not internal, communications network.
    Answer (A) is incorrect because basic purposes of an organization's internal communications network include establishing a common focus. Answer (C) is incorrect because basic purposes of an organization's internal communications network include aiding decision making. Answer (D) is incorrect because basic purposes of an organization's internal communications network include integrating employee efforts.

26. Communication plays an important role in the successful operation of all organizations. Which of the following statements concerning organizational communications is false?

    A. Communication involves at least two people: a sender and a receiver.

    B. Communication is what the sender says, not what the receiver understands.

    C. Every act of communication influences the organization in some way.

    D. Management spends the majority of its time communicating with other members of the organization.

Answer (B) is correct. *(CIA, adapted)*
    REQUIRED: The false statement concerning organizational communications.
    DISCUSSION: The communication process has five elements: the sender, the symbols in which the message is encoded, the medium through which the message flows, the receiver, and feedback. Because the effectiveness of communication can be known only by its impact on the receiver and the perceived change in the receiver's behavior, the received message must govern the definition. The sent message may be garbled in encoding, in transmission, or in the receiver's decoding.
    Answer (A) is incorrect because communication involves at least a sender and a receiver. Answer (C) is incorrect because an organization is, by definition, two or more people gathered together for a common purpose. These people agree on organizational goals via communicating their objectives, and management spends the majority of its time influencing the achievement of goals by communicating with other members of the organization. Answer (D) is incorrect because an organization is, by definition, two or more people gathered together for a common purpose. These people agree on organizational goals via communicating their objectives, and management spends the majority of its time influencing the achievement of goals by communicating with other members of the organization.

27. Which of the following terms does not apply to noise in communication?

    A. Encoding.

    B. Sending.

    C. Interpretation.

    D. Decoding.

Answer (C) is correct. *(Publisher)*
    REQUIRED: The term that does not apply to noise in communication.
    DISCUSSION: Interpretation is a subprocess of perception. Noise is a disruption that impedes the communication process.
    Answer (A) is incorrect because encoding is part of the communication process that can be disrupted by noise. Answer (B) is incorrect because sending is a part of the communication process that can be impeded by noise. Answer (D) is incorrect because decoding is part of the communication process that can be impeded by noise.

28. Which of the following statements is false according to communications theory?

A. The process has three elements: sender, medium, receiver.

B. Two-directional communication is usually most effective.

C. Communication is the message actually received, not what is transmitted.

D. Informal communications are used by effective managers.

Answer (A) is correct. *(Publisher)*
REQUIRED: The false statement about communications.
DISCUSSION: The communication process has five elements: the sender, the symbols in which the message is encoded, the medium through which the message is sent, the receiver, and feedback.
Answer (B) is incorrect because two directional communication is usually most effective. Answer (C) is incorrect because communication is the message received. Answer (D) is incorrect because effective managers use informal communications.

29. Which one of the following is not an example of formal internal communication?

A. Input for the yearly budget provided by the Purchasing Department to the director of budgeting.

B. Environmental impact statements.

C. Expense account reports.

D. Safety bulletins.

Answer (B) is correct. *(CMA, adapted)*
REQUIRED: The item not a formal internal communication.
DISCUSSION: A formal communication is conducted through the formal structure of the organization. Informal communication operates outside of officially established channels. An internal communication is one that is both generated and received within the organization. An environmental impact statement is generated within the organization, but the recipient (a governmental body) is outside the organization.
Answer (A) is incorrect because input for the yearly budget is a form of communication that is both generated internally and received by a person within the organization. Answer (C) is incorrect because expense reports are a form of communication that is both generated internally and received by a person within the organization. Answer (D) is incorrect because safety bulletins are a form of communication that is both generated internally and received by a person within the organization.

30. Which of the following is least appropriate with regard to management's approach to informal group or grapevine communication? Management should

A. Use it to supplement communication channels of the formal organization.

B. Try to suppress it as a possible source of conflicting information.

C. Take advantage of it as a device to correct misinformation.

D. Make use of it as a means of transmitting information not appropriate for formal communication channels.

Answer (B) is correct. *(CIA, adapted)*
REQUIRED: The least appropriate management actions regarding the grapevine.
DISCUSSION: Suppressing grapevine networks is difficult, if not impossible. Recognizing that the grapevine exists and can be used effectively for several kinds of messages makes better managerial sense.
Answer (A) is incorrect because management can use a grapevine or informal communication network to supplement the formal communication process. Answer (C) is incorrect because management can use a grapevine or informal communication network to correct misinformation. Answer (D) is incorrect because management can use a grapevine or informal communication network to transmit information not appropriate for formal communication channels.

31. The biggest advantage of oral communication over written communication is that it

A. Tends to be more accurate.

B. Promotes feedback.

C. Is less time-consuming.

D. Does not provide a permanent record.

Answer (B) is correct. *(Publisher)*
REQUIRED: The biggest advantage of oral communication over written communication.
DISCUSSION: Oral communication promotes immediate feedback so that the sender knows that the message has been clearly received by the receiver.
Answer (A) is incorrect because written communication tends to be more accurate than oral communication. Answer (C) is incorrect because, although oral communication is less time-consuming than written communication, immediate feedback is a greater advantage. Answer (D) is incorrect because providing a permanent record is advantageous.

32. Which one of the following statements regarding communication along the grapevine in an organization is false?

A. By maintaining open channels of communication, managers can minimize the damage the grapevine can do in an organization.

B. Attempts to totally eliminate the grapevine are unlikely to succeed.

C. The grapevine communication network can exist in several patterns.

D. The grapevine is rumor-mongering, and managers should not use it.

Answer (D) is correct.   *(CMA, adapted)*
REQUIRED: The false statement about communication along a grapevine.
DISCUSSION: A grapevine is the name of the informal communication channel that exists in all organizations. The grapevine exists wherever there are people. Although the grapevine is usually accurate, it can carry gossip and rumor. The effective manager stays tuned into the grapevine and uses it constructively.
Answer (A) is incorrect because managers can minimize the damage that a grapevine can cause by transmitting accurate and timely information and maintaining open channels of communication. Answer (B) is incorrect because attempts to eliminate the grapevine are likely to strengthen it. Answer (C) is incorrect because grapevines can exist in several patterns. For example, one person may tell one other person who tells one other person, etc.; one person may tell all people in a group; individuals may tell selected others; or individuals may tell others at random.

33. All of the following statements about communication are true except

A. Written communication inhibits feedback.

B. Managers spend more of their workday involved in oral communication than written communication.

C. Written communication provides a permanent record.

D. Written communication is usually better when the message is nonroutine and personal.

Answer (D) is correct.   *(CMA, adapted)*
REQUIRED: The false statement about communication.
DISCUSSION: Written communication is usually better when the message is routine and impersonal. A nonroutine message can be better communicated orally. Written communication also offers the advantage of providing a permanent record of the message, but it inhibits immediate feedback because the two parties are not in direct contact. Breakthroughs in electronic technology, such as computers that can recognize the human voice, may in the future blur the distinction between oral and written communication.
Answer (A) is incorrect because written communication does inhibit feedback. Answer (B) is incorrect because most managers do spend more time involved with oral than with written communication. Answer (C) is incorrect because written communication does provide a permanent record of the message.

34. Which of the following is the best indicator of the effectiveness of a communication on a receiver?

A. Understanding of message received.

B. Clarity of message.

C. Change in receiver's attitude.

D. Change in receiver's behavior.

Answer (D) is correct.   *(CIA, adapted)*
REQUIRED: The best indicator of a communication's effectiveness.
DISCUSSION: The best indicator of the effectiveness of a communication on the receiver is the change in the receiver's behavior in the direction requested or required by the communication. The sender has the responsibility to solicit feedback (or observe results) to determine the communication's effectiveness.
Answer (A) is incorrect because a receiver who understands a message may change attitude but may not necessarily change behavior. Answer (B) is incorrect because, although the clarity of the message is a receiver perception necessary to understanding (believing) the message, the receiver must respond appropriately before the message is effective. Answer (C) is incorrect because a receiver who understands a message may change attitude but may not necessarily change behavior.

35. A company is rumored to be considering downsizing. Because a manager stops the use of all temporary employees, the staff concludes that some jobs will be lost. Which of the following is true about the manager's communication about job losses?

    A. The staff decoded the formal communication sent by the manager correctly.

    B. The manager properly encoded the idea in a message.

    C. The lack of a formal message had a negative impact on staff.

    D. The channel through which the message was sent was appropriate.

Answer (C) is correct. *(CIA, adapted)*
    REQUIRED: The true statement about the manager's communication regarding job losses.
    DISCUSSION: Management's lack of formal communication regarding possible downsizing caused the employees to draw their own negative conclusions based on a manager's actions. Management should formally communicate the reasons for eliminating the use of temporary employees or refute the rumor about downsizing.

36. When evaluating communication, the accountant should be aware that nonverbal communication

    A. Is independent of a person's cultural background.

    B. Is often imprecise.

    C. Always conveys a more truthful response.

    D. Always conveys less information than verbal communication.

Answer (B) is correct. *(CIA, adapted)*
    REQUIRED: The true statement about nonverbal communication.
    DISCUSSION: Nonverbal communication (body language) consists of facial expressions, vocal intonations, posture, gestures, and appearance, and physical distance. Thus, by its nature, nonverbal communication is much less precise than verbal communication.
    Answer (A) is incorrect because nonverbal communication is heavily influenced by culture. For example, a nod of the head may have opposite meanings in different cultures. Answer (C) is incorrect because nonverbal communication is not necessarily more truthful. Answer (D) is incorrect because nonverbal communication can sometimes convey more information.

37. Nancy Ashburn is the cost accounting manager for Imperial Aluminum's extrusion plant. Her job involves coordinating and summarizing monthly production department variance reports that are prepared by various staff accountants. She then provides the relevant variances to her colleagues, the production departmental managers. The accounting reports communicated by Ashburn are an example of

    A. Downward communication.

    B. Hierarchical communication.

    C. Informal communication.

    D. Horizontal communication.

Answer (D) is correct. *(CMA, adapted)*
    REQUIRED: The type of communication represented by variance reports.
    DISCUSSION: Communication can be downward (from superior to subordinate), upward (from subordinate to superior), or horizontal (from one peer to another). It may also be formal or informal. A variance report prepared in the accounting department and sent to production departments is a formal horizontal communication because it occurs among peers laterally through an officially established channel.
    Answer (A) is incorrect because downward communication is from a superior to a subordinate. Answer (B) is incorrect because hierarchical communication is either upward or downward. Answer (C) is incorrect because informal communication operates outside of formal structural channels; a grapevine is an example.

38. Arthur Bell is the superintendent of a production department. Every month, Bell sends copies of his department's production variance reports to his supervisory staff asking them to explain variances that exceed certain prescribed limits. Bell's communication of variances to his supervisory staff and their explanation to him of the variances are examples of

    A. Horizontal communication and upward communication, respectively.

    B. Formal and informal communication, respectively.

    C. Informal communication and the grapevine, respectively.

    D. Downward communication and upward communication, respectively.

Answer (D) is correct. *(CMA, adapted)*
    REQUIRED: The types of communication represented by a supervisor's request for an explanation of variances and the subordinates' responses.
    DISCUSSION: Communication can be downward (from superior to subordinate), upward (from subordinate to superior), or horizontal (from one peer to another). Bell's communication of variance reports to his subordinates is downward communication. The subordinates' replies are upward communications.
    Answer (A) is incorrect because no communication among peers occurred. Answer (B) is incorrect because both forms of communication were within the formal organizational structure. Answer (C) is incorrect because both forms of communication were within the formal organizational structure.

39. An advisable strategy for a participant in a meeting of the employees would be to

A. Read the agenda and supporting materials for the meeting during the early part of the meeting to prepare for later discussion.

B. Present strong opinions on one side of a proposal right away.

C. Present views as trial balloons that can be researched later.

D. Consider the opinions and information needs of other participants before speaking.

Answer (D) is correct. *(CIA, adapted)*
REQUIRED: The strategy for a participant in a meeting of the employees.
DISCUSSION: Analyzing the audience assists a speaker to gather the right information for the meeting. Moreover, understanding the other participants' opinions and needs enables the speaker to express his/her ideas in the way best calculated to be persuasive.
Answer (A) is incorrect because the most effective meeting participants come to meetings prepared. The agenda and other materials should be read in advance. Answer (B) is incorrect because, unless the speaker is certain of others' opinions (or is the most powerful person in the organization), (s)he should not commit to a position until the degree of support for that view can be estimated. Answer (C) is incorrect because ideas should be researched in advance of the meeting so that the participant appears to be prepared and productive.

40. At Marshall Inc., accounting clerks log incoming invoices, and the controller determines the amount and timing of invoice payments. For this type of situation, the most efficient and accurate communication network is the

A. All-channel network.

B. Circle network.

C. Chain network.

D. Wheel network.

Answer (D) is correct. *(CMA, adapted)*
REQUIRED: The best communication network to use for a system in which clerks log invoices and the controller determines the amount and timing of payments.
DISCUSSION: In the wheel form of communication network, the leader acts as a central conduit for all communications. Because the controller must process all payments, a wheel network offers the most efficient and accurate communication channel in these circumstances.
Answer (A) is incorrect because an all-channel network is inappropriate. All members of this group have no need to communicate with each other. Answer (B) is incorrect because a circle network is inappropriate. Each member of the group must communicate with the controller. Answer (C) is incorrect because a chain network is inappropriate. Each member of the group must communicate with the controller.

41. Which of the following is an example of upward communication?

A. Management's notices on bulletin boards.

B. Grievance actions.

C. Informational inserts in pay envelopes.

D. Personnel policy manuals.

Answer (B) is correct. *(CIA, adapted)*
REQUIRED: The item that is an example of upward communication.
DISCUSSION: Grievance actions are a formal means of bringing employee dissatisfaction to the attention of management, i.e., from the bottom upward.
Answer (A) is incorrect because this is an example of downward communication. Official changes in procedures or benefits can be announced by notices on bulletin boards. Answer (C) is incorrect because this is an example of downward communication. Official changes in procedures or benefits can be announced by notices on bulletin boards. Answer (D) is incorrect because this is an example of downward communication. Official changes in procedures or benefits can be announced by notices on bulletin boards.

42. Nonverbal communication consists of messages conveyed by

I. The physical distance between the sender and the receiver

II. The facial expressions used when speaking

III. Electronic means of communication such as e-mail

IV. Unconscious actions of the speaker while speaking

    A. III only.

    B. IV only.

    C. I and II only.

    D. I, II, and IV.

Answer (D) is correct. *(CIA, adapted)*
    REQUIRED: The true statement(s) about nonverbal communication.
    DISCUSSION: Physical distance and positioning convey many nonverbal messages that depend on cultural differences. For example, Americans tend to prefer a large personal space. Facial expressions provide almost limitless variations of meaning thanks to the dozens of facial muscles and the possibilities created by different contexts, cultures, and individual personalities. In addition to facial expressions, other unconscious actions of the speaker affect the message sent. They include gestures, posture, movement, touch, mode of dress, surroundings, and voice characteristics.
    Answer (A) is incorrect because e-mail is electronic communication, not a nonverbal communication. Answer (B) is incorrect because the physical distance between the sender and the receiver and the facial expressions used when speaking are also nonverbal signals. Answer (C) is incorrect because the speaker's unconscious actions are part of nonverbal communication.

43. Effective communication is most likely to take place when

    A. The sender and receiver share similar frames of reference.

    B. The message is stated in general rather than specific terms.

    C. The message is delivered as quickly as possible.

    D. The sender ignores any underlying assumptions.

Answer (A) is correct. *(CIA, adapted)*
    REQUIRED: The situation most likely to encourage effective communication.
    DISCUSSION: Effective communication is likely to have the least amount of distortion when the sender and the receiver share similar frames of reference. If both sender and receiver understand the symbols used to communicate and the underlying assumptions concerning the problem, the message will be easier to write, to send, and to understand.
    Answer (B) is incorrect because stating a message in general terms will not create effective communication if the message concerns a specific problem. Answer (C) is incorrect because haste can make waste. A message cannot be effective if it is coded too quickly or if some is lost in transit. Answer (D) is incorrect because the sender should not assume that the receiver will recall all underlying assumptions. If both ends of the message share a frame of reference, underlying assumptions need not be spelled out, but they should not be ignored.

5.4 Problems in Communication

44. Which of the following does not describe perception?

    A. Selectivity.

    B. Organization.

    C. Objective.

    D. Interpretation.

Answer (C) is correct. *(Publisher)*
    REQUIRED: The term not describing perception.
    DISCUSSION: Perception is the process through which someone gives meaning to the surrounding environment. Perception consists of three subprocesses: selectivity, organization, and interpretation. Objectives focus upon the purpose of communication rather than the receipt and interpretation (perception).
    Answer (A) is incorrect because selectivity is a perception subprocess by which one screens out certain stimuli to focus on details. Without selectivity, one would be overwhelmed by sensory overload. Answer (B) is incorrect because organization is a perception subprocess by which disorganized stimuli are grouped to give meaning to otherwise meaningless information. Answer (D) is incorrect because interpretation is a perception subprocess by which meaning is given to a set of stimuli based on the individual's experience.

45. In which one of the following statements is the use of accounting jargon an impediment to communication between accountants and nonaccounting professionals?

    A. "Labor standards tell us how much time workers should take to assemble a computer."

    B. "I am trying to decide whether the million dollar disbursement should be expensed or capitalized."

    C. "In carrying out variance analysis, I am seeking the possible reasons why the net income shown in the financial statements for the year 1996 is 20% less than expected."

    D. "An accounting department in a factory is classified as a service because it allows the departments actually involved in the making of products freedom from bookkeeping chores."

Answer (B) is correct. *(CMA, adapted)*
    REQUIRED: The statement in which accounting jargon impedes communication.
    DISCUSSION: The use of jargon leads to communication problems when a specialist tries to send a message to a nonspecialist. The use of the phrase "expensed or capitalized" is a use of jargon in that a nonaccountant might not understand the technical meaning of the terms. Thus, the recipient of the message may not be able to provide a clear answer.
    Answer (A) is incorrect because this statement is straightforward in that it defines the technical term labor standards. Answer (C) is incorrect because the technical term is described in layman's terms. Answer (D) is incorrect because no technical accounting terms are used.

46. Noise may disrupt communication during transmission. All of the following are examples of noise except

    A. Selective perception.

    B. Static on a telephone line.

    C. A letter lost because it was interspersed with junk mail.

    D. A participant in a conversation being called away for a meeting.

Answer (A) is correct. *(CMA, adapted)*
    REQUIRED: The item that is not an example of noise.
    DISCUSSION: Noise in a communication channel is an outside disruption that impedes the flow of a message. It can vary from real noise, such as loud machines running and static on a phone line, to disruptions such as phone calls during a face-to-face conversation. Selective perception on the part of either the sender or the receiver of a message is not noise because it is not an outside disruption.
    Answer (B) is incorrect because static on a phone line is noise that might affect the quality of a communication. Answer (C) is incorrect because a lost letter is a random event that can cause a disruption in communication. Answer (D) is incorrect because an interruption during a conversation disrupts the communication.

47. In some organizations, first-line supervisors withhold or alter unfavorable information that they do not want higher management to know. This selective withholding of information is widely known as

    A. Selective reception.

    B. Filtering.

    C. Regulating information flow.

    D. Perceptual defense.

Answer (B) is correct. *(CIA, adapted)*
    REQUIRED: The true term for withholding information from higher management.
    DISCUSSION: Communication within an organization must be clear, appropriate, and properly transmitted. Distortion can be unintentional (e.g., a phone line going dead), or it may follow from deliberate filtering either by the sender or an intermediary. The auditor should watch for indications that first-line or lower-level management is "filtering" out bad news or covering up irregularities.
    Answer (A) is incorrect because selective reception (perceptual defense), the tendency for people to hear what they want or expect to hear, is filtering by the recipient. Answer (C) is incorrect because regulating information flow deals more with volume than content. Answer (D) is incorrect because selective reception (perceptual defense), the tendency for people to hear what they want or expect to hear, is filtering by the recipient.

48. In his report, an internal auditor stated that communication in the auditee area was poor with employees deciding in advance which information should be given to management so as to present themselves in the best possible light. This is an example of

    A. Filtering.

    B. Selective perception.

    C. Emotion.

    D. Language.

Answer (A) is correct. *(IIA, adapted)*
    REQUIRED: The definition of filtering.
    DISCUSSION: Filtering of a message is the sender's manipulation of information so that it will be viewed more favorably by the receiver. Filtering is a typical problem in upward communication, e.g., from employee to manager.
    Answer (B) is incorrect because selective perception involves the receiver selectively interpreting what they see or hear based on their interest, background, experience, and attitudes. Answer (C) is incorrect because emotions affect the interpretation of the message, not the contents. Answer (D) is incorrect because choice of language involves the personal selection of words to communicate the same message without distorting it.

49. A manager found that instructions given to a subordinate were not followed. A review of the cause of the failure revealed that the manager was interrupted by several telephone calls while issuing the instructions. In terms of problems in the communications chain, the interruptions are

A. Noise.

B. Nonverbal feedback.

C. Semantics.

D. Closure.

Answer (A) is correct. *(CIA, adapted)*
REQUIRED: The interruptions encountered in the communications process.
DISCUSSION: Noise in the communication channel refers to any disruption that impedes the encoding, sending, or receipt of a message, such as being interrupted by several telephone calls while issuing instructions.
Answer (B) is incorrect because nonverbal feedback, or body language, encompasses the facial expressions, gestures, and posture that send various messages. Answer (C) is incorrect because semantics is the study of meanings, especially connotative nuances. Answer (D) is incorrect because closure is the process of filling in the blanks of an incomplete message.

50. A purchasing agent placed a rush telephone order with a supplier. The clerk in the supplier's office repeated the order specifications back to the purchasing agent. No written confirmations were exchanged. When the shipment arrived, it was late and of the wrong quantity. However, the purchasing agent was unable to prove that the shipment was unsatisfactory. What link of the communication chain has failed in this scenario?

A. Encoding.

B. Decoding.

C. Medium.

D. Feedback.

Answer (C) is correct. *(CIA, adapted)*
REQUIRED: The link of the communication chain that failed.
DISCUSSION: In the communication process, the medium is the channel through which the communication flows. The failure in this case was caused by the choice of a medium that did not create a permanent record of the facts of the communication.
Answer (A) is incorrect because the order information was repeated back correctly to the sender, so it was encoded properly. Answer (B) is incorrect because the order information was repeated back correctly to the sender, so it was decoded properly. Answer (D) is incorrect because the supplier's clerk gave accurate verbal feedback on the essentials of the order.

Questions 51 and 52 are based on the following information. A multinational firm was attempting to buy a controlling interest in a medium size ($10 million annual sales) Brazilian metal-working firm. Its negotiator in Brazil sent the following telegram: "They won't deal unless 51% ownership." The executive committee of the multinational firm, not wanting a minority interest, then canceled the deal. Upon returning to the multinational firm, the negotiator pointed out that the Brazilian firm wanted to sell no more than 51% ownership so they could retain at least 49%. Thus, the deal could have been made.

---

51. The telegram received by the executive committee was faulty. In terms of the links in the communications process, the error occurred because of

A. Noise in the communication chain.

B. The sender's perception.

C. Message encoding.

D. The choice of transmission medium.

Answer (C) is correct. *(CIA, adapted)*
REQUIRED: The reason for the communications error.
DISCUSSION: Encoding is the sender's packaging of an idea for better understanding. It entails translating the message into symbols that can be transmitted through the chosen medium of communication and then decoded by the recipient. In this example, the sender's wording of the message was misleading.
Answer (A) is incorrect because the message was received exactly as transmitted. Answer (B) is incorrect because the sender had the correct perception of the message as it was actually encoded. Answer (D) is incorrect because no transmission errors occurred.

52. The faulty telegram led to a communications error by the executive committee of the multinational firm. The error was in

A. Decoding of the message.

B. Choice of transmission medium.

C. Understanding of the message.

D. Response to the message.

Answer (C) is correct. *(CIA, adapted)*
REQUIRED: The nature of the communications error.
DISCUSSION: Because of faulty encoding, the message was open to two different interpretations. The committee chose the wrong one.
Answer (A) is incorrect because words were properly decoded. Answer (B) is incorrect because the medium was capable of completing the exchange. Answer (D) is incorrect because the action matched the committee's understanding of the message.

53. Studies of managerial communications have indicated that

    A. Most managers are excellent communicators.

    B. Managers spend most of their time communicating.

    C. Written communication takes more of a manager's time than oral communication.

    D. Most effective communicators will be good managers.

Answer (B) is correct. *(CIA, adapted)*
    REQUIRED: The true statement concerning managerial communications.
    DISCUSSION: Because communication is the process of conveying meaning or understanding from one person to another, managers must spend most of their time communicating with subordinates, peers, and superiors. They communicate organizational goals and plans downward, lower-level results and problems upward, and coordinating information horizontally (among peers or across organizational channels).
    Answer (A) is incorrect because one of the problems within management is the inability of many managers to clearly and concisely communicate ideas, concepts, directives, policies, results, etc. Answer (C) is incorrect because managers spend more time in oral than in written communication. Answer (D) is incorrect because good management requires more than just effective communication. If a manager cannot motivate subordinates, even clearly communicated information will be ineffective to achieve organizational objectives.

54. Which one of the following statements about human perception and its role in the communication process is false?

    A. Perception is used to interpret information from the environment.

    B. Perception can distort communication only at the end of the communication process.

    C. Selective perception refers to the tendency to remember what we prefer and to forget what we are uncomfortable with.

    D. Stereotyping is a form of perceptual organization.

Answer (B) is correct. *(CMA, adapted)*
    REQUIRED: The false statement about human perception and its role in the communication process.
    DISCUSSION: Managers must always consider the perceptions of a message recipient. Recipients vary in their perception of messages because of background, language, education, attitudes toward the sender (such as stereotyping) and job, etc. This variance can result in communication distortion at any stage of the communication process.
    Answer (A) is incorrect because perception is the process of giving meaning to the environment, e.g., to determine the meaning of messages. Answer (C) is incorrect because selectivity is the necessary process of filtering external stimuli. Answer (D) is incorrect because stereotyping is a way of organizing and interpreting experience. Unfortunately, it entails drawing inferences based on inadequate information.

55. Which of the following is an example of a badly encoded message?

    A. Inattention or disinterest in the message.

    B. Inconsistency between verbal and nonverbal messages.

    C. Gesturing to someone who cannot see the gesture.

    D. Sender's dislike of receiver.

Answer (B) is correct. *(Publisher)*
    REQUIRED: The example of a badly encoded message.
    DISCUSSION: If body language or tone of voice send a message different from the spoken words, the receiver will not be clear about the meaning of the message.
    Answer (A) is incorrect because inattention or disinterest in the message is an example of nonreception in which the receiver fails to receive any communication. Answer (C) is incorrect because gesturing to someone who cannot see the gesture is an example of faulty channel selection. Answer (D) is incorrect because the sender's dislike of the receiver is an example of interpersonal problems.

56. Which one of the following statements about the nature of communication is true?

    A. Communication occurs only when we deliberately and consciously decide to communicate.

    B. Accounting terms such as expense, revenue, net income, and variance mean the same to all users.

    C. Because managerial accounting reports classify and summarize vast amounts of data, they do not add to the information overload within an organization.

    D. Communication between departments is affected by the level of functional specialization within departments.

Answer (D) is correct. *(CMA, adapted)*
    REQUIRED: The true statement about the nature of communication.
    DISCUSSION: Communication between departments is sometimes affected by the level of functional specialization within those departments. Noise of any sort can inhibit communication, and that noise can be physical or nonphysical. An example of nonphysical noise is the difference in expertise between the sender and the recipient. A sender must establish a climate that encourages the elimination of interpersonal barriers to communication.
    Answer (A) is incorrect because communication can be unconscious, e.g., body language. Answer (B) is incorrect because accounting terms can mean different things to different people; that is why some companies use an accounting manual to promote consistent treatment of similar items. Answer (C) is incorrect because accounting reports can add to information overload, particularly for people who do not understand them.

57. Which of the following is unlikely to cause changes in attitudes?

A. Make sure that the message is credible.

B. Present many different issues in as short a time as possible.

C. Shape the argument to the listener.

D. Focus the presentation on its ultimate objective.

Answer (B) is correct. *(CIA, adapted)*

REQUIRED: The communication technique unlikely to cause changes in attitudes.

DISCUSSION: Presenting many different issues in as short a time as possible will confuse the listener and cause the message to be lost or disregarded. To convey a persuasive message effectively, the communicator should make a clear presentation that focuses on the ultimate objective. The argument should be stated one idea at a time, and unrelated subjects and jumping from issue to issue should be avoided. The presentation should guide the recipient of the communication directly to the desired conclusion.

Answer (A) is incorrect because trust, competence, objectivity, and high ethical standards are important in changing attitudes. Answer (C) is incorrect because effective persuasion demands flexibility so that the arguments presented have a better chance of changing the person's attitudes. Answer (D) is incorrect because, to convey a persuasive message effectively, the communicator should make a clear presentation that focuses on the ultimate objective.

58. "But I mailed the order 4 weeks ago, giving the supplier plenty of time," said the parts manager when asked why a critical part was not available. The most likely reason for this failed communication between the parts manager and the supplier was

A. Lack of feedback.

B. Confusing language.

C. Inappropriate medium.

D. Perceptual selectivity.

Answer (A) is correct. *(CIA, adapted)*

REQUIRED: The most likely reason for failed communication between the parts manager and the supplier.

DISCUSSION: The effectiveness of communication can be determined only by the sender's seeking feedback and observing the impact of the communication on the receiver. The sender is obligated to solicit feedback to ensure that the communication process is complete. The receiver should give feedback to the sender. The importance of feedback to check the effectiveness of the communication process indicates the limitations of one-way communications (e.g., memos). Effectiveness can only be measured when the sender perceives a change in the receiver's behavior. Thus, the parts manager (the sender) should have sought and the supplier (the receiver) should have provided, feedback.

Answer (B) is incorrect because the facts do not suggest that the language used was confusing. Answer (C) is incorrect because the mail is an acceptable medium of transmission. Answer (D) is incorrect because the supplier had no reason to ignore (selectively screen out) an order. A supplier's perceptual selection obviously includes rather than excludes customer orders.

Questions 59 and 60 are based on the following information. The supervisor of purchasing reviewed a memorandum prepared for a buyer in the department. The memo read, "Effective September 30, the corporation has determined that your functions will be absorbed into our parent company's small-unit purchasing function. This will reduce operating costs, improve communications, and facilitate production engineering changes. You will be provided with outplacement support." "That should cover the situation," thought the supervisor. "It's too bad that I am leaving on vacation before the buyer returns from vacation, but this memo will give the buyer the general idea."

---

59. What link in the communications chain is defective?

A. The meaning of the message would be unclear to the buyer.

B. The supervisor chose the wrong channel for the communication.

C. The supervisor should not be the source of this type of communication.

D. The supervisor did not account for the noise in the communication chain.

Answer (B) is correct. *(CIA, adapted)*

REQUIRED: The link in the communications chain that is defective.

DISCUSSION: In the communications process, the medium is the channel through which the communication flows. The defect in this case was the channel chosen to inform the employee of his/her loss of job. The supervisor should have spoken directly with the employee.

Answer (A) is incorrect because the buyer will readily understand that (s)he has been fired. Answer (C) is incorrect because the buyer's supervisor should have conveyed the news of the termination. Answer (D) is incorrect because there is no noise (interference) in the communication channel.

60. Refer to the information preceding question 59. Select an additional deficiency in the communication chain.

   A. The receiver of the communication was inappropriate; the personnel department should have received the memorandum and then informed the buyer.

   B. The message is improperly encoded because the buyer does not know why the termination is to be completed.

   C. Because the supervisor and buyer have conflicting vacation schedules, no possibility exists for feedback.

   D. The supervisor should not be the sender of the memorandum; the personnel department is the appropriate source.

Answer (C) is correct. *(CIA, adapted)*
   REQUIRED: The additional deficiency in the communications chain.
   DISCUSSION: The communications process has five elements: (1) the sender of the message, (2) symbols used to encode the message, (3) the medium chosen to send the message, (4) the receiver of the message, and (5) feedback acknowledging interpretation of the message by the receiver. Because the supervisor and buyer have conflicting vacation schedules, no possibility exists for feedback, and the buyer is not referred to anyone else in the organization for any additional information.
   Answer (A) is incorrect because, although the message should also be routed through the personnel department, the notification of a termination appropriately comes from the direct superior. Answer (B) is incorrect because the memorandum included the reasons for the termination. Answer (D) is incorrect because communication of a direct job-related impact should be transmitted by the employee's immediate superior.

61. All of the following statements about communication are false except

   A. Managers spend more of their workday involved in written communication than oral communication.

   B. Written communication encourages feedback.

   C. Breakthroughs in electronic technology will blur the distinctions between written and oral communications.

   D. The grapevine rarely provides accurate information.

Answer (C) is correct. *(Publisher)*
   REQUIRED: The false statement about communication.
   DISCUSSION: Breakthroughs in electronic technology may lead to oral messages being recorded and subsequently written out.
   Answer (A) is incorrect because managers spend more time communicating orally than they do communicating in writing. Answer (B) is incorrect because written communication inhibits feedback. Answer (D) is incorrect because the grapevine provides accurate information more often than not.

5.5 Listening and Electronic Communication

62. Which of the following is a potential disadvantage to listening by a manager?

   A. Demonstrates concern for subordinates by the manager.

   B. Concentration may be focused on the words spoken to the exclusion of the ideas.

   C. Gain more information about the workplace.

   D. May result in higher employee morale.

Answer (B) is correct. *(Publisher)*
   REQUIRED: The advantages to effective listening.
   DISCUSSION: If a manager is focused on the words spoken by someone else and not the intended ideas, there is a decoding problem. Effective listening requires understanding the message the communicating party is trying to convey.
   Answer (A) is incorrect because effective listening has a positive effect on both superiors and subordinates through showing concern for each others views. Answer (C) is incorrect because effective listening by managers often gives the manager a better idea of what employees are thinking and potential problems. Answer (D) is incorrect because effective listening by a manager shows subordinates that their input is valued and often raises employee morale.

63. Which of the following is false with regard to e-mail policies?

   A. Employees may use informal writing because e-mail is often informal in nature.

   B. Employees should understand that the organization has a legal right to monitor their use of the e-mail system.

   C. Filters should be used to protect against spam.

   D. E-mails should be concisely written.

Answer (A) is correct. *(Publisher)*
   REQUIRED: The policies associated with e-mail use in an organization.
   DISCUSSION: The principles of good writing still apply to e-mails. Therefore, e-mails should be written like any other formal communication within the organization.
   Answer (B) is incorrect because employers are legally permitted to keep track of employee activities while employees are at work, including monitoring e-mails. Answer (C) is incorrect because filters should be used to prevent incoming spam. If spam eludes the filters, it should be deleted. Answer (D) is incorrect because e-mails are still supposed to be written with good writing skills.

64. Organizational characteristics that may be barriers to effective communications include all of the following except

    A. Organizational status differences.

    B. Lack of formal channels.

    C. Listening problems.

    D. Departmental needs and goals.

Answer (C) is correct. *(Publisher)*
    REQUIRED: The statement that is not an organizational characteristic that may be a barrier to effective communication.
    DISCUSSION: Listening problems are personal characteristics, not organizational characteristics that may cause communication problems.
    Answer (A) is incorrect because organizational status and power differences are characteristics that may inhibit effective communication. Answer (B) is incorrect because lack of formal channels is a characteristic that may inhibit effective communication. Answer (D) is incorrect because departmental needs and goals are characteristics that may inhibit effective communication.

65. The benefits of electronic communication for a company and its employees include

    A. More efficient use of resources to increase profitability.

    B. Creation of redundant tasks that allow employees to develop expertise.

    C. Constant development of new procedures.

    D. Elimination of simulation models.

Answer (A) is correct. *(Publisher)*
    REQUIRED: The benefit of electronic communication for a company and its employees.
    DISCUSSION: The benefits of electronic communication include better control of information, more timely information, elimination of tedious tasks, improvement of competitiveness due to improved technology, standardization of procedures by computer programs, assistance for strategic planning, and optimization of organizational resources to improve productivity.
    Answer (B) is incorrect because electronic communication eliminates redundant tasks. Answer (C) is incorrect because procedures and operations are standardized by electronic communication. Answer (D) is incorrect because simulation is enhanced by computerization.

66. Which of the following is a benefit of implementing an electronic communication system?

    A. Relatively low capital expenditures are required.

    B. The company's comparative advantage over smaller firms that cannot afford such a system will increase.

    C. There is little need for additional resource allocation to facilitate implementation of the system.

    D. The sophistication of electronic communication systems eliminates the need for backup files and data recovery systems.

Answer (B) is correct. *(Publisher)*
    REQUIRED: The benefit of implementing an electronic communication system.
    DISCUSSION: Implementation of an electronic communication system improves the technology of a company. This increases the company's comparative advantage over smaller companies that cannot afford electronic communication systems.
    Answer (A) is incorrect because the initial capital expenditures for acquisition and set-up costs are large. Answer (C) is incorrect because additional resources must be allocated for implementation. Answer (D) is incorrect because no system can positively ensure against data loss. Backup files and data recovery systems are essential.

67. Telecommuting, working away from the office and communicating via electronic media, has become more widespread as advances in communication devices have made this more practical. All of the following are problems that are beginning to be associated with employees using telecommuting except that the telecommuting employees

    A. Fall behind in their fields of specialization.

    B. Lack strong working relationships.

    C. Experience a loss of career opportunities.

    D. Lack sufficient communication skills.

Answer (D) is correct. *(CMA, adapted)*
    REQUIRED: The item that is not a problem associated with employees who telecommute from their homes.
    DISCUSSION: People who are computer literate have in recent years begun working from their homes via telecommunication devices. Problems include lack of reliable telephone lines, a potential increase in management's work load, the loss of in-office contributions, a tendency to fall behind in fields of specialization, a lack of strong working relationships with other employees, a loss of career opportunities, and inadequate socialization. The primary strength of these individuals, however, has been their communication skills.
    Answer (A) is incorrect because telecommuters have tended to fall behind in their fields of specialization. Answer (B) is incorrect because telecommuters may be unable to form normal manager-employee and employee-employee relationships. Interaction with telecommuters poses obvious problems. Answer (C) is incorrect because telecommuters sometimes experience a loss of career opportunities as a result of not being in the office on a day-to-day basis.

STUDY UNIT SIX
ORGANIZATIONAL STRUCTURE AND EFFECTIVENESS

(17 pages of outline)

This study unit addresses the organizing function of management. It outlines the major theories of organizational design and describes the elements of organizational effectiveness. Particular emphasis is placed on the contingency approach to design developed from systems thinking. Other subunits concern some of the principal formats for integrating and coordinating an organization's activities.

6.1 THE ORGANIZING PROCESS

1. **Edgar Schein** describes the following elements of organizations:

   a. **Coordination of effort** in a cooperative social arrangement
   b. A **common goal or purpose**
   c. **Division of labor** (efficient specialization)
   d. A **hierarchy of authority**

      1) Authority is the right to direct, and to expect performance from, other people. Those people are **accountable** to their superiors in the hierarchy.

2. **Kreitner** (Management, 9th ed., Houghton Mifflin, pages 285-287) classifies organizations as follows:

   a. **Businesses** are engaged in economic activities with the intent to make a profit.
   b. **Nonprofit service organizations**, such as charities and universities, serve particular groups of clients. Money may come from donations, appropriations, or grants.
   c. **Mutual benefit organizations** are groups that exist to serve their members, e.g., labor unions, political parties, or credit unions.
   d. **Commonweal organizations** provide a standard service to all members of a population. Examples are local police departments and public school systems.

3. **Organizational charts** represent the formal organizational structure in two dimensions: vertical hierarchy and horizontal specialization. They often resemble a pyramid, with the chief executive on top and the operating workforce on bottom. Recent trends in management, including increased span of control and decreased hierarchy, have resulted in flatter organizational charts.

   a. The typical organizational chart can be designed to

      1) Reflect classical, formal vertical authority channels (**chain of command**).
      2) Show reporting relationships and task groupings (**departmentation**).
      3) Describe communication channels.
      4) Identify location of sources of organizational expertise.
      5) Show promotional or career tracks.
      6) Depict the span of control and number of organizational levels.
      7) Show major **functions** and their respective relationships (**horizontal specialization**).

b. **Shortcomings of organizational charts** include a

1) Limited presentation of information, a shortcoming that can be overcome by supplementing the chart with a detailed manual.
2) Tendency to quickly become obsolete due to rapid change.
3) Failure to show informal communication, influence, power, or friendships.
4) Tendency to ignore informal job trade-offs among titles on the chart.
5) Possibility of misleading management by giving an appearance of structure and order that might not exist.
6) Possibility that position titles do not reflect actual functions.

4. **Theories of organizing** may be roughly divided into two categories: traditional, closed-system theories and modern, open-system theories.

a. The **closed-system perspective** treats the organization as focused on economic efficiency in a reasonably predictable environment. Planning and control processes can substantially eliminate uncertainty.

1) The **scientific school of management** was the first major school to develop. It focused on the production process and ways to make it more efficient. It is based on the work of **Frederick W. Taylor**, who advocated a systematic quantitative approach oriented towards individual job design. Taylor's **principles of scientific management** are

a) Scientific analysis of work.
b) Scientific selection, training, and development of workers.
c) Cooperation among work planners and operators.
d) Equal sharing of responsibility by labor and management, who perform the tasks for which they are best suited.

2) **Henri Fayol** (a Frenchman publishing in 1916), sometimes called the father of administration, advocated the separation of administration from technical, commercial, financial, and accounting operations. Fayol's **functions of management** listed below form the foundation for the modern functional or process approach to classifying a manager's activities.

a) Planning
b) Organizing
c) Commanding
d) Coordinating
e) Controlling

3) Taylor, Fayol, and other traditionalists advocated the creation of authoritarian organizations characterized by narrow spans of control, close supervision, and the top-down flow of authority.

a) The **hierarchy of authority** should be precisely determined to foster pursuit of common objectives (**unity of objective**).
b) The **principle of unity of command** should be followed. Each subordinate should have only one superior (though a superior may have as many subordinates as allowed by the superior's span of control). Violation of this principle leads to confusion and frustration for the subordinate.
c) **Authority should be** proportionate to **responsibility**. Thus, a person should not be held accountable for performance unless (s)he has the power to perform.
d) Authority but not responsibility may be **delegated**.

4) **Max Weber**, a nineteenth-century German sociologist, coined the term **bureaucracy**. It described a traditionalist organization founded on efficient military principles, including "impartiality," or the making of personnel decisions based on merit.

    a) Despite its bad reputation, bureaucracy is a feature of every large organization. Because bureaucracy (characterized by division of labor, a hierarchy of authority, a framework of rules, and impersonality) is necessary, managers should be aware of the symptoms of an inefficient and otherwise **dysfunctional bureaucracy**.

        i) A high degree of bureaucratization

        ii) Too many boring jobs

        iii) Obedience to authority at all costs

        iv) Development of rules that are pointless or that obscure accountability

        v) Impersonality in the sense of ignoring the human needs of customers and employees

b. The **open-system perspective** treats the organization as focused on survival in an uncertain environment. The organization itself and the environment contain variables that may not be controllable.

    1) **Chester Barnard** (1938) argued that an organization is a **cooperative system** with a bottom-up flow of authority. His **acceptance theory of authority** is based on the premise that a manager's leadership depends on employees' acceptance of it. Thus, compliance with a message from a superior is dependent on employees'

        a) Understanding of the message.

        b) Belief that it serves an organizational objective.

        c) Belief that it serves their objectives.

        d) Ability to comply.

    2) The open-systems perspective reflects the reality that a successful organization must **adapt** rapidly to changes in such factors as technology progress, product evolution, market fluctuations, competitive challenges, and globalization.

    3) An **organizational system** is a group or set of things (subsystems) that are interrelated or interdependent so as to form a part of a larger whole. The open-systems perspective recognizes that understanding an organization is impossible without considering the larger context or system of which it is a part.

        a) It also considers both human relations and structural issues.

        b) Systems may be closed or open. **Closed systems** are closed to the external environment. Few systems are truly closed, but boundaries may be artificially drawn to facilitate analysis by treating a system as if it were closed.

            i) Classical viewpoints treated management as a closed system and ignored most things external to the organization. Such policy is limited and dangerous in that effective management of a social system is not deterministic or mechanistic.

c) **Open systems** are not self-sufficient. They must be open to, and have interaction with, an **external environment**. The **system boundaries** are drawn to reflect external inputs and system outputs.

   i)   A closed system suffers **entropy**, or progressive degradation and disorganization. An open system seeks replenishment through its boundaries with the larger system (environment). Accordingly, an open system is in **dynamic equilibrium**. For example, a business may obtain external financing to modernize its plant.

   ii) Closed-systems management writers viewed the environment as beyond their concern; open-systems writers see the environment as vital.

d) An open system is characterized by **synergism**, the interaction of its parts so that the total effect exceeds the sum of the effects of the separate parts.

e) Another attribute of open systems is **equifinality**, or the ability to achieve desired results by using different methods. Thus, a manufacturer may vary such inputs into the production process as labor and materials.

f) A business or other open system obtains **inputs** (information, capital, labor, materials, etc.) and produces **outputs** (goods, services, earnings, nonrecycled scrap, etc.).

g) An open system may be viewed as consisting of the following:

   i)   The **technical subsystem** (the production function)

   ii) The **boundary-spanning subsystem**, which interacts with the environment (sales, purchasing, public relations, planning, etc.)

   iii) The **management subsystem**, which coordinates the other subsystems

h) An open-systems organization should also be a **learning organization**. According to David Garvin, it should effectively create, acquire, and transfer knowledge. It must also succeed in changing its behavior in response.

   i)   Organizational learning proceeds by **cognition** (acquiring new knowledge), **behavior** (acquiring new skills), and **performance**.

   ii) The **skills** required for an organization to prosper as it copes with inevitable change are

   - Problem solving
   - Learning by systematic experimentation
   - Learning from its experience
   - Learning from customers, competitors, and others
   - Transferring and implementing what has been learned, e.g., through training and communication

5. **Organizational effectiveness**

   a.   In the narrowest sense, effectiveness is achievement of objectives. It is contrasted with **efficiency**, which is the ratio of output to input. In the broadest sense, an organization must achieve its objectives efficiently to be considered effective.

   1)   Economists define **productivity** as the ratio of real output to a unit of input.

b.   Continued profitability and growth are the obvious effectiveness criteria for businesses. However, **society's expectations** expressed through laws and regulations (antitrust, securities regulation, labor law, worker safety, environmental protection, pension security, antidiscrimination, consumer protection, etc.) provide many other criteria.

1)   The weighting of these concerns raises difficult issues for all businesses.

c.   **Time** is a component of organizational effectiveness. Accordingly, an organization should strive to be effective and efficient, grow, be profitable, satisfy society's and its stakeholders' expectations, learn, adapt, develop, and survive over a period of years.

1)   The organization needs to be effective and efficient and meet expectations of society, owners, employees, customers, and creditors in the **near term** (about 1 year).

2)   It must **adapt** to change and **develop** its capacities in the **intermediate term** (about 2-4 years).

3)   It must **survive** in an uncertain environment full of obstacles and opportunities in the **long term** (about 5 years or more).

d.   **Organizational decline** (loss of effectiveness and efficiency coupled with inflexibility) may lead to downsizing, merger, reorganization, or liquidation. It results from decreased demand, resource limitations, or mismanagement.

1)   The following are **characteristics** of organizations that are stable or in decline:

   a)   Centralization
   b)   Lack of long-term planning because of a short-term crisis mentality
   c)   Lack of innovation
   d)   A tendency to place blame on leaders
   e)   Rejection of change when most needed
   f)   High turnover of the best leaders
   g)   Poor morale
   h)   Not setting priorities for cutbacks
   i)   Conflict over control and resources when teamwork is most needed

2)   **Management complacency** has been identified as the most important cause of organizational decline. Its characteristics are

   a)   A lack of innovation
   b)   Faulty perception of markets and competition
   c)   Failure to observe or properly appraise the initial warnings of decline
   d)   Not focusing on daily objectives

3)   An **adaptive organization**

   a)   Monitors problems and watches for the symptoms of decline.

   b)   Restates and clarifies its objectives on a timely basis.

   c)   Identifies the best markets and customers and the most threatening competitors.

   d)   Promotes experimentation, communication, and participation.

   e)   Recognizes that it may be the most vulnerable when it is the most successful. Arrogant overconfidence tends to be greatest then.

4)   Downsizing results from organizational decline, changes in the business cycle, or business combinations. The objectives are cost reduction, improved efficiency, and higher profits.

   a)   These purposes are often not achieved. Many organizations follow cycles of hiring, firing, and rehiring that do not yield the expected benefits to offset the harm to terminated employees, the loss of morale of the survivors, and the damage to communities.

b)   Downsizing also tends to have a disproportionate effect on women and members of minorities, who tend to be the last hired and first fired.

c)   The more enlightened view is that employees are not readily disposable commodities but valuable resources who should be terminated only as a last resort. This view seeks alternatives to involuntary termination.

i)   Redeployment involves retraining or transferring employees or lending them to other companies.

ii)   Voluntary retirement programs offer accelerated retirement benefits, severance allowances, or other compensation.

iii)   Employees may share jobs or be shifted to lower-level positions.

iv)   All employees may be asked to accept reduced hours or pay.

v)   Outplacement assists laid-off employees in finding new jobs.

vi)   The law may require notice. In the U.S., companies with 100 or more employees must give 60 days' notice of facilities' closings or layoffs.

vii)   A job bank provides downsized employees with work that is usually outsourced.

viii)   Counseling and training may be offered to counter the stress felt by employees who are retained.

6.   Stop and review! You have completed the outline for this subunit. Study multiple-choice questions 1 through 9 beginning on page 171.

6.2 THE CONTINGENCY APPROACH

1.   The contingency approach is derived from **open systems** thinking. It stresses that the search for answers to organizational design problems depends on contingencies that can be discovered and studied. Accordingly, no one design format fits all organizations.

a.   Because this approach argues for situationally determined answers, the key is finding the relevant factors in the organization's **environment**.

b.   Moreover, the greater the environmental uncertainty, the more **adaptive** the organization must be.

2.   Contingency design determines the **structure** that suits the **environmental (state) uncertainty** faced by the organization. Environmental uncertainty is a function of, among other things,

a.   Stability of demand for the organization's goods or services.

b.   Reliability of supply.

c.   Rate of technological change.

d.   Socioeconomic and political pressures.

3.   **Burns and Stalker** distinguished between mechanistic and organic organizations.

a.   In a **mechanistic organization** (an inflexible bureaucracy), tasks are specifically defined and have little flexibility. Moreover, knowledge tends to be task-specific. Hierarchical authority is strong, with an emphasis on employee obedience, and communication is mostly top-down. Rights and obligations are clearly defined, but how individual efforts relate to achieving organizational objectives is not.

1)   Mechanistic organizations are most likely to succeed in **stable and certain environments**.

    b. An **organic organization** is adaptive. Tasks are broadly and flexibly defined, and the relationship of individual effort and organizational objectives is clear. In addition, knowledge tends to be professional. Work methods, rights, and obligations are purposely left unclear. Self-control is preferred to hierarchical control. Thus, superiors have an informational and advisory role. Communication is participative and horizontal.

        1) Organic organizations are most likely to succeed in **unstable and uncertain environments**.

4. **Lawrence and Lorsch** addressed the relationship between environmental complexity and the organization's balance between differentiation and integration.

    a. **Differentiation** is caused by the division of labor and technical specialization. Thus, specialists in, for example, marketing and IT may have substantial differences in skills, attitudes, and behavior. Differentiation leads to organizational fragmentation because specialists tend to have a narrow focus.

    b. **Integration** is the coordination of effort required for achievement of mutual objectives. Typical structural arrangements for achieving integration include a hierarchy of authority, a framework of rules, departmentation, formation of cross-functional groups, computer systems, liaison bodies, and human relations training.

    c. In successful organizations (and in their subunits), a **dynamic equilibrium** exists between the tendencies of fragmentation and coordination. Furthermore,

        1) Differentiation and integration are directly correlated with **environmental complexity**.

        2) The higher the differentiation, the greater the obstacles to integration.

        3) An unsuccessful organization in a complex environment is likely to be highly differentiated but poorly integrated.

5. According to Henry Mintzberg, an organization has five components. Depending on which is in control, one of five different structures will evolve. The five organizational components include the

    a. **Operating core** -- workers who perform the basic tasks related to production
    b. **Strategic apex** -- top managers
    c. **Middle line** -- managers who connect the core to the apex
    d. **Technostructure** -- analysts who achieve a certain standardization in the organization
    e. **Support staff** -- indirect support services

6. Mintzberg's five organizational structures include the following:

    a. A **simple structure**, such as that of a small retailer, has a low complexity and formality, and authority is centralized. Its small size and simplicity usually precludes significant inefficiency in the use of resources. The strategic apex is the dominant component.

    b. A **machine bureaucracy** is a complex, formal, and centralized organization that performs highly routine tasks, groups activities into functional departments, has a strict chain of command, and distinguishes between line and staff relationships. The technostructure dominates.

c. A **professional bureaucracy** (e.g., a university or library) is a complex and formal but decentralized organization in which highly trained specialists have great autonomy. Duplication of functions is minimized. For example, a university would have only one history department. Thus, the operating core is in control.

d. A **divisional structure** is essentially a self-contained organization. Hence, it must perform all or most of the functions of the overall organization of which it is a part. It is characterized by substantial duplication of functions compared with more centralized structures. The middle line dominates.

e. An **adhocracy** (an organic structure) has low complexity, formality, and centralization. Vertical differentiation is low and horizontal differentiation is high. The emphasis is on flexibility and response. Thus, the support staff dominates.

7. Stop and review! You have completed the outline for this subunit. Study multiple-choice questions 10 through 12 on page 174.

6.3 DEPARTMENTATION

1. **Division of labor** breaks complex processes into their simpler components. This makes task specialization by employees possible. However, dividing labor creates a need for efficient coordination of those performing the separate tasks. One response to the problem is departmentation, a structural format for organizational integration that is intended to promote coordination. It is the grouping of related activities into significant organizational subsystems (groups, divisions, units, departments, etc.).

a. **Departmentation by function** is found in almost every organization at some level whether for-profit or nonprofit. The most common departments in for-profit organizations are marketing, production, and finance (though other terms may be used). These often extend upward in the organizational chart to the level below the chief executive.

1) Advantages include occupational specialization, simplified training, and representation of primary functions at the top level of the organization.

2) Disadvantages include lack of coordination among primary functions and absence of profit centers within the organization.

b. **Departmentation by territory** (geographic location) is favored by national or multi-national firms and government agencies with scattered resources, offices, or plants.

1) Advantages include quicker reaction to local market changes, greater familiarity with local problems or unique geographic concerns, and logistical savings in freight costs and travel time.

2) Disadvantages include more delegation of authority to regional managers, problems of control for headquarters, and duplication of facilities and service functions (personnel, purchases, etc.).

a) Advances in telecommunications counteract some of the disadvantages.

c. **Departmentation by product or service** is growing in importance for multiline, large-scale enterprises. It is often an outgrowth of functional departmentation. The result is that product-service subunits may be treated as separate businesses with a high degree of autonomy. Managers must therefore have a broad perspective, not a merely functional orientation.

1) Advantages include better use of specialized capital and skills, ease of coordination, simpler assignment of profit responsibility, compatibility with a decentralization strategy, and a basis for allocating capital efficiently to products or services likely to achieve the best returns.

2) Disadvantages include the requirement for a greater number of persons with managerial ability, duplication of facilities and service functions, and difficulty integrating operations.

d. **Departmentation by customer** allows for service to a particular customer to be provided under the management of a subunit. This form of departmentation seldom appears at the top level of an organizational structure, but it is common at middle levels (e.g., the loan officer of a large bank who handles one account exclusively). Customer departmentation is typical in the sales department of a firm organized by function.

1) Advantages include improved customer service as a result of greater expertise in a particular business and ease in identifying contributions to profit by different types and locations of customers.

2) Disadvantages include difficulties in coordination with other units in the organization, pressure to give preferential treatment to a given manager's customers, and duplication of facilities and service functions.

e. **Project departmentation** is appropriate for experimental or one-time activities, e.g., the construction of a ship, a large building, or a major design project (such as a military weapons system).

1) Advantages include specialization and ease of communication and coordination of efforts required within a particular project.

2) Disadvantages include need for reorganization at the end of the project, problems of recruitment at the start of the project, and difficulty of maintaining control at the central office.

f. **Matrix design** may be a combination of any of the previously mentioned approaches. For example, a manager for each product may be appointed to supervise personnel who simultaneously report to a manager for each function. This form is used in R & D and in **project management**.

1) The emphasis of the arrangement is on the result or the product.

2) The functional organization remains, but parts of it are temporarily lent or assigned to a given project.

3) The project may be to make a product indefinitely or to accomplish a limited but lengthy task, such as construction of a submarine.

4) Matrix design provides the security and accountability of the functional form. However, it also provides expert personnel to the project only when needed and only to the extent required. It allows personnel as well as functions to be most effectively and efficiently used.

5) The technical ability of employees is better appraised by the functional managers than by the project manager.

6) Practical applications skills can be appraised by the project manager on site.

7) Unnecessarily large swings in levels of personnel and equipment are minimized.

a) The major disadvantage is that the **unity-of-command** principle is violated. Hence, the authority, responsibility, and accountability of the parties involved must be clearly defined to avoid confusion and employee dissatisfaction.

b) A second disadvantage is the possible inefficient use of employees. Individuals may be idle while waiting for project assignments that require their specific talents.

8) It is difficult for large organizations to use matrix design because they typically have many levels (both vertical and horizontal), thus slowing communications.

g. **Lean production** is a management concept that focuses on minimization of everything from inventories to labor hours. Invented by Toyota, lean production is becoming a dominant paradigm in manufacturing. It has driven many of the performance improvements now being made in industry. The objective is to identify and eliminate waste. These improvements benefit all of the organization's stakeholders, including customers and shareholders. Society as a whole also benefits because the waste traditionally embedded in the manufacturing process is removed, releasing resources for other uses.

1) Lean production's basic premise is that better designed products, avoidance of defects, increased speed and flexibility, and reduced inventory buffers translate to decreased costs of doing business.

2) Many organizations use **benchmarking** as a tool to determine how low inventories and costs can be.

3) An organization cannot become a lean producer overnight. Management must build and nurture the logic and machinery that drive lean production.

4) Implementing lean production usually means breaking old patterns and installing new ones.

5) Strategic planning is an important cornerstone of lean production.

6) Effective lean production requires partnering with suppliers.

h. **Departmentation by work flow process** is used in reengineered organizations.

1) Reengineering involves starting anew to redesign an organization's core processes rather than attempting to improve the current system. Reengineering is not merely downsizing or continuous improvement, but a complete change in ways of doing business.

a) In the modern, highly competitive business environment, an organization needs to adapt quickly and radically to change. Thus, reengineering is usually a cross-functional process of innovation requiring substantial investment in information technology and retraining. Successful reengineering may bring dramatic improvements in customer service and the speed with which new products are introduced.

2) Organizations that use **work flow process** design are known as **horizontal organizations**. Their objective is an outward focus on customer satisfaction. For this purpose, the horizontal work flow between **identification of customer needs** and satisfaction of those needs is to be managed quickly and efficiently.

2. Stop and review! You have completed the outline for this subunit. Study multiple-choice questions 13 through 21 beginning on page 174.

6.4 LINE AND STAFF DESIGN

1. **Major Approaches**

a. The **classical** approach views **line** activities as those directly responsible for the primary function, product, or service of the organization. Staff members provide supporting technical expertise. In **mechanistic organizations**, a line-and-staff design helps to preserve unity of command.

1) Production is a line activity, but more current writers include sales (marketing) and sometimes finance, depending on the objectives of the organization.

2) **Staff** activities are advisory. They are necessary to the organization but secondary to the line functions. A distinction should be made between **personal staff** and **specialized staff**. The former are individuals assigned to a given manager, and the latter are functions that serve the whole organization.

b. **Behavioral theorists'** concerns with **acceptance of authority** distinguish their approach to line and staff relationships. They see exercise of **informal authority** as a very important constraint on formal chains of command.

1) Advice offered by senior staff is akin to a command. They have access to senior management and can exercise more informal authority than a junior line manager.

2) Even the classical school acknowledged the dilemma of how to ensure adoption of specialized staff advice without subverting line authority. If line management refuses to accept staff's advice, what can senior management do?

3) A staff group with **advisory authority** can only offer suggestions, prepare plans for consideration by line managers, and evaluate organizational performance.

a) A staff member often has an area of technical expertise, such as law, industrial labor relations, operations research, or personnel.

b) The staff member's goal is the approval (or rejection) of a complete recommended solution, but a line manager may want a quick fix to a problem rather than a complete solution.

c) Consultation with line personnel is essential.

4) A staff group may have **concurrent** authority. Line management must persuade experts in specified areas to agree to an action or decision.

a) EXAMPLE: A line production manager may be required to obtain a second signature on a lease agreement from the legal department.

5) A staff group may be given complete authority in a specialized area, and its specialized activities are separated from line management.

a) Unlike advisory activities, the line manager must use the services of the staff organization.

b) Examples include information systems, purchasing, and personnel.

6) A staff group may occasionally be given **control** authority. Thus, line authority may be superseded by that of the specialist staff designated by higher levels of management to make certain decisions in the area of staff expertise.

a) Control staff authority appears to violate classical principles of unity of command. However, there is no violation when the control staff act as agents for the higher-level line manager, who has delegated authority to the staff.

i) EXAMPLE: Quality-control inspectors have the authority to reject marginal products, but because this authority is exercised on behalf of the manufacturing manager, the chain of command actually remains intact.

7) If the organization adopts **TQM** concepts with an emphasis on internal as well as external service, line managers and staff personnel may be viewed as having a **customer-service provider** relationship.

2.   A hybrid of the control authority relationship of staff and line is called a **functional authority**. This kind of design is common in **organic organizations**.

    a.   An individual is given functional authority outside the chain of command for certain specified activities. The individual may be either a line or a staff manager who is a specialist in a particular field.

        1)   EXAMPLE: The vice president in charge of sales may be given functional authority over manufacturing executives in scheduling customer orders, packaging, or making service parts available.

    b.   Functional authority may be created for numerous reasons when a line manager is not the person best suited to oversee a given activity, for example, lack of special knowledge, inability to supervise processes, or a danger of diverse interpretations of policies.

        1)   EXAMPLE: The vice president for industrial labor relations may have functional authority over the production manager for the purpose of negotiating a new labor contract, though no line relationship exists at other times.

    c.   Functional specialists have the authority to determine the appropriate standards in their own field of specialization and to enforce those standards.

        1)   EXAMPLE: The chief engineer of an airline may have the authority to remove airplanes from service, overriding the wishes of the vice president for operations.

3.   **Line and staff conflicts** are almost inevitable given the considerable difference in their backgrounds and activities. These individuals tend to have different training and education, perspectives on the organization, career and other objectives, and temperaments.

    a.   Line and staff conflicts are classic examples of the **differentiation and fragmentation** process discussed earlier in this study unit.

    b.   Operating executives with line authority often see a high potential for harm in staff activity. A staff member with vaguely defined authority from a chief executive effectively usurps the authority of subunit managers.

    c.   Staff are not responsible for the success of a line department, but only for generating suggestions. If an implemented suggestion fails, line managers will blame the suggestion, and staff will blame the poor implementation of the suggestions.

    d.   Setting staff apart from line responsibilities gives them the time and environment in which to think, but this separation can also lead to thinking in a vacuum and suggestions by staff that are inappropriate or not feasible.

    e.   Excessive staff activity may violate the principle of **unity of command**. Subordinates may become confused and wonder whether they are primarily responsible to the staff member or to their line manager.

4.   Line-staff conflicts may be **minimized** by

    a.   Clearly defining areas of activity and authority.

    b.   Sharply defining the nature and place of line and staff. For example, line may have authority and responsibility, and staff may be required to sell their ideas to line.

    c.   Stressing the systems approach to all employees, whether line or staff, to encourage them to work together toward organizational goals.

    d.   Reducing areas of possible conflict, e.g., keeping functional authority to a minimum and providing feedback to staff of line's reaction to proposals.

    e.   Using the concept of **completed staff work** when possible. Thus, recommendations should be complete enough to make possible yes-or-no response from line managers. Advice should be clear and complete.

5. The modern approach to line and staff is based on **systems theory**.

   a. Every position and task must contribute to achievement of organizational objectives.

   b. Distinctions between producers and helpers are irrelevant.

   c. The changing nature of work environments from predominantly production firms to predominantly service providers makes it harder to pinpoint who exactly is responsible for producing.

      1) EXAMPLE: At a motor inn with the objective of customer satisfaction, who is line and who is staff?

6. Stop and review! You have completed the outline for this subunit. Study multiple-choice questions 22 through 25 beginning on page 177.

6.5 SPAN OF CONTROL

1. **Span of control** (span of management or span of authority) is an upper limit to the number of people who can be effectively and efficiently supervised by one person.

2. The **classical view** holds that the universal span of control is five or six people.

3. The **behavioral school** advocates expanding the span of control if possible. The advantages are

   a. **Increasing autonomy and morale** of individual workers by reducing the time available to a manager to direct them (the more people per manager, the less time available per person).

   b. **Decreasing communication problems** by reducing organizational levels (given a fixed number of employees, the narrower the span of control, the taller the organization, and the greater the number of levels).

4. The **modern or contingency approach** suggests that the appropriate span of control varies widely. It identifies the situational variables that determine the span of control, including

   a. The supervisor's training, interests, abilities, personality, time available to supervise, etc.

   b. Workers' interests, drives, commitment to the job, training, attitudes, aptitudes, etc.

   c. The work situation, including the technological process used (job shop, mass production, continuous process), frequency of change in job method, complexity of the task, dependence on the work of others, and supervision required.

   d. The organization's environment, including how rapidly it is compelled to change by technological innovation or market pressure and the amount of **uncertainty** in the environment.

5. Spans of control tend to move from wider to narrower as

   a. The work done becomes **less similar**.
   b. Workers being supervised become more **dispersed** geographically.
   c. The work done becomes more **complex**.
   d. The frequency and intensity of **required supervision** increase.
   e. The time needed for **coordination** with other supervisors increases.
   f. The time needed for **planning** increases.

6. The number of levels in an organization will be greatly influenced by the span of control.

   a. **Flat organizational structures** have relatively few levels from top to bottom. Thus, they have wide spans of control.

      1) Flat structures provide fast information flow from top to bottom of the organization and increased employee satisfaction.

        2)   Disadvantages of reduced supervision are poorer employee training, lack of coordination, and behavioral problems.

    b.   **Tall organizational structures** have many levels between top and bottom. Hence, they have relatively narrow spans of control.

        1)   Tall structures are faster and more effective at problem resolution than flat structures because of increased frequency of interaction between superior and employee and the greater order imposed by the hierarchical structure.

        2)   Disadvantages are slow decision making, excessive supervision, greater administrative costs, and lack of initiative resulting from too little delegation of authority.

    c.   Studies do not indicate great advantages for either flat or tall structures.

7.   Stop and review! You have completed the outline for this subunit. Study multiple-choice questions 26 through 36 beginning on page 178.

6.6 CENTRALIZATION AND DECENTRALIZATION

1.   Major design issues are the concentration of authority in an organization, its degree, and the levels at which it occurs.

2.   Centralization and decentralization are relative terms. Absolute centralization or decentralization is impossible.

3.   **Classicists** view decentralization with some distrust because they seek to avoid any dilution of control by senior managers.

4.   **Behavioralists** view decentralization in the same way as delegation, that is, as a good way to improve motivation and morale of lower-level employees.

5.   The **modern or contingency view** is that neither centralization nor decentralization is good or bad in itself. The degree to which either is stressed depends upon a given situation.

    a.   Decisions cannot be decentralized to those who do not have necessary **information**, e.g., knowledge of job objectives or measures for evaluation of performance.

    b.   Decisions cannot be decentralized to people who do not have the training, experience, knowledge, or **ability** to make them.

    c.   Decisions requiring a **quick response** should be decentralized to those near the action.

    d.   Decentralization should not occur below the organizational level at which **coordination** must be maintained (e.g., each supervisor on an assembly line cannot be allowed to decide the reporting time for employees).

    e.   Decisions that are of **critical importance** to the survival of the organization should not be decentralized.

    f.   Decentralization has a positive influence on **morale**.

6.   Decentralization is a philosophy of organizing and managing. Careful selection of which decisions to push down the hierarchy and which to hold at the top is required. The **degree of decentralization** will be greater if

    a.   More decisions are made lower in the hierarchy.
    b.   More of the important decisions are made lower in the hierarchy.
    c.   More functions are affected by decisions made at lower levels.
    d.   Fewer decisions made lower in the hierarchy are monitored by senior management.

7. Organizational design should achieve a **balance** between centralization and decentralization. The main benefits of centralization are more **effective control and reduced costs** through resource sharing. The main benefits of decentralization are **flexibility and adaptability** that permit a rapid response to changes in circumstances.

    a. The more centralized organization tends to thrive in a relatively stable and certain environment.

    b. The more decentralized organization tends to be more successful in a relatively unstable and uncertain environment.

8. Establishment of **strategic business units (SBUs)** is a means of decentralization used by large corporations seeking to enjoy the entrepreneurial advantages of smaller entities.

    a. An SBU in principle is permitted by its parent to function as an **independent business**, including development of its own strategic plans. A true SBU

        1) Is not merely a supplier of the parent, but serves its own markets.
        2) Encounters competition.
        3) Is a **profit center**.
        4) Makes all important decisions about its business although it may share resources with the parent.

9. **Delegation** is the formal process of assigning authority downward. Delegation is similar to decentralization in philosophy, process, and requirements.

    a. The **classical approach** is to avoid delegation because the superior is deemed to be both responsible and knowledgeable. Under that view, delegation avoids responsibility.

    b. The **behavioral view** sees delegation as useful in every organization because no one has time to make every decision, and employees like to make decisions affecting their work.

    c. The **modern or contingency approach** is to view delegation as dependent on the situation and the people involved. Delegation requires

        1) Skill, self-confidence, and knowledge of organizational objectives.
        2) A feedback system to allow objective assessment of performance.
        3) Faith in employees' abilities.
        4) Clear recognition of the basic need to delegate.
        5) Willingness to accept risk.
        6) Desire to develop and train employees.

    d. The **delegation process** involves

        1) Determination of results expected.
        2) Assignment of tasks and responsibilities.
        3) Delegation of authority for accomplishing these tasks.
        4) Recruitment of responsible people for the accomplishment of tasks.
        5) Clear communication of what is expected in objective terms.
        6) Follow-up because **ultimate responsibility** still resides with the delegator.

    e. The **benefits of delegation** are time savings for the delegator, training and development of lower-level managers, and improved morale.

f.   **Obstacles to delegation**

1)   The delegator is a perfectionist, has low self-esteem, fears criticism or competition, lacks confidence in lower-level managers, or has low risk tolerance.

2)   Jobs are poorly defined.

3)   Controls are ineffective.

4)   Superiors are not role models for delegation.

g.   The continuum of delegation

1)   Investigation and reporting
2)   Investigation and submission of recommendations
3)   Investigation and advising about plans
4)   Investigation and undertaking action, with reporting on what was done
5)   Investigation and undertaking action

10.   **New types of organizations** tend to have **flatter structures** (fewer layers), make more use of **teams**, and avoid the disadvantages of the complex large entity by creating **entrepreneurial units**.

a.   An **hourglass organization** has three layers:

1)   The strategic layer determines the mission of the organization and ensures that it is successful.

2)   A small group of middle managers coordinates a variety of lower-level cross-functional activities. These managers are generalists, not specialists, and they are not simply conduits for operating information. Computer systems can instantly transfer such information directly to the top layer.

3)   On the lowest level are empowered technical specialists who are most often self-supervised. They lack promotion possibilities, but are motivated by lateral transfers, challenging work, training in new skills, and pay-for-performance plans.

b.   A **cluster organization** is in essence a group of teams. Workers are multiskilled and shift among teams as needed. Communication and group skills are vital, requiring special training and team-building exercises. Pay is for knowledge.

c.   **Network organizations**. The relative independence of the various firms in a network differentiates it from a vertically integrated organization.

1)   A network is not based on the price mechanism or on a hierarchical relationship but on coordination through adaptation.

2)   It is a long-term, strategic relationship based on implicit contracts without specific legal ties.

3)   A network allows member firms to gain a competitive advantage against competitors outside the network.

4)   A network may be viewed as a group of activities involving suppliers and customers that add value. Each activity may be performed internally at an internal cost or subcontracted at an external cost.

a)   When an activity is subcontracted, a transaction cost will be incurred.

b)   A technological restriction on the existence of a network is that external costs must be less than internal costs. The firms in the network must be able to reduce the transaction costs so that the combination of external and transaction costs is less than internal costs.

        c)   The difference between a network and a normal market is that transaction costs in the market are low enough for any player.

             i)   In a network, the participating firms reduce initially high transaction costs through cooperative efforts.

     5)   A network is an ultimate expression of **outsourcing**, which entails obtaining goods or services from outside sources that could be acquired internally. For example, a firm may choose to outsource its computer processing or legal work, and a manufacturer may buy rather than make components.

  d. **Virtual organizations** are "flexible networks of value-adding subcontractors, linked by the Internet, e-mail, fax machines, and telephones" (Kreitner, 9th ed., pages 343-344).

     1)   The emphasis is on speed and constant, if not too rapid, change.
     2)   Constant learning is essential.
     3)   Cross-functional teams are emphasized.
     4)   Stress is high.

11.   Stop and review! You have completed the outline for this subunit. Study multiple-choice questions 37 through 49 beginning on page 181.

QUESTIONS

6.1 The Organizing Process

1. The organizational chart

A. Is used only in centralized organizations.

B. Is applicable only to profit-oriented companies.

C. Depicts only line functions.

D. Depicts the lines of authority linking various positions.

Answer (D) is correct. *(CMA, adapted)*
    REQUIRED: The true statement about an organizational chart.
    DISCUSSION: An organizational chart is used to represent the organizational structure of an entity. It normally resembles a pyramid, with the chief executive on top and the operating work force on the bottom. Lines show reporting relationships, lines of authority, and task groupings. An organizational chart depicts promotional or career tracks and illustrates the span of control and the number of organizational levels.
    Answer (A) is incorrect because an organizational chart can be used in decentralized as well as centralized organizations. Answer (B) is incorrect because not-for-profit agencies use organizational charts for the same reasons as profit-oriented companies. Answer (C) is incorrect because both staff and line functions are depicted on organizational charts.

2. Which type of organization is based upon strategic long-term relationships based upon implicit contracts and coordination through adaptation?

A. Hourglass organization.

B. Cluster organization.

C. Network organization.

D. Virtual organization.

Answer (C) is correct. *(Publisher)*
    REQUIRED: The organization based upon strategic long-term relationship based upon implicit contracts and coordination through adaption.
    DISCUSSION: A network organization is a network based upon coordination through adaptation. It also is based upon long-term relationships without specific legal ties.
    Answer (A) is incorrect because an hourglass organization has three layers consisting of a strategic layer, a group of middle managers, and lower level technical specialists. There are also specific legal contracts in the form of employer-employee contracts. Answer (B) is incorrect because a cluster organization is essentially a group of teams. The teams are still part of an organization with explicit contracts such as employer-employee contracts. Answer (D) is incorrect because a virtual organization is a network of value-adding subcontractors who are linked by electronic mediums.

3. A public university would be considered which type of organization?

- A. Commonweal organization.
- B. Business organization.
- C. Nonprofit service organization.
- D. Mutual benefit organization.

Answer (C) is correct. *(Publisher)*
REQUIRED: The classification of a university.
DISCUSSION: Nonprofit service organizations include charities and universities. Nonprofit service organizations serve particular groups of clients.
Answer (A) is incorrect because a commonweal organization provides a standard service to all members of the population. Examples include fire stations and police departments. Answer (B) is incorrect because business organizations are engaged in to make a profit. Answer (D) is incorrect because a mutual benefit organization is comprised of groups that serve their members such as labor unions or political parties.

4. Organizational charts often represent the formal structure of an organization. Often the organizational chart represents a pyramid with the chief executive on the top and the operating workforce on the bottom. Which of the following would not be included in a typical organizational chart?

- A. The span of control and the number of organizational levels.
- B. Communication channels.
- C. Promotional or career tracks.
- D. Informal influence or friendships.

Answer (D) is correct. *(Publisher)*
REQUIRED: The limitations of organizational charts.
DISCUSSION: Organizational charts often show the formal relationships between employers and employees. However a shortcoming of organizational charts is that they do not show informal relationships between the upper and lower levels of the corporate hierarchy.
Answer (A) is incorrect because the span of control and the number of organizational levels is demonstrated by the pyramid. The chief executive at the top has the greatest control over the organization and then the levels of the pyramid show the number of organizational levels. Answer (B) is incorrect because the communication channels are often up the pyramid and is shown on the organizational chart. Answer (C) is incorrect because the higher levels of the pyramid are the levels that employees can be promoted to.

5. Which of the following concepts is not consistent with a successful authoritarian organization?

- A. Each subordinate should only have one superior.
- B. Superiors may have as many subordinates as possible within the superior's span of control.
- C. Responsibility may be delegated.
- D. The hierarchy of authority should be precisely defined.

Answer (C) is correct. *(Publisher)*
REQUIRED: The characteristics of a successful authoritarian organization.
DISCUSSION: Taylor, Fayol, and other traditionalists advocated the creation of authoritarian organizations. One of the criteria for success was the ability to delegate authority but not responsibility. Responsibility should always remain with the person who made the decision.
Answer (A) is incorrect because the unity of command principle states that each subordinate should only have one superior in order to prevent confusion and frustration. Answer (B) is incorrect because the unity of command principle states that a superior can have as many subordinates as he or she can reasonably manage. Answer (D) is incorrect because the unity of objective principle requires that the hierarchy of authority be precisely defined to pursue common objectives.

6. Although bureaucracy is often perceived negatively by the public, it is a feature of nearly every large company. Which of the following is a sign that a bureaucracy is dysfunctional?

- A. A diversity of jobs.
- B. Rules that obscure responsibility.
- C. A large number of rules necessary for day to day operations.
- D. Obedience to authority.

Answer (B) is correct. *(Publisher)*
REQUIRED: The symptoms of a dysfunctional bureaucracy.
DISCUSSION: A sign that a bureaucracy is dysfunctional is the development of rules that are meaningless or that obscure accountability. A lack of accountability shows that the bureaucracy is ineffective at identifying the source problems and creating solutions to solve the problems.
Answer (A) is incorrect because a diversity of jobs prevents employees from becoming bored with routine and unchallenging tasks. Answer (C) is incorrect because many bureaucracies have rules to guide day to day operations. As long as the rules have a purpose and are not meaningless then the rules do not create a dysfunctional environment. Answer (D) is incorrect because obedience to authority is required for a corporation's operations to run smoothly. However, obedience at all costs is a sign that the bureaucracy is dysfunctional.

7. London Corporation adheres to an open-systems perspective belief that the organization must adapt to changes in the environment to be successful. Which of the following would be inconsistent with London Corporation following an open-systems framework?

    A. London Corporation attempts to utilize resources in order to be self-sufficient.

    B. London Corporation experiments with different production methods to find the method that is the most efficient and effective.

    C. London Corporation emphasizes the overall result of projects instead of the individual inputs.

    D. London Corporation requires employees to undergo monthly training seminars.

Answer (A) is correct. *(Publisher)*
    REQUIRED: The characteristics of an open-system organization.
    DISCUSSION: Open-systems acknowledge the need to interact with their environment and therefore are not able to be self-sufficient. Self-sufficiency is a quality inherit in closed-systems because closed-systems try to avoid interaction with the external environment.
    Answer (B) is incorrect because equifinality is the ability to achieve desired results by using different methods which is an attribute of open-system organizations. Answer (C) is incorrect because synergism is the emphasis of the total effect exceeding the sum of the parts. Synergism is an attribute of an open-system. Answer (D) is incorrect because an open-system organization focuses on learning by its employees.

8. Faced with 3 years of steadily decreasing profits despite increased sales and a growing economy, which of the following is the healthiest course of action for a chief executive officer to take?

    A. Set a turnaround goal of significantly increasing profits within 2 months. Set clear short-term objectives for each operating unit that, together, should produce the turnaround.

    B. Reduce staff by 10% in every unit.

    C. Classify all job functions as either (a) adding value in the eyes of the customer (such as production and sales) or (b) not adding value in the eyes of the customer (such as accounting and human resources). Reduce staff in the non-value-adding functions by 20%.

    D. Implement a plan to encourage innovation at all levels. Use early retirement and reemployment programs to trim staff size.

Answer (D) is correct. *(CIA, adapted)*
    REQUIRED: The healthiest course of action given decreasing profits despite increasing sales.
    DISCUSSION: Organizational decline has been found to have the following characteristics: greater centralization, lack of long-term planning, reduced innovation, scapegoating, resistance to change, high turnover of competent leaders, low morale, nonprioritized downsizing, and conflict. Reversing these characteristics is the key to reversing organizational decline, for example, by encouraging innovation in all aspects of the organization's activities and by redeploying personnel.
    Answer (A) is incorrect because this response illustrates two of the characteristics of organizational decline: increased centralization of decision making and lack of long-term planning. The exclusive emphasis on short-term results is likely to be counterproductive. Answer (B) is incorrect because another characteristic of organizational decline is nonprioritized downsizing. By itself, downsizing rarely turns a company around. Answer (C) is incorrect because reducing staff disproportionately in control functions could have disastrous consequences.

9. Which of the following has been identified as the most important cause of organizational decline?

    A. Centralization.

    B. Management complacency.

    C. Poor employee morale.

    D. Lack of innovation.

Answer (B) is correct. *(Publisher)*
    REQUIRED: The most important cause of organizational decline.
    DISCUSSION: Management complacency often is characterized by a lack of innovation, faulty perception of markets and competition, failure to observe or appraise the initial indicators of decline, and not focusing on daily objectives. Therefore, the characteristics listed are the product of poor management.
    Answer (A) is incorrect because centralization is a characteristic of many successful corporations and does not necessarily indicate organizational decline. Answer (C) is incorrect because poor employee morale can be addressed by management that is attentive and involved in the employee's activities. Answer (D) is incorrect because a lack of innovation can be corrected by management if the proper corrective actions are taken such as investing more in research and development or benchmarking.

6.2 The Contingency Approach

10. Which of the following is true with regard to the contingency approach to solving problems within an organization?

    A. The organization's environment plays the largest role in finding situationally determined answers.

    B. The organization may be less adaptive when the environment is more uncertain.

    C. The organization should search for a design format that can be used in all cases.

    D. The contingency approach focuses on a closed systems thinking.

Answer (A) is correct. *(Publisher)*
    REQUIRED: The true statement regarding the contingency approach to solving problems within an organization.
    DISCUSSION: The contingency approach argues for situationally determined answers, the key is finding the relevant factors in the organization's environment.
    Answer (B) is incorrect because the organization should be more adaptive when the environment is uncertain. Answer (C) is incorrect because no single design format fits all organizations and situations. Answer (D) is incorrect because the contingency approach focuses on an open systems thinking.

11. In a dynamic equilibrium, successful organizations have a balance between fragmentation and coordination. Which of the following may cause an organization to risk the loss of this equilibrium?

    A. A framework of rules.

    B. A hierarchy of authority.

    C. Formation of cross-functional groups.

    D. Division of labor and technical specialization.

Answer (D) is correct. *(Publisher)*
    REQUIRED: The problems encountered with integration.
    DISCUSSION: The division of labor and technical specialization often lead to differentiation within an organization. Differentiation leads to fragmentation because specialists often have a narrow focus and make integration more difficult.
    Answer (A) is incorrect because a framework of rules is necessary for an organization to coordinate to achieve mutual objectives. Answer (B) is incorrect because a hierarchy of authority prevents fragmentation of the organization by having a central authority direct when necessary. Answer (C) is incorrect because the formation of cross-functional groups helps employees integrate into the organization and prevents the fragmentation of specialization.

12. Which of the following is a characteristic of a mechanistic organization?

    A. Knowledge by employees tends to be task-specific.

    B. Self-control is preferred to hierarchical control.

    C. Superiors usually have an informational and advisory role.

    D. Communication is horizontal.

Answer (A) is correct. *(Publisher)*
    REQUIRED: The characteristics of a mechanistic organization.
    DISCUSSION: A mechanistic organization designs tasks that are specifically designed and have little flexibility. Therefore, the mechanistic organization focuses on task-specific knowledge by its employees.
    Answer (B) is incorrect because an organic organization prefers self-control instead of hierarchical control. Answer (C) is incorrect because, in most organic organizations, management often plays an informal role and allows employees to make many decisions providing input as needed. Answer (D) is incorrect because organic organizations focus on communication that is participative and horizontal.

6.3 Departmentation

13. Departmentation is the grouping of organizational subsystems. The greatest advantage of functional departmentation is that it

    A. Provides the benefits of specialization.

    B. Facilitates communication between primary functions.

    C. Helps to focus on achievement of organizational goals.

    D. Is appropriate for geographically dispersed companies.

Answer (A) is correct. *(Publisher)*
    REQUIRED: The greatest advantage of functional departmentation.
    DISCUSSION: Departmentation by function is the most widely used method and is found in almost every enterprise at some level. The most common departments are selling, production, and finance (though other terms may be used). These often extend upward in the organizational chart to the level below the chief executive. If persons within a department have similar knowledge, skills, and interests, they can specialize in the solution of particular problems. Thus, problem solving becomes more efficient.
    Answer (B) is incorrect because departmentation by function facilitates communication and coordination within rather than between departments. Answer (C) is incorrect because the focus may tend to be on departmental, not organizational, goals. Answer (D) is incorrect because territorial departmentation may be preferable for these companies.

14. Departmentalization may be performed by

I. Function
II. Product
III. Geography

    A. I only.

    B. II only.

    C. I and II only.

    D. I, II and III.

Answer (D) is correct. *(IIA, adapted)*
    REQUIRED: The way departmentation may be performed.
    DISCUSSION: Departmentation may be performed by function, product, and geography. Departmentation by function is found in almost every organization at some level whether for-profit or nonprofit. The most common departments in for-profit organizations are marketing, production, and finance (though other terms may be used). These often extend upward in the organizational chart to the level below the chief executive. Departmentation by product or service is growing in importance for multiline, large-scale enterprises. It is often an outgrowth of functional departmentation. The result is that product-service subunits may be treated as separate businesses with a high degree of autonomy. Managers must therefore have a broad perspective, not a merely functional orientation. Departmentation by territory (geographic location) is favored by national or multinational firms and government agencies with scattered resources, offices, or plants.
    Answer (A) is incorrect because departmentation may be performed by product and geography. Answer (B) is incorrect because departmentation may be performed by function. Answer (C) is incorrect because departmentation may be performed by geography.

15. Departmentalization is a common form of business integration. Grouping together all related jobs, activities, and processes for a given business objective into a major organizational subunit is an example of

    A. Product-service departmentalization.

    B. Functional departmentalization.

    C. Geographic location departmentalization.

    D. Customer classification departmentalization.

Answer (A) is correct. *(IIA, adapted)*
    REQUIRED: The type of departmentation defined.
    DISCUSSION: Departmentation by product or service is growing in importance for multiline, large-scale enterprises and is an outgrowth of functional departmentation. The result is product-service subunits may be treated as seperate businesses with a high degree of autonomy. Managers must therefore have a broad perspective, not a merely functional orientation.
    Answer (B) is incorrect because functional departmentation categorizes jobs according to the activity performed. Answer (C) is incorrect because geographic location departmentation categorizes based upon the area in which a part of the business is located. Answer (D) is incorrect because customer classification departmentation categorizes based upon the differing needs of discrete groups of customers.

16. The form of departmentation that most readily lends itself to use of profit centers is

    A. Project.

    B. Functional.

    C. Product.

    D. Matrix.

Answer (C) is correct. *(Publisher)*
    REQUIRED: The form of departmentation most appropriate for use of profit centers.
    DISCUSSION: Departmentation by product is growing in importance for multiline, large-scale enterprises. It is an outgrowth of functional departmentation and permits extensive authority for a division executive over a given product or product line. Its advantages include better use of specialized resources and skills, ease of coordination of the activities for a given product, and simpler assignment of profit responsibility. It is compatible with a decentralization strategy and provides, via product profit centers, a basis for allocating capital more efficiently.
    Answer (A) is incorrect because a profit center is an organizational unit responsible for costs and revenues on an ongoing basis, not just for a one-time activity. Answer (B) is incorrect because the profitability of a single function is difficult to measure. Answer (D) is incorrect because it is used for a specific project or for R & D.

17. Dual reporting is most characteristic of which method of departmentation?

    A. Territorial.

    B. Functional.

    C. Product.

    D. Matrix.

Answer (D) is correct. *(Publisher)*
    REQUIRED: The method of departmentation of which dual reporting is most characteristic.
    DISCUSSION: A matrix organization consists of a project team of people from various functional areas within the organization. These specialists report simultaneously to the project manager and the managers of their functional departments. At the end of the project, the team is disbanded.
    Answer (A) is incorrect because departmentation by territory does not require violation of the unity of command principle. Answer (B) is incorrect because departmentation by function does not require violation of the unity of command principle. Answer (C) is incorrect because departmentation by product does not require violation of the unity of command principle.

18. Which particular type of organization structure will likely have unity-of-command problems unless there is frequent and comprehensive communication between the various functional and project managers?

    A. Line and staff.

    B. Strategic business unit.

    C. Centralized.

    D. Matrix.

Answer (D) is correct. *(CIA, adapted)*
  REQUIRED: The organization structure with unity-of-command problems absent frequent communication among managers.
  DISCUSSION: A matrix structure allows authority to flow both vertically and horizontally. A manager is appointed for each project and draws on personnel who are organized by function and report to a manager for each function. This violates the principle of unity of command, which states that each subordinate should have only one superior.
  Answer (A) is incorrect because a line and staff structure is designed to maximize unity of command by giving only line managers the authority to make decisions affecting those in their chain of command. Answer (B) is incorrect because a strategic business unit is a subunit that is treated as an independent business. Thus, unity of command is not an issue for a strategic business unit. Answer (C) is incorrect because a centralized structure need not have unity-of-command problems if management is organized in a line and staff fashion.

19. Of the following entities, a matrix organization would be most appropriate for

    A. A company operating a set of geographically dispersed telephone call centers that provide technical support.

    B. A company which starts several complex, multidisciplinary engineering and construction projects each year.

    C. A retail company, which sells to customers through multiple stores, located in shopping malls, as well as through a website and mailed catalogs.

    D. A company that provides temporary staffing help to a wide variety of commercial and governmental agencies.

Answer (B) is correct. *(IIA, adapted)*
  REQUIRED: The entity most appropriate for a matrix organization.
  DISCUSSION: A matrix organization consists of a project team of people from various functional areas within the organization. These specialists report simultaneously to the project manager and the managers of their functional departments. At the end of the project, the team is disbanded. Accordingly, a matrix organization that assigns specialists as needed to various projects is appropriate for such a company.
  Answer (A) is incorrect because individuals assigned to work in a call center have only one supervisor. Moreover, they are not employees from different functions. Answer (C) is incorrect because, although multichannel sales require coordination, staff are not necessarily moved from one sales channel to another for project work, and they are not likely to report to different supervisors. Answer (D) is incorrect because temporary staff do not report to any manager within a temporary agency. They simply work for a wide variety of employers who have full authority. They are not necessarily "specialized staff." If not needed, they are simply not paid.

20. In what form of organization does an employee report to multiple managers?

    A. Bureaucracy.

    B. Matrix.

    C. Departmental.

    D. Mechanistic.

Answer (B) is correct. *(CIA, adapted)*
  REQUIRED: The organization in which an employee reports to multiple managers.
  DISCUSSION: A matrix organization (project management) is characterized by vertical and horizontal lines of authority. The project manager borrows specialists from line functions as needed. This manager's authority is limited to the project, and the specialists will otherwise report to the line managers.
  Answer (A) is incorrect because, in a bureaucracy, each subordinate reports to a single manager. Answer (C) is incorrect because departmental organization structures represent the typical organization with unified and clear single lines of authority. Answer (D) is incorrect because mechanistic organization structure is another term for a bureaucracy.

21. Which of the following elements of an organization requires people to be accountable to their superiors?

    A. Coordination of effort.

    B. Division of labor.

    C. Common goal or purpose.

    D. Hierarchy of authority.

Answer (D) is correct. *(Publisher)*
  REQUIRED: The element requiring people to be accountable to their superiors.
  DISCUSSION: A hierarchy of authority requires people to be accountable to their superiors in the hierarchy.
  Answer (A) is incorrect because coordination of effort involves cooperation in the social environment of the organization. Answer (B) is incorrect because division of labor ensures efficient specialization of employees. Answer (C) is incorrect because a common goal or purpose is relevant to the employees and employer achieving a common objective.

6.4 Line and Staff Design

Questions 22 and 23 are based on the following information.

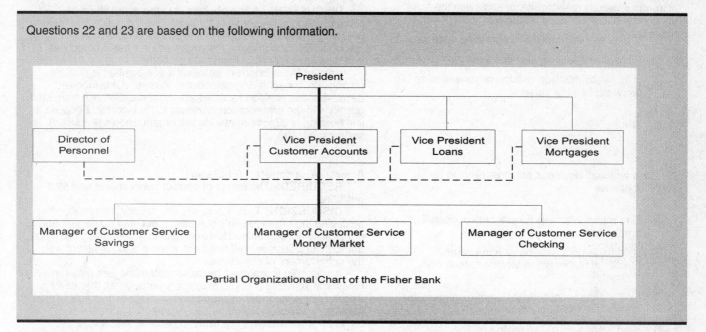

Partial Organizational Chart of the Fisher Bank

22. Which of the following is a staff position in the Fisher Bank?

A. The manager of customer service-checking, the department that handles checking account inquiries and transactions.

B. The director of personnel, the department that handles the hiring, firing, promotion, etc., of all employees.

C. The chief loan officer, who is in charge of final approval of all loans.

D. The vice president in charge of the mortgage department, which handles mortgages on business and residential property.

Answer (B) is correct. *(Publisher)*
REQUIRED: The example of a staff position in a bank.
DISCUSSION: Staff positions in any organization advise and support the line positions. They indirectly help to achieve the organization's basic objective. Each staff position's authority is, at most, functional. Such authority is exercised only over activities related to the staff's function or specialty.
Answer (A) is incorrect because this is an example of a line position that is directly involved in the achievement of the organization's objectives and which is directly related to the service(s) and/or product(s) offered by the firm. Answer (C) is incorrect because this is an example of a line position that is directly involved in the achievement of the organization's objectives and which is directly related to the service(s) and/or product(s) offered by the firm. Answer (D) is incorrect because this is an example of a line position that is directly involved in the achievement of the organization's objectives and which is directly related to the service(s) and/or product(s) offered by the firm.

23. The manager of customer service checking at Fisher Bank is most likely to encounter conflict(s) because of

A. The department's reliance on the savings manager and the money market manager.

B. His/her providing services for customers who do not have checking accounts.

C. The requirement that (s)he must report directly to both the president and the vice president for customer accounts.

D. A potential disagreement with the director of personnel about a subordinate's performance appraisal.

Answer (D) is correct. *(Publisher)*
REQUIRED: The conflict most likely to be encountered by a line manager.
DISCUSSION: The director of personnel (DP) must coordinate all employee evaluations. Although the manager of checking services is in a line position that is not under the DP, (s)he works with the DP when hiring, dismissing, transferring, or evaluating employees.
Answer (A) is incorrect because the manager of checking is a line position which does not rely on the other customer service managers. Answer (B) is incorrect because the department only provides services for the customers with checking accounts. Answer (C) is incorrect because the manager of checking reports to the president indirectly through a vice president.

24. A line position

A. Is indirectly responsible for achieving the organization's basic objectives.

B. Makes administrative and operating decisions.

C. Advises and assists staff positions.

D. Is indirectly involved with the organization's product(s) and/or services.

Answer (B) is correct.   *(Publisher)*
REQUIRED: The characteristic of a line position in the organization.
DISCUSSION: A line position is in the direct chain of command and is responsible for administering policy and making operating decisions. People in line positions have direct responsibility for achieving the organization's basic objectives and thus have formal or legitimate authority.
Answer (A) is incorrect because a line position is directly responsible for achieving objectives. Answer (C) is incorrect because a line position receives advice and assistance from staff positions in the organization. Answer (D) is incorrect because a line position is directly related to the organization's product(s) and/or service(s).

25. Line and staff positions are most likely to be in conflict because

A. Line managers have no authority over staff employees.

B. Staff managers consider line managers' functional authority threatening to their own authority.

C. Line managers believe that staff managers are resistant to their advice.

D. Staff managers dislike relying on line expertise.

Answer (A) is correct.   *(Publisher)*
REQUIRED: The cause of conflict between line and staff positions.
DISCUSSION: Line managers are directly responsible for achieving the organization's objectives, but staff managers are not directly accountable. However, line managers may have no authority to influence staff behavior when it is inconsistent with the achievement of objectives.
Answer (B) is incorrect because staff managers may have functional authority that line managers perceive as threatening. Answer (C) is incorrect because staff managers give line managers advice, not vice versa. Answer (D) is incorrect because line managers are likely to become reliant on staff expertise.

6.5 Span of Control

26. Which of the following factors is least likely to affect a manager's direct span of control?

A. Frequency of supervisor-subordinate contact.

B. The manager's willingness to delegate authority.

C. The manager's training and communication skills.

D. Number of people in the corporation.

Answer (D) is correct.   *(CIA, adapted)*
REQUIRED: The factor least likely to affect a manager's direct span of control.
DISCUSSION: The optimal span of control is the number of subordinates that a given manager can effectively supervise. It is a function of many situational factors. However, the total number of people in an organization has no bearing on the optimal span of control of a particular manager.
Answer (A) is incorrect because managers who can contact subordinates frequently are able to control more people than those who have relatively infrequent contact with subordinates. Answer (B) is incorrect because managers who delegate authority have more time to control the subordinates who report to them. These individuals can therefore supervise more people than managers who prefer not to delegate authority. Answer (C) is incorrect because managers who have received effective training and are skillful communicators are equipped to control more individuals than managers who are untrained and/or have deficient communication skills.

27. Which of the following is generally true regarding a manager's span of control?

A. Narrow spans of control are typically found in flat organizations, those with few hierarchical levels.

B. An organization with narrow spans of control needs more managers than those with wide spans.

C. Wider spans of control mean higher administrative expense and less self-management.

D. Wider spans of control help ensure good internal controls and policy compliance throughout an organization.

Answer (B) is correct.   *(IIA, adapted)*
REQUIRED: The true statement regarding a manager's span of control.
DISCUSSION: Span of control (span of management or span of authority) is an upper limit to the number of people who can be effectively and efficiently supervised by one person. Narrow spans of control mean that the ratio of those supervised (subordinates) to those doing the supervision (managers) is lower. Hence, more managers are required.
Answer (A) is incorrect because narrow spans of control mean a tall organization with many more levels. Answer (C) is incorrect because narrow spans of control result in higher administrative expense (coordination) and less self-management. Answer (D) is incorrect because wider spans of control give subordinates more discretion.

28. When determining the appropriate span of control, the most important consideration is

- A. The set of policies and procedures currently in effect.
- B. The typical span of control used by other entities.
- C. The preference of the company's creditors.
- D. That all departments will be evaluated, whether or not they will be affected.

Answer (A) is correct. *(Publisher)*
REQUIRED: The factor that is most important when choosing a span of control.
DISCUSSION: The most important factors to consider are the employees' and manager's preferences and skills, the firm's culture, the tasks involved, physical location of the department, and established policies and procedures.
Answer (B) is incorrect because, although examining similar entities may be useful, it is not one of the most important considerations. Answer (C) is incorrect because this consideration would only be necessary if required by an agreement with the creditors. Answer (D) is incorrect because this is not normally considered in a span-of-control decision.

29. The difference between a tall organization structure and a flat organization structure is that in the former

- A. The communication process takes longer and is of poorer quality.
- B. Maintenance of the organization is less costly.
- C. The morale of lower-level employees is generally higher.
- D. A higher degree of coordination and cooperation is created.

Answer (A) is correct. *(CIA, adapted)*
REQUIRED: The difference between tall and flat organization structures.
DISCUSSION: "Flat" organizational structures have relatively few levels from top to bottom. "Tall" organizational structures have many levels between top and bottom. Flat structures have the advantages of fast information flow from top to bottom of the organization and increased employee satisfaction. Tall structures are faster and more effective at problem resolution because of the increased frequency of interaction between superior and subordinate, and the greater order imposed by the hierarchy. Studies do not indicate great advantages for either flat or tall structures.

30. The most likely span of control to apply over 14 data-entry clerks who do essentially the same job and work in the same office would be

- A. Close.
- B. Narrow.
- C. Moderate.
- D. Wide.

Answer (D) is correct. *(CIA, adapted)*
REQUIRED: The span-of-control category that would be most applicable.
DISCUSSION: In any situation, there are underlying variables that influence the number of subordinates a manager can supervise. In general, if jobs are similar, procedures are standardized, and physical dispersion is minimized, a wide span of control is most effective.
Answer (A) is incorrect because close is not a span-of-control category. Answer (B) is incorrect because a narrow span of control is useful where jobs are dissimilar, procedures are not standardized, and subordinates are more dispersed. Answer (C) is incorrect because a moderate span of control is useful in situations that have some characteristics of both extremes, wide and narrow.

31. In which of the following situations would a narrower span of control be more appropriate?

- A. Managers do not spend a great deal of time on planning or strategic management.
- B. Managers must spend a great deal of time coordinating with other managers.
- C. Subordinates work in the same area rather than being geographically dispersed.
- D. Work performed by subordinates is substantially identical.

Answer (B) is correct. *(IIA, adapted)*
REQUIRED: The situation in which a narrower span of control is appropriate.
DISCUSSION: If substantial coordination is required, a manager benefits from reduced supervision requirements. In addition, increased coordination implies that the work done by subordinates is not standardized. As spans of control move from wider to narrower, the work done becomes less similar and more complex.
Answer (A) is incorrect because, if substantial planning is required, a manager benefits from the reduced supervision requirements characteristic of a wider span of controls. Also, increased planning implies a changing environment in which work of subordinates will be changing over time, requiring significant managerial work for training. Answer (C) is incorrect because geographical dispersion of subordinates justifies a narrow span of control. Answer (D) is incorrect because, when subordinates perform very similar work, they can train one another, provide backup if one subordinate is not present, and verify one another's work. In addition, work procedures are relatively easy to document, and a manager can be knowledgeable about the work of everyone. Thus, a wider span of control is appropriate.

32. A flat organization structure is one with relatively few levels of hierarchy and is characterized by wide spans of management control. A tall organization has many levels of hierarchy and narrow spans of control. Which of the following situations is consistent with a flat organization structure?

A. Tasks require little direction and control of subordinates.

B. Work areas are geographically dispersed.

C. Tasks are highly complex and varied.

D. Subordinates perform distinctly different tasks.

Answer (A) is correct. *(CIA, adapted)*
REQUIRED: The situation consistent with a flat organization structure.
DISCUSSION: Flat structures have the advantages of fast information flow from top to bottom of the organization and increased employee satisfaction. Tall structures are faster and more effective at problem resolution because of the increased frequency of interaction between superior and subordinate and the greater order imposed by the hierarchy. For a flat structure to be successful, employees must be able to work without supervision much of the time because a manager with many employees has little time for each one.
Answer (B) is incorrect because geographically dispersed work areas are very difficult for a manager with many subordinates to control. Answer (C) is incorrect because tasks that are highly complex and varied are more appropriate for a narrow span of control. Answer (D) is incorrect because a narrow span of control (a tall structure) is more appropriate when subordinates perform distinctly different tasks.

33. The optimal span of control of a manager is contingent upon several situational variables. For instance, a manager supervising workers within the same work area who are performing identical tasks that are simple and repetitive would best be able to supervise

A. An unlimited number of employees.

B. Only a few workers (a narrow span of control).

C. A relatively large number of employees (a wide span of control).

D. Fewer workers than if the workers were geographically dispersed.

Answer (C) is correct. *(CIA, adapted)*
REQUIRED: The optimal span of control of a manager supervising workers within the same work area who are performing identical tasks that are simple and repetitive.
DISCUSSION: In any situation, there are underlying variables that influence the number of subordinates a manager can supervise. In general, if jobs are similar, procedures are standardized, and physical dispersion is minimized, a wide span of control is most effective.
Answer (A) is incorrect because, although a manager under these conditions would be able to supervise a large number of employees, an upper limit must exist. Answer (B) is incorrect because the conditions described support a wide rather than a narrow span. Answer (D) is incorrect because geographical dispersion would decrease rather than increase the span of control.

34. Which of the following is an advantage of a tall organizational structure?

A. The flow of communications from top to bottom and bottom to top is improved.

B. The organization's overall objectives are familiar to all employees.

C. More opportunity to advance.

D. Labor expenses are reduced.

Answer (C) is correct. *(Publisher)*
REQUIRED: The advantage of a tall organizational structure.
DISCUSSION: The organizational structure consists of the order, disposition, and relationships of positions and lines of responsibility within an entity. In a tall organizational structure, decision-making responsibility is shared by many levels.
Answer (A) is incorrect because it is an advantage of a flat organizational structure, which concentrates decision-making power at one level. Answer (B) is incorrect because it is an advantage of a flat organizational structure, which concentrates decision-making power at one level. Answer (D) is incorrect because it is an advantage of a flat organizational structure, which concentrates decision-making power at one level.

35. Which of the following is a disadvantage of a flat organizational structure?

A. Employees are not encouraged to be creative.

B. The input of fresh ideas from outside the company is limited because employee turnover is low.

C. Managers spend too much time training individuals and not enough time supervising.

D. Employees may not be performing work tasks properly.

Answer (D) is correct. *(Publisher)*
REQUIRED: The disadvantage of a flat organizational structure.
DISCUSSION: A flat organizational structure concentrates decision-making authority at one level. Tasks and performance objectives may be unclear to employees because of a lack of supervision.
Answer (A) is incorrect because a lack of supervision increases employee flexibility. Answer (B) is incorrect because the number of management levels limits the opportunity for advancement, which may cause high employee turnover. Answer (C) is incorrect because managers spend too much time supervising, and employees do not receive enough training.

36. Which of the following is a likely effect of a narrow span of control?

A. The manager closely supervises employees.

B. Each employee is given more responsibility.

C. The organizational structure is flexible.

D. The manager's control over employees is limited.

Answer (A) is correct. *(Publisher)*
REQUIRED: The effect most likely to result from a narrow span of control.
DISCUSSION: The span of control is the number of subordinates for which a manager or supervisor is responsible. When the span of control is narrow, a few subordinates are tightly controlled. A narrow span of control is typical of tall organizational structures.
Answer (B) is incorrect because it is a likely effect of a wide span of control, which is likely to be found in flat organizational structures. Answer (C) is incorrect because it is a likely effect of a wide span of control, which is likely to be found in flat organizational structures. Answer (D) is incorrect because it is a likely effect of a wide span of control, which is likely to be found in flat organizational structures.

6.6 Centralization and Decentralization

37. Centralization and decentralization are defined according to the relative delegation of decision-making authority by top management. Many managers believe that decentralized organizations have significant advantages over centralized organizations. A major advantage of a decentralized organization is that

A. Decentralized organizations are easier to control.

B. Decentralized structures streamline organizations and eliminate duplication of resources.

C. Decentralized organizations have fewer managers than centralized organizations.

D. Decentralized organizations encourage increased initiative among employees.

Answer (D) is correct. *(CIA, adapted)*
REQUIRED: The major advantage of a decentralized organization.
DISCUSSION: A decentralized organization allows lower level employees to participate in decision making. This increased involvement encourages initiative and creative thinking and is especially appropriate in complex and rapidly changing environments.
Answer (A) is incorrect because decentralized organizations are more difficult to control. Answer (B) is incorrect because centralized structures streamline organizations and eliminate duplication of resources. Answer (C) is incorrect because the number of managers is not related to the degree of centralization or decentralization but is a function of the span of control.

38. A claimed advantage of decentralizing is

A. Concentration of authority.

B. Manager development.

C. Elimination of duplication of effort.

D. Departmentalization.

Answer (B) is correct. *(CIA, adapted)*
REQUIRED: The advantage of decentralizing an organization.
DISCUSSION: When an organization changes from a centralized to a decentralized structure, top management is delegating more authority to middle and lower levels. Thus, managers at these lower levels are usually hired and developed more rigorously than under the centralized structure.
Answer (A) is incorrect because authority is more concentrated in centralized management structures. Answer (C) is incorrect because some effort will inevitably be duplicated under decentralization, of which departmentalization is a moderate form. Answer (D) is incorrect because departments are formed when one manager can no longer supervise the entire organization; departmentalization is therefore a characteristic of centralized as well as decentralized organizations.

39. A network organizational structure is one in which

A. An employee reports to two bosses.

B. Authority and responsibility are concentrated at the top of the organization.

C. Labor is specialized.

D. Major business functions are subcontracted to third party providers.

Answer (D) is correct. *(Publisher)*
REQUIRED: The definition of a network organizational structure.
DISCUSSION: The subcontracting of major business functions to others is a feature of network structures.
Answer (A) is incorrect because this is a distinguishing feature of a matrix structure. Answer (B) is incorrect because this is a characteristic of centralization. Answer (C) is incorrect because this is a characteristic of bureaucracy.

40. Which of the following is a benefit of decentralization?

    A. The head of the company is aware of and can influence all decisions before they are made.

    B. The company is operated as one unit.

    C. Specialists for a particular product have no authority but advise the company's top management.

    D. Decisions are made on a more timely basis.

Answer (D) is correct. *(Publisher)*
REQUIRED: The benefit of decentralization.
DISCUSSION: Decentralization is the extent to which decision-making power is delegated within an entity. When approval from upper-level management is not required, lower-level managers can make more timely decisions because they are closer to the necessary sources of information.
    Answer (A) is incorrect because this typifies a highly centralized entity. Answer (B) is incorrect because operating the company as one unit typifies a highly centralized entity. Answer (C) is incorrect because decentralization would give these specialists more authority.

41. Which of the following is a reason for delegating?

    A. The manager wants to make more decisions.

    B. Subordinates lack initiative.

    C. The manager wants to remain the sole expert in his/her field.

    D. Subordinates have too many responsibilities.

Answer (B) is correct. *(Publisher)*
REQUIRED: The reason for delegating authority within a firm.
DISCUSSION: Delegation is the assignment of a manager's authority and/or workload to his/her subordinates. By increasing subordinates' responsibilities, the manager gives them more opportunity to exercise judgment and become more confident.
    Answer (A) is incorrect because delegation passes some decision-making power to subordinates. Answer (C) is incorrect because delegation gives subordinates the opportunity to increase their expertise. Answer (D) is incorrect because delegation gives subordinates more responsibilities.

42. Which of the following is a reason that a manager may be reluctant to delegate?

    A. The manager fears being held accountable for the subordinate's performance.

    B. The manager fears (s)he may fail because of some lack of knowledge.

    C. The manager did not monitor the subordinate's work.

    D. The manager fears unknown goals.

Answer (A) is correct. *(Publisher)*
REQUIRED: The reason a manager is reluctant to delegate.
DISCUSSION: Managers fear delegating because of insecurity, mistrust, insufficient planning, and/or aversion to the risk of being responsible for subordinates' actions.
    Answer (B) is incorrect because this is a fear that subordinates have about delegation. Answer (C) is incorrect because it states a potential implementation problem. Answer (D) is incorrect because this is a fear that subordinates have about delegation.

43. Advantages of decentralization include all of the following except

    A. Decisions are more easily made.

    B. Managers' motivation increases.

    C. Greater uniformity in decisions.

    D. Problems can be dealt with on the spot.

Answer (C) is correct. *(IIA, adapted)*
REQUIRED: The statement that is not an advantage of decentralization.
DISCUSSION: Organizational design should achieve a balance between centralization and decentralization. The main benefits of centralization are more effective control and reduced costs through resource sharing. The main benefits of decentralization are flexibility and adaptability that permit a rapid response to changes in circumstances. Accordingly, increased uniformity in decision making is an advantage of centralization. It reflects the benefit of more effective control.
    Answer (A) is incorrect because ease of decision making is an advantage of decentralization. Answer (B) is incorrect because an increase in managers' motivation is an advantage of decentralization. Answer (D) is incorrect because immediacy of problem resolution is an advantage of decentralization.

44. Which of the following is not a characteristic of decentralized organizations?

- A. Decentralized organizations are usually more flexible.
- B. Decentralized organizations have reduced costs through resource sharing.
- C. Decentralized organizations have fewer decisions made lower in the hierarchy that are monitored by senior management.
- D. Decentralization has a positive influence on morale.

Answer (B) is correct. *(Publisher)*
REQUIRED: The characteristics of decentralized organizations.
DISCUSSION: The main benefits of centralization are more effective control and reduced costs through resource sharing. In a centralized organization, senior management is able to direct control over subordinates and direct the flow of resources. Senior management is able to allocate reduce costs most effectively because they are aware of where expenses can be reduced across departments within an organization.
Answer (A) is incorrect because the main benefit to decentralized organizations is that they are more flexible and quickly adapt to changes. Therefore, decentralized organizations tend to thrive in relatively unstable or uncertain environments. Answer (C) is incorrect because a main feature of decentralization is for senior management to allow subordinates make decisions without constant supervision or approval. Answer (D) is incorrect because decentralization has been shown to improve employee morale by empowering employees to make decisions on their own.

45. The primary difference between centralization and decentralization is

- A. Separate offices for all managers.
- B. Geographical separation of divisional headquarters and central headquarters.
- C. The extent of freedom of decision making by many levels of management.
- D. The relative size of the firm.

Answer (C) is correct. *(Publisher)*
REQUIRED: The primary difference between centralization and decentralization.
DISCUSSION: The primary distinction between centralization and decentralization is in the degree of freedom of decision making by managers at many levels. In decentralization, decision making is at as low a level as possible. The premise is that the local manager can make better (more informed) decisions than a centralized manager. Centralization is based on the theory that decision making must be consolidated so that activities throughout the organization may be more effectively coordinated. In most organizations, a mixture of these approaches is found to be best.
Answer (A) is incorrect because the concept of centralization and decentralization involves levels of decision making, not whether all managers have separate offices. Answer (B) is incorrect because geographical separation of divisional and central headquarters can support either a centralized or decentralized environment. Answer (D) is incorrect because the relative size of the firm may be a factor in determining whether to maintain a centralized or decentralized environment, but relative size is not a primary difference between centralization and decentralization.

46. Which of the following is most likely to be a disadvantage of decentralization?

- A. Lower-level employees will develop less rapidly than in a centralized organization.
- B. Top management will have less time available to devote to unique problems.
- C. Lower-level managers may make conflicting decisions.
- D. Lower-level managers may lose motivation.

Answer (C) is correct. *(CIA, adapted)*
REQUIRED: The item most likely to be a disadvantage of decentralization.
DISCUSSION: The disadvantages of decentralization include a tendency to focus on short-run results to the detriment of the long-term health of the entity, an increased risk of loss of control by top management, the increased difficulty of coordinating interdependent units, and less cooperation and communication among competing decentralized unit managers.
Answer (A) is incorrect because decentralization encourages development of lower-level managers. They will have greater responsibilities and authority. Answer (B) is incorrect because top managers will be freed from operating problems. Answer (D) is incorrect because decision-making power should motivate lower-level managers.

47. Which of the following is not a cost of decentralization?

A. Dysfunctional decision making owing to disagreements of managers regarding overall goals and subgoals of the individual decision makers.

B. A decreased understanding of the overall goals of the organization.

C. Increased costs for developing the information system.

D. Increased costs of corporate-level staff services and management talent.

Answer (D) is correct. *(Publisher)*
REQUIRED: The item not a cost of decentralization.
DISCUSSION: The costs of centralized staff may actually decrease under decentralization. On the other hand, the corporate staff and the various services they provide may have to be duplicated in various divisions, thereby increasing overall costs. Suboptimal decisions may result from disharmony among organizational goals, subgoals of the division, and the individual goals of managers. The overall goals of the firm may more easily be misunderstood because individual managers may not see the larger picture. Moreover, the information system necessary for adequate reporting in a decentralized mode will tend toward redundancy, which increases costs.
Answer (A) is incorrect because dysfunctional decision-making is a cost of decentralization. Answer (B) is incorrect because a decreased understanding of the overall goals of an organization is a cost of decentralization. Answer (C) is incorrect because increased costs for developing the information system is a cost of decentralization.

48. Halo Corporation is consistent of ten groups of teams that each consists of multi-skilled workers. Workers are often transferred between teams when needed and communication among and within groups is emphasized. Halo Corporation would be classified as an

A. Hourglass organization.

B. Cluster organization.

C. Network organization.

D. Virtual organization.

Answer (B) is correct. *(Publisher)*
REQUIRED: The characteristics of a cluster organization.
DISCUSSION: A cluster organization is essentially a group of teams. The workers are often multi-skilled and shift among teams as needed. The workers undergo special training and team-building exercises. The pay is also based upon knowledge.
Answer (A) is incorrect because an hourglass organization has three layers consisting of a strategic layer, a group of middle managers, and lower level technical specialists. Answer (C) is incorrect because a network organization is a group of members who do not have legal ties but form a strategic relationship to have an advantage over competition. Answer (D) is incorrect because a virtual organization is typically a group of sub-contractors who are linked via the internet, fax machines, and telephones.

49. The CEO of a rapidly growing high-technology firm has exercised centralized authority over all corporate functions. Because the company now operates in four geographically dispersed locations, the CEO is considering the advisability of decentralizing operational control over production and sales. Which of the following conditions probably will result from and be a valid reason for decentralizing?

A. Greater local control over compliance with governmental regulations.

B. More efficient use of headquarters staff officials and specialists.

C. Less overall operating costs.

D. Quicker and better operating decisions.

Answer (D) is correct. *(CIA, adapted)*
REQUIRED: The condition that would be a valid reason for decentralizing.
DISCUSSION: Decentralization results in greater speed in making operating decisions because they are made by lower level managers instead of being referred to top management. The quality of operating decisions should also be enhanced, assuming proper training of managers, because those closest to the problems should be the most knowledgeable about them.
Answer (A) is incorrect because compliance with governmental regulations is probably more easily achieved by centralization. A disadvantage of decentralization is the difficulty of assuring uniform action by units of the entity that have substantial autonomy. Answer (B) is incorrect because decentralization may result in duplication of efforts, resulting in less efficient use of headquarters staff officials and specialists. Answer (C) is incorrect because decentralization may result in duplication of efforts, thereby increasing overall costs.

Use Gleim's *CIA Test Prep* for interactive testing with over 2,000 additional multiple-choice questions!

STUDY UNIT SEVEN
MANAGING GROUPS

(10 pages of outline)

This study unit addresses the nature and types of groups, their characteristics and behavior, how they evolve, and how they should be managed.

7.1 GROUP DYNAMICS

1.   Management should improve the **social capital** of the organization by enhancing the relationships of the groups within its structure. A **group** has the following characteristics:

 a.   It consists of at least two individuals.
 b.   They interact freely.
 c.   They recognize themselves as group members (**common identity**).
 d.   They agree on the reason for the group (**common purpose**).

2.   **Informal groups**. People naturally seek association and group acceptance and tend to form both formal and informal groups as a result. Thus, effective managers recognize, accept, and take advantage of the **informal organization**.

 a.   Informal groups are created within organizations because of

  1)   Authority interrelationships that cannot be charted
  2)   Unwritten rules of conduct
  3)   Group preferences

 b.   **Characteristics of informal groups**

  1)   They develop primarily to satisfy esteem needs (friendship).
  2)   Almost all employees, including managers, are members of some informal group(s).
  3)   Members react to group pressures. These pressures are difficult to resist, and most members conform.
  4)   Informal groups tend to be small and are often very complex. They develop their own leaders, exist to fill the needs of the members, and usually result from the frequent interaction among individuals in the course of their work.

 c.   **Favorable effects of informal groups** include

  1)   Reducing tension and encouraging production
  2)   Improving coordination and reducing supervision required
  3)   Aiding in problem-solving situations
  4)   Providing another (often faster) channel of communication

   a)   The **grapevine** is the informal, unofficial communication system found in every kind of organization. The emergence of computer networks in the workplace has only served to strengthen the grapevine.

  5)   Providing social satisfactions that supplement job satisfaction

d.   Informal groups have **potentially unfavorable effects**, for example,

1)   Circumventing managerial actions

2)   Reducing production (slowdowns caused by counterproductive social interactions)

3)   Causing dissension in the formal organization

4)   Spreading rumors and distorting information

5)   Adding to the cost of doing business

6)   Forming subgroups that hinder group cohesiveness

7)   Pressuring members to adopt group norms that may be contrary to the objectives of the organization

8)   Developing dominant members

3.   **Formal groups** are work groups (designated as committees, teams, etc.) within the organization assembled to perform a productive activity.

a.   Individuals are assigned to formal groups based on the organization's purposes and their qualifications for serving those purposes.

b.   Formal groups have explicitly designated **leaders** with authority and responsibility for directing the members.

c.   **Membership** in formal groups is relatively more permanent than in informal groups.

1)   Membership in informal groups may not be the same as in formal groups.

d.   Formal groups are more **structured** than informal groups.

4.   Commitment to a group depends on its attractiveness and cohesiveness.

a.   **Attractiveness** is a favorable view from the outside.

b.   **Cohesiveness** is the tendency of members to adhere to the group and unite against outside pressures.

c.   Group attractiveness and cohesiveness are fostered by its prestige and status, cooperation among the members, substantial member interaction, small size of the group, similarity of members, good public image, and common external threat.

d.   Group attractiveness and cohesiveness are diminished by its unpleasant demands on members, disagreements about activities and procedures, bad experiences with the group, conflict between the group's demands and those of other activities, bad public image, and possibility of joining other groups.

5.   **Role playing** is an important concept that emerged from group dynamics theory. A **role** is the behavior expected of a person who occupies a particular position. Everyone is expected to play or assume different roles in different situations.

a.   The term also refers to actual behavior.

b.   Different people in the same position should behave similarly.

c.   **Role conflict** emerges when two or more roles, making conflicting demands, are simultaneously expected of, or imposed on, a person.

1)   **Role models** may be crucial in helping individuals resolve role conflicts.

d.   Roles may be formally defined, for example, in job descriptions and procedures manuals.

6. **Norms** have a more general effect than roles. From earliest observations, groups have been found to be guided by self-set standards of performance and behavior, usually based on a composite of the personal and social backgrounds of the individuals on the job as well as those of people outside the group and outside the job.

   a. Norms vary from culture to culture and most often are unwritten.

   b. The **functions of norms** are to

      1) Protect the group (survival)
      2) Better define role behavior and expectations
      3) Safeguard members from loss of face (self-image)
      4) Reinforce the group's values and common identity

   c. **Enforcement of norms** in the positive sense follows from attention, recognition, and acceptance (social reinforcement).

      1) Enforcement of norms in the negative sense may be by ridicule, condescension, or criticism. The ultimate sanction is **ostracism**, or rejection by the group.

7. An important element of group dynamics is **conformity**, defined by Kreitner (9th ed., p. 478) as "complying with prevailing role expectations and norms."

   a. The **benefit** of conformity is predictability of behavior, e.g., performance of assigned tasks. The **cost** of conformity may, in the extreme, be tolerance of illegal, unethical, or incompetent conduct.

   b. Irving Janis researched conformity in **cohesive groups**. As a result, he identified one of the perils of such groups as **groupthink**, or the tendency to conform and ignore relevant individual input that is at variance with the perceived group opinion.

      1) Although, at the same time, consensus is desirable, individuals with a deep commitment to the group may be unable to maintain their critical objectivity.

      2) **Symptoms** of groupthink are

         a) Over-optimism
         b) Assumed morality of the preferred action
         c) Intolerance of dissent
         d) An urgent search for unanimity

      3) **Avoiding groupthink** can be done by

         a) Being aware of its dangers.
         b) Encouraging members to think critically.
         c) Seeking outside opinions.
         d) Expressly assigning a member of the group to advocate contrary positions.
         e) Expressly considering ramifications of different actions.
         f) Not using a group as a rubber stamp for a decision already made by senior management.

      4) Groupthink may have been a major factor in recent **corporate governance scandals**. Directors often failed to perform their duty to protect shareholders by critically evaluating the actions of senior management.

      5) **Cooperative (constructive) conflict** has been advocated as a means, not only of managing change, but also as a way of avoiding groupthink.

8. **Group Decision Making**

   a. Group decision making and problem solving has the following advantages:

      1) The group has greater knowledge and experience than an individual.
      2) The group provides multiple perspectives.

3) Members participating in a group process tend to have a better understanding of the reasons for different actions.

4) Those actively participating in the group process tend to accept, and have ownership of, the result.

5) Group involvement provides training for the less experienced members.

b. The following are the disadvantages:

1) The social pressure to conform may inhibit creativity.

2) The group may be dominated by a few aggressive members.

3) The decision or solution may be a product of logrolling (political dealing).

4) The goal of reaching a good decision or solution may be displaced by a secondary concern, e.g., competing with a rival.

5) The process may suffer from groupthink, or preference for unanimity over the quality of the decision or solution.

c. The following are methods that may be applied to improve the creativity:

1) **Attribute listing** is applied primarily to improve a tangible object. It lists the parts and essential features of the object and systematically analyzes modifications intended as improvements.

2) **Brainstorming** is an unstructured approach that relies on the spontaneous contribution of ideas from all members of a group. This technique breaks down broadly based problems into their essentials. A nonjudgemental environment is necessary.

3) **Creative leap** is a process that formulates an ideal solution and then works back to a feasible one.

4) The **Delphi technique** is an approach in which the manager solicits opinions on a problem from experts in the field, summarizes the opinions, and feeds the summaries back to the experts (without revealing any of the participants to each other). The process is reiterated until the opinions converge on an optimal solution. This method attempts to avoid **groupthink** (the tendency of individuals to conform to what they perceive to be the consensus).

5) The **Edisonian approach** is a trial-and-error experimental method. It should usually not be applied unless other approaches have been unsuccessful.

6) **Forced relationship** is a structured adaptation of free association. The elements of a problem are analyzed and the associations among them are identified so as to detect patterns that may suggest new ideas.

7) **Free association** is a method of idea generation that reports the first thought to come to mind in response to a given stimulus, for example, a symbol or analogy pertaining to a product for which an advertising slogan is sought. The objective is to express the content of consciousness without censorship or control.

8) **Morphological matrix analysis** is a structured technique that plots decision variables along the axes of a matrix. The relationships of these variables are found in the squares within the chart.

9) **Synectics** is a highly structured group approach to problem statement and solution based on creative thinking. It involves free use of analogies and metaphors in informal exchange within a carefully selected small group of individuals of diverse personality and areas of specialization.

9. Stop and review! You have completed the outline for this subunit. Study multiple-choice questions 1 through 20 beginning on page 194.

7.2 STAGES OF GROUP DEVELOPMENT

1. The process of group development proceeds through a succession of stages in which conflicts over power, authority, and interpersonal relationships must be overcome.

    a. Mutual understanding, trust, and commitment to the group tend to be absent in the beginning.

    b. Group objectives, members' roles, and leadership are initially uncertain.

2. A **mature group**, that is, the end stage of group development, tends to be effective and productive compared with groups in earlier stages of development. A mature group has the following traits according to L. N. Jewell and H. J. Reitz:

    a. Member awareness of individuals' strengths and weaknesses in relation to the group's function.

    b. Acceptance of individuals' differences.

    c. Acceptance of group authority and interpersonal relationships.

    d. Rational discussion of decisions with tolerance of dissent and no attempt to force unanimity.

    e. Limitation of conflict to substantive rather than emotional issues, e.g., group objectives and the means of reaching them.

    f. Members' awareness of their roles in group processes.

3. Jewell and Reitz have also defined the **stages of group development**. The principal issue in the early stages is uncertainty about power and authority relationships. The principal issue in the later stages is uncertainty about interpersonal relationships.

    a. In its **orientation stage**, the group is the least mature, effective, and efficient. Uncertainties are high and temporary leaders emerge.

    b. During the **conflict and challenge stage**, emerging leaders are opposed by people or subgroups with differing agendas. Redistribution of power and authority may occur during what may be a lengthy stage. It also may be the final stage if conflicts cannot be resolved.

    c. The consolidation of the power shifts begun during the conflict and challenge stage occurs during the **cohesion stage**. The members reach agreement about authority, structure, and procedures. They also begin to identify with the group. If progress is to continue, the stage should be brief.

    d. The **delusion stage** is a period during which the members must surmount a false sense that all emotional issues have been resolved. Hence, harmony is emphasized at the expense of properly addressing problems.

    e. When the group reaches the **disillusion stage**, cohesiveness diminishes as the members realize that their expectations are not being met. Absenteeism increases. Some members take the risk of urging the group to do better.

    f. Groups that evolve into the **acceptance stage** of group development tend to be both effective and efficient. This stage is characterized by personal and mutual understanding, tolerance of individual differences, constructive conflict about substantive matters, realistic expectations about group performance, and acceptance of the authority structure. The resulting trust engenders cohesiveness and a free exchange of information among group members.

4. Stop and review! You have completed the outline for this subunit. Study multiple-choice questions 21 through 23 on page 200.

7.3 ORGANIZATIONAL POLITICS

1.   Organizational politics, or **impression management**, is defined by Andrew DuBrin as "the pursuit of self-interest at work in the face of real or imagined opposition."

2.   Managers must understand organizational politics as a matter of self-interest. Moreover, they also must understand its negative effects on morale, the effectiveness of needed change, and ethical behavior.

3.   Self-interested behaviors are those not based solely on competence and diligence or resulting from good fortune.

   a.   **Positive political behaviors** include coalition building, networking, and seeking mentors.

   b.   **Negative political behaviors** include whistleblowing, sabotage, threats, taking credit for others' work or ideas, and building revolutionary coalitions.

4.   The **organizational culture** may encourage politics by creating unreasonable obstacles to group and individual advancement.

5.   Research suggests that the following **perceptions about organizational politics** are widely held:

   a.   Political behavior increases as managers rise in the hierarchy.

   b.   The frequency of political behavior increases as the organization grows.

   c.   Line managers are less political than staff managers.

   d.   Marketing managers are the most political, and production managers are the least.

   e.   Reorganization results in more political behavior than other changes.

   f.   Political behavior aids career advancement.

   g.   Political behavior may be beneficial to the organization by promoting ideas, building teams, enhancing communication, and lifting morale.

   h.   Political behavior may have a negative effect on the organization by distracting managers from focusing on entity objectives.

6.   The following are among the common **political tactics** identified by DuBrin:

   a.   **Posturing** is an attempt to make a good impression, for example, by taking credit for others' work or seeking to stay one jump ahead of a rival (one-upmanship).

   b.   **Empire building** is an attempt to control greater resources. Thus, a manager with a larger budget may believe that (s)he is in a safer position and is more influential.

   c.   **Making the supervisor look good** is an effort to impress the person who controls one's career path.

   d.   **Collecting and using social IOVs** is a tactic employed by someone who views favors as the currency of advancement, not as unselfish acts. Such a manager may help another to look good or not to look bad, for example, by concealing a mistake.

   e.   **Creating power and loyalty cliques** is a tactic based on the premise that a cohesive group has more power than an individual.

   f.   **Engaging in destructive competition** includes such behaviors as gossip, lying, and sabotage.

7. **Limiting organizational politics** is desirable because such behavior may hinder the achievement of organizational objectives. To avoid this result, DuBrin suggests

    a. Creating an open, trusting environment.
    b. Focusing on performance.
    c. Not modeling political behavior for lower-level managers.
    d. Using work and career planning to make individual objectives congruent with organizational objectives.
    e. Job rotation to develop a broader perspective and understanding of the problems of others.

8. Stop and review! You have completed the outline for this subunit. Study multiple-choice questions 24 through 27 on page 201.

7.4 TEAM BUILDING

1. **Participative management** gives employees greater control of the workplace when they can establish objectives, be involved in decision making, solve problems, or effect organizational change. Employees are more highly motivated and productive and turnover is lower when effective participative management programs are in place. Quality control circles, self-managed teams, and open-book management reflect the participative principle.

    a. **Quality circles (QCs)** are groups, usually of five to ten employees (management or subordinates), doing similar work who volunteer to meet at a specified time (e.g., once a week for an hour) to discuss and solve problems associated with their work areas.

        1) The objectives of QCs are to use employee capabilities more fully, build a more congenial workplace, and contribute to the improvement and development of both the organization and individual employees.
        2) Introduction of QCs is evolutionary through training, support, and team building. They are not imposed by management directive.
        3) The mechanics of a QC include the following problem-solving steps:

            a) Circle members bring problems before the group.
            b) The problems or projects are analyzed.
            c) Solutions are developed and presented to management.
            d) Management follows up on the suggestions by either approving or disapproving the ideas, with feedback to circle members.
            e) Members help to implement and evaluate the solutions.

        4) **Advantages of quality circles**

            a) Easy implementation without major organizational change
            b) More efficient and effective operation of the organization
            c) Better-quality products
            d) Improved employee morale and better cohesion among coworkers

        5) **Disadvantages of quality circles**

            a) Objections from unions
            b) Reduced morale if suggestions are not accepted by management and management fails to explain nonacceptance adequately
            c) Potential loss of management control

b. **Self-managed teams** are a facet of total quality management (TQM). They are autonomous groups that go beyond quality circles because they represent a major organizational change.

   1) Team members are not volunteers, but have been assigned to the teams.

   2) Teams are assembled to produce a complete product or service. Accordingly, they are empowered to perform traditional management tasks, such as scheduling, ordering materials, and even hiring.

   3) Members' jobs are enriched or **vertically loaded** not only by performing some management functions but also by cross-training and job rotation.

   4) The benefits of teams flow from the principle that employee self-management (and self-organization) is best.

      a) Motivation is improved because decision making is decentralized. The increased authority of autonomous work groups is intended to create a sense of ownership in the work product. Better decision making, productivity, quality, and goal congruence should be the results.

      b) An advantage of cross-functional teams is improved communication because all members have a better understanding of all facets of team activities.

      c) If teams are staffed appropriately and have the necessary resources and support from management, they should be able to improve the processes of production. The individuals who perform the work have the power to make decisions about the way it is done.

   5) **Managerial resistance** is the primary obstacle to adoption of self-managed teams. Fundamental organizational change is difficult. Thus, tradition-oriented managers tend to regard self-managed teams as endangering their status.

c. **Open-book management (OBM)** involves sharing important financial information with trained and empowered employees. This approach is founded on trusting employees, commitment to their training, and waiting patiently for results (usually at least two years). Kaj Aggarwal and Betty Simkins developed the **STEP** (share, teach, empower, pay) model for OBM described below.

   1) Step one is to **share** important financial information (sales, expenses, profits, stock prices). It should be displayed prominently, e.g., on an internal website or in hallways.

   2) Step two is to **teach** employees how to understand this information and the organization's operations. Simulations and board games are possible methods.

   3) Step three is to **empower** employees to make needed changes.

   4) Step four is to **pay** employees fairly as recognition of their accomplishments. Profit-sharing, stock options, and bonuses are among the methods of compensation.

d. The success of participative management rests upon **employee support**. According to David Levine, this support is most likely when four conditions are present:

   1) Profit-sharing
   2) Job security (a long-term relationship)
   3) Strong efforts to sustain group cohesiveness
   4) Protection of employee rights

2. A **team** is a group whose members work intensively with each other to achieve a specific common goal. A **group** consists of two or more people who interact with each other to accomplish a goal. All teams are groups, but not all groups are teams.

   a. Teams can improve organizational performance, but they are often difficult to form because it takes time for members to learn to work together. Normally, the smaller the team, the better. A maximum of nine members is recommended.

   b. A team differs from a group because team leadership often rotates, and team members are accountable to each other.

   c. Members of a team are empowered when they are properly trained and equipped, have the relevant information they need, are fully involved in decision making, and receive fair compensation for their work. Teams can be empowered by monitoring their progress and offering timely feedback on performance.

   d. A **cross-functional** team includes members who have different areas of expertise. A **research-and-development team** is an example of a team that is typically cross-functional in that many skills are needed to identify and create a new product.

      1) A cross-functional team need not be **self-managed**, but a self-managed team ordinarily is cross-functional.

      2) Unlike the members of a quality circle, cross-functional team members are assigned.

      3) The major difficulty is to integrate the work of individuals from diverse specialties (and possibly cultures).

   e. A **virtual team** uses computer and telecommunications technology (e-mail, voice mail, fax, Internet-based project software, videoconferencing, etc.) so that geographically distant members can work together on projects and reach common goals.

      1) Such a team may be able to work faster than a traditional team. Nevertheless, experience indicates that occasional in-person interaction and trust- and team-building procedures are still vital.

      2) Roles, expectations, performance standards, objectives, and deadlines must be clearly communicated.

      3) Deborah Duarte and Nancy Snyder recommend the following procedure for **building a virtual team**:

         a) Specify the individuals (sponsors and other stakeholders) who connect the team to the organization's power centers.

         b) Draft a charter stating the team's purposes and objectives.

         c) Choose the members. Core members are regular participants, extended members provide support, and ancillary members approve the work.

         d) Introduce the members. At this first meeting, leaders make certain determinations about members. For example, members should know why they were chosen, their computers should be compatible, they should have a way of finding answers to questions, and they should not be working on too many other projects.

         e) Conduct an in-person team orientation that includes an overview of the charter and guidance regarding the development of team norms. Examples of these team norms are the choice of, and the etiquette for, various communications media; how work is to be reviewed; the scheduling of meetings; and which meetings will be in-person.

         f) The team process should address such matters as management of the work, information storage and sharing, designation of the reviewers of documents, and frequency of review.

    f. **Team effectiveness** is reflected in achievement of objectives, innovation, adaptability, commitment, and favorable evaluations by senior management. According to Hans Thamhain, team effectiveness is determined by three sets of interdependent factors. Team effectiveness requires that all factors need to be addressed continually. A high performance team is committed to the personal growth of its team members.

        1) **People** - Job satisfaction, trust and team spirit, effective communication, successful conflict resolution, and job security.

        2) **Organization** - Stability, job security, supportive management, a fair compensation system, and stable objectives and priorities.

        3) **Tasks** - Clear objectives, direction, and planning; capable technical management; leadership; stimulating work; employee independence; experienced employees; team involvement; and visibility of the task.

    g. **Trust** is a key factor in any participative management approach. According to Douglas Houston, it is "a belief in the integrity, character, or ability of others." Thus, management should take action to build trust from the time that teams or other work groups are formed.

        1) The following is Dale Zand's **model for building trust**:

            a) A commitment to **trust** means that managers strive to improve personal interaction by being open, honest, and willing to change.

            b) Managers' commitment to trust includes disclosure of **information**, emotions, and opinions.

            c) The commitment to trust also extends to receptiveness to **influence** by others.

            d) When mutual trust is achieved, **control** will be self-imposed. Direct supervision will not be necessary when all persons involved know that others will perform.

        2) Fernando Bartolomé states that managers build trust through

            a) Timely and accurate **communication**
            b) **Supportive behavior**
            c) Showing **respect**, e.g., by delegation and effective listening
            d) **Fairness** of evaluations
            e) **Predictability** of behavior and promise-keeping
            f) **Competence** exemplified by sound judgment and technical proficiency

        3) Trust inspires trust. Hence, **being trusted** tends to lead to **trust in others**.

    3. Stop and review! You have completed the outline for this subunit. Study multiple-choice questions 28 through 39 beginning on page 202.

QUESTIONS

7.1 Group Dynamics

1. Which of the following can be a limiting factor associated with group decision making?

  A. Groups generally do not analyze problems in enough depth.

  B. It is very difficult to get individuals to accept decisions made by groups.

  C. Groups have a difficult time identifying the important components of decision making.

  D. Accountability is dispersed when groups make decisions.

Answer (D) is correct. *(IIA, adapted)*

    REQUIRED: The limiting factor associated with group decision making.

    DISCUSSION: The difficulty associated with group-aided decision making is accountability for the decision. If a decision is made by a group, no one person is responsible. The best method is for the group to recommend a decision but for a manager to assume responsibility for making the final decision.

    Answer (A) is incorrect because groups may analyze problems in greater depth. Answer (B) is incorrect because individuals who participate in the decision may accept it more readily. Answer (C) is incorrect because greater experience and expertise of a group may render it more effective than a single manager in identifying key components of decision making.

2. Which one of the following is generally not beneficial to group decision making in an organization?

A. More information.

B. Acceptance.

C. More knowledge.

D. Dominant members.

Answer (D) is correct. *(CMA, adapted)*
REQUIRED: The item that is not beneficial to group decision making in an organization.
DISCUSSION: Group decision making, such as by committee, works better when the committee is small and the members accept each other as contributing parts of the group. A dominant member is not desirable. The chair should act as a moderator and not be considered threatening or overbearing by the other members.
Answer (A) is incorrect because a group decision, like an individual decision, is better when based on sufficient information. Answer (B) is incorrect because acceptance of each member of the committee and the goals of the committee is essential. Answer (C) is incorrect because the more knowledge that group members possess, the better the decision is likely to be.

3. Which of the following is not an advantage of group decision making as compared to individual decision making?

A. Groups obtain an increased degree of acceptance of a solution so that it may be more easily implemented.

B. Group decision making is consistent with democratic methods.

C. Group members bring more complete information and knowledge into the decision process.

D. Group members avoid expressing opinions that deviate from what appears to be the group consensus.

Answer (D) is correct. *(CIA, adapted)*
REQUIRED: The item that is not an advantage of group decision making.
DISCUSSION: The groupthink phenomenon is undesirable. Groupthink occurs when group members accept what appears to be the group consensus rather than giving their honest input. The result may be decisions with which some members of the group are not happy.
Answer (A) is incorrect because, if members of the group are responsible for the decision making, their participation in the implementation process will increase the ease with which the decisions are carried out. Answer (B) is incorrect because group decision making adds legitimacy to the solution by following democratic methods. Answer (C) is incorrect because a group possesses greater resources than an individual.

4. Which of the following statements about group decision making is generally considered false?

A. There is a lack of responsibility for group decisions.

B. Group decision making is almost always less efficient than individual decision making.

C. The desire by individual members to be accepted by the group often restrains open disagreement.

D. Group decision making tends to be less creative than individual decision making.

Answer (D) is correct. *(IIA, adapted)*
REQUIRED: The false statement about group decision making.
DISCUSSION: Groups tend to be more creative than individuals because diversity of member views generally results in groups considering more alternatives for solving a problem.
Answer (A) is incorrect because individuals do not accept responsibility for group decisions. Answer (B) is incorrect because group decision making almost always takes more time than individual decision making, except when the need for diverse views is so great that an individual decision maker needs to consult many people or perform research. Answer (C) is incorrect because group members generally have diverse views, but their common need to be accepted and respected by the group often restrains the full, open expression of their views when they fear strong disagreement.

5. Informal groups often have many favorable effects on the members. Which of the following is one of the favorable effects informal groups have on members but that may have an unfavorable effect on the organization?

A. Informal groups aid in problem-solving situations.

B. Informal groups improve coordination and reduce supervision required.

C. Informal groups reduce tension and encourage production.

D. Informal groups provide another channel of communication.

Answer (D) is correct. *(Publisher)*
REQUIRED: The favorable effect that informal groups have on members but which also have an unfavorable effect on the organization.
DISCUSSION: The additional channel of communication is a benefit to the informal group but may cause problems for the organization depending upon what messages are being communicated. This grapevine may cause the spread of false rumors or information and could be detrimental to the organization.
Answer (A) is incorrect because aiding in problem-solving situations is advantageous to both the informal group members and the organization. Answer (B) is incorrect because improved coordination and reduced supervision is a benefit to both the informal group and the organization. Answer (C) is incorrect because the reduced tension and increased production is a benefit to both the informal group and the organization.

6. Which of the following is not true with regard to informal groups?

    A. Members of the group are susceptible to group pressure.

    B. The groups develop primarily to satisfy esteem needs.

    C. Almost all employees and managers are members of an informal group.

    D. Informal groups tend to be small and have simple relationships.

Answer (D) is correct.   *(Publisher)*
    REQUIRED: The false statement regarding informal groups.
    DISCUSSION: Informal groups tend to be small and are often very complex. They develop their own leaders and usually result from the frequent interaction among individuals in the course of their work.
    Answer (A) is incorrect because group pressure is often a major characteristic of informal groups and the pressure is often hard to resist because members seek acceptance from the group. Answer (B) is incorrect because informal groups often form to establish friendships which satisfy esteem needs. Answer (C) is incorrect because almost everyone in an organization forms some type of friendship or other informal relationship with others in the organization.

7. An audit manager allowed a work group to make a decision about whether to adopt a new work procedure. In allowing the group to make the decision, the manager should be aware that groups tend to make

    A. Very conservative decisions and do not want to assume risk.

    B. Faster decisions than do individuals because groups have more expertise than does any one person.

    C. Decisions that are less accurate than those made by individuals.

    D. Riskier decisions than do individuals, and individual responsibility for the group's decision is lessened.

Answer (D) is correct.   *(IIA, adapted)*
    REQUIRED: The decisions made by work groups.
    DISCUSSION: Groups tend to make riskier decisions, and individual responsibility is reduced. Groups can become complex and members must react to pressures.
    Answer (A) is incorrect because groups tend to make riskier decisions than individuals (part of the group shift phenomenon). Answer (B) is incorrect because group decisions take longer than individual decisions. Answer (C) is incorrect because group decisions tend to be more accurate than individual decisions.

8. During which stage of group development does a group exhibit a consolidation of power and reach an agreement among members about authority, structure, and procedures?

    A. Conflict and challenge stage.

    B. Disillusion stage.

    C. Acceptance stage.

    D. Cohesion stage.

Answer (D) is correct.   *(Publisher)*
    REQUIRED: The stage of group development during which a group exhibits a consolidation of power and reaches an agreement about authority, structure, and procedures.
    DISCUSSION: The consolidation of power shifts begun during the conflict and challenge stages occurs during the cohesion stage. Members often reach an agreement on authority, structure, and procedures.
    Answer (A) is incorrect because in the conflict and challenge stage, emerging leaders are opposed by people or subgroups with differing agendas. Answer (B) is incorrect because cohesiveness diminishes as the members realize that their expectations are not being met. Answer (C) is incorrect because the acceptance stage involves personal and mutual understanding, tolerance of individual differences, and acceptance of the authority structure. The acceptance stage has demonstrated more progress than the cohesion stage, which has only agreed with the authority, structure, and procedures.

9. Under "groupthink"

    A. There is a tendency to conform to the majority's will and to ignore relevant individual input that is at variance with group opinion.

    B. The group is not required to reach consensus.

    C. The extent of groupthink is proportional to the size of the group.

    D. There are too many alternatives to facilitate decision making.

Answer (A) is correct.   *(IIA, adapted)*
    REQUIRED: The true statement regarding "groupthink."
    DISCUSSION: Groupthink is the tendency to conform to the majority's will when individual input is at variance with the group opinion. Groupthink is a cause of faulty decision making in a group. Groups may not consider all alternatives because they desire unanimity at the expense of quality decisions. Groupthink occurs when groups are highly cohesive and under considerable pressure to make a decision.
    Answer (B) is incorrect because consensus is desirable even when groupthink is avoided. Answer (C) is incorrect because groupthink is not limited to groups of only certain sizes. Answer (D) is incorrect because few alternatives may be addressed by a group afflicted with groupthink.

10. Formal groups are work groups within the organization assembled to perform a productive activity. How is a formal group similar to an informal group?

A. Membership in both informal and formal groups tends to be permanent.

B. Informal and formal groups develop their own leaders to fill the needs of the group.

C. Informal and formal groups usually provide social satisfaction that supplements job satisfaction.

D. Informal and formal groups are based on the organization's purpose and needs.

Answer (C) is correct. *(Publisher)*
REQUIRED: The similarity between formal and informal groups.
DISCUSSION: The use of groups in organizations has often led to a higher degree of social satisfaction because members feel that they have contributed to a part of the group and gained the acceptance of their peers. Both informal and formal groups usually provide an employee with greater job satisfaction than the employee would otherwise have on his or her own.
Answer (A) is incorrect because membership in formal groups is relatively more permanent than in informal groups. Answer (B) is incorrect because formal groups have explicitly designated leaders with authority while informal groups develop their own leaders. Answer (D) is incorrect because formal groups are formed based upon an organization's purpose and needs. Informal groups are often developed by the employees of the organization without regard to the organization's purpose or needs.

11. Which of the following is not a characteristic of informal groups?

A. They are developed to establish friendships.

B. Informal groups tend to be small and very complex.

C. Membership in informal groups lasts longer than membership in formal groups.

D. Informal groups develop their own leaders.

Answer (C) is correct. *(Publisher)*
REQUIRED: The statement that does not characterize informal groups.
DISCUSSION: Membership in formal groups tends to last longer than membership in informal groups. Membership in both groups is usually different as well.
Answer (A) is incorrect because informal groups are often developed to satisfy esteem needs such as the desire to form friendships. Answer (B) is incorrect because informal groups are often small and complex because they evolve from interaction in the course of work. There are no predetermined leaders and therefore the structure of the group is complex. Answer (D) is incorrect because informal groups often develop their own leaders from interaction during the course of work.

12. A weakness of cohesive groups may be

A. Conformity.

B. Groupthink.

C. The development of norms.

D. Commitment by members.

Answer (B) is correct. *(Publisher)*
REQUIRED: The weakness of cohesive groups.
DISCUSSION: Groupthink occurs when a cohesive group's members tend to conform and ignore a relevant individual input that is at variance with the perceived group opinion.
Answer (A) is incorrect because conformity is important for a group to successfully complete its objective. Members must be able to put aside individual differences to accomplish the objective. Answer (C) is incorrect because the development of norms is not usually a bad side effect. Norms often are beneficial if they help a group achieve an objective with more cooperation than would be the case without norms. Answer (D) is incorrect because commitment by group members is necessary for a group to be successful in accomplishing an objective.

13. Groupthink is defined as

A. The tendency to conform and ignore relevant individual input that is at variance with the majority opinion.

B. The guidance of groups based upon self-set standards of performance and behavior.

C. The members of a group developing a solution to a problem after all the relevant information has been considered.

D. A way of brainstorming ideas to address an issue presented to a group by management.

Answer (A) is correct. *(Publisher)*
REQUIRED: The definition of groupthink.
DISCUSSION: Research into cohesive groups has revealed the prevalence of groupthink. Groupthink is conformity to a group's opinion despite information that it may be incorrect.
Answer (B) is incorrect because norms are defined as the guidance of groups based upon self-set standards of performance and behavior. Answer (C) is incorrect because considering all relevant information avoids the problem of groupthink. The group addresses issues that may change its opinion. Answer (D) is incorrect because groupthink is not a way of developing ideas to address an issue. Groupthink is using the ideas of the group to address an issue, regardless of outside information.

14. When compared to individuals, groups have advantages and disadvantages for decision making. Which of the following is true regarding group decisions?

	Advantage	Disadvantage
A.	Increased personal accountability	Disagreements do not surface because of pressures to conform
B.	Increased acceptance of a decision by participants	Takes more time to arrive at a decision
C.	Takes less time to arrive at a decision	Lack of personal accountability
D.	Increased diversity of expertise	Reduced acceptance of decision by participants

Answer (B) is correct. *(IIA, adapted)*
REQUIRED: The advantages and disadvantages of group decision making.
DISCUSSION: Group decision making and problem solving has the following advantages: (1) the group has greater knowledge and experience than an individual; (2) the group provides multiple perspectives; (3) members participating in a group process tend to have a better understanding of the reasons for different actions; (4) those actively participating in the group process tend to accept, and have ownership of, the result; and (5) group involvement provides training for the less experienced members. The following are the disadvantages: (1) the social pressure to conform may inhibit creativity; (2) the group may be dominated by a few aggressive members; (3) the decision or solution may be a product of logrolling (political dealing); (4) the goal of reaching a good decision or solution may be displaced by a secondary concern, e.g., competing with a rival; and (5) the process may suffer from groupthink, or preference for unanimity over the quality of the decision or solution.
Answer (A) is incorrect because group decisions lead to lack of personal accountability. Answer (C) is incorrect because an individual makes decisions more quickly then a group. Answer (D) is incorrect because those who participated in a group process are more likely to accept and support the group's decisions.

15. Which of the following characteristics do both informal and formal groups share?

A. They are both structured similarly.

B. Commitment to both groups depends on the group's attractiveness and cohesiveness.

C. Membership in both groups is usually the same.

D. Both groups exist within the community to perform a productive activity.

Answer (B) is correct. *(Publisher)*
REQUIRED: The characteristics that informal and formal groups share.
DISCUSSION: The commitment to a group depends on the group's attractiveness and cohesiveness. Employees are more likely to join a group that has a favorable view from the outside and whose group members adhere to the group and resist outside pressure.
Answer (A) is incorrect because formal groups are often more structured than informal groups. Answer (C) is incorrect because membership in formal groups may not be the same as in informal groups. Answer (D) is incorrect because informal groups form to fill the needs of the members, not to perform a productive activity.

16. Which of the following is true with regard to norms?

A. Norms are similar from culture to culture.

B. Norms reinforce the group's values and common identity.

C. Norms may be enforced by ridicule or criticism.

D. Norms are often written in an organization's policy manual.

Answer (B) is correct. *(Publisher)*
REQUIRED: The true statement regarding norms.
DISCUSSION: Norms often provide a common identity for a group. Members feel they are part of a cohesive group with members who also share the same values.
Answer (A) is incorrect because norms vary from culture to culture. Answer (C) is incorrect because enforcement of norms in the negative sense may be done with ridicule and criticism. Answer (D) is incorrect because norms are often unwritten.

17. Groups have often evolved by self-set standards of performance and behavior, usually based on the personal and social backgrounds of the individuals on the job. This establishment of a group culture is referred to as developing

A. Role models.

B. Cohesiveness.

C. Conformity.

D. Norms.

Answer (D) is correct. *(Publisher)*
REQUIRED: The definition of norms.
DISCUSSION: Norms are the standards of behavior adopted by a group when it is in its early stages. The norms of the group are often a composite of the personal and social backgrounds of the individuals who comprise the group.
Answer (A) is incorrect because role models set an example for other employees to follow but role models are not usually responsible for establishing the culture of a group. Answer (B) is incorrect because cohesiveness is the tendency of members to adhere to the group and unite against outside pressures. Answer (C) is incorrect because conformity involves complying with the prevailing role expectations and norms of a group.

18. A lack of cohesiveness and attractiveness in a group may lead to

- A. A lack of commitment by the members.
- B. Dissention in the formal organization.
- C. Cooperation among group members.
- D. Substantial group member interaction.

Answer (A) is correct. *(Publisher)*
REQUIRED: The result of a lack of cohesiveness and attractiveness in a group.
DISCUSSION: Commitment to a group depends on the group's attractiveness and cohesiveness. A lack of commitment may lead to members joining other groups and bad experiences with the group.
Answer (B) is incorrect because dissention in the formal organization would be too extreme for a single group to cause. Answer (C) is incorrect because the opposite is likely to happen. A lack of cohesiveness and attractiveness will most likely make group member cooperate less. Answer (D) is incorrect because group member interaction will most likely decrease as members consider joining other groups or become frustrated with the group.

19. One of the keys to successful redesigning of jobs in order to motivate employees is

- A. Creating autonomous work teams.
- B. Enlarging jobs by adding more tasks similar to those being performed.
- C. Rotating workers to different jobs to provide them with variety.
- D. Changing the content of jobs so that they fit each worker's need for growth.

Answer (D) is correct. *(IIA, adapted)*
REQUIRED: The way to motivate employees with redesigned jobs.
DISCUSSION: One of the major principles of successful job design and redesign is to consider employee needs and skills and match them with jobs. An alternative is to change the jobs to fit those needs and skills. The objective is to conform to strengths and to avoid weaknesses.
Answer (A) is incorrect because creating autonomous work teams is only one type of job enrichment. It is not applicable in many situations. Answer (B) is incorrect because adding more similar tasks does not fundamentally redesign jobs. It may be demotivating if existing tasks are difficult or boring. Answer (C) is incorrect because rotating workers provides only a temporary challenge. It does not suit most employees who want additional challenges.

20. A new production team has been formed by taking experienced high achievers from existing teams within the factory. The members of the new team have not been required to learn any new skills, and the machines used are identical to those used in their former teams. The team's production supervisor is a longtime employee of the organization but has not previously worked with any members of the new team. Despite the abilities and previous individual achievements of the individual team members, management is surprised by the mediocre performance of the new team. The best approach for the production supervisor to improve performance would be to

- A. Increase pressure on the team through higher goals and reprimands.
- B. Replace these individuals on the team.
- C. Provide opportunities for the team members to socialize with each other.
- D. Do nothing now because it is too soon to draw any conclusions.

Answer (C) is correct. *(CIA, adapted)*
REQUIRED: The best approach for improving team performance.
DISCUSSION: As the team members work and socialize, cohesiveness will be enhanced because of the opportunity to discover commonalities and share experiences. However, performance may or may not improve as cohesiveness increases. Improvement is also contingent on the group's performance norms. A cohesive group enforces norms. Thus, if norms are high, greater cohesiveness should result in better performance.
Answer (A) is incorrect because external pressure sometimes increases group cohesiveness and improves performance. However, these team members do not know each other well, and they may perceive that the team will not respond adequately to adversity. Answer (B) is incorrect because group cohesiveness has not had sufficient opportunity to develop. Starting over will be counterproductive. Answer (D) is incorrect because cohesiveness will probably improve over time, but the supervisor can speed the process by encouraging social interaction.

7.2 Stages of Group Development

21. Which of the following characteristics is common with a mature group?

A. Harmony is emphasized at the expense of addressing the problems.

B. No attempt to force unanimity.

C. Members begin to identify with the group.

D. Redistributions of power and authority may occur.

Answer (B) is correct. *(Publisher)*
REQUIRED: The characteristics of a mature group.
DISCUSSION: A mature group is in the end stage of group development and tends to be more effective and productive compared to groups in earlier stages. A mature group engages in rational discussion of decisions with tolerance of dissent and no attempt to force unanimity.
Answer (A) is incorrect because harmony is emphasized at the expense of addressing problems during the delusion stage when members have the false sense that all emotional issues have been resolved. Answer (C) is incorrect because members begin to identify with the group during the cohesion stage. In a mature group, members already identify with the group. Answer (D) is incorrect because redistributions of power and authority occur during the conflict and challenge stage when leaders are opposed by members of the group with differing agendas.

22. A mature group lacks which of the following characteristics?

A. Acceptance of individuals' differences.

B. Members' awareness of their roles in group processes.

C. Attempts to compel unanimity.

D. Acceptance of group authority and interpersonal relationships.

Answer (C) is correct. *(Publisher)*
REQUIRED: The characteristic not found in a mature group.
DISCUSSION: A mature group has rational discussion of decisions with tolerance of dissent and no attempt to force unanimity. Groups that are in their early stages attempt to force unanimity.
Answer (A) is incorrect because a mature group acknowledges that each member is unique and that the objectives can be accomplished without each group member being the same. Answer (B) is incorrect because members of a group are often aware of the role they play in a mature group. Answer (D) is incorrect because a mature group already has structured itself so that each member understands the hierarchy of authority and the interpersonal relationships.

23. During which stages do the primary issues among group members involve uncertainty about power and authority relationships?

	Early Stages	Later Stages
A.	Yes	Yes
B.	Yes	No
C.	No	Yes
D.	No	No

Answer (B) is correct. *(Publisher)*
REQUIRED: The identification of the principal issues encountered in the early and later stages in groups.
DISCUSSION: According to Jewell and Reitz, the principal issue in the early stages is uncertainty about power and authority relationships. The principal issue in the later stages is uncertainty about interpersonal relationships.
Answer (A) is incorrect because groups in later stages of development already have defined power and authority relationships and there is little uncertainty. Answer (C) is incorrect because groups in early stages of development have problems defining power and authority relationships while groups in later stages of development do not. Answer (D) is incorrect because groups in early stages of development have problems defining power and authority relationships.

7.3 Organizational Politics

24. Which of the following tactics may employees use when they feel their individual power is insignificant?

- A. They may engage in posturing by taking credit for the work of a coworker.
- B. They may engage in destructive competition by spreading false rumors.
- C. They may engage in creating power and loyalty cliques with other coworkers.
- D. They may attempt to conceal errors made by their supervisor in order to aid their future advancement within the corporation.

Answer (C) is correct. *(Publisher)*
REQUIRED: The tactics employees engage in when they feel a cohesive group has more power than an individual.
DISCUSSION: Employees will often form groups when they feel their collective bargaining power is greater than the power of an individual.
Answer (A) is incorrect because posturing is the attempt to make a good impression and is often used when an individual feels his or her power is adequate. Answer (B) is incorrect because engaging in destructive competition does not reveal that an individual feels their power is insignificant. Answer (D) is incorrect because concealing errors by an employee demonstrates that they feel their power is great enough to hide errors and not get caught.

25. In which of the following situations would organizational politics most likely have a significant impact?

- A. When space allocations are made according to objective criteria.
- B. When the budget allows for generous salary increases for all employees.
- C. When promotions are based on an employee's attitude.
- D. When performance outcomes are clearly stated and objective.

Answer (C) is correct. *(IIA, adapted)*
REQUIRED: The situation significantly affected by organizational politics.
DISCUSSION: Organizational politics, or impression management, is defined by Andrew DuBrin as "the pursuit of self-interest at work in the face of real or imagined opposition." Also, employees tend to believe that pursuit of self-interest at work in the form of career advancement is aided by playing politics. Hence, employees will try to, among other things, manage the impression of their attitudes held by superiors.
Answer (A) is incorrect because space allocations are not affected by politics. Answer (B) is incorrect because, if each employee receives a salary increase, politics will be irrelevant. Answer (D) is incorrect because, if an employee meets his or her objectives, politics should not significantly affect his or her performance evaluations.

26. Which of the following factors plays a key role in encouraging organizational politics?

- A. Unreasonable obstacles to group and individual advancement.
- B. Several managers are not promoting employees on an entirely merit-based system.
- C. A lack of a code of ethics for the organization.
- D. Low employee morale.

Answer (A) is correct. *(Publisher)*
REQUIRED: The key factor in encouraging organizational politics.
DISCUSSION: The organizational culture plays a large role in encouraging organizational politics. The organizational culture may encourage politics by creating unreasonable obstacles to group and individual advancement.
Answer (B) is incorrect because promotions are often based on merit but other factors are often considered when deciding who to promote. Other factors may be personality and communication skills relevant to the new position. Answer (C) is incorrect because a lack of a code of ethics may play a factor in organizational politics but the culture of an organization plays a larger role because a culture reveals more about an organization's activities than a book. Answer (D) is incorrect because low employee morale is often the end result of organizational politics.

27. The organizational culture may encourage politics by creating unreasonable obstacles to group and individual advancement. Which type of political tactic involves taking credit for another person's work?

- A. Loyalty cliques.
- B. Destructive competition.
- C. Empire building.
- D. Posturing.

Answer (D) is correct. *(Publisher)*
REQUIRED: The type of political tactic involving taking credit for another person's work.
DISCUSSION: Posturing is an attempt to make a good impression, for example, by taking credit for others' work or seeking to stay one jump ahead of a rival.
Answer (A) is incorrect because creating power and loyalty cliques is a tactic based on the premise that a cohesive group has more power than an individual. Answer (B) is incorrect because engaging in destructive competition includes activities such as gossip, lying, and sabotage. Answer (C) is incorrect because empire building is an attempt to control greater resources. A manager who supervises many employees may feel more secure and influential.

7.4 Team Building

28. Which of the following is not one of the advantages of self-managed teams?

   A. Motivation is improved because decision making is decentralized.

   B. Improved processes of production if the teams are supported properly.

   C. Managerial acceptance by tradition-oriented managers.

   D. Improved communication because all members understand the team's activities better.

Answer (C) is correct. *(Publisher)*
REQUIRED: The characteristic that is not an advantage of self-managed teams.
DISCUSSION: Managerial resistance is often the primary obstacle of self-managed teams. Organizational change is difficult and tradition-oriented managers tend to regard self-managed teams as a threat to their status.
   Answer (A) is incorrect because the increased authority of autonomous work groups creates a sense of ownership of the final product. Answer (B) is incorrect because teams are often able to improve production processes if the team is properly supported by management. Answer (D) is incorrect because cross-functional teams result in improved communication because all the members have a better understanding of the team activities.

29. Which of the following is false with regard to quality circles and self-managed teams?

   A. Managerial acceptance by tradition-oriented managers.

   B. Self-managed teams are assigned by management and quality circle teams are voluntary.

   C. Self-managed teams and quality circles often have better cohesion among members.

   D. Self-managed teams and quality circles are often able to help the organization to operate more efficiently and effectively.

Answer (A) is correct. *(Publisher)*
REQUIRED: The false statement regarding quality circles and self-managed teams.
DISCUSSION: Managerial acceptance is the primary obstacle to adoption of self-managed teams. Tradition-oriented managers often perceive the loss of authority to a self-managed team as a threat to their status.
   Answer (B) is incorrect because self-managed teams are assigned while quality circles often include employee who meet at specified times to discuss and solve problems. Answer (C) is incorrect because teams in general tend to have better cohesion among member than employees who are not part of teams. Answer (D) is incorrect because both types of teams function to improve the organization overall. Quality circles often try to improve the quality of products and operations while self-managed teams are assembled to accomplish a specified task or group of tasks.

30. Which of the following is key to any plan to empower teams?

   A. Give structure to team members.

   B. Monitor progress and offer timely feedback on performance.

   C. Reduce authority of the team when mistakes are made.

   D. Avoid tension and conflict within the team.

Answer (B) is correct. *(IIA, adapted)*
REQUIRED: The key item to any plan to empower teams.
DISCUSSION: Members of a team are empowered when they are properly trained and equipped, have the relevant information they need, are fully involved in decision making, and receive fair compensaion for their work. Monitoring and feedback are keys to maintaining empowerment because they are necessary to team effectiveness. Team effectiveness is reflected in achievement of objectives, innovation, adaptability, commitment, and favorable evaluations by senior management.
   Answer (A) is incorrect because empowered team members may determine their own structure. Answer (C) is incorrect because a tolerance for problems and mistakes is part of empowerment. Answer (D) is incorrect because tension and conflict are a normal part of team development.

31. The sharing of important financial information with employees based upon a foundation of trust and commitment to training is known as

   A. Self-managed teams.

   B. Open-book management.

   C. Quality circles.

   D. Impression management.

Answer (B) is correct. *(Publisher)*
REQUIRED: The definition of open-book management.
DISCUSSION: Open-book management involves sharing important financial information with trained and empowered employees. This approach is founded on trusting employees, commitment to their training, and waiting patiently for results.
   Answer (A) is incorrect because self-managed teams involve teams that are empowered to perform traditional management tasks. Self-managed teams may be able to view financial information, but not in all cases. Answer (C) is incorrect because quality groups usually meet to discuss and solve problems associated with their work areas. Quality circles are usually not able to view important financial information without management approval. Answer (D) is incorrect because impression management is the pursuit of self-interest in the fear of a real or perceived risk.

32. Which of the following actions can management take to build trust with groups?

    A. Disclose information, emotions, and opinions.

    B. Engaging in timely and accurate communication.

    C. Showing respect to the group.

    D. All of the answers are correct.

Answer (D) is correct. *(Publisher)*
    REQUIRED: The actions management can take to build trust with groups.
    DISCUSSION: The three factors that show that management desires to build a trusting relationship between the group and management.
    Answer (A) is incorrect because engaging in timely and accurate communication and showing respect to the group will also help build mutual trust. Answer (B) is incorrect because disclosing information, emotions, and opinions also help build mutual trust. Showing respect to the group also demonstrates that management desires a trusting relationship. Answer (C) is incorrect because disclosure of information, emotions, and opinions and engaging in timely and accurate communication also demonstrates that management desires to build trust with the group.

33. Which of the following factors is critical for the success of participative management?

    A. Trust.

    B. Control.

    C. Information.

    D. Influence.

Answer (A) is correct. *(Publisher)*
    REQUIRED: The factor critical to the success of participative management.
    DISCUSSION: Trust is the key factor in any participative management approach. Management should take action to build trust as soon as groups are formed. If there is a lack of trust, then success is unlikely because both the team and management will act in their own self-interest and not the interest of the organization.
    Answer (B) is incorrect because control comes after there is mutual trust. Direct supervision will be unnecessary if both management and the teams trust that each will act in the organization's best interest. Answer (C) is incorrect because managers will not disclose information if they do not trust the team first. Answer (D) is incorrect because neither party will be able to influence the other if there is not mutual trust for each party's position.

34. Which of the following is not an appropriate approach to team building?

    A. Ensuring a balance of complementary team roles.

    B. Choosing members who need to improve their skills.

    C. Developing clear and shared values.

    D. Selecting team members based on how they are likely to relate to each other.

Answer (B) is correct. *(IIA, adapted)*
    REQUIRED: The inappropriate approach to team building.
    DISCUSSION: A team is most likely to be effective when it is fully empowered. Empowerment follows from properly training and equipping team members, and providing them with all necessary information. A team will not be effective if its members lack the needed skills.
    Answer (A) is incorrect because role definition is a recognized approach to team building. Answer (C) is incorrect because value development is a recognized approach to team building. Answer (D) is incorrect because interpersonal relations is a recognized approach to team building.

35. Which of the following statements regarding virtual teams is false?

    A. Virtual teams may be able to work faster than a traditional team.

    B. In-person interaction and team-building exercises are unnecessary.

    C. Roles and objectives must be clearly communicated.

    D. Team leaders should meet their members in person before the members are chosen for participation in the group.

Answer (B) is correct. *(Publisher)*
    REQUIRED: The false statement regarding a virtual team.
    DISCUSSION: In-person and team-building exercises are often necessary to create the cohesion and trust for a group to operate effectively. If there are no team-building exercises, the team may fracture and become ineffective at achieving its objective.
    Answer (A) is incorrect because virtual teams have an advantage of being able to meet anywhere at anytime and therefore may be able to complete tasks faster than traditional teams. Answer (C) is incorrect because in any group, roles and objectives should be clearly communicated to ensure that the team is working together productively towards a common goal. Answer (D) is incorrect because it is recommended that team leaders meet with prospective team members to ensure that the members are compatible with the group and are not working on too many other projects.

36. The STEP model is consistent with which organizational philosophy?

    A. Self-managed teams.

    B. Open-book management.

    C. Impression management.

    D. Group development.

Answer (B) is correct. *(Publisher)*
    REQUIRED: The organizational philosophy that is consistent with the STEP model.
    DISCUSSION: Open-book management involves sharing important financial information with trained and empowered employees. The first step is to share (S) the financial information with the employees. Next, management must teach (T) the employees how to understand the information and use it to the benefit of the organization. Then, management empowers (E) the employees to act on the information given. Finally, the employees are paid (P) for their accomplishments.
    Answer (A) is incorrect because self-managed teams are not part of the STEP model. The STEP model involves providing employees with important financial information and teaching the employees how to use it. Answer (C) is incorrect because impression management involves acting in self-interest in the face of a real or perceived threat. Answer (D) is incorrect because group development is the stages in bringing a group together from development to maturity.

37. A team is a group whose members work together to achieve a specific common goal. Which of the following is true with respect to teams?

    A. All groups are teams but not all teams are groups.

    B. Teams improve organizational performance because teams are easy to form.

    C. A team is similar to a group because team leadership often rotates and members are accountable to each other.

    D. Smaller teams are recommended.

Answer (D) is correct. *(Publisher)*
    REQUIRED: The characteristics of teams.
    DISCUSSION: Normally smaller teams are recommended. Two to nine members is recommended because working in teams requires accepting a diversity of ideas and opinions. Larger groups require more time for each of the members to develop trust in one another and to work together productively.
    Answer (A) is incorrect because all teams are groups but not all groups are teams. Each team, by definition, is a group of people. Answer (B) is incorrect because teams often improve organizational performance but teams are not easy to form because it takes time for group members to learn to work together. Answer (C) is incorrect because a team differs from a group because team leadership often rotates and team members are accountable to each other.

38. Which of the following indicates a high performance team?

    A. Pride in the team leader.

    B. Quick agreement on the first proposed solution for problems facing the team.

    C. Care in risk-taking.

    D. Commitment to personal growth of team members.

Answer (D) is correct. *(IIA, adapted)*
    REQUIRED: The characteristic that indicates a high performance team.
    DISCUSSION: Team effectiveness is reflected in achievement of objectives, innovation, adaptability, commitment, and favorable evaluations by senior management. According to Hans Thamhain, team effectiveness is determined by three sets of interdependent factors. Team effectiveness requires that all factors need to be addressed continually. A high performance team is committed to the personal growth of its team members.
    Answer (A) is incorrect because high performance teams recognize the value of all members. Answer (B) is incorrect because quick agreement reflects a lack of diversity characteristic of "groupthink." Answer (C) is incorrect because individuals tend to be more risk averse than teams.

39. Which one of the following statements about quality circles is false?

    A. A quality circle is typically comprised of a group of 8 to 10 subordinates and supervisors.

    B. Part of the quality circle concept includes teaching participants communication skills, quality strategies, and problem analysis techniques.

    C. Quality circles meet on the company premises and on company time.

    D. The quality circle has the final control over implementation of recommended solutions.

Answer (D) is correct. *(CIA, adapted)*
    REQUIRED: The false statement about quality circles.
    DISCUSSION: Use of quality circles is a form of participative management. A quality circle is a group of up to 10 individuals (managers and subordinates) who do similar work and who volunteer to meet weekly to discuss and solve work-related problems. However, management retains the right to make the final decisions.
    Answer (A) is incorrect because a quality circle is a small group of subordinates and supervisors, usually 8 to 10 people. Answer (B) is incorrect because each member is responsible for the success of the circle, and success depends on the ability of members to analyze and solve problems. Answer (C) is incorrect because quality circles are used by companies to accomplish objectives. Participation is part of each worker's job.

STUDY UNIT EIGHT
INFLUENCE AND LEADERSHIP

(9 pages of outline)

This study unit describes the research on influence processes used by managers in organizations. Such processes range from influence tactics, the application of various sources of power, employee empowerment, and behavior modification to the many theories of leadership and its development.

8.1 INFLUENCE AND POWER

1. Kreitner (9th ed., page 496) defines **influence** in the work environment as "any attempt by a person to change the behavior of superiors, peers, or lower-level employees." Influence may be exerted in many ways, including the use of power and the exercise of leadership.

2. Management literature (Kipnin, Schmidt, Wilkinson, and others) describes **generic influence tactics** that may be used in any direction (upward to influence superiors, laterally to influence peers, and downward to influence lower-level employees).

    a. The following are the generic influence tactics noted by researchers:

        1) **Consultation** permits the other person(s) to participate in the decision or change.

        2) **Rational persuasion** tries to convince others by reliance on a detailed plan, supporting evidence, and reason.

        3) **Inspirational appeals** are calls to superordinate goals. They are appeals to emotions, values, or ideals.

        4) **Ingratiating tactics** attempt to raise the other person's self-esteem prior to a request.

        5) **Coalition tactics** seek the aid of others to persuade someone to agree.

        6) **Pressure tactics** involve intimidation, threats, and demands.

        7) **Upward appeals** are based on the formal or informal support of higher management.

        8) **Exchange tactics** entail an exchange of favors, a reminder of a past favor, or an offer of a personal sacrifice.

    b. The most commonly used influence tactics are consultation, rational persuasion, and inspirational appeals. The least commonly used are pressure tactics, upward appeals, and exchange tactics.

        1) Research suggests that male and female managers do not differ significantly in their use of influence tactics.

        2) Upward influence methods used by employees of **authoritarian managers** are most likely to consist of ingratiating tactics and upward appeals.

        3) Rational persuasion is the method used most often by employees of **participative managers**.

3.   **Power** is the ability to influence employees to do what they would not ordinarily do. It has also been defined as the ability to use people, information, and material resources to accomplish something (Morgan McCall, Jr.). Power and influence may be wielded formally or informally.

    a.   **Power sources** include

        1)   Legitimate or position power (closely associated with formal authority)

            a)   Human nature is such that employees tend not to completely obey someone who relies solely on legitimate authority. Moreover, managers may not have the right to direct (exert formal authority over) some people whom they need to influence.

        2)   Expertise

            a)   The most notable example today is the influence wielded by IT professionals.

        3)   Referent power (derived from the leader's charisma or employees' identification with the leader)

            a)   The negative aspect of referent power is that the individuals who have it often seem prone to abuse it.

        4)   Coercive

            a)   A power rooted in the fear or threat of punishment.

        5)   Control of rewards

    b.   The greater the sources of power possessed by a manager, the more likely an employee will be inclined to accept his/her authority. In other words, a manager who has both formal and informal sources of power will be more influential than someone with only one source.

    c.   **Authority** is the **right** to manage others. Thus, it differs from power, the **ability** to accomplish something. A manager may have one without the other.

    d.   The dimensions of power include the ability to control others, act freely, or resist control by others.

    e.   The exercise of power affects the **decisions** made by employees, for example, as the result of advice offered by someone with expert power. It also affects **behavior**, for example, as the result of a warning from someone with coercive power. Moreover, the exercise of power affects **situations**, for example, a change in the nature or type of resources used in operations effected by someone with any base of power.

    f.   Modern management theory emphasizes **employee empowerment**. The question is not whether employees should be empowered but the circumstances in which it should occur.

        1)   Individuals need to be honest, trustworthy, unselfish, and skilled.

        2)   Empowerment is not synonymous with lack of control. Appropriate oversight is necessary.

        3)   Employees should have adequate training, relevant information, and other necessary tools.

        4)   Employees should participate fully in making important decisions.

        5)   Employees should be fairly compensated.

        6)   The paradox is that managers who appropriately surrender power by empowering employees actually gain power. They have an increased ability to achieve desired results.

4. **Behavior modification** is the management of environmental factors to encourage desirable behavior and to discourage undesirable behavior. Environmental factors include antecedents and consequences of behavior.

    a. **Antecedents** are cues that encourage but do not cause a given behavior. Managing antecedents involves eliminating barriers to good performance and replacing them with helpful aids.

        1) **Barriers** include unattainable objectives, poor training, confusing rules, and conflicting directions from management.

        2) **Aids** include challenging but attainable objectives, clear instructions, realistic plans, constructive suggestions, and acceptable work rules.

    b. **Consequences** include the following:

        1) **Positive reinforcement** provides rewards for certain responses. It focuses on desirable rather than undesirable behavior. Theorists regard positive reinforcement as the most effective approach.

            a) Examples are the awarding of merit-based salary bonuses or paying on a sliding scale relative to production.

            b) **Continuous reinforcement** rewards every occurrence of a desirable new behavior.

            c) **Intermittent reinforcement** provides occasional rewards for an established behavior. **Variable-interval schedules** of intermittent reinforcement lead to better performance. Employees are more alert because of the uncertainty involved, and performance and reward are connected. **Fixed-interval schedules** of reinforcement do not clearly link performance and reward.

        2) **Negative reinforcement** is the withdrawal of an existing unpleasant condition (such as a threat) when the desired behavior occurs.

        3) **Extinction** discourages a behavior by ignoring it (not reinforcing it).

        4) **Punishment** discourages a behavior by immediately following it with a negative consequence.

5. Stop and review! You have just completed the outline for this subunit. Study multiple-choice questions 1 through 12 beginning on page 213.

8.2 LEADERSHIP

1. Leadership is the act or process of influencing, inspiring, and guiding people so they will strive willingly toward the achievement of group objectives through common effort.

    a. **Formal leadership** pursues the organization's objectives, but **informal leadership** may pursue objectives at variance with the organization's.

        1) Formal (but not informal) leaders ordinarily have formal authority and legitimate power. However, both kinds of leaders may wield any of the other types of power.

        2) Informal leaders whose objectives are the same as (different from) those of the organization are assets (liabilities).

    b. The **classical position** focused on the idea that, although authority, decision making, and responsibility may all be decentralized to some extent, leadership is a characteristic of the individual's personality and cannot be subdivided.

c. The **traitist approach** attempts to identify traits possessed by leaders. It has produced such a long list of leadership traits that, in effect, it identifies nothing. Nevertheless, a few traits do seem to have significant correlation with a leader's effectiveness.

1) Intelligence
2) Scholarship
3) Dependability
4) Social participation and interest
5) Socioeconomic status (in comparison with nonleaders)

d. A more recent traitist approach is based on the **emotional intelligence** of leaders, that is, their social skills and judgment, maturity, and emotional control. These abilities can be learned, especially when a manager or employee understands that immaturity, erratic behavior, and uncontrolled negative emotions have a bad effect on the workplace. According to Daniel Goleman, a leader can acquire social capital through exhibiting the following **leadership traits**:

1) **Self-awareness** is knowing oneself.
2) **Self-management** is the ability to prevent one's mood swings from interfering with positive relationships.
3) **Social awareness** is understanding the actions and emotions of others. This ability helps a person to adapt in a productive way.
4) **Relationship management** is an ability possessed by a person who communicates and resolves conflict effectively. Humor and a benign approach are characteristics of people who develop good relationships.

e. Some writers have argued that men and women have different leadership traits. However, the research indicates male and female managers do not match the stereotypes (task orientation versus relationship orientation, respectively).

2. With so little useful guidance from the leader characteristics approach, behavior-oriented researchers examined **leader behavior** to determine whether leaders conduct themselves in certain ways.

a. **Styles of leadership** are emphasized in behavioral approaches. The personal background of the manager is also a determining factor, as are the personalities and backgrounds of the employees being supervised. These styles have been characterized as

1) **Authoritarian.** The manager dictates all decisions to the employees, so communication is downward. Moreover, tasks are clearly defined. This is considered the classical approach to leadership. Employees are not allowed to give input. Authoritarian leaders rely on threats and punishment and do not trust employees. However, such leadership can sometimes be the most effective, such as when there is limited time to make a decision or when employees do not respond to any other leadership style. Performance is on time and predictable.

2) **Democratic (participative).** The leader delegates substantial authority. Employees participate in defining and assigning tasks. Communication is actively upward as well as downward. Thus, employees are more committed.

3) **Laissez faire** (free rein). Employees in a group are given the authority and responsibility to make their own decisions. Communication is mostly horizontal. This style works best when employees show personal initiative, but the group also may flounder without the leader's guidance.

4) **Consultative.** The manager takes the employee's view into account but still makes the decisions.

5) **Bureaucratic**. A manager manages "by the book." Everything must be done according to procedure or policy. If there is no policy to cover a situation, the manager refers to the next level above himself. Bureaucratic leaders are essentially policemen rather than leaders. Bureaucratic leaders are sometimes necessary when employees are working with dangerous or highly delicate equipment or chemicals. Cash handling functions are sometimes policed by a bureaucratic leader.

    a) Management theoretician Max Weber argued that bureaucracy is essential in structuring governments and administrations. He viewed it as functional, efficient, and necessary for capitalism to be successful. Within the bureaucratic type there are specific rules and regulations for every goal. These rules must be followed by employees. Officials are subject to a hierarchy and fulfill their duties impersonally. Weber began by discussing how work is carried out within the bureaucratic organization. Activities for governing are official duties and are assigned by a set of rules that determine who will perform what specialized task. These are completed only by employees who have received the adequate education. In this manner, the functions become bureaucratic authority. Within the bureaucracy there exists labor hierarchy directed by more regulations. That is, there are levels of authority. Supervision by a higher official ensures that management remains orderly. Also, subordinate officials have the opportunity to appeal a decision to a higher authority.

b. According to a model developed at Ohio State University, two behavior patterns that are consistently found in the study of leadership are the **initiation of structure** and **consideration** by the leader (production-centered versus employee-centered behavior).

    1) Initiating structure behavior is directed towards accomplishing tasks. Structure includes

        a) Defining duties
        b) Establishing procedures
        c) Planning and organizing work

    2) Consideration behavior is the establishment of a personal relationship between the leader and the subordinate. High consideration by the leader includes

        a) Warmth toward the employee as a person
        b) Psychological support for the employee
        c) Helpfulness with problems in the work

    3) Both structure initiation and consideration behavior are present in all job situations. The relative amounts of each must be appropriate to the situation. For example,

        a) A highly structured situation (e.g., assembly-line work) may respond negatively to further structure initiated by the manager, but positively to increased consideration.

        b) A manager of R & D may find the initiation of structure much more productive than increased consideration. Creative personnel working on a disorganized project may find a better defined project plan much more satisfying than a demonstration of concern by the manager.

4) The following are the four leadership styles in the Ohio State model:

   a) **Low structure and consideration** indicates a passive leader.

   b) **Low structure and high consideration** results from an emphasis on satisfying employee needs.

   c) **High structure and low consideration** results from a primary focus on task accomplishment.

   d) **High structure and high consideration** reflect a strong emphasis on both task accomplishment and satisfying employee needs.

c. The **leadership grid** developed by Robert Blake and Jane Mouton is a trademarked classification scheme. **Concern for production** is on the horizontal axis, and **concern for people** is on the vertical axis.

   1) Concern for production emphasizes output, cost control, and profit.

   2) Concern for people emphasizes friendship, aiding employees in accomplishing tasks, and addressing employee issues (e.g., compensation).

   3) Each axis has a scale of 1 to 9. Thus, the primary styles are the following:

      a) **1,1**: Little concern for production or people (impoverished management)

      b) **1,9**: Primary concern for people, little concern for production (country club management)

      c) **9,1**: Primary concern for production, little concern for people (authority-compliance management)

      d) **5,5**: Moderate concern for production and people to maintain status quo (middle-of-the-road management)

      e) **9,9**: Great concern for production and people, trust, teamwork, and commitment (team management)

         i) Blake and his associates assert that the 9,9 style is best because it produces the best operating results, health outcomes, and conflict resolutions.

3. **Situational theories** of leadership argue that the appropriate style depends on the situation. The emphasis is on flexibility because no one leadership style is best in every situation.

   a. According to Fred E. Fiedler's **contingency theory**, people become leaders not only because of personality attributes, but also because of various situational factors and the interaction between the leaders and the situation.

      1) Thus, the right person at the right time may rise to a position of leadership if his/her personality and the needs of the situation complement each other. The same person might not become a leader in different circumstances because of failure to interact successfully with that situation.

      2) The contingency theory model has **three dimensions**:

         a) **Position power** is a function of the formal authority structure. It is the degree to which the position held enables a leader to evaluate, reward, punish, or promote the group members. It is independent of other sources of power, such as personality or expertise.

         b) **Task structure** is how clearly and carefully members' responsibilities for various tasks are defined. Quality of performance is more easily controlled when tasks are clearly defined.

         c) **Leader-member relations** reflect the extent to which group members like and trust and are willing to follow a leader.

3) The "least preferred coworker" test is one way to assess the leadership styles of individuals. It asks them to rank coworkers on 16 contrasting traits (e.g., efficient or inefficient) from least to most preferred. For example, if the least preferred coworker is described relatively favorably, the person doing the rating is likely to be primarily interested in a personal relationship.

4) Fiedler's research showed that leaders tend to be task-motivated or relationship-motivated.

   a) The **task-motivated style** is most effective when the situation is very favorable or very unfavorable.

      i) The situation is **very favorable** when the leader's position of power is high, tasks are well defined, and leader-member relations are good. The situation is **very unfavorable** when the reverse is true.

      ii) In the favorable situation, a leader has little need to address relationship issues and should therefore concentrate on the work. In the unfavorable situation, the leader must emphasize close supervision.

   b) The **relationship-motivated style** is most effective in the middle, less extreme situations when favorable and unfavorable factors are mixed.

5) The most effective leadership style is contingent upon the degree to which the three dimensions are present in a situation.

6) Leadership is therefore as much a responsibility of the organization's placement of leaders as it is of the leaders themselves. An organization should identify leadership situations and its managers' leadership styles and engineer the job to suit the manager if necessary.

b. According to Hersey and Blanchard's **situational leadership theory**, the appropriate leadership style depends on the followers' maturity, which is their degree of willingness to be responsible for directing their behavior. Four styles of leadership are described in a situational leadership model created by Paul Hersey and Ken Blanchard. Its dimensions are task and relationship behaviors.

1) **Selling.** A selling leadership style explains decisions and provides opportunity for clarification (high task and high relationship).

2) **Telling.** A telling leadership style provides specific instructions and closely supervises performance (high task and low relationship).

3) **Participating.** A participating leadership style encourages the sharing of ideas and facilitates decision making (low task and high relationship).

4) **Delegating.** A delegating leadership style turns over responsibility for decisions and implementation (low task and low relationship).

c. **Path-goal theory** emphasizes **motivation**. It combines the research on initiating structure and consideration with expectancy theory.

1) Leaders should motivate employees by clarifying employees' understanding of

   a) Work goals,

   b) The relationship of achievement of those goals with rewards that matter to employees, and

   c) How the goals may be achieved.

2) Leaders should increase payoffs, define the path to success, remove obstacles, and increase the chances of individual satisfaction while the path is being traveled.

3) According to path-goal theory, two groups of contingency factors affect the relationship between leadership behavior and the outcomes of employee performance and satisfaction.

    a) **Environmental factors** are those beyond employees' control (task structure, the formal authority system, and the work group).

    b) **Subordinate factors** include the employees' locus of control, experience, and perceived ability.

4) A leadership style should be chosen that complements but does not duplicate the factors in the environment and is consistent with employees' characteristics.

    a) The **directive** leader lets employees know what is expected of them, schedules work to be done, and gives specific guidance on how to accomplish tasks.

        i) A directive style is most effective when the employees are externally controlled, tasks are ambiguous or stressful, and substantial conflict exists in the work group. Thus, a directive style is appropriate when employees do not have high perceived ability or experience.

    b) The **supportive** leader is friendly and shows concern for the needs of the employees.

        i) The supportive style is best when tasks are highly structured and the authority relationships are clear and bureaucratic.

        ii) This approach depends on people who want to work, grow, and achieve.

        iii) The supportive style may be best when tasks are unsatisfying.

    c) The **participative** leader consults with employees and uses their suggestions before making a decision.

        i) The participative style is most useful when employees believe they control their own destinies, that is, when they have an internal locus of control. Such individuals may be resentful if they are not consulted.

    d) The **achievement-oriented** leader is a facilitator who sets challenging goals and expects employees to perform at their highest level.

        i) Achievement-oriented leadership is appropriate when tasks are nonrepetitive and ambiguous and employee competence is high.

5) In contrast with Fiedler's approach, path-goal theorists believe that managers are able to adapt their styles to the situation.

4. A **transformational leader** combines initiating structure and consideration with such other behaviors as charisma. The transformational leader is able to inspire the members of the organization to aspire to, and to achieve, more than they thought was possible.

    a. Transformational leadership emphasizes vision, development of the individual, empowerment of the worker, and the challenging of traditional assumptions.

    b. Transformational leaders articulate a vision, use nontraditional thinking, encourage individual development, provide workers with regular feedback, use participative decision-making, and promote a cooperative and trusting work environment.

c. The transformational leader normally has charisma, is inspirational, provides intellectual stimulation to workers, and gives individualized consideration.

d. A **transactional leader** emphasizes monitoring of employees so that they adhere to standards. Thus, the transactional leader ensures that expectations are met, but the transformational leader motivates employees to go beyond expectations.

5. Robert Greenleaf's philosophy of **servant leaders** is founded on the following principles:

a. They have an instinctive desire to serve others and must therefore consciously decide to become leaders.

b. They clearly define a vision (goals).

c. They are trusted by their followers.

d. They listen first.

e. They accept people, if not their performance.

f. They have intuitive foresight that allows them to make sound judgments.

g. They believe that every problem begins inside themselves. Thus, personal development is their focus.

6. **Mentoring** is systematic development of leadership by providing career counseling and social nurturing. According to Abraham Zalegnick, it requires intensive tutoring, coaching, and guidance.

a. Some organizations have formal mentoring programs that assign mentors to junior employees. However, some research indicates that a mentoring arrangement that occurs informally and voluntarily may have better results.

b. According to Kathy Kram's research, mentoring serves career and psychosocial functions.

1) **Career functions** include sponsorship, visibility, coaching, protection, and assigning challenges.

2) **Psychosocial functions** include role modeling, acceptance, confirmation, counseling, and friendship.

c. Mentors also may benefit from intrinsic pleasure in helping others to succeed or from gaining power by transferring values and skills to the people they mentor.

7. Stop and review! You have just completed the outline for this subunit. Study multiple-choice questions 13 through 37 beginning on page 217.

QUESTIONS

8.1 Influence and Power

1. A manager can use power and authority to accomplish objectives. The relationship between these two important concepts is best explained as follows:

A. Power is the right to do things, while authority is the ability to do things.

B. Authority is the right to do things, while power is the ability to do things.

C. Power and authority are both required to accomplish a task.

D. Power and authority are simply two words that describe the same concept -- how to get things done in organizations.

Answer (B) is correct. *(CIA, adapted)*
REQUIRED: The relationship between power and authority.
DISCUSSION: Authority is the officially sanctioned privilege to direct others. A clear hierarchy of authority enhances coordination and accountability. Power is the ability to marshal organizational resources to obtain results. A manager may have both authority and power, or one without the other.
Answer (A) is incorrect because authority is the right to do things, and power is the ability to do things. Answer (C) is incorrect because a manager may accomplish a task without having formal authority. Answer (D) is incorrect because authority is the right to do things, and power is the ability to do things.

2. A company's decisions are made solely by Ed Smith, the president and major shareholder. Which of the following powers is Smith least likely to have over the other shareholders to whom he has delegated some authority?

    A. Coercive power.

    B. Legitimate power.

    C. Referent power.

    D. Reward power.

Answer (C) is correct. *(Publisher)*
    REQUIRED: The power that Smith is least likely to have over the other shareholders.
    DISCUSSION: A person who is the head of a company may exert influence through five types of power. Referent power is the capacity for the individual's personality and style to cause others to identify with or like him/her.
    Answer (A) is incorrect because coercive power is the ability of the individual to make others cooperate by applying pressure. Answer (B) is incorrect because legitimate power is the leader's right to expect cooperation from others. Answer (D) is incorrect because reward power is the individual's ability to influence others through their expectation that good behavior will be rewarded.

3. Some behavioral models stress employee participation as a key to motivation. A limitation of the participative approach is

    A. Workers are intrinsically lazy and must be driven.

    B. A number of dissatisfiers must be present in order for the approach to work.

    C. It is difficult to elicit the participation of all employees.

    D. Unresolvable conflicts arise when a mature, capable, creative person joins a structured, demanding, and limiting organization.

Answer (C) is correct. *(CIA, adapted)*
    REQUIRED: The limitation of the participative approach.
    DISCUSSION: For a participative management approach to succeed, the parties must have sufficient time, the issues must be relevant to employees' interests, employees must have the abilities (training and communication skills) to participate, and the company culture should support participation. Accordingly, a limitation of the participative approach is that it is unlikely that all employees are willing to participate in decision making.
    Answer (A) is incorrect because the participative approach assumes that workers are positively motivated. Answer (B) is incorrect because the presence of dissatisfiers is not consistent with the participative approach. Answer (D) is incorrect because such conflicts arise when the needs of individuals are not integrated with the needs of the organization.

4. Which of the following is true concerning generic influence tactics?

    A. Consultation involves appealing to emotions, values, or ordeals.

    B. Ingratiating tactics attempt to raise the other person's self-esteem prior to a request.

    C. Coalition tactics try to convince others by reliance on a detailed plan, supporting evidence, and reason.

    D. Pressure tactics are based on the formal or informal support of higher management.

Answer (B) is correct. *(Publisher)*
    REQUIRED: The true statement concerning generic influence tactics.
    DISCUSSION: Management literature describes generic influence tactics that may be used in any direction. As noted by researchers, ingratiating tactics attempt to raise the other person's self-esteem prior to a request.
    Answer (A) is incorrect because consultation permits the other person to participate in the decision or change. Answer (C) is incorrect because coalition tactics seek the aid of others to persuade someone to agree. Answer (D) is incorrect because pressure tactics involve intimidation, threats, and demands.

5. Which of the following is not an example of positive reinforcement of behavior?

    A. Paying a bonus to employees who had no absences for any four-week period.

    B. Giving written warnings after only every other absence.

    C. Assigning a mentor to each employee.

    D. Having a lottery every month where 10% of the employees with no absences receive a $200 bonus.

Answer (B) is correct. *(CIA, adapted)*
    REQUIRED: The action not an example of positive reinforcement.
    DISCUSSION: Negative reinforcement removes an unpleasant condition when the desired behavior occurs, whereas positive reinforcement rewards the desired behavior. Thus, attending class is reinforced by the removal of something unpleasant, i.e., the receipt of a written warning. Because a warning is given after every other absence, the reinforcement is intermittent, not continuous.
    Answer (A) is incorrect because paying a bonus is a positive reinforcement. Answer (C) is incorrect because assigning a mentor is a positive reinforcement. The firm is attempting to link each individual with a positive role model. Answer (D) is incorrect because holding a lottery is an intermittent positive reinforcement.

6. The director of internal auditing for a large company has established an excellent reputation because of her strong professional credentials and tactful but firm handling of auditor-auditee relationships. With regard to auditees, she must rely upon what sources of power?

    A. Expert, coercive.

    B. Referent, reward.

    C. Referent, expert.

    D. Legitimate, coercive.

Answer (C) is correct. *(Publisher)*
    REQUIRED: The sources of power relied on by a particular manager.
    DISCUSSION: The internal audit director has no formal (legitimate or position) power over auditees. Nor does she have the power to coerce (punish) or reward them. Rather, her ability to exert power (influence others) must derive from her specialized ability and knowledge and the force of her personal qualities.
    Answer (A) is incorrect because she does not have the power to coerce others. Answer (B) is incorrect because she has no power to reward others. Answer (D) is incorrect because she does not have the power to coerce others.

7. The punishing of employees is made less effective by

    A. Stating the offending behavior specifically.

    B. Postponing the start of disciplinary procedures.

    C. Permitting employees to challenge their culpability.

    D. Focusing the discussion on the offending behavior instead of the offender.

Answer (B) is correct. *(CIA, adapted)*
    REQUIRED: The action that renders the discipline process less effective.
    DISCUSSION: Effective discipline requires immediate corrective action to eliminate the negative effects of the undesirable employee conduct and to establish and reinforce appropriate behavior. Delay merely invites more serious consequences. Moreover, the punishment should be commensurate with the offense, and the employee should clearly perceive the relationship between the punishment and the behavior.
    Answer (A) is incorrect because stating the undesirable behavior clarifies for the employee the link between conduct and consequences. Answer (C) is incorrect because, in U.S. legal culture, the accused has the right to be heard in his/her defense. Answer (D) is incorrect because focusing on the offense rather than the offender is less likely to engender fear and resentment on the part of the employee.

8. Power is synonymous with leadership. Simply, it is the ability to influence other people. The sources of power are various. For example, the kind of power arising from the strength of the leader's personality is known as

    A. Coercive power.

    B. Legitimate power.

    C. Expert power.

    D. Referent power.

Answer (D) is correct. *(Publisher)*
    REQUIRED: The kind of power arising from the strength of the leader's personality.
    DISCUSSION: Power may be classified as reward power (the leader controls resources), coercive power (the leader may punish the subordinate), legitimate power (the leader has the right to lead), referent power (the leader has fame, charisma, etc.), and expert power (the leader has specialized ability or knowledge).

9. A leader who is able to gain compliance from a group based solely on personal attraction is said to have

    A. Reward power.

    B. Coercive power.

    C. Referent power.

    D. Legitimate power.

Answer (C) is correct. *(CIA, adapted)*
    REQUIRED: The type of power held by a leader who uses personal attraction to gain compliance from a group.
    DISCUSSION: Referent power is based on identification of subordinates with a superior. Thus, personal magnetism (charisma) may be a basis for influencing others to comply with a manager's directives.
    Answer (A) is incorrect because reward power is based on a person's ability to grant benefits. Answer (B) is incorrect because coercive power is rooted in the fear or threat of punishment. Answer (D) is incorrect because legitimate power is based on a person's superior position.

10. A manager believes that positive reinforcement is the most appropriate way to deal with employees. Which of the following actions demonstrates the principle of positive reinforcement?

    A. Employees are given 2-day suspension without pay if errors exceed a predefined level.

    B. Employees are praised when the detected error rate in their work stays below a predefined level.

    C. Time budgets, which have forced employees to rush and consequently make errors, are eliminated.

    D. Employees are not required to work overtime if errors stay below a predefined level.

Answer (B) is correct. *(CIA, adapted)*
    REQUIRED: The action that demonstrates positive reinforcement.
    DISCUSSION: Positive reinforcement is a behavior modification technique that provides rewards for certain responses. It focuses on desirable rather than undesirable behavior. The practice of praising employees when the detected error rate in their work stays below a predefined level demonstrates positive reinforcement.
    Answer (A) is incorrect because suspending employees is punishment. Answer (C) is incorrect because eliminating time budgets is extinction, which is the elimination of reinforcement that is maintaining a behavior. Answer (D) is incorrect because not requiring employees to work overtime is negative reinforcement, which is the elimination of something unpleasant when a desired behavior occurs.

11. When supervising employees, the behavior most likely to attain long-term positive results for a manager would be to

    A. Discipline employees immediately using oral reprimands, written warnings, and temporary suspensions.

    B. Hold weekly meetings during which employees are reminded of work procedures and are praised for the week's accomplishments.

    C. Praise employees on a random schedule and link rewards to performance.

    D. Tell employees that working overtime now will result in a better performance review in 6 months.

Answer (C) is correct. *(CIA, adapted)*
    REQUIRED: The supervisory behavior most likely to have long-term positive results.
    DISCUSSION: Variable-interval schedules of reinforcement lead to higher performance. Employees are more alert because of the uncertainty involved, and performance and reward are connected.
    Answer (A) is incorrect because punishment only leads to short-term suppression of the behavior and may cause the staff member to avoid the manager, who is seen as punishing rather than helpful. Answer (B) is incorrect because fixed-interval reinforcement schedules do not clearly link performance and rewards. Answer (D) is incorrect because 6 months is too long an interval for linking performance and reward.

12. A production worker in a plant often speaks for the entire work force when problems arise between labor and management. Although this individual has the same level of authority and expertise as his/her co-workers, the worker seems to possess a degree of power that others do not have. What type of power does this individual apparently have?

    A. Coercive.

    B. Referent.

    C. Legitimate.

    D. Reward.

Answer (B) is correct. *(CIA, adapted)*
    REQUIRED: The type of power held by a worker who leads fellow workers despite having no advantage in expertise or authority.
    DISCUSSION: Referent power is based on identification of subordinates with a superior. Thus, personal magnetism (charisma) may be a basis for influencing others to comply with a manager's directives.
    Answer (A) is incorrect because coercive power is rooted in fear or threat of punishment. Answer (C) is incorrect because legitimate power is based on formal authority or the organizational position held by a leader. Answer (D) is incorrect because reward power is based on a person's ability to grant benefits.

8.2 Leadership

13. According to the contingency theory of leadership, a manager will be most effective when (s)he

   A. Consistently initiates structure.

   B. Adapts his/her style to specific circumstances.

   C. Is task-oriented.

   D. Is relationship-oriented.

Answer (B) is correct. *(Publisher)*

REQUIRED: The most effective management approach according to contingency theory.

DISCUSSION: Fred E. Fiedler's contingency theory of management holds that no single style of directing is best for all occasions. A successful director (leader) must, for each situation, balance his/her formal authority, the task structure, and the leader's relationships with the pertinent group members.

Answer (A) is incorrect because a relationship (employee)-oriented approach may be preferable when tasks are highly structured. Answer (C) is incorrect because a relationship (employee)-oriented approach may be preferable when tasks are highly structured. Answer (D) is incorrect because, when tasks are ill-defined, the more effective manager may be one who concentrates on defining and organizing the jobs to be done rather than on motivating employees.

14. Which of the following leadership types is best known as an agent of change?

   A. Participative leader.

   B. Traitist leader.

   C. Transformational leader.

   D. Free-rein leader.

Answer (C) is correct. *(Publisher)*

REQUIRED: The leadership style that is best used when an agent of change is needed.

DISCUSSION: A transformational leader is an agent of change who attempts to inspire the members of the organization to aspire to, and to achieve, more than they thought was possible. Transformational leadership emphasizes vision, development of the individual, empowerment of the worker, and the challenging of traditional assumptions. The transformational leader normally has charisma, is motivational, provides intellectual stimulation to workers, and gives individualized consideration.

Answer (A) is incorrect because a participative leader is simply one who allows employees to have input into the decision making process. Answer (B) is incorrect because "traitist leader" is essentially a nonsense term as used here; the traitist approach was a field of study that attempted to identify the traits possessed by leaders. Answer (D) is incorrect because a free-rein leader is one who allows employees to make their own decisions.

15. Which of the following is true regarding the most recent traitist approach to leadership?

   A. It attempts to identify traits possessed by leaders.

   B. It has produced such a long list of leadership traits that, in effect, it identifies nothing.

   C. It is based on scholarship, dependability, and social participation.

   D. It is based on social skills, judgment, maturity, and emotional control.

Answer (D) is correct. *(Publisher)*

REQUIRED: The true statement regarding the most recent approach to traitist leadership.

DISCUSSION: The most recent traitist approach is based on the emotional intelligence of leaders, that is, their social skills and judgment, maturity, and emotional control. These abilities can be learned, especially when a manager or employee understands that immaturity, erratic behavior, and uncontrolled negative emotions have a bad effect on the workplace.

16. Leadership situations vary with regard to the degree to which the leader can determine what subordinates will do, how they will do it, and what the results will be. According to Fiedler's contingency theory, a leader with a relationship-oriented management style will be most effective when (s)he exerts

   A. Great control.

   B. Moderate control.

   C. Little control.

   D. Great or little control.

Answer (B) is correct. *(Publisher)*
   REQUIRED: The situation in which a relationship-oriented management style will be most effective.
   DISCUSSION: A relationship-oriented manager is employee centered. His/her self-esteem is strongly affected by personal interactions with subordinates. Fiedler indicated that such a manager is most effective when not faced with the extremes of high or low control situations. High control follows from strong position power, a structured task, and good leader-member relations. A low control situation has just the opposite characteristics. In a high-control environment, a concern for personal relations may be unimportant. In a low-control situation, the relationship-oriented leader may be unable to provide the needed task structuring. Thus, the moderate control situation is best. An example is an assembly-line situation (a structured task) in which leader-member relations are poor.

17. Of the following, the most important for success as a project manager is

   A. Budgeting and accounting knowledge.

   B. People management skills, such as conflict resolution and negotiation.

   C. Statistical analysis and process design experience.

   D. Strategic management tools and training.

Answer (B) is correct. *(Publisher)*
   REQUIRED: The most important item for success as a project manager.
   DISCUSSION: Projects are outside the normal organizational hierarchy or chain of command, so a project leader cannot rely on direct authority to accomplish what must be done by the various parts of an organization that are participating in a project.
   Answer (A) is incorrect because projects are ad hoc and temporary, and most challenges involve people and technical/technology issues. Answer (C) is incorrect because statistical analysis and process design are skills that, if necessary in a project, would be employed by a subordinate, not the project manager. Answer (D) is incorrect because strategic management is long-term, broad-based, and starts with relatively few constraints other than existing resources organization-wide, while project management is shorter-term and focused on a project that has been approved with specific resources.

18. If a supervisor uses a supportive management approach, evidenced by positive feelings and concern for subordinates, a problem might result because

   A. An approach based on pure power makes it difficult to motivate staff.

   B. This approach depends on material rewards for the worker.

   C. This approach depends on people who want to work, grow, and achieve.

   D. The manager must believe in the teamwork approach.

Answer (C) is correct. *(CIA, adapted)*
   REQUIRED: The problem that could result from using a supportive management approach.
   DISCUSSION: Supportive management techniques orient workers toward performance rather than obedience or happiness. The leader should have positive feelings for his/her employees and should attempt to encourage participation and involvement. This approach is effective when used with employees who are motivated to work, improve themselves and their abilities, and accomplish goals.
   Answer (A) is incorrect because an approach based on pure power is an autocratic style of leadership, not a supportive approach. Answer (B) is incorrect because the custodial model depends on material rewards for the worker. This model is predicated on the belief that a happy worker is a productive worker. Answer (D) is incorrect because the manager's beliefs are not sufficient. The workers must also believe in the system.

19. Which of the following statements is true regarding leadership styles?

   A. The manager dictates all decisions to the employees, so communication is downward and tasks are clearly defined in authoritarian leadership.

   B. Employees in a group are given the authority and responsibility to make their own decisions in democratic leadership.

   C. The leader delegates substantial authority and employees participate in defining and assigning tasks in laissez faire leadership.

   D. None of the answers are correct.

Answer (A) is correct. *(Publisher)*
   REQUIRED: The true statement regarding leadership styles.
   DISCUSSION: When a manager uses an authoritarian leadership style, he/she dictates all decisions to the employees, so communication is downward. Moreover, tasks are clearly defined. This is considered the classical approach to leadership. Employees are not allowed to give input.
   Answer (B) is incorrect because the leader delegates substantial authority in democratic leadership. In addition, employees participate in defining and assigning tasks. Therefore, communication is actively upward as well as downward. Answer (C) is incorrect because employees in a group are given the authority and responsibility to make their own decisions in laissez faire leadership. Answer (D) is incorrect because one of the answer choices is correct.

Questions 20 through 23 are based on the following information.

The following question presents a scenario in which a manager needs to decide what leadership style to use to obtain employee satisfaction and effective employee performance. For the purposes of this question, the manager has a choice of four styles.

- The <u>directive</u> leader lets subordinates know what is expected of them, schedules work to be done, and gives specific guidance on how to accomplish tasks.
- The <u>supportive</u> leader is friendly and shows concern for the needs of the subordinates.
- The <u>participative</u> leader consults with subordinates and uses their suggestions before making a decision.
- The <u>achievement-oriented</u> leader sets challenging goals and expects subordinates to perform at their highest level.

20. The manager of a team of actuaries has been asked to develop the basic pricing structure for a new health insurance product. The team has successfully designed other pricing structures in recent years. The manager was assigned to the team 6 months ago. What is the best leadership style for the manager of this team?

    A. Directive.

    B. Supportive.

    C. Participative.

    D. Achievement-oriented.

Answer (C) is correct. *(CIA, adapted)*
REQUIRED: The best leadership style for a new manager of a team that has successfully completed similar projects.
DISCUSSION: Participative style is most useful when subordinates believe they control their own destinies, that is, when they have an internal locus of control. Such individuals may be resentful if they are not consulted.
Answer (A) is incorrect because directive leadership provides highest subordinate satisfaction when a team encounters substantive internal conflict, when tasks are ambiguous, and when subordinates' locus of control is external. Answer (B) is incorrect because supportive style is best when tasks are highly structured and the authority relationships are clear and bureaucratic. Answer (D) is incorrect because achievement-oriented style will increase subordinates' expectations that high performance will result from their best efforts.

21. The workers in a factory have been told that their machines are obsolete and will be replaced by new, computer-assisted machines. The workers must be retrained and are eager to learn everything about the new machines. The manager was recently hired from a company where the new machines were extensively used and is very familiar with them. In this case, what is the best leadership style for the manager?

    A. Directive.

    B. Supportive.

    C. Participative.

    D. Achievement-oriented.

Answer (A) is correct. *(CIA, adapted)*
REQUIRED: The best leadership style for the manager when workers must be retrained and are eager to learn.
DISCUSSION: According to path-goal theory, two groups of contingency factors affect the relationship between leadership behavior and outcomes (performance and satisfaction): environmental factors beyond subordinates' control (task structure, the formal authority system, and the work group) and subordinate factors. The latter include the subordinate's locus of control, experience, and perceived ability. A leadership style should be chosen that complements but does not duplicate the factors in the environment and is consistent with subordinates' characteristics. A directive style is most effective when the subordinate's locus of control is external, tasks are ambiguous or stressful, and substantial conflict exists in the work group. Thus, a directive style is appropriate when subordinates do not have high perceived ability or experience.
Answer (B) is incorrect because subordinates who are neither competent nor confident are best led using the directive style. Answer (C) is incorrect because subordinates with an internal locus of control need a leader with a participative style. Answer (D) is incorrect because achievement-oriented leadership is appropriate when tasks are nonrepetitive and ambiguous and employee competence is high.

22. Refer to the information preceding question 20. A production team has been together for several years and has worked well together. However, severe arguments have recently occurred between two members of the group, and other members have begun to take sides. This problem has had a negative effect on production performance. The best leadership style for the manager in this situation is

- A. Directive.
- B. Supportive.
- C. Participative.
- D. Achievement-oriented.

Answer (A) is correct. *(CIA, adapted)*
REQUIRED: The best leadership style for the manager given substantive internal conflict.
DISCUSSION: Directive leadership provides highest subordinate satisfaction when a team encounters substantive internal conflict. Thus, directive leadership is the appropriate complement to the environmental factors. The leader should intervene to compensate for the stress and strife in the workplace.
Answer (B) is incorrect because supportive style is best when tasks and authority relationships are highly structured. Answer (C) is incorrect because participative style is most useful when subordinates believe they control their own destinies. Answer (D) is incorrect because achievement-oriented leadership is appropriate when tasks are nonrepetitive and ambiguous and employee competence is high.

23. Refer to the information preceding question 20. A manager in a government agency supervises a section of clerical employees who review license applications for approval or denial. The clerical jobs are well defined procedurally and are covered by government regulations. In this case, what is the best leadership style for the manager?

- A. Directive.
- B. Supportive.
- C. Participative.
- D. Achievement-oriented.

Answer (B) is correct. *(CIA, adapted)*
REQUIRED: The best leadership style for the manager of clerical workers.
DISCUSSION: A supportive style is best when tasks are highly structured and the authority relationships are clear and bureaucratic. This approach depends on people who want to work, grow, and achieve. The supportive style may be best when tasks are unsatisfying.
Answer (A) is incorrect because a directive style is most effective when the employees' locus of control is external, tasks are ambiguous or stressful, and substantial conflict exists in the work group. Thus, a directive style is appropriate when employees do not have high perceived ability or experience. Answer (C) is incorrect because a participative style is most useful when subordinates believe they control their own destinies. Answer (D) is incorrect because achievement-oriented leadership is appropriate when tasks are nonrepetitive and ambiguous and employee competence is high.

24. A leader who explains decisions and provides opportunity for clarification is described as having which leadership style?

- A. Selling.
- B. Telling.
- C. Participating.
- D. Delegating.

Answer (A) is correct. *(IIA, adapted)*
REQUIRED: The leadership style that includes explaining decisions and providing an opportunity for clarification.
DISCUSSION: According to Hersey and Blanchard, a selling style of leadership provides a high degree of task orientation and a high degree of relationship orientation. This type of leader explains decisions and provides opportunities for clarification. Thus, upward and downward, two-way communication is active. This approach is more democratic than authoritarian.
Answer (B) is incorrect because a telling leadership style (high task and low relationship) provides specific instructions and closely supervises performance. Answer (C) is incorrect because a participating leadership style (low task and high relationship) encourages the sharing of ideas and facilitates decision-making. Answer (D) is incorrect because a delegating leadership style (low task and low relationship) turns over responsibility for decisions and implementation.

25. An Internal Audit Department adopts a training posture that provides training to management on fraud awareness including an overview of the corporate fraud policy and hotline. This training posture best demonstrates that the Internal Audit Department is taking which of the four leadership roles?

A. Pathfinding which focuses on "What is our purpose and how will we achieve it?"

B. Aligning which focuses on "How do we align systems and processes to achieve our purpose?"

C. Empowering which focuses on "How do we cultivate our people to have the right authority, responsibility, and commitment to help us best achieve our purpose?"

D. Modeling which focuses on "How do we demonstrate the values to convince others to follow us and take responsibility for achieving our purpose?"

Answer (C) is correct. *(Publisher)*
REQUIRED: The leadership role that best demonstrates the training posture.
DISCUSSION: Empowering is the best answer because fraud awareness training as noted in the question provides individuals with the information and guidance they need to take responsibility and commit to tasks required to achieve a purpose. Fraud awareness training makes sure they know policy and how to report suspected issues.
Answer (A) is incorrect because pathfinding addresses establishment of purpose, or mission and vision. Answer (B) is incorrect because, while fraud awareness could be deemed part of the alignment process, it is not the best answer because it is only one component of an overall fraud program. Answer (D) is incorrect because modeling addresses the values established to be followed by subordinates.

26. Which of the following constitute initiating structure behavior?

I. Defining duties.
II. Planning and organizing work.
III. Helping with problems in the work.

A. I and II only.

B. I and III only.

C. II and III only.

D. I, II, and III.

Answer (A) is correct. *(Publisher)*
REQUIRED: The definition of initiating structure behavior.
DISCUSSION: Initiating structure behavior is directed towards accomplishing tasks. Structure includes defining duties, establishing procedures, planning and organizing work. Consideration on the other hand, is the establishment of a personal relationship between the leader and the subordinate. High consideration by the leader includes warmth towards the employee as a person, psychological support for the employee, and helpfulness with problems in the work.
Answer (B) is incorrect because helping with problems in the work is consideration behavior. Answer (C) is incorrect because helping with problems in the work is consideration behavior. Answer (D) is incorrect because helping with problems in the work is consideration behavior.

27. A production team has been together for several years and has worked well together. However, severe arguments have recently occurred between two members of the group, and other members have begun to take sides. This problem has had a negative effect on production performance. The best leadership style for the manager in this situation is

A. Directive.

B. Supportive.

C. Participative.

D. Achievement-oriented.

Answer (A) is correct. *(Publisher)*
REQUIRED: The leadership style that prevents a negative effect on production performance.
DISCUSSION: The directive leader lets employees know what is expected of them, schedules work to be done, and gives specific guidance on how to accomplish tasks.
Answer (B) is incorrect because the supportive leader is friendly and shows concern for the needs of the employees. Answer (C) is incorrect because the participative leader consults with employees and uses their suggestions before making a decision. Answer (D) is incorrect because the achievement-oriented leader is a facilitator who sets challenging goals and expects employees to perform at their highest level.

28. A manager implementing the directive leader approach should

A. Closely supervise each employee.

B. Display confidence in each employee's ability.

C. Work with the employee when developing goals.

D. Clearly signal that the employee is expected to be successful.

Answer (A) is correct. *(Publisher)*
REQUIRED: The action that should be taken by a manager using the directive leader approach.
DISCUSSION: The situational approach to leadership (called path-goal theory) allows a manager to choose one of four approaches for implementing his/her leadership style. One of these is the best directive leader approach in which a manager provides close guidance to the employee through the use of specific rules, policies, and procedures.

29. Which of the following is true regarding Fiedler's studies of contingency theory?

A. The three dimensions to contingency theory are position power, task structure, and relationship structure.

B. The two types of leaders that emerged from his studies include task-oriented style and leader-member style.

C. Placement of leaders in the organization is not as important as their leadership skills.

D. People become leaders not only because of personality attributes, but also because of various situational factors and the interaction between the leaders and the situation.

Answer (D) is correct. *(Publisher)*
REQUIRED: The true statement concerning Fiedler's studies of contingency theory.
DISCUSSION: According to Fred E. Fiedler's contingency theory, people become leaders not only because of personality attributes, but also because of various situational factors and the interaction between the leaders and the situation. Thus, the right person at the right time may rise to a position of leadership if his/her personality and the needs of the situation complement each other.
Answer (A) is incorrect because the three dimensions to contingency theory are position power, task structure, and leader-member relations. Answer (B) is incorrect because the two types of leaders that emerged from Fiedler's studies are task-oriented style and relationship-oriented style. Answer (C) is incorrect because leadership is as much a responsibility of the organization's placement of leaders as it is of the leaders themselves.

30. Which of the following is a benefit of implementing the achievement-oriented leader approach rather than the directive leader approach?

A. Employee development is enhanced.

B. The structured environment allows employees to better achieve the organization's goals.

C. Closer supervision is provided for those who perform better in a structured work atmosphere.

D. Employees have more opportunities to develop creativity and meet challenges.

Answer (D) is correct. *(Publisher)*
REQUIRED: The benefit of using the achievement-oriented leader approach.
DISCUSSION: The benefits to the company of the achievement-oriented leader approach include greater employee confidence and commitment, more employee decision making, increased employee creativity, more challenging objectives, and reduced supervision for employees who work best independently.
Answer (A) is incorrect because employee development is also enhanced under the directive leader approach. Answer (B) is incorrect because this benefit results from the directive leader approach. A structured environment is not a characteristic of the achievement-oriented leader approach. Answer (C) is incorrect because this benefit results from the directive leader approach. Close supervision is not a characteristic of the achievement-oriented leader approach.

31. Which of the following is not a factor to consider when assessing readiness for change in an organization?

A. Benefit and risk.

B. Avoiding mistakes.

C. Speed of implementation.

D. Impact on people.

Answer (B) is correct. *(Publisher)*
REQUIRED: The factor that is not considered when assessing readiness for change in an organization.
DISCUSSION: This is a factor in the implementation of change.
Answer (A) is incorrect because the level of uncertainty to anticipated benefits is an important indicator of readiness for change. Answer (C) is incorrect because the speed of obtaining results is an important indicator of readiness for change. Answer (D) is incorrect because the impact on employees and customers is an important indicator of readiness for change.

32. Rupert is a manager who believes that his department's most valuable resource is the employees' time. He enforces a set of rigid rules for employees. A characteristic of this leadership style is that

A. Employees are encouraged to participate in decision making.

B. Personal interaction among employees is limited.

C. Organizational objectives are coordinated with each employee's goals.

D. The manager's perceptions are similar to McGregor's Theory Y.

Answer (B) is correct. *(Publisher)*
REQUIRED: The characteristic of a leadership style based on the importance of time and a set of rigid rules.
DISCUSSION: The characteristics of a leadership style based on deadlines and strict rules include an emphasis on relatively inflexible congruence with the organization's overall goals, perceptions related to McGregor's Theory X, and limitations on interaction and communication among employees.
Answer (A) is incorrect because employee participation is decreased by this leadership style. Answer (C) is incorrect because organizational goals are strongly emphasized, whereas individual employee goals are de-emphasized. Answer (D) is incorrect because Theory Y is optimistic about employees' motivation, ability, and self-discipline. In this situation, the manager's perceptions are similar to Theory X, which suggests that employees dislike work and need constant direction or coercion.

33. Using the leadership grid developed by Robert Blake and Jane Mouton where each axis has a scale of 1 to 9, a primary style of 9, 9 would indicate

A. Little concern for production or people (impoverished management).

B. Moderate concern for production and people to maintain status quo (middle-of-the-road management).

C. Great concern for production and people, trust, teamwork, and commitment (team management).

D. Primary concern for production, little concern for people (authority-compliance management).

Answer (C) is correct.   *(Publisher)*
REQUIRED: The true statement concerning the leadership grid.
DISCUSSION: A primary style that rates 9, 9 on a scale of 1 to 9 indicates that it is at a maximum on both axes. Thus, there is great concern for production and great concern for people. This leadership style would emphasize output, cost control, and profit in addition to friendship, aiding employees, and addressing employee issues.
Answer (A) is incorrect because little concern for production or people would be equivalent to 1, 1 on the leadership grid. Answer (B) is incorrect because moderate concern for production and people to maintain status quo would be equivalent to a 5, 5 on the leadership grid. Answer (D) is incorrect because primary concern for production with little concern for people would be equivalent to a 9, 1 on the leadership grid.

34. A staff auditor is technically outstanding and works well with audit clients, but is not good at leading an audit team. To improve the auditor's performance, the auditor should be

A. Put in charge of the biggest project; the only way to learn is by performing the task.

B. Put in charge of small projects with set milestones and a fully trained staff.

C. Sent to school for management theory classes.

D. Left alone and given assignments that accentuate personal strengths and avoid personal weaknesses.

Answer (B) is correct.   *(Publisher)*
REQUIRED: The method for improving an auditor's performance.
DISCUSSION: The auditor can learn to lead small teams which will in turn prepare him/her to lead larger projects.
Answer (A) is incorrect because the auditor cannot start with the biggest project since (s)he lacks leadership experience. Answer (C) is incorrect because theory classes do not change the leadership style of an auditor. Answer (D) is incorrect because leaving the auditor alone does not promote leadership nor give the auditor the chance to become a successful leader.

35. Marianne is a manager who believes that positive employee attitudes are extremely important. She cooperates with employees in solving problems. A likely effect on employee behavior of this leadership style is

A. Mistrust of the manager.

B. A lack of extraordinary performance.

C. High employee turnover.

D. Increased employee creativity.

Answer (D) is correct.   *(Publisher)*
REQUIRED: The effect on employee behavior most likely to result from the described leadership style.
DISCUSSION: When a manager works to maintain a positive attitude among employees and cooperates with them in problem solving, employees are likely to be more motivated, confident, and creative. This leadership style should also improve communication and decrease absenteeism.

36. Which of the following is false regarding transformational leadership?

A. Transformational leadership emphasizes vision, development of the individual, empowerment of the worker, and the challenging of traditional assumptions.

B. Transformational leaders use traditional thinking to monitor employees so that they adhere to standards.

C. Transformational leaders have charisma and provide intellectual stimulation to the workers.

D. Transformational leaders expect employees to achieve more than they thought was possible.

Answer (B) is correct.   *(Publisher)*
REQUIRED: The false statement regarding transformational leadership.
DISCUSSION: Transformational leaders have charisma and provide intellectual stimulation to the workers. In addition they will emphasize vision, focus on development of the individual, empowerment of the worker, and the challenging of traditional assumptions. A transactional leader, on the other hand, would monitor employees to ensure that they adhered to standards.

37. Leadership styles differ depending upon the personality type of the individual leader. A risk averse leader will generally

    A. Make decisions more slowly.

    B. Require less information than a risk taker.

    C. Maintain status differences between themselves and others.

    D. Work well in participative efforts where joint responsibility is assumed by several people.

Answer (A) is correct. *(Publisher)*
    REQUIRED: The trait generally attributed to a risk averse leader.
    DISCUSSION: A risk averse leader will avoid risky situations, make decisions more slowly, and seek more information than a person who is described as a risk taker.
    Answer (B) is incorrect because a risk averse person requires more information than a risk taker. Answer (C) is incorrect because the maintenance of status differences is an aspect of authoritativeness, not of risk aversion. Answer (D) is incorrect because less authoritative individuals work well in participative efforts; this is not related to risk aversion.

Use Gleim's *CIA Test Prep* for interactive testing with over 2,000 additional multiple-choice questions!

STUDY UNIT NINE
TIME MANAGEMENT

(9 pages of outline)

This study unit begins with a discussion of how an individual manager may improve his/her mastery of daily workflow by applying time management skills. It continues with a subunit on automated workflow management. The study unit concludes with a detailed presentation on project planning techniques.

9.1 TIME MANAGEMENT SKILLS

1.   To function effectively, managers must learn to manage time properly. The **key principle** is to focus on results rather than on staying busy.

   a.   This idea is reflected in **Pareto analysis** (named for an Italian economist). It states the **80:20 rule**, which argues that typically 80% of unfocused effort generates only 20% of results. Thus, a manager needs to concentrate time and energy on the tasks with the highest payoffs or the most benefit.

   b.   Time management is actually self management. The skills needed to manage others are the same: the ability to plan, delegate, organize, direct, and control.

   c.   Time management does require self-discipline and control until it becomes an everyday habit. Plans and schedules for managing time are useless if one does not follow them.

2.   The following are **common techniques for effective time management**:

   a.   **Finding out how much time is worth**. A manager should calculate how much money (s)he costs the organization each year, including salary, office space, equipment, facilities, and taxes. After adding to that amount (a negative) the annual expected profit (a positive) to be generated by the manager, the total should be divided by the annual hours expected to be worked. The result is the manager's **hourly worth** to the organization.

      1)   If the net benefit of the manager's performing a task is less than this amount, it should be delegated to an assistant whose time is less costly.

      2)   A manager can free up considerable time by appropriate delegation.

   b.   **Prioritizing work**. One technique is for the manager to concentrate on the things that (s)he enjoys. The result should be better quality work.

      1)   A second method is for the manager to concentrate on tasks most closely related to his/her strengths.

      2)   A third method is for the manager to determine how (s)he is being evaluated and to prioritize tasks accordingly. This approach requires the manager to pose certain questions, for example,

         a)   What is the purpose of this job?
         b)   What are the measures of success?
         c)   What are the deadlines?
         d)   What are the resources available?

    c.   **Keeping an activity log for about a week**. The log should be an accurate record of how long is spent doing different tasks. Most people are surprised at how much time they waste on unproductive activities such as talking to colleagues or making coffee. Thus, the log raises awareness and promotes avoidance of time-wasting behavior.

        1)   The log also helps a manager determine when during the day (s)he is the most (least) productive. Identifying the pattern of productivity permits managers to schedule the most important tasks when they are at their best.

    d.   **Developing an action plan**. This tool requires listing all the tasks that need to be performed to achieve a goal.

        1)   It is not a to-do list, which focuses on different tasks that need to be done during the day. An action plan focuses on a single goal. During any given day, a manager may follow several action plans to achieve multiple short-term goals.

    e.   **Creating a prioritized to-do list**. This tool is best used when a manager has many different, unrelated tasks to perform during the day. It consists of all the tasks completed during a day ranked according to their importance.

        1)   A manager should start with the most important task and finish with the least important.

    f.   **Learning to say "NO."** This tool is often overlooked but can save a lot of time. People may make offers that are not part of the daily plan and will not help the manager to complete any necessary tasks. In these circumstances, the manager must learn to politely say no.

3.   Stop and review! You have completed the outline for this subunit. Study multiple-choice questions 1 through 4 beginning on page 233.

9.2 WORKFLOW MANAGEMENT

1.   Workflow is the automation of a part or of a whole business process.

2.   A **workflow management system** defines, manages, and executes workflows by using computer software that has been programmed for the organization's workflow logic. It should distribute the work in an efficient manner to achieve an organizational goal. All workflow management systems have common features:

    a.   **Process definition**. A business process is translated into a formal, computer processable definition using a process definition tool.

    b.   **Workflow management control software**. This component is used to create and delete processes, add activities to user worklists within the operational process, and control interaction between workers and IT application tools.

    c.   **Human interaction with the control software**. Any human interaction that occurs in the business process must be capable of being entered into the control software. This software can also facilitate the efforts of workers and managers by allowing them to access relevant information or IT application tools.

    d.   **The ability to distribute tasks and information**. This can be accomplished in a variety of ways, such as electronic mail or message passing. It may also involve transferring information between different vendors on separate subnetworks.

3. Workflow management systems can be implemented to fit a wide variety of scenarios. The following are some of their key benefits:

   a. A more efficient business process as a result of being able to eliminate unnecessary steps,

   b. Improved control over the business process as a result of standardized work methods and easily traceable audit trails,

   c. More flexibility as a result of having processes controlled by software that can be changed to meet the needs of customers, and

   d. Better customer service due to a more consistent business process that allows for more predictable responses to customers.

4. Stop and review! You have completed the outline for this subunit. Study multiple-choice questions 5 through 8 beginning on page 234.

9.3 PROJECT MANAGEMENT TECHNIQUES

1. Project management techniques are designed to aid the planning and control of large-scale projects having many interrelated activities. They have increased in importance as organizations have become more project-centered. Because of rapid technological change, organizations must reduce project times to be competitive. The most important characteristic for success as a project manager is people management skills, such as conflict resolution and negotiation.

   a. A **project** is a temporary undertaking with specified objectives. It often requires that a cross-functional team work outside customary organizational lines under a deadline. Hence, interpersonal skills are at a premium in project management. A manager may not have line authority over some team members.

   b. The **project life cycle** consists of

      1) **Conceptualization** (setting overall objectives, budgets, and schedules)
      2) **Planning** (obtaining resources, assigning duties, and coordinating activities)
      3) **Execution** (monitoring, correcting, meeting expectations, and finishing the project within time and budgetary limits)

         a) Most resources are used during this stage.

      4) **Termination** (turning the project over to the user and redistributing project resources)

   c. **Project management software** should be flexible and transparent so as to provide timely reports of all the key components of a project. Among other things, it should

      1) Specify and schedule required activities.
      2) Perform sensitivity analysis of the effects of changes in plans.
      3) Calculate a project's critical path.
      4) Establish priorities.
      5) Be able to modify or merge plans.
      6) Manage all types of project resources.
      7) Monitor progress, including adherence to time budgets for activities.

   d. Example applications

      1) Building construction
      2) Research and development projects
      3) New product planning
      4) Feasibility studies
      5) Audit studies
      6) Movie production
      7) Conversion to a new computer information system

    e.   Project planning has unique characteristics.

        1)   Results, including meeting deadlines and making quick decisions, are more important than adherence to a process.

        2)   Overall objectives must be kept in view even when attending to daily, routine matters and coping with numerous distractions.

        3)   Sufficient resources, including time, should be allocated to planning despite the pressure for results.

        4)   The deadline is a strong motivator. It shapes individual and team objectives.

    f.   **Enterprise resource planning (ERP)** is the latest phase in the development of computerized systems for planning and controlling organizational resources. ERP is intended to integrate enterprise-wide information systems by creating one database linked to all of the organization's applications.

        1)   ERP connects all operations (personnel, the financial accounting system, production, marketing, distribution, etc.). It also connects the organization with its suppliers (supply-chain management) and customers (customer-relationship management).

        2)   Thus, ERP facilitates demand analysis and materials requirements planning. By decreasing lead times, it improves just-in-time inventory management. Even more importantly, ERP's coordination of all operating activities permits flexible responses to shifts in supply and demand.

        3)   The disadvantages of ERP are its extent and complexity, which make customization of the software difficult and costly.

2.   Some of the more common project scheduling techniques are Gantt or bar charts, flowcharting, PERT, and CPM. **Gantt charts** or **bar charts** are simple to construct and use. The project is divided into logical subprojects called activities or tasks, and the start and completion times for each activity are estimated. The resulting bar chart shows each activity as a horizontal bar along a time scale.

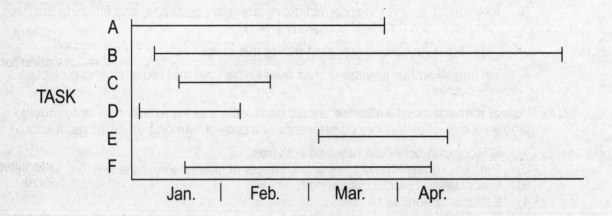

    a.   The major advantage of the Gantt chart is its simplicity. It forces the planner to think ahead and define logical activities. As the project progresses, actual completion times can be compared with planned times. Furthermore, the technique requires no special tools or mathematics and can be used on small projects as well as large ones.

    b.   The major disadvantage is that interrelationships among activities are not shown. Several special methods have been developed to show these on a Gantt chart, but they are feasible only for simple relationships.

3. **Flowcharting** is commonly used in computer programming for determining program logic and in total quality management for simplifying work processes. However, flowcharts are also useful for establishing the desirable **sequence** of activities and decisions.

    a. A simple flowchart developed for this purpose might use **arrows** to indicate the direction of flow, **diamonds** to signify decisions, and **rectangles** to signify activities.

    b. Flowcharts do not indicate the time required for decisions and activities. They also become less feasible as projects become more complicated.

    c. Software is available for flowcharting.

4. **Program Evaluation and Review Technique** was developed to help managers in planning and controlling large-scale projects. PERT diagrams are free-form networks showing each activity as a line between events. A sequence of lines shows interrelationships among activities. PERT diagrams are more complex than Gantt charts, but they have the advantages of incorporating probabilistic time estimates and identifying the critical path.

    a. **Events** are discrete moments in time representing the start or finish of an activity. They consume no resources.

    b. **Activities** are tasks to be accomplished. They consume resources (including time) and have a duration over time.

    c. The **network diagram** is formed by

        1) The lines (activities) connected from left to right in the necessary sequence of their accomplishment. They can be marked with time lengths.

        2) Circles representing events and numbered for identification.

    d. The **critical path** is the longest path in time through the network. It is critical because, if any activity on the critical path takes longer than expected, the entire project will be delayed. Every network has at least one critical path. Some have more than one.

        1) The **mean completion time** for the critical path is the sum of the means of the activity times.

        2) The **standard deviation of the completion time** for the critical path is the square root of the sum of the variances (squares of the standard deviations) of the activity times.

            a) EXAMPLE: If the critical path has two activities, and the standard deviations of the completion times are 3 and 4, the standard deviation for the critical path is

$$\sqrt{3^2 + 4^2} = 5$$

    e. Paths that are not critical have **slack time**. One advantage of PERT is that it identifies slack time, which represents unused resources that can be diverted to the critical path.

    f. Several techniques have been developed to include cost information in the analyses. This variation of PERT is often called **PERT-Cost**. It entails combining activities into work packages to facilitate cost control. By estimating costs for each work package, a manager can develop a budget that indicates when costs should be incurred.

    g. **Activity times** can be expressed probabilistically. Computer programs are available to make the calculations and find critical paths.

h.   PERT analysis includes probabilistic estimates of activity completion times. **Three time estimates** are made – optimistic, most likely, and pessimistic.

1)   The time estimates for an activity are assumed to approximate a **beta probability distribution**. In contrast with the normal distribution, this distribution has finite endpoints (the optimistic and pessimistic estimates) and is unimodal; that is, it has only one mode (the most likely time).

2)   PERT approximates the mean of the beta distribution by dividing the sum of the optimistic time, the pessimistic time, and four times the most likely time (the mode) by six.

3)   The **standard deviation** is approximated by dividing the difference between the pessimistic and optimistic times by six. The basis for the latter approximation is that various probability distributions have tails that lie about plus or minus three standard deviations from the mean. For example, 99.9% of observations in the normal distribution are expected to lie within this range.

i.   EXAMPLE: If an activity can be completed in 6 days (optimistic time) 10 days (most likely time), or 20 days (pessimistic time), the expected duration is 11 days {[6 + (4 × 10) + 20] ÷ 6}.

1)   Thus, the most likely time is weighted the most heavily.
2)   The standard deviation is 2.33 [(20 – 6) ÷ 6].

j.   EXAMPLE:

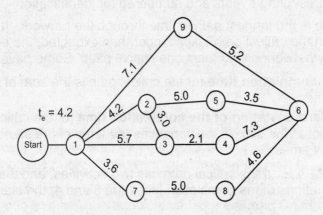

1)   For the network above, the following are the paths and path times:

Path	Time (hours)
Start-1-9-6	16.5
Start 1-2-5-6	16.9
Start-1-2-3-4-6	20.8
Start-1-3-4-6	19.3
Start-1-7-8-6	17.4

2)   Path Start-1-2-3-4-6 is the critical path because it has the longest time.

k.   In the second example above, path 1-3 takes only 5.7 hours, whereas the critical path events (1-2-3) take 7.2 hours. The slack time represented by path 1-3 is thus 7.2 – 5.7, or 1.5. People assigned to path 1-3 have an extra 1.5 hours to help elsewhere.

5.   The **critical path method (CPM)** was developed independently of PERT and is widely used in the construction industry. CPM may be thought of as a subset of PERT. Like PERT, it is a network technique. Unlike PERT, it uses deterministic time and cost estimates. Its advantages include cost estimates plus the concept of "crash" efforts and costs.

   a.   Activity times are estimated for normal effort and crash effort. **Crash time** is the time to complete an activity assuming that all available resources were devoted to the task (overtime, extra crew, etc.).

   b.   Activity costs are also estimated for normal and crash efforts.

   c.   These estimates allow the project manager to estimate the costs of completing the project if some of the activities are completed on a crash basis.

   d.   The **network diagram** is constructed in the same manner as PERT diagrams. Once the diagram is constructed, the critical paths are found for normal and crash times. More than one critical path may exist for each diagram.

   e.   **Crashing the network** means finding the minimum cost for completing the project in minimum time.

   f.   CPM computer programs allow updating of the solution as work proceeds.

6.   **Network models** are used to solve managerial problems pertaining to project scheduling, information systems design, and transportation systems design. Networks consisting of nodes and arcs may be created to represent in graphic form problems related to transportation, assignment, and transshipment. The shortest-route, minimal spanning tree, and maximal flow problems are other applications of network models.

   a.   A **shortest-route algorithm** minimizes total travel time from one site to each of the other sites in a transportation system.

   b.   The **maximal flow algorithm** maximizes throughput in networks with distinct entry (source node) and exit (sink node) points. Examples of applications are highway transportation systems and oil pipelines. Flows are limited by capacities of the arcs (e.g., highways or pipes).

   c.   The **minimal spanning tree algorithm** identifies the set of connecting branches having the shortest combined length. A spanning tree is a group of branches (arcs) that connects each node in the network to every other node. An example problem is the determination of the shortest telecommunications linkage among users at remote sites and a central computer.

7.   **Management by objectives (MBO)** is a behavioral, communications-oriented, responsibility approach to management and employee self direction. MBO is a comprehensive management approach and therefore is relevant to the **planning and control** of projects.

   a.   MBO is based on the Theory Y philosophy that employees

   1)   Want to work hard if they know what is expected.
   2)   Like to understand what their jobs actually entail.
   3)   Are capable of self-direction and self-motivation.

   b.   MBO requires

   1)   Senior management participation and commitment to the program. These managers must

   a)   Determine the overall direction and objectives for the organization.
   b)   Communicate these effectively in operational or measurable terms.
   c)   Coordinate subordinates' objectives with overall objectives.
   d)   Follow up at the end of the MBO cycle period to reward performance and review problems.

2) Integration of the objectives for all subunits into a compatible, balanced system directed toward accomplishment of the overall objectives.

3) Provisions for regular periodic reporting of performance toward attainment of the objectives.

4) Free and honest communications between supervisor and subordinate.

5) A commitment to a Theory Y philosophy on the part of supervisors.

6) An organizational climate that encourages mutual trust and respect.

c. **Objectives** are commitments to reach measurable outcomes within a specified time. Thus, they are targets, standards, and motivators.

1) Setting objectives is a top-down process that creates a **means-end** hierarchy that ties together the levels of the organization. Thus, one level's ends (objectives) provide the next higher levels means for reaching its ends.

2) MBO allows an individual to understand how his/her job objectives provide the means for the accomplishment of the superior's job objectives.

d. **Steps necessary to implement an MBO program** include establishing objectives and action plans (the planning steps) and periodic review and final appraisal (the control steps).

1) Each subordinate should define his/her job objectives and the specific actions (s)he would like to take over the next time period to help reach those job objectives.

2) The subordinate's objectives and activities should be reviewed within the context of the objectives at higher levels.

3) When the subordinate's objectives are at odds with upper-level objectives, a **coaching session** is necessary.

a) This process frequently represents the acid test of MBO because the supervisor must avoid dictating the subordinate's objectives if the spirit of participation is to be preserved.

b) If the subordinate's objectives are deemed by the supervisor to be inappropriate, and the subordinate cannot be coached out of them, the supervisor can either

i) Let the subordinate learn by failing in doing the job his/her way, or
ii) Overrule on this particular issue.

c) A commitment to Theory Y, trust in subordinates, and the supervisor's job security (the confidence to allow subordinates still more latitude) will play important roles.

d) The clearer the definition of job and organizational objectives and the greater the degree of trust and communication between supervisor and subordinate, the easier it is to avoid these dilemmas in implementing MBO.

4) The supervisor and subordinate should mutually set and agree on a realistic action plan that can be accomplished by the end of the period.

5) Flexibility should be maintained during the period to accommodate unforeseen changes. Thus, after developing objectives and action plans, the next step is the **periodic review**.

a)   At regular intervals, objectives should be reconsidered to determine whether they are appropriate in the light of changed circumstances. Otherwise, progress toward achievement of the established objectives should be evaluated and feedback provided.

6)   At the end of the MBO cycle, the supervisor and subordinate should meet for a **final performance appraisal**. They should review the results, analyze and discuss differences, and use the discussion for learning and performance feedback (not as correction or discipline).

7)   The MBO cycle should then be repeated.

8.   Stop and review! You have completed the outline for this subunit. Study multiple-choice questions 9 through 27 beginning on page 235.

QUESTIONS

9.1 Time Management Skills

1. All of the following are skills that managers must focus on when attempting to manage time properly except

   A. The ability to focus on results.

   B. Striving to stay busy.

   C. Concentrating time and energy on tasks with the highest payoffs.

   D. The ability to plan, delegate, organize, direct, and control.

Answer (B) is correct. *(Publisher)*
REQUIRED: The skill not necessary for effective time management.
DISCUSSION: To function effectively, managers must learn to manage time properly. The key principle is to focus on results rather than on staying busy. Time management is actually self-management. The skills needed to manage others are the same skills needed to manage oneself. Time management requires self-discipline and control until it becomes an everyday habit.
Answer (A) is incorrect because the key principle behind effective time management is to focus on results. Answer (C) is incorrect because a manager needs to concentrate time and energy on the tasks with the highest payoffs or the most benefits so that results are optimized. Answer (D) is incorrect because these specific skills are necessary to manage time.

2. Which of the following are common techniques for effective time management?

   I. Finding out how much time is worth
   II. Developing an action plan
   III. Learning to say "No"

   A. I only.

   B. I and II only.

   C. II and III only.

   D. I, II, and III.

Answer (D) is correct. *(Publisher)*
REQUIRED: The common techniques for effective time management.
DISCUSSION: For effective time management, there are several techniques that a manager can use. By finding out how much his/her time is worth, a manager can assess whether there is a net benefit or a net loss to the organization when the manager performs a particular duty. Developing an action plan can help manage time because it allows an individual to focus on a single goal. By learning to say "No," managers can avoid performing tasks that are not part of the daily plan, which can be crippling to proper time management.

3. The technique that calls for the manager to concentrate on tasks that are most closely related to his/her strengths is

   A. Keeping an activity log for about a week.

   B. Creating a prioritized to-do list.

   C. Prioritizing work.

   D. Developing an action plan.

Answer (C) is correct. *(Publisher)*
REQUIRED: The method that requires an assessment of the tasks that are most closely related to a manager's strengths.
DISCUSSION: The are several common techniques that managers use for effective time management. One of those techniques is prioritizing work. There are three methods that can be employed to prioritize work. The first one is for the manager to concentrate on the things that (s)he enjoys. The second is for the manager to concentrate on tasks most closely related to his/her strengths. The third method is for the manager to determine how (s)he is being evaluated and to prioritize tasks accordingly.
Answer (A) is incorrect because this technique just requires that the manager keep an accurate log of how long is spent doing different tasks. Answer (B) is incorrect because this technique calls for the manager to compile a list of all the tasks performed and/or completed during a day ranked according to their importance. Answer (D) is incorrect because the technique requires listing all the tasks that need to be performed to achieve a goal.

4. After performing an assessment to find out how much his time is worth, Lance, the manager of Mathew Corporation, determined that the net benefit to the organization for performing a particular task is less than his hourly worth to the organization. Which of the following statements is most true in relation to this situation?

A. Lance should delegate this task to an assistant whose time is less costly.

B. Lance should continue performing the task because there is no way to change this outcome.

C. If Lance receives a raise in his salary, the gap between the net benefit and his hourly worth will decrease.

D. Lance should work more hours so that his hourly worth increases.

Answer (A) is correct. *(Publisher)*
REQUIRED: The true statement with regard to finding out how much time is worth.
DISCUSSION: A manager should calculate how much money (s)he costs the organization each year, including salary, office space, equipment, etc. After adding to that amount the annual expected profit to be generated by the manager, the total should be divided by the annual hours expected to be worked. The result is the manager's hourly worth to the organization. If the net benefit to the organization of the manager's performing a task is less than his/her hourly worth, it should be delegated to an assistant whose time is less costly.
Answer (B) is incorrect because Lance can correct this inefficiency by delegating this task to his assistant. Answer (C) is incorrect because a raise in his salary will widen the gap between the net benefit and his hourly worth. Answer (D) is incorrect because if he works more hours, his hourly worth will decrease.

9.2 Workflow Management

5. Which of the following statements is false with regard to a workflow management system?

A. Workflow management systems can be implemented to fit a wide variety of scenarios.

B. Workflow management systems should distribute the work in an efficient manner to achieve an organizational goal.

C. Workflow management systems define, manage, and execute workflows by using firm-specific software.

D. A common feature of workflow management systems is activity plan developing.

Answer (D) is correct. *(Publisher)*
REQUIRED: The false statement regarding workflow management systems.
DISCUSSION: A workflow management system defines, manages, and executes workflows by using computer specific software that has been programmed for the organization's workflow logic. It should distribute the work in an efficient manner to achieve an organizational goal. It can be implemented to fit a wide variety of scenarios.

6. All workflow management systems have common features. Those features include

I.   Process definition
II. The ability to distribute tasks and information

A. I only.

B. II only.

C. Both I and II.

D. Neither I nor II.

Answer (C) is correct. *(Publisher)*
REQUIRED: The common features of a workflow management system.
DISCUSSION: Workflow management systems define, manage, and execute workflows by using firm-specific software. All workflow management systems have common features. These features include process definition, workflow management control software, human interaction with the control software, and the ability to distribute tasks and information.

7. Which of the following is not a key benefit of a workflow management system?

A. A more efficient business process.

B. Less flexibility.

C. Improved control over the business process.

D. Better customer service.

Answer (B) is correct. *(Publisher)*
REQUIRED: The key benefits of a workflow management system.
DISCUSSION: Workflow management systems have several key benefits. These benefits include: a more efficient business process as a result of being able to eliminate unnecessary steps, improved control over the business process as a result of standardized work methods and easily traceable audit trails, and better customer service due to a more consistent business process that allows for more predictable responses to customers. Workflow management systems actually offer more flexibility, not less, as a result of having processes controlled by software that can be changed to meet the needs of customers.

8. Which of the following features of workflow management systems describes a component that is used to add activities to user worklists within the operational process?

    A. Workflow management control software.

    B. Human interaction with the control software.

    C. Process definition.

    D. The ability to distribute tasks and information.

Answer (A) is correct. *(Publisher)*

REQUIRED: The definition of workflow management control software.

DISCUSSION: All workflow management systems have common features. Among those features is workflow management control software. This component is used to create and delete processes, add activities to user worklists within the operational process, and control interaction between workers and IT application tools.

Answer (B) is incorrect because this feature describes the requirement that any human interaction that occurs in the business process must be capable of being entered into the control software. Answer (C) is incorrect because a process definition is the act of using a process definition tool to translate a business process into a formal, computer processable definition. Answer (D) is incorrect because this feature describes the system's ability to relay information through various means, such as electronic mail or message passing.

9.3 Project Management Techniques

9. Which of the following statements most accurately describes the conceptualization stage of the project life cycle?

    A. Obtaining resources, assigning duties, and coordinating activities.

    B. Setting overall objectives, budgets, and schedules.

    C. Monitoring, correcting, meeting expectations, and finishing the project within time and budgetary limits.

    D. Turning the project over to the user and redistributing project resources.

Answer (B) is correct. *(Publisher)*

REQUIRED: The description of the conceptualization stage of the project life cycle.

DISCUSSION: The project life cycle consists of four general stages: conceptualization, planning, execution, and termination. During the conceptualization stage, overall objectives, budget, and schedules are generated and set.

Answer (A) is incorrect because these are activities that are performed during the planning stage. Answer (C) is incorrect because these are activities that are performed during the execution stage. Answer (D) is incorrect because these are activities that are performed during the termination stage.

10. Project management software should, among other things, possess the ability to

I. Perform sensitivity analysis of the effects of changes in the plan.

II. Modify or merge plans.

III. Manage those project resources that are only specific to planning.

    A. I only.

    B. II only.

    C. Both I and II.

    D. Both I and III.

Answer (C) is correct. *(Publisher)*

REQUIRED: The characteristics that project management software should possess.

DISCUSSION: Project management software should be flexible and transparent so as to provide timely reports of all key components of a project. Among other things, it should perform sensitivity analysis of the effects of changes in plans, and be able to modify or merge plans. This software should also be able to manage all types of project resources, not just those related to one specific area or stage of the project.

Answer (A) is incorrect because this is not the only characteristic that project management software should possess. Answer (B) is incorrect because this is not the only characteristic that project management software should possess. Answer (D) is incorrect because managing project resources specific to planning is not required of project management software.

11. Which of the following devices operates as a means to integrate enterprise-wide information systems by creating one database linked to all of the organization's applications?

    A. Enterprise resource planning.

    B. Project management software.

    C. Program evaluation and review technique.

    D. Project conceptualization.

Answer (A) is correct.   *(Publisher)*
REQUIRED: The description of enterprise resource planning (ERP).
DISCUSSION: ERP is the latest phase in the development of computerized systems for planning and controlling organizational resources. ERP is intended to integrate enterprise-wide information systems by creating one database linked to all of the organization's applications.
Answer (B) is incorrect because project management software is a device that provides timely reports of all key components of a project. Answer (C) is incorrect because program evaluation and review technique is a device that helps managers in planning and controlling large-scale projects. Answer (D) is incorrect because project conceptualization is the first stage of the project life cycle.

12. The disadvantage of using a Gantt chart as a project scheduling technique is that

    A. It forces the planner to think ahead and define logical activities.

    B. As the project progresses, actual completion times can be compared with planned times.

    C. It requires no special tools or mathematics.

    D. Interrelationships among activities are not shown.

Answer (D) is correct.   *(Publisher)*
REQUIRED: The disadvantage of using Gantt charts.
DISCUSSION: Gantt charts take a project and divide it into logical subprojects called activities or tasks, and the start and completion times for each activity are estimated. The major disadvantage of using Gantt charts is that interrelationships among activities are not shown. Several special methods have been developed to show these on a Gantt chart, but they are feasible only for simple relationships.

13. Most of the resources are used during which stage of the project life cycle?

    A. Conceptualization.

    B. Planning.

    C. Execution.

    D. Termination.

Answer (C) is correct.   *(Publisher)*
REQUIRED: The stage of the project life cycle when most of the resources are used.
DISCUSSION: The project life cycle consists of four stages: conceptualization, planning, execution, and termination. During the execution stage, activities that are performed include monitoring, correcting, meeting expectations, and finishing the project within time and budgetary limits. Most resources are used during this stage.

14. Which of the following project scheduling techniques is commonly used in total quality management for simplifying work processes?

    A. Gantt charts.

    B. Flowcharting.

    C. Program evaluation and review technique.

    D. Critical path method.

Answer (B) is correct.   *(Publisher)*
REQUIRED: The description of flowcharting.
DISCUSSION: Flowcharting is commonly used in computer programming for determining program logic and in total quality management for simplifying work processes. However, they are also used for establishing the desirable sequence of activities and decisions.
Answer (A) is incorrect because Gantt charts divide projects into subprojects and then estimate start and completion times for them. Answer (C) is incorrect because program evaluation and review technique helps managers in planning and controlling large-scale projects. Answer (D) is incorrect because the critical path method is a network technique widely used in the construction industry that uses deterministic time and cost estimates.

15. Which of the following statements is false regarding program evaluation and review technique (PERT)?

A. PERT diagrams are more complex than Gantt charts.

B. PERT diagrams are free-form networks showing each activity as a line between events.

C. Like Gantt charts, PERT diagrams do not show interrelationships among activities.

D. PERT is especially useful for scheduling large-scale projects.

Answer (C) is correct. *(Publisher)*
REQUIRED: The false statement regarding PERT.
DISCUSSION: PERT was developed to help managers in planning and controlling large-scale projects. PERT diagrams are free-form networks showing each activity as a line between events. PERT diagrams are more complex than Gantt charts, but they have the advantages of incorporating probabilistic time estimates and identifying the critical path. Unlike Gantt charts, PERT diagrams include a sequence of lines that show interrelationships among activities.

16. If the critical path has two activities, and the standard deviations of the completion times are 5 and 12, what is the standard deviation of the completion time of the critical path?

A. 13

B. 4.12

C. 7.75

D. 10.91

Answer (A) is correct. *(Publisher)*
REQUIRED: The calculation of the standard deviation of the completion time of the critical path.
DISCUSSION: The standard deviation of the completion time for the critical path is the square root of the sum of the variances (squares of the standard deviations) of the activity times. In this case, to calculate the standard deviation of the completion time of the critical path, the standard deviations must be squared and then summed up with each other: $[(5 \times 5) + (12 \times 12)] = 169$. The final step is to take the square root of the result: square root of $169 = 13$. This is the standard deviation of the completion time for the critical path.
  Answer (B) is incorrect because the standard deviations must be squared before they are summed up and the square root is taken. Answer (C) is incorrect because the standard deviations must first be squared and then summed up, not multiplied by each other. Answer (D) is incorrect because the squares of the standard deviations are summed up, not subtracted from each other.

17. Which of the following is correct with regard to the critical path in a PERT diagram?

A. The critical path is the shortest path in time through the network.

B. The mean completion time for the critical path is the sum of the means of the activity times.

C. If any activity on the critical path takes longer than expected, the slack time of the critical path will ensure that the entire project is not delayed.

D. Every PERT network has more than one critical path.

Answer (B) is correct. *(Publisher)*
REQUIRED: The correct statement regarding the critical path in a PERT diagram.
DISCUSSION: The program evaluation and review technique (PERT) utilized network diagrams that are formed by lines (activities), usually marked with time lengths, connected from left to right in the necessary sequence of their accomplishment, and circles representing events, which are usually numbered for identification. The critical path is the longest path in time through the network. The mean completion time for the critical path is the sum of the means of the activity times.
  Answer (A) is incorrect because the critical path is the longest path in time through the network. Answer (C) is incorrect because if any activity on the critical path takes longer than expected, the entire project will be delayed. There is no slack time on the critical path. Answer (D) is incorrect because not every PERT network has more than one critical path. Each network has at least one critical path.

18. A PERT analysis shows that an activity can be completed at an optimistic time of 8 days, a most likely time of 10 days, and a pessimistic time of 18 days. What is the expected duration of the activity?

    A. 6 days.

    B. 8.66 days.

    C. 11 days.

    D. 15 days.

Answer (C) is correct. *(Publisher)*
REQUIRED: The correct calculation of the expected duration of an activity.
DISCUSSION: PERT approximates the mean of the beta distribution, also known as the expected duration, by dividing the sum of the optimistic time, the pessimistic time, and four times the most likely time by six. This gives the most likely time the heaviest weight. Given the facts, the expected duration would be 11 days, calculated as follows: $\{[8 + (4 \times 10) + 18] \div 6\}$.
Answer (A) is incorrect because the most likely time must be multiplied by four. Answer (B) is incorrect because the most likely time is multiplied by four, not the optimistic time. Answer (D) is incorrect because the most likely time is multiplied by four, not the pessimistic time.

19. A PERT analysis shows that an activity can be completed at an optimistic time of 8 days, a most likely time of 10 days, and a pessimistic time of 18 days. What is the standard deviation of the completion time of the activity?

    A. 4.33

    B. 1.33

    C. 0.33

    D. 1.67

Answer (D) is correct. *(Publisher)*
REQUIRED: The correct calculation of the standard deviation of the completion time of the activity.
DISCUSSION: The standard deviation is approximated by dividing the difference between the pessimistic time and the optimistic time by six. The basis for the latter approximation is that various probability distributions have tails that lie about plus or minus three standard deviations from the mean. Given the facts, the standard deviation of the completion time of the activity is 1.67, calculated as follows: $[(18 - 8) \div 6]$.
Answer (A) is incorrect because the optimistic time is subtracted from the pessimistic time, not added. Answer (B) is incorrect because the difference is taken between the optimistic time and the pessimistic time, not the most likely time and the pessimistic time. Answer (C) is incorrect because the difference is taken between the optimistic time and the pessimistic time, not the optimistic time and the most likely time.

20. Brad is the project manager who is in charge of planning an upcoming large-scale project. He wishes to be able to make a valid estimate of time. Also, in the event that all the resources available must be devoted to a specific task during the project, Brad wants to be able to estimate any added costs to the total project. Which project scheduling technique is best suited for Brad's wishes?

    A. Critical path method.

    B. Project evaluation and review technique.

    C. Gantt charts.

    D. Flowcharting.

Answer (A) is correct. *(Publisher)*
REQUIRED: The characteristics of the critical path method.
DISCUSSION: The critical path method is a network technique that uses deterministic time and cost estimates. Its advantages include cost estimates plus the concept of "crash" efforts and costs. Crash time is the time to complete an activity assuming that all available resources were devoted to the task. Activity costs are estimated for normal and crash efforts. These estimates allow the project manager to estimate the costs of completing the project if some of the activities are completed on a crash basis.
Answer (B) is incorrect because traditional PERT diagrams do not include estimates of costs. Answer (C) is incorrect because traditional Gantt charts do not include estimates of costs. Answer (D) is incorrect because traditional flowcharts do not include estimates of costs.

21. With regard to the critical path method (CPM), what does the phrase "crashing the network" refer to?

    A. Finding the minimum cost for completing the project in the minimum time.

    B. Finding the maximum cost for completing the project in the minimum time.

    C. Finding the minimum cost for completing the project in the maximum time.

    D. Finding the maximum cost for completing the project in the maximum time.

Answer (A) is correct. *(Publisher)*
REQUIRED: The definition of crashing the network.
DISCUSSION: The critical path method is a network technique that uses deterministic time and cost estimates. Its advantages include cost estimates plus the concept of "crash" efforts and costs. Crash time is the time to complete an activity assuming that all available resources were devoted to the task. Crashing the network means finding the minimum cost for completing the project in the minimum time.

22. Which network model algorithm maximizes throughput in networks with distinct entry and exit points?

    A. Minimal spanning tree algorithm.

    B. Longest-route algorithm.

    C. Maximal flow algorithm.

    D. Shortest-route algorithm.

Answer (C) is correct. *(Publisher)*
    REQUIRED: The definition of the maximal flow algorithm.
    DISCUSSION: Network models are used to solve managerial problems pertaining to project scheduling, information systems design, and transportation systems design. The shortest-route, minimal spanning tree, and maximal flow problems are other applications of network models. The maximal flow algorithm maximizes throughput in networks with distinct entry and exit points. Examples of applications are highway transportation systems and oil pipelines.
    Answer (A) is incorrect because the minimal spanning tree algorithm identifies the set of connecting branches having the shortest combined length. Answer (B) is incorrect because a longest-route algorithm is not an existing algorithm used in network models. Answer (D) is incorrect because a shortest-route algorithm minimizes total travel time from one site to each of the other sites in a transportation system.

23. Management by objectives is based on the Theory Y philosophy on employees. All of the following statements are facets of the Theory Y philosophy except

    A. Employees want to work hard if they know what is expected.

    B. Employees will lose focus without the clear presence of an overwhelming authoritative figure.

    C. Employees like to understand what their jobs actually entail.

    D. Employees are capable of self-direction and self-motivation.

Answer (B) is correct. *(Publisher)*
    REQUIRED: The facets of the Theory Y Philosophy on employees.
    DISCUSSION: The Theory Y philosophy is the frame of mind on which management by objectives (MBO) is based. This philosophy promotes the ideal that it is not necessary for management to take a dictator type role in order to get employees to do their job. It concludes that employees want to work hard if they know what is expected, they like to understand what their jobs actually entail, and they are capable of self-direction and self-motivation. Thus, the Theory Y philosophy does not conclude that employees will lose focus without the clear presence of an overwhelming authoritative figure.

24. Which of the following are requirements of a management by objectives approach?

    I. Free and honest communications between supervisor and subordinate.

    II. Provisions for regular periodic reporting of performance toward attainment of the objectives.

    A. I only.

    B. II only.

    C. Both I and II.

    D. Neither I nor II.

Answer (C) is correct. *(Publisher)*
    REQUIRED: The requirements of a management by objectives approach.
    DISCUSSION: Management by objective (MBO) is a behavioral, communications-oriented, responsibility approach to management and employee self direction. MBO is a comprehensive approach and therefore is relevant to the planning and control of projects. Among other things, MBO requires provisions for regular periodic reporting of performance toward attainment of the objectives. It also requires free and honest communications between supervisor and subordinate.

25. In an MBO program, when is a coaching session necessary?

    A. When the subordinate is attempting to define his/her job objectives.

    B. When the subordinate's objectives are at odds with upper-level objectives.

    C. When the subordinate identifies that specific actions (s)he would like to take over the next time period to help reach his/her job objectives.

    D. When it is time for the supervisor and the subordinate to mutually agree on an action plan that can be accomplished by the end of the period.

Answer (B) is correct. *(Publisher)*
REQUIRED: The scenario in an MBO program that requires a coaching session.
DISCUSSION: Steps necessary to implement an MBO program include establishing objectives and action plans (the planning steps) and periodic review and final appraisal (the control steps). During the planning steps, the subordinate's objectives and activities should be reviewed within the context of the objectives at higher levels. When the subordinate's objectives are at odds with upper-level objectives, a coaching session is necessary.
    Answer (A) is incorrect because this step is performed prior to the subordinate's objectives being reviewed to make sure that it is in line with upper-level objectives. Answer (C) is incorrect because this step is performed prior to the subordinate's objectives being reviewed to make sure that it is in line with upper-level objectives. Answer (D) is incorrect because at this point, any discrepancy regarding objectives should have been resolved and there is no longer a need for a coaching session.

26. During a coaching session, the supervisor and subordinate are not able to resolve a discrepancy between objectives. The supervisor can either

    I.   Let the subordinate learn by failing in doing the job his/her way.

    II.   Overrule on this particular issue.

    III.   Suspend the employee for not conforming to the required objectives.

    A. I and III only.

    B. II and III only.

    C. I, II, and III.

    D. I and II only.

Answer (D) is correct. *(Publisher)*
REQUIRED: The steps a supervisor can take when the coaching session does not resolve the issue.
DISCUSSION: When the subordinate's objectives are at odds with upper-level objectives, a coaching session is necessary. If the subordinate's objectives are deemed to be inappropriate by the supervisor, and the subordinate cannot be coached out of them, the supervisor can either let the subordinate learn by failing in doing the job his/her way, or overrule on this particular issue. If this is an MBO program, the supervisor should not suspend the subordinate because of a discrepancy between the subordinate's objectives and upper-level objectives.

27. During the final performance appraisal of the MBO cycle, the supervisor and subordinate should perform all of the following steps except

    A. Review the results of the action plan.

    B. Analyze and discuss differences between the actual results and the action plan.

    C. Provide learning and performance feedback.

    D. Figure out a way for disciplining the subordinate for not accomplishing certain activities on the action plan.

Answer (D) is correct. *(Publisher)*
REQUIRED: The step not to be performed during the final performance appraisal of the MBO cycle
DISCUSSION: At the end of the MBO cycle, the supervisor and subordinate should meet for a final performance appraisal. They should review the results, analyze and discuss differences, and use the discussion for learning and performance feedback. There should not be any behaviors exhibited that will lend themselves to corrective or disciplinary action.

Use Gleim's *CIA Test Prep* for interactive testing with over 2,000 additional multiple-choice questions!

STUDY UNIT TEN
CONFLICT AND NEGOTIATION

(5 pages of outline)

This study unit concerns the related subjects of conflict management and negotiation. The nature and causes (triggers) of conflict and the means of resolving it are discussed. After negotiation is defined, the elements of effective negotiation are described.

10.1 CONFLICT

1. Effective interpersonal relationships and organizational change are closely tied to conflict management.

   a. According to Dean Tjosvold, **conflict** entails "incompatible behaviors; one person interfering, disrupting, or in some other way making actions less effective."

      1) However, conflict may be cooperative as well as competitive.

   b. **Cooperative conflict** is constructive. The existence of cooperative (shared) goals is the basis for treating the conflict as a mutual problem.

      1) In this context, the parties may be able to trust each other's motives and believe what the other says.

      2) Discussions are productive, the attitude (and the result) is win-win, and the parties move ahead together.

   c. **Competitive conflict** is destructive. Opposite goals are pursued, and neither side trusts or believes the other.

      1) The parties avoid genuine dialogue, and the attitude is win-lose.
      2) Ultimately, the parties take separate paths.

2. **Conflict triggers** raise the probability of conflict between groups or individuals.

   a. They should be allowed to exist if they cause cooperative conflict. Otherwise, they should be eliminated.

   b. Conflict may be triggered by

      1) Badly defined job descriptions (jurisdictional boundaries).

         a) Reorganization may be the solution.

      2) Scarcity of people, funds, or other resources.

         a) Increasing resources may be the solution.

      3) Failure of communication.

         a) Removing obstacles that hinder effective two-way communication is essential, but the problem is perennial.

      4) Deadlines. Time pressure may induce better performance (constructive) or anger and frustration (destructive).

      5) Policies, procedures, rules, or other standards viewed by employees as unfair.

         a) If very unpopular, they should be changed to avoid competitive conflict.

      6)   Individual personality differences.

          a)   Reassignment or termination of employees may be the solution.

      7)   Differences in status, an issue in any hierarchical entity.

          a)   The remedy is respect for the ideas, values, and concerns of lower-level employees.

      8)   Not meeting expectations.

          a)   The problem can be avoided through clarifying in advance the expectations employees have about their jobs.

3.   Managers may address competitive conflicts in a variety of ways.

    a.   **Problem solving** is a means of resolving the conflict by confronting it and removing its causes. The emphasis is on facts and solutions, not personalities and assignment of blame.

      1)   The disadvantage is that problem solving is time consuming.

    b.   **Smoothing** is a short-term avoidance approach. The parties in conflict are asked by management to submerge their differences temporarily, e.g., until a project is completed. It does not resolve the conflict.

    c.   **Forcing** occurs when a superior uses his/her formal authority to order a particular outcome. It does not resolve the conflict. Indeed, forcing may intensify it.

    d.   **Superordinate goals** are the overriding goals of the entity to which subunit and personal goals are subordinate. An appeal to these goals is another short-term solution that does not resolve the conflict.

    e.   **Compromise** entails negotiation by the parties in conflict. The conflict is resolved through a process by which each side makes concessions. Thus, the parties both gain and lose.

      1)   However, if the negotiators on both sides are not skillful (see the earlier description of cooperative conflict), the conflict is suppressed, not resolved.

      2)   The disadvantage of fully negotiating a compromise is that the process is time consuming.

    f.   **Expanding resources** resolves conflicts that result from scarcity.

    g.   **Avoidance** is nonaction. It withdraws from and suppresses the conflict but does not solve the underlying problem.

    h.   **Accommodation** is the willingness of one party to the conflict to place another's needs and concerns above his/her own.

4.   Cooperative conflict may result in better decision making, a reduction in complacency, more self-criticism, greater creativity, and solutions to problems. Cooperative conflict drives the change processes that all organizations need to survive and prosper.

    a.   Thus, **intentional stimulation of conflict** may be desirable. For example, management may intentionally trigger conflict by

      1)   Making changes in the organizational structure;

      2)   Hiring new employees with different values, managerial styles, attitudes, and backgrounds; or

      3)   Designating individuals to oppose the majority views of the group.

5.   Stop and review! You have completed the outline for this subunit. Study multiple-choice questions 1 through 8 beginning on page 245.

10.2 NEGOTIATION

1. Kreitner cites Northwestern University scholars who define **negotiation** as "a decision-making process among interdependent parties who do not share identical preferences." The parties to the relationship must decide through bargaining what values will be exchanged (given and taken) by each side.

    a. This definition is broad enough to encompass negotiating processes of all kinds from private interpersonal relations to commercial activities to agreements among nations.

    b. Two-party and three-party negotiations are common.

        1) For example, a **two-party negotiation** occurs when a person sells his/her car to a used car dealer.

        2) An example of a **three-party negotiation** is a person's sale of stock through a broker.

2. **Effective negotiation** allows the parties to meet their needs and to establish the **trust** necessary for future bargaining.

    a. Effective negotiation emphasizes a **win-win attitude**.

        1) In some cultures, the dominant approach is **competitive**. Rewards are given for winning and punishment is given for losing.

            a) This **win-lose attitude** views negotiation using a sports metaphor, that is, as a zero-sum game.

            b) The win-win attitude is to treat negotiation as a positive-sum game.

        2) The win-win attitude is **cooperative**, seeking mutual benefit and satisfaction.

            a) It is founded on the principle that resources are sufficient for all and that the **third alternative** (not one side's way or the other side's way) is preferable.

            b) An advantage of win-win negotiation is that it promotes support of, and commitment to, the agreement.

        3) For a successful negotiation, the negotiator should understand the implications for both sides if the negotiation fails.

        4) The negotiator should present facts and precedents in an organized manner when negotiating with an analytical personality.

    b. Effective negotiators understand their **best alternative to a negotiated agreement (BATNA)**, an idea developed by Harvard University researchers.

        1) The BATNA is the acceptable minimum outcome if a negotiator cannot obtain the desired result.

        2) Understanding the BATNA helps a negotiator to avoid the following two mistakes:

            a) Accepting an unfavorable agreement
            b) Rejecting a favorable agreement

        3) A reasonable BATNA protects against bad decisions caused by the following:

            a) **Framing error** is a perceptual problem. The presentation or context of information may bias its interpretation and the resulting decision.

      i)   Accordingly, favorably (unfavorably) presented information may be viewed more (less) favorably than is justified.

- For example, a job seeker may hope that the attractive appearance of a resumé will sway the judgment of a potential employer.
- Purely semantic effects may also result in framing error. For example, a glass still holds 50% of its capacity whether it is described as half full or half empty. However, the former (latter) characterization may lead to a more (less) favorable opinion of the content.

  b) **Escalation of commitment** is adherence to a failing course of action when a purely objective decision maker would abandon it. This irrational tendency to persist in error is based on a variety of organizational, social, and psychological factors.

      i)   Structural resistance to change in an organization

      ii)   Organizational politics

      iii) Organizational culture, e.g., values that stress persistence in the face of obstacles

      iv) Societal approval of those who persevere and overcome obstacles

      v)   Personal desire to avoid the embarrassment of conceding defeat

      vi) Perceived opportunity to reverse the trend of events

      vii) Competitive desire to win

      viii) Attempted justification of prior decisions

  c) **Overconfidence** is the common tendency to overestimate the chances of success. It tends, paradoxically, to be directly related to the difficulty of the undertaking.

      i)   One explanation for this phenomenon is that overconfidence may be necessary to develop the fortitude to embark on a very difficult course of action.

  d) A primary disadvantage of forcing another party to accept terms in a negotiation is that it damages the relationship between the negotiators.

4) The BATNA also helps to define the **bargaining zone**. It is the difference between the BATNAs belonging to each side, i.e., the set of outcomes acceptable to both.

  a) **Example**: A parent wishes to sell a subsidiary for $1.5 billion, with a BATNA of $1.2 billion. A buyer wishes to acquire the subsidiary for $1 billion, with a BATNA of $1.3 billion. Hence, negotiation is feasible because a bargaining zone (buyer's BATNA of $1.3 billion – seller's BATNA of $1.2 billion) exists.

  b) Negotiation is **not feasible** in the absence of a bargaining zone. In the example above, if the seller's BATNA were $1.4 billion, negotiation would be fruitless.

  c) Negotiation is **not necessary** if the parties do not disagree. For example, they may have contracted to accept the result of a formal appraisal of the value of something to be bought and sold.

  d) Determining the other side's BATNA may be the most difficult aspect of a negotiation. Each side has an incentive to keep its BATNA confidential.

      i)   Thus, the other side's BATNA must be estimated so that, in turn, the negotiating zone may be estimated.

3. The steps to overcoming unexpected resistance from another party are as follows:

   a. Attempt to determine the reason behind the resistance (first step).
   b. Stop the meeting and address the other party's concerns privately.
   c. Restate the negotiator's position regarding the issue.
   d. Research the other party to determine its views and requirements.

4. **Added-value negotiating** was developed by Karl and Steve Albrecht. It is applied when something more than the elements of negotiation described in this subunit is necessary. Its basic concept is that the two sides make **multiple deals** to "add value" to the process.

   a. Step one is for the parties mutually to **clarify interests**.

      1) These interests may be subjective as well as objective. The purpose is to isolate commonalities.

   b. Step two is to **identify options**.

      1) The purpose is to establish a "marketplace of value," i.e., the range of values each side can give the other.

   c. Step three is to **design alternative deal packages**.

      1) The distinctive feature of added-value negotiation is that it provides for multiple win-win offers. Each consists of groups of the values identified in step two.

   d. Step four is to **select a deal** after the parties have considered the deal packages designed in step three.

      1) They evaluate each possible deal's "value, balance, and fit." The "mutually acceptable deal" is then chosen.

   e. Step five is to **perfect the deal**.

      1) Details are negotiated, and the deal is put in written form.
      2) The process creates **relationships** that will benefit later negotiations.
      3) The keys are openness, flexibility, and mutuality in the quest for a "successful exchange of value."

5. Stop and review! You have completed the outline for this subunit. Study multiple-choice questions 9 through 21 beginning on page 247.

QUESTIONS

10.1 Conflict

1. Matthew and Nick are working on similar projects. After looking at Nick's work, Matthew informs him that his project contains many errors and is not acceptable. Matthew discusses with Nick ways to improve on the quality of his work in order to prevent this from happening again. Nick acknowledges his mistakes and vows to work harder. He listens to Matthew's suggestions, corrects the errors on the current project, and returns a high quality project. This is an example of

A. Cooperative conflict.

B. Competitive conflict.

C. Destructive conflict.

D. None of the answers are correct.

Answer (A) is correct. *(Publisher)*
REQUIRED: The example of cooperative conflict.
DISCUSSION: Matthew's conflict with Nick is productive because dialogue between the two workers is productive. They share the same goals for a high quality project.
Answer (B) is incorrect because the two employees are not competing with each other. Matthew is desiring to help Nick with his project. Answer (C) is incorrect because Matthew and Nick both displayed constructive behavior. Answer (D) is incorrect because the situation is an example of cooperative conflict.

2. Conflict may be

I.   Cooperative
II. Competitive

    A.   I only.

    B.   II only.

    C.   Both I and II.

    D.   Neither I nor II.

Answer (C) is correct. *(Publisher)*
    REQUIRED: The accurate description of conflict.
    DISCUSSION: Conflict may be either cooperative or competitive. Cooperative conflict is constructive and competitive conflict is destructive.
    Answer (A) is incorrect because conflict may be cooperative or competitive. Answer (B) is incorrect because conflict may also be cooperative. Answer (D) is incorrect because conflict may be both cooperative and competitive.

3. Which of the following conflict triggers is best resolved by reorganization?

    A.   Scarcity of people, funds, or other resources.

    B.   Badly defined job descriptions.

    C.   Failure of communication.

    D.   Deadlines.

Answer (B) is correct. *(Publisher)*
    REQUIRED: The conflict trigger best resolved by reorganization.
    DISCUSSION: If badly designed job descriptions occur, then the best resolution is reorganization.
    Answer (A) is incorrect because the scarcity of people, funds, or other resources is best resolved by increasing resources. Answer (C) is incorrect because failure of communication is best resolved by removing obstacles to effective two-way communication. Answer (D) is incorrect because deadlines may induce better performance or anger and frustration. Reorganization is not the best solution for conflicts with deadlines.

4. Which of the following conflict resolution techniques has the goal of maintaining harmonious relationships by placing another's needs and concerns above your own?

    A.   Accommodation.

    B.   Compromise.

    C.   Collaboration.

    D.   Avoidance.

Answer (A) is correct. *(IIA, adapted)*
    REQUIRED: The conflict resolution technique with a goal of maintaining harmonious relationships.
    DISCUSSION: The goal of accommodation is maintaining harmonious relationships by placing an emphasis on another's needs and concerns.
    Answer (B) is incorrect because compromise resolves conflict through a process in which each side makes concessions. Answer (C) is incorrect because collaboration resolves conflict. The parties work together to obtain a solution. Answer (D) is incorrect because avoidance does not resolve conflict. It is nonaction.

5. Time consumption is a disadvantage when managers address conflict by

    A.   Smoothing.

    B.   Forcing.

    C.   Problem-solving.

    D.   None of the answers are correct.

Answer (C) is correct. *(Publisher)*
    REQUIRED: The way in which managers address conflict that uses excessive time.
    DISCUSSION: Problem-solving is a way managers address conflicts, but it requires a large amount of time to resolve.
    Answer (A) is incorrect because smoothing is a short-term avoidance approach. Answer (B) is incorrect because forcing occurs when a superior uses his or her formal authority to order a particular outcome. Answer (D) is incorrect because problem-solving takes managers a long time to resolve conflicts.

6. Which of the following are conflict triggers?

    A.   Deadlines.

    B.   Policies, procedures, rules, or other standards viewed by employees as unfair.

    C.   Not meeting expectations.

    D.   All of the answers are correct.

Answer (D) is correct. *(Publisher)*
    REQUIRED: The example(s) of conflict triggers.
    DISCUSSION: Deadlines are conflict triggers because time pressures may induce better performance (constructive) or anger and frustration (destructive). Polices, procedures, rules, or other standards viewed by employees as unfair are conflict triggers and should be changed to avoid competitive conflict if very unpopular. Not meeting expectations is a conflict trigger, but the problem can be avoided through clarifying in advance the expectations employees have about their jobs.
    Answer (A) is incorrect because deadlines are a conflict trigger. Answer (B) is incorrect because policies, procedures, rules, or other standards viewed by employees as unfair are conflict triggers. Answer (C) is incorrect because not meeting expectations is a conflict trigger.

7. Intentional stimulation of conflict can be triggered by

I.   Making changes to the organizational structure.

II.   Hiring new employees with different values, attitudes, and backgrounds.

III. Assigning an employee the role of devil's advocate to oppose the majority views.

    A. I only.

    B. I, II, and III.

    C. I and III only.

    D. II only.

Answer (B) is correct. *(Publisher)*
REQUIRED: The action(s) that cause intentional stimulation of conflict.
DISCUSSION: Intentional stimulation of conflict is triggered by making changes in the organizational structure, hiring new employees with different values, attitudes, backgrounds, and assigning an employee to be devil's advocate to oppose the majority views of the group.
Answer (A) is incorrect because hiring new employees with different values, attitudes, backgrounds, and assigning an employee the role of devil's advocate to oppose the majority views are also triggers of intentional stimulation of conflict. Answer (C) is incorrect because hiring new employees with different values, attitudes, and backgrounds is another trigger of intentional stimulation of conflict. Answer (D) is incorrect because making changes to the organizational structure and assigning an employee the role of devil's advocate to oppose the majority views are additional ways to trigger intentional stimulation of conflict.

8. Carling, a manager, resolves a conflict between two employees, Philip and John, by recommending concessions to be made by both employees. The two employees agree to the concessions and the conflict is resolved. Both Philip and John gain and lose. Which of the following describes the way Carling addressed the conflict?

    A. Forcing.

    B. Smoothing.

    C. Compromise.

    D. Problem solving.

Answer (C) is correct. *(Publisher)*
REQUIRED: The ways in which managers address conflicts.
DISCUSSION: Compromise entails negotiation by the parties in conflict. The conflict is resolved through a process by which each side makes concessions. Thus, the parties both gain and lose. Because Philip and John each made concessions, the conflict was resolved through compromise.
Answer (A) is incorrect because forcing occurs when a superior uses his or her formal authority to order a particular outcome. It does not resolve the conflict. Forcing may intensify it. Answer (B) is incorrect because smoothing is a short-term avoidance approach. The parties in conflict are asked by management to submerge their differences temporarily until a project is completed. Answer (D) is incorrect because problem solving is a means of resolving the conflict by confronting it and removing its causes. The emphasis is on facts and solutions, not personalities and assignment of blame.

10.2 Negotiation

9. Which of the following is an example of a two-party negotiation?

    A. A person sells his or her car to a used car dealer.

    B. A person requests a financial institution to pay another person.

    C. A person sells stock through a broker.

    D. A person sells his or her house through a real estate agent.

Answer (A) is correct. *(Publisher)*
REQUIRED: The true example of a two-party negotiation.
DISCUSSION: A person who sells his or her car to a used car dealer is the correct example of a two-party negotiation since only the seller and dealer are involved in the negotiations.
Answer (B) is incorrect because a person who requests a financial institution to pay another person is an example of a three-party negotiation. The three parties involved are the person requesting the financial institution to use funds from his or her account to pay another individual, the financial institution responsible for paying the payee, and the person receiving the funds from the financial institution. Answer (C) is incorrect because a person who sells stock through a broker is another example of a three-party negotiation. The seller, broker, and buyer are involved in these negotiations. Answer (D) is incorrect because this is an example of three-party negotiations involving the seller, real estate agent, and the buyer of the house.

10. A reasonable BATNA (best alternative to a negotiated agreement) protects against bad decisions caused by the following

I.   Framing error.
II. Escalation of commitment.
III. Overconfidence.

    A. I and III only.

    B. I, II, and III.

    C. I only.

    D. II and III only.

Answer (B) is correct.   *(Publisher)*
    REQUIRED: The problems a reasonable BATNA protects against.
    DISCUSSION: A reasonable BATNA protects against bad decisions caused by the following: framing error, escalation of commitment, and overconfidence. Framing error is a perceptual problem. The presentation or context of information may bias its interpretation and the resulting decision. Escalation of commitment is adherence to a failing course of action when a purely objective decision maker would abandon it. Overconfidence is the common tendency to overestimate the chances of success.
    Answer (A) is incorrect because a reasonable BATNA also protects against escalation of commitment. Answer (C) is incorrect because a reasonable BATNA also protects against escalation of commitment and overconfidence. Answer (D) is incorrect because a reasonable BATNA also protects against framing errors.

11. In regard to effective negotiation, a win-win attitude is characterized by

    A. Seeking mutual benefit and satisfaction.

    B. Cooperative.

    C. It promotes support of, and commitment to, the agreement.

    D. All of the answers are correct.

Answer (D) is correct.   *(Publisher)*
    REQUIRED: The characteristic(s) of a win-win attitude.
    DISCUSSION: In regards to effective negotiation, a win-win attitude is characterized by seeking mutual benefit and satisfaction, being cooperative, and promoting support of, and commitment to, the agreement. In contrast to a win-win attitude, a win-lose attitude is competitive and is a zero-sum game instead of a positive-sum game.
    Answer (A) is incorrect because cooperation and promoting support and commitment to the agreement are additional characteristics of a win-win attitude. Answer (B) is incorrect because seeking mutual benefit and satisfaction and supporting and committing to the agreement are characteristics of a win-win attitude. Answer (C) is incorrect because two additional characteristics of a win-win attitude are seeking mutual benefit and satisfaction and being cooperative.

12. When planning for successful negotiations, the negotiator should

    A. Understand the implications for both sides if the negotiation fails.

    B. Concentrate solely on the issues in the negotiation at hand.

    C. Not deviate from stated positions.

    D. Depend on the initial research prepared for the negotiation.

Answer (A) is correct.   *(IIA, adapted)*
    REQUIRED: The necessary action when planning for successful negotiations.
    DISCUSSION: Negotiators should assess the best alternatives for both themselves and the other parties to determine their relative strength in the negotiation process. If alternatives are not readily available or are unattractive, a party is under additional pressure to make the negotiation work.
    Answer (B) is incorrect because the negotiator should evaluate all alternatives to avoid placing undue pressure on the success of the negotiation. Answer (C) is incorrect because an objective perspective may assist the negotiator in identifying alternatives. Answer (D) is incorrect because additional research may be required to fully understand the other party's alternatives to negotiation.

13. When negotiating with an analytical personality, the negotiator should

    A. Present facts and precedents in an organized manner.

    B. Push the other party for quick closure of negotiations.

    C. Focus on creating a bond with the other party.

    D. Include unimportant items in the proposal for bargaining.

Answer (A) is correct.   *(IIA, adapted)*
    REQUIRED: The necessary action when negotiating with an analytical personality.
    DISCUSSION: An analytical person tends to be drawn to details and swayed by factual information.
    Answer (B) is incorrect because pushing an analytical person may result in increased resistance. Answer (C) is incorrect because analytical personalities make decisions based on facts rather than on emotions. Answer (D) is incorrect because the analytical person tends not to enjoy negotiation games as much as other personality types. If the other party believes the negotiator to be deceitful, they may be unwilling to cooperate or even stop negotiations altogether.

14. Which of the following is the acceptable minimum outcome if a negotiator cannot obtain the desired result?

    A. Win-win attitude.

    B. Cooperation.

    C. Best alternative to a negotiated agreement (BATNA).

    D. Win-lose attitude.

Answer (C) is correct. *(Publisher)*
    REQUIRED: The acceptable minimum outcome if a negotiator cannot obtain the desired result.
    DISCUSSION: BATNA is the acceptable minimum outcome if a negotiator cannot obtain the desired result. The BATNA helps a negotiator to avoid accepting an unfavorable agreement and rejecting a favorable agreement.
    Answer (A) is incorrect because a win-win attitude is cooperative. It is founded on the principle that resources are sufficient for all and a third alternative is preferable. Answer (B) is incorrect because cooperation is the act of seeking mutual benefit and satisfaction. Answer (D) is incorrect because a win-lose attitude is competitive. It results as a zero-sum game.

15. Understanding the best alternative to a negotiated agreement (BATNA), helps a negotiator to avoid which of the following?

I. Accepting an unfavorable settlement.
II. Rejecting a favorable settlement.

    A. I only.

    B. II only.

    C. I and II.

    D. Neither I nor II.

Answer (C) is correct. *(Publisher)*
    REQUIRED: The mistakes avoided by understanding the BATNA.
    DISCUSSION: Accepting an unfavorable settlement and rejecting a favorable settlement are two mistakes avoided by understanding the BATNA. The BATNA is the acceptable minimum outcome if a negotiator cannot obtain the desired result.
    Answer (A) is incorrect because rejecting a favorable settlement is avoided by understanding the BATNA. Answer (B) is incorrect because accepting an unfavorable settlement is avoided by understanding the BATNA. Answer (D) is incorrect because accepting an unfavorable settlement and rejecting a favorable settlement are avoided by understanding the BATNA.

16. Which of the following is an example of framing error?

I. A job seeker may hope that the attractive appearance of a resume will sway the judgment of a potential employer.

II. A glass still holds 50% of its capacity whether it is described as half full or half empty. However, the former (latter) characterization may lead to a more (less) favorable opinion of the content.

    A. I only.

    B. I and II.

    C. II only.

    D. Neither I nor II.

Answer (B) is correct. *(Publisher)*
    REQUIRED: The true example of framing error.
    DISCUSSION: Framing error is a perceptual problem. The presentation or context of information may bias its interpretation and the resulting decision. Thus, favorably (unfavorably) presented information may be viewed more (less) favorably than its merits warrant. Both I and II are examples of framing errors.
    Answer (A) is incorrect because situation II is also an example of framing error. The favorably (unfavorably) presented information may be viewed more (less) favorably than its merits warrant. Answer (C) is incorrect because situation I is also a correct example of framing error. Answer (D) is incorrect because both of the situations listed are examples of framing error since the presentation or context of information may bias its interpretation and the resulting decision.

17. The negotiator, when encountering unexpected resistance from another party, should first

    A. Attempt to determine the reason behind the resistance.

    B. Stop the meeting and address the other party's concerns privately.

    C. Restate the negotiator's position regarding the issue.

    D. Research the other party to determine its views and requirements.

Answer (A) is correct. *(IIA, adapted)*
    REQUIRED: The negotiator's actions when encountering unexpected resistance.
    DISCUSSION: The first step in overcoming unexpected resistance is to attempt to determine the reason behind the resistance. Without knowing the reason, the negotiator is unable to counter it effectively. For example, knowing whether the other party is concerned about a major issue or a detail will affect the negotiator's response.
    Answer (B) is incorrect because, generally, a resolution should be attempted at the time. Only if one or both parties to the negotiation need additional time to evaluate new information or calm down should a break be taken. Answer (C) is incorrect because the negotiator should first work with the other party to determine the cause of disagreement. Answer (D) is incorrect because research regarding the other party should occur prior to the initial negotiation meeting.

18. A parent wishes to sell a subsidiary for $1.6 billion. A buyer wishes to acquire the subsidiary for $1.1 billion, with the best alternative to a negotiated agreement (BATNA) of $1.4 billion. What is an acceptable BATNA for the seller in order for negotiation to be feasible?

    A. $1.3 billion.

    B. $1.5 billion.

    C. $1.7 billion.

    D. $1.75 billion.

Answer (A) is correct. *(Publisher)*
    REQUIRED: The acceptable BATNA for the offer to be feasible.
    DISCUSSION: $1.3 billion is an acceptable BATNA because the BATNA of the buyer is $1.4 billion. Any amount over $1.4 billion would cause negotiation to not be feasible.
    Answer (B) is incorrect because $1.5 billion is higher than the $1.4 billion BATNA of the buyer. The buyer will not be willing to negotiate with the seller. Answer (C) is incorrect because $1.7 billion is higher than the buyer's BATNA of $1.4 billion. Once again, negotiation is not feasible in this situation. Answer (D) is incorrect because $1.75 billion BATNA is higher than the $1.4 billion BATNA of the buyer.

19. Angela and Leticia negotiate the details and put the deal in written form. Angela and Leticia have developed a good relationship and future negotiations will benefit. During what step of the value-added negotiating process has taken place?

    A. Perfect the deal.

    B. Identify options.

    C. Design alternative deal packages.

    D. Select a deal.

Answer (A) is correct. *(Publisher)*
    REQUIRED: The steps in the added-value negotiation process.
    DISCUSSION: Angela and Leticia performed step five of value-added negotiation by perfecting the deal. This step is characterized by negotiating details and putting the deal in written form. The process creates relationships that will benefit later negotiations.
    Answer (B) is incorrect because the purpose of identifying options is to establish a "marketplace of value," i.e., the range of values each side can give the other. Answer (C) is incorrect because designing alternative deal packages exemplifies the distinctive feature of added-value negotiation which provides for multiple win-win offers. Answer (D) is incorrect because selecting a deal is completed after the parties have considered the deal packages.

20. Steps in a negotiation include clarifying interests, identifying options, designing alternative deal packages, selecting a deal, and perfecting the deal. The type of negotiation described is

    A. Two-party.

    B. Three-party.

    C. Added-value.

    D. Ineffective.

Answer (C) is correct. *(Publisher)*
    REQUIRED: The type of negotiation.
    DISCUSSION: In added value negotiating, the two sides make multiple deals to "add value" to the process. Clarifying interests, identifying options, designing alternative deal packages, selecting a deal, and perfecting a deal are all steps in added-value negotiating.
    Answer (A) is incorrect because a two-party negotiation occurs between two persons, for example, when a person sells his or her car to a used car dealer. Answer (B) is incorrect because a three-party negotiation occurs between three persons, for example, when a person sells his or her stock through a broker. Answer (D) is incorrect because added-value negotiating is an example of effective negotiation.

21. What is a primary disadvantage of forcing another party to accept terms in a negotiation?

    A. Damage of the relationship between the negotiators.

    B. Lack of achievement of the negotiator's goals.

    C. Increased time involved in reaching an agreement.

    D. Reduction in internal support for the negotiator's tactics.

Answer (A) is correct. *(IIA, adapted)*
    REQUIRED: The primary disadvantage of forcing another party to accept a negotiation's terms.
    DISCUSSION: In future negotiations, the "forced" opponent will be less likely to work with the negotiator to achieve mutual goals. Negotiations in which one or both parties feel they must "win" at the expense of the other party ultimately do not build a relationship of trust and cooperation.
    Answer (B) is incorrect because the negotiator has achieved the goals of this negotiation. Answer (C) is incorrect because often a collaborative approach to a negotiation will take longer due to the time taken in understanding the other party's needs and concerns and then resolving the issue to the benefit of both parties. Answer (D) is incorrect because the negotiator's tactics should be supported or condoned, so long as the negotiation resulted in favorable terms for the firm.

Use Gleim's *CIA Test Prep* for interactive testing with over 2,000 additional multiple-choice questions!

APPENDIX A
THE IIA CONTENT SPECIFICATION OUTLINES (CSOs)

We have reproduced The IIA's Content Specification Outlines (CSOs) verbatim from their website (www.theiia.org) for your convenience. Please visit The IIA's website for updates and more information about the exam. Rely on the Gleim book and software to pass each part of the exam. We have researched and studied The IIA's CSOs as well as questions from prior exams to provide you with an excellent review program.

PART I – THE INTERNAL AUDIT ACTIVITY'S ROLE IN GOVERNANCE, RISK, AND CONTROL

A. **COMPLY WITH THE IIA'S ATTRIBUTE STANDARDS (15 - 25%)** (proficiency level)

1. Define purpose, authority, and responsibility of the internal audit activity.

   a. Determine if purpose, authority, and responsibility of internal audit activity are clearly documented/approved.

   b. Determine if purpose, authority, and responsibility of internal audit activity are communicated to engagement clients.

   c. Demonstrate an understanding of the purpose, authority, and responsibility of the internal audit activity.

2. Maintain independence and objectivity.

   a. Foster independence.

      1) Understand organizational independence.
      2) Recognize the importance of organizational independence.
      3) Determine if the internal audit activity is properly aligned to achieve organizational independence.

   b. Foster objectivity.

      1) Establish policies to promote objectivity.
      2) Assess individual objectivity.
      3) Maintain individual objectivity.
      4) Recognize and mitigate impairments to independence and objectivity.

3. Determine if the required knowledge, skills, and competencies are available.

   a. Understand the knowledge, skills, and competencies that an internal auditor needs to possess.

   b. Identify the knowledge, skills, and competencies required to fulfill the responsibilities of the internal audit activity.

4. Develop and/or procure necessary knowledge, skills, and competencies collectively required by internal audit activity.

5. Exercise due professional care.

6. Promote continuing professional development.

   a. Develop and implement a plan for continuing professional development for internal audit staff.
   b. Enhance individual competency through continuing professional development.

7. Promote quality assurance and improvement of the internal audit activity.

   a. Establish and maintain a quality assurance and improvement program.

   b. Monitor the effectiveness of the quality assurance and improvement program.

   c. Report the results of the quality assurance and improvement program to the board or other governing body.

   d. Conduct quality assurance procedures and recommend improvements to the performance of the internal audit activity.

8. Abide by and promote compliance with The IIA Code of Ethics.

B. **ESTABLISH A RISK-BASED PLAN TO DETERMINE THE PRIORITIES OF THE INTERNAL AUDIT ACTIVITY (15 - 25%)** (proficiency level)

1. Establish a framework for assessing risk.
2. Use the framework to:

   a. Identify sources of potential engagements (e.g., audit universe, management request, regulatory mandate)
   b. Assess organization-wide risk
   c. Solicit potential engagement topics from various sources
   d. Collect and analyze data on proposed engagements
   e. Rank and validate risk priorities

3. Identify internal audit resource requirements.
4. Coordinate the internal audit activity's efforts with:

   a. External auditor
   b. Regulatory oversight bodies
   c. Other internal assurance functions (e.g., health and safety department)

5. Select engagements.

   a. Participate in the engagement selection process.
   b. Select engagements.
   c. Communicate and obtain approval of the engagement plan from board.

C. **UNDERSTAND THE INTERNAL AUDIT ACTIVITY'S ROLE IN ORGANIZATIONAL GOVERNANCE (10 - 20%)** (proficiency level)

1. Obtain board's approval of audit charter.
2. Communicate plan of engagements.
3. Report significant audit issues.
4. Communicate key performance indicators to board on a regular basis.
5. Discuss areas of significant risk.
6. Support board in enterprise-wide risk assessment.
7. Review positioning of the internal audit function within the risk management framework within the organization.
8. Monitor compliance with the corporate code of conduct/business practices.
9. Report on the effectiveness of the control framework.
10. Assist board in assessing the independence of the external auditor.
11. Assess ethical climate of the board.
12. Assess ethical climate of the organization.
13. Assess compliance with policies in specific areas (e.g., derivatives).
14. Assess organization's reporting mechanism to the board.
15. Conduct follow-up and report on management response to regulatory body reviews.
16. Conduct follow-up and report on management response to external audit.
17. Assess the adequacy of the performance measurement system, achievement of corporate objective.
18. Support a culture of fraud awareness and encourage the reporting of improprieties.

D. **PERFORM OTHER INTERNAL AUDIT ROLES AND RESPONSIBILITIES (0 - 10%)** (proficiency level)

1. Ethics/compliance

   a. Investigate and recommend resolution for ethics/compliance complaints.
   b. Determine disposition of ethics violations.
   c. Foster healthy ethical climate.
   d. Maintain and administer business conduct policy (e.g., conflict of interest).
   e. Report on compliance.

2. Risk management

   a. Develop and implement an organization-wide risk and control framework.
   b. Coordinate enterprise-wide risk assessment.
   c. Report corporate risk assessment to board.
   d. Review business continuity planning process.

3. Privacy

   a. Determine privacy vulnerabilities.
   b. Report on compliance.

4. Information or physical security

   a. Determine security vulnerabilities.
   b. Determine disposition of security violations.
   c. Report on compliance.

E. **GOVERNANCE, RISK, AND CONTROL KNOWLEDGE ELEMENTS (15 - 25%)**

1. Corporate governance principles (awareness level)
2. Alternative control frameworks (awareness level)
3. Risk vocabulary and concepts (proficiency level)
4. Risk management techniques (proficiency level)
5. Risk/control implications of different organizational structures (proficiency level)
6. Risk/control implications of different leadership styles (awareness level)
7. Change management (awareness level)
8. Conflict management (awareness level)
9. Management control techniques (proficiency level)
10. Types of control (preventive, detective, input, output) (proficiency level)

F. **PLAN ENGAGEMENTS (15 - 25%)** (proficiency level)

1. Initiate preliminary communication with engagement client.
2. Conduct a preliminary survey of the area of engagement.

   a. Obtain input from engagement client.
   b. Perform analytical reviews.
   c. Perform benchmarking.
   d. Conduct interviews.
   e. Review prior audit reports and other relevant documentation.
   f. Map processes.
   g. Develop checklists.

3. Complete a detailed risk assessment of the area (prioritize or evaluate risk/control factors).
4. Coordinate audit engagement efforts with

   a. External auditor
   b. Regulatory oversight bodies

5. Establish/refine engagement objectives and identify/finalize the scope of engagement.
6. Identify or develop criteria for assurance engagements (criteria against which to audit).
7. Consider the potential for fraud when planning an engagement.

   a. Be knowledgeable of the risk factors and red flags of fraud.
   b. Identify common types of fraud associated with the engagement area.
   c. Determine if risk of fraud requires special consideration when conducting an engagement.

8. Determine engagement procedures.
9. Determine the level of staff and resources needed for the engagement.
10. Establish adequate planning and supervision of the engagement.
11. Prepare engagement work program.

FORMAT: 125 multiple-choice questions

PART II – CONDUCTING THE INTERNAL AUDIT ENGAGEMENT

A. **CONDUCT ENGAGEMENTS (25 - 35%)** (proficiency level)

1. Research and apply appropriate standards:

   a. IIA Professional Practices Framework (Code of Ethics, Standards, and Practice Advisories)
   b. Other professional, legal, and regulatory standards

2. Maintain an awareness of potential for fraud when conducting an engagement.

   a. Notice indicators or symptoms of fraud.
   b. Design appropriate engagement steps to address significant risk of fraud.
   c. Employ audit tests to detect fraud.
   d. Determine if any suspected fraud merits investigation.

3. Collect data.
4. Evaluate the relevance, sufficiency, and competence of evidence.
5. Analyze and interpret data.
6. Develop workpapers.
7. Review workpapers.
8. Communicate interim progress.
9. Draw conclusions.
10. Develop recommendations when appropriate.

11. Report engagement results.

    a. Conduct exit conference.
    b. Prepare report or other communication.
    c. Approve engagement report.
    d. Determine distribution of report.
    e. Obtain management response to report.

12. Conduct client satisfaction survey.
13. Complete performance appraisals of engagement staff.

B. **CONDUCT SPECIFIC ENGAGEMENTS (25 - 35%)** (proficiency level)

1. Conduct assurance engagements.

    a. Fraud investigation

        1) Determine appropriate parties to be involved with investigation.
        2) Establish facts and extent of fraud (e.g., interviews, interrogations, and data analysis).
        3) Report outcomes to appropriate parties.
        4) Complete a process review to improve controls to prevent fraud and recommend changes.

    b. Risk and control self-assessment

        1) Facilitated approach

            a) Client-facilitated
            b) Audit-facilitated

        2) Questionnaire approach
        3) Self-certification approach

    c. Audits of third parties and contract auditing
    d. Quality audit engagements
    e. Due diligence audit engagements
    f. Security audit engagements
    g. Privacy audit engagements
    h. Performance (key performance indicators) audit engagements
    i. Operational (efficiency and effectiveness) audit engagements
    j. Financial audit engagements
    k. Information technology (IT) audit engagements

        1) Operating systems

            a) Mainframe
            b) Workstations
            c) Server

        2) Application development

            a) Application authentication
            b) Systems development methodology
            c) Change control
            d) End user computing

        3) Data and network communications/connections (e.g., LAN, VAN, and WAN)
        4) Voice communications
        5) System security (e.g., firewalls, access control)
        6) Contingency planning
        7) Databases
        8) Functional areas of IT operations (e.g., data center operations)
        9) Web infrastructure
        10) Software licensing
        11) Electronic Funds Transfer (EFT)/Electronic Data Interchange (EDI)
        12) E-Commerce
        13) Information protection/viruses
        14) Encryption
        15) Enterprise-wide resource planning (ERP) software (e.g., SAP R/3)

    l. Compliance audit engagements

2. Conduct consulting engagements.

    a. Internal control training
    b. Business process review
    c. Benchmarking
    d. Information technology (IT) and systems development
    e. Design of performance measurement systems

C. **MONITOR ENGAGEMENT OUTCOMES (5 - 15%)** (proficiency level)

    1.   Determine appropriate follow-up activity by the internal audit activity
    2.   Identify appropriate method to monitor engagement outcomes
    3.   Conduct follow-up activity
    4.   Communicate monitoring plan and results

D. **FRAUD KNOWLEDGE ELEMENTS (5 - 15%)**

    1.   Discovery sampling (awareness level)
    2.   Interrogation techniques (awareness level)
    3.   Forensic auditing (awareness level)
    4.   Use of computers in analyzing data (awareness level)
    5.   Red flag (proficiency level)
    6.   Types of fraud (proficiency level)

E. **ENGAGEMENT TOOLS (15 - 25%)**

    1.   Sampling (awareness level)

        a.   Nonstatistical (judgmental)
        b.   Statistical

    2.   Statistical analyses (process control techniques) (awareness level)
    3.   Data gathering tools (proficiency level)

        a.   Interviewing
        b.   Questionnaires
        c.   Checklists

    4.   Analytical review techniques (proficiency level)

        a.   Ratio estimation
        b.   Variance analysis (e.g., budget vs. actual)
        c.   Other reasonableness tests

    5.   Observation (proficiency level)
    6.   Problem solving (proficiency level)
    7.   Risk and control self-assessment (CSA) (awareness level)
    8.   Computerized audit tools and techniques (proficiency level)

        a.   Embedded audit modules
        b.   Data extraction techniques
        c.   Generalized audit software (e.g., ACL, IDEA)
        d.   Spreadsheet analysis
        e.   Automated workpapers (e.g., Lotus Notes, Auditor Assistant)

    9.   Process mapping including flowcharting (proficiency level)

  FORMAT: 125 multiple-choice questions

PART III – BUSINESS ANALYSIS AND INFORMATION TECHNOLOGY

A. **BUSINESS PROCESSES (15 - 25%)**

    1.   Quality management (e.g., TQM) (awareness level)
    2.   The International Organization for Standardization (ISO) framework (awareness level)
    3.   Forecasting (awareness level)
    4.   Project management techniques (proficiency level)
    5.   Business process analysis (e.g., workflow analysis and bottleneck management, theory of constraints) (proficiency level)
    6.   Inventory management techniques and concepts (proficiency level)
    7.   Marketing- pricing objectives and policies (awareness level)
    8.   Marketing- supply chain management (awareness level)
    9.   Human Resources (individual performance management and measurement, supervision, environmental factors that affect performance, facilitation techniques, personnel sourcing/staffing, training and development, and safety) (proficiency level)
    10.   Balanced Scorecard (awareness level)

B. **FINANCIAL ACCOUNTING AND FINANCE (15 - 25%)**

    1.   Basic concepts and underlying principles of financial accounting (statements, terminology, relationships) (proficiency level)
    2.   Intermediate concepts of financial accounting (e.g., bonds, leases, pensions, intangible assets, R & D) (awareness level)
    3.   Advanced concepts of financial accounting (e.g., consolidation, partnerships, foreign currency transactions) (awareness level)

4.   Financial statement analysis (proficiency level)
5.   Cost of capital evaluation (awareness level)
6.   Types of debt and equity (awareness level)
7.   Financial instruments (e.g., derivatives) (awareness level)
8.   Cash management (treasury functions) (awareness level)
9.   Valuation models (awareness level)

    a.   Inventory valuation
    b.   Business valuation

10. Business development life cycles (awareness level)

C. **MANAGERIAL ACCOUNTING (10 - 20%)**

1.   Cost concepts (e.g., absorption, variable, fixed) (proficiency level)
2.   Capital budgeting (awareness level)
3.   Operating budget (proficiency level)
4.   Transfer pricing (awareness level)
5.   Cost-volume-profit analysis (awareness level)
6.   Relevant cost (awareness level)
7.   Costing systems (e.g., activity-based, standard) (awareness level)
8.   Responsibility accounting (awareness level)

D. **REGULATORY, LEGAL, AND ECONOMICS (5 - 15%)** (awareness level)

1.   Impact of government legislation and regulation on business
2.   Trade legislation and regulations
3.   Taxation schemes
4.   Contracts
5.   Nature and rules of legal evidence
6.   Key economic indicators

E. **INFORMATION TECHNOLOGY (IT) (30 - 40%)** (awareness level)

1.   Control frameworks (e.g., SAC, COBIT)
2.   Data and network communications/connections (e.g., LAN, VAN, and WAN)
3.   Electronic funds transfer (EFT)
4.   E-Commerce
5.   Electronic data interchange (EDI)
6.   Functional areas of IT operations (e.g., data center operations)
7.   Encryption
8.   Viruses
9.   Information protection
10. Evaluate investment in IT (cost of ownership)
11. Enterprise-wide resource planning (ERP) software (e.g., SAP R/3, Peoplesoft)
12. Operating systems
13. Application development
14. Voice communications
15. Contingency planning
16. Systems security (e.g., firewalls, access control)
17. Databases
18. Software licensing
19. Web infrastructure

FORMAT: 125 multiple-choice questions

PART IV – BUSINESS MANAGEMENT SKILLS

A. **STRATEGIC MANAGEMENT (20 - 30%)** (awareness level)

1.   Global analytical techniques

    a.   Structural analysis of industries
    b.   Competitive strategies (e.g., Porter's model)
    c.   Competitive analysis
    d.   Market signals
    e.   Industry evolution

2.   Industry environments

    a.   Competitive strategies related to:

        1)   Fragmented industries
        2)   Emerging industries
        3)   Declining industries

       b.   Competition in global industries

           1)   Sources/impediments
           2)   Evolution of global markets
           3)   Strategic alternatives
           4)   Trends affecting competition

   3.   Strategic decisions

       a.   Analysis of integration strategies
       b.   Capacity expansion
       c.   Entry into new businesses

   4.   Portfolio techniques of competitive analysis
   5.   Product life cycles

B. GLOBAL BUSINESS ENVIRONMENTS (15 - 25%) (awareness level)

   1.   Cultural/legal/political environments

       a.   Balancing global requirements and local imperatives
       b.   Global mindsets (personal characteristics/competencies)
       c.   Sources and methods for managing complexities and contradictions
       d.   Managing multicultural teams

   2.   Economic/financial environments

       a.   Global, multinational, international, and multilocal compared and contrasted
       b.   Requirements for entering the global market place
       c.   Creating organizational adaptability
       d.   Managing training and development

C. ORGANIZATIONAL BEHAVIOR (20 - 30%) (awareness level)

   1.   Motivation

       a.   Relevance and implication of various theories
       b.   Impact of job design, rewards, work schedules, etc.

   2.   Communication

       a.   The process
       b.   Organizational dynamics
       c.   Impact of computerization

   3.   Performance

       a.   Productivity
       b.   Effectiveness

   4.   Structure

       a.   Centralized/decentralized
       b.   Departmentalization
       c.   New configurations (e.g., hourglass, cluster, network)

D. MANAGEMENT SKILLS (20 - 30%) (awareness level)

   1.   Group dynamics

       a.   Traits (cohesiveness, roles, norms, groupthink, etc.)
       b.   Stages of group development
       c.   Organizational politics
       d.   Criteria and determinants of effectiveness

   2.   Team building

       a.   Methods used in team building
       b.   Assessing team performance

   3.   Leadership skills

       a.   Theories compared/contrasted
       b.   Leadership grid (topology of leadership styles)
       c.   Mentoring

   4.   Personal time management

E.   **NEGOTIATING (5 - 15%)** (awareness level)

    1.   Conflict resolution

        a.   Competitive/cooperative
        b.   Compromise, forcing, smoothing, etc.

    2.   Added-value negotiating

        a.   Description
        b.   Specific steps

    FORMAT: 125 multiple-choice questions

APPENDIX B
THE IIA EXAMINATION BIBLIOGRAPHY

The Institute has prepared a listing of references for the CIA exam, reproduced beginning below. These publications have been chosen by the Board of Regents as reasonably representative of the common body of knowledge for internal auditors. However, all of the information in these texts will not be tested. When possible, questions will be written based on the information contained in the suggested reference list. This bibliography is reorganized in an alphabetical listing by part to give you an overview of the scope of each part. The IIA also indicates that the examination scope includes

1. Articles from *Internal Auditor* (The IIA periodical)
2. IIA research reports
3. IIA pronouncements, e.g., The IIA Code of Ethics and SIASs
4. Past published CIA examinations

The IIA bibliography is reproduced for your information only. The texts you will need to acquire (use) to prepare for the CIA exam will depend on many factors, including

1. Innate ability
2. Length of time out of school
3. Thoroughness of your undergraduate education
4. Familiarity with internal auditing due to relevant experience

SUGGESTED REFERENCES FOR THE CIA EXAM

PART I: THE INTERNAL AUDIT ACTIVITY'S ROLE IN GOVERNANCE, RISK, AND CONTROL

Sawyer, et al, *Sawyer's Internal Auditing*, 5th Ed., The Institute of Internal Auditors.

OR Sears, *Internal Auditing Manual*, WG&L Financial Reporting & Management.

The American Institute of Certified Public Accountants, *Internal Control - Integrated Framework*, 1994.

The Institute of Internal Auditors, Inc., *Professional Practices Framework*, 2002.

OR *Other Control and Governance Frameworks*.

Supplemental:

Albrecht, Wernz, and Williams, *Fraud: Bringing Light to the Dark Side of Business*, Irwin Professional Publishing.

Murphy and Parker, *Handbook of IT Auditing*, Warren, Gorham & Lamont.

Reider, *Complete Guide to Operational Auditing*, John Wiley & Sons, Inc.

PART II: CONDUCTING THE INTERNAL AUDIT ENGAGEMENT

Sawyer, et al, *Sawyer's Internal Auditing*, 5th Ed., The Institute of Internal Auditors.

OR Sears, *Internal Auditing Manual*, WG&L Financial Reporting & Management.

The Institute of Internal Auditors, Inc., *Professional Practices Framework*, 2002.

Supplemental:

Kreitner, *Management*, 9th Ed., Houghton Mifflin Co., 2004.

PART III: BUSINESS ANALYSIS AND INFORMATION TECHNOLOGY

Information Systems and Control Foundation, *Cobit: Governance, Control, and Audit for Information and Related Technology*, 3rd Ed., 2000.

International Accounting Standards Committee, *International Accounting Standards*, 2002.

Kieso, Warfield, and Weygandt, *Intermediate Accounting*, 11th Ed., John Wiley & Sons, Inc., 2004.

Kreitner, *Management*, 9th Ed., Houghton Mifflin Co., 2004.

Sawyer, et al, *Sawyer's Internal Auditing*, 5th Ed., the Institute of Internal Auditors.

OR Sears, *Internal Auditing Manual*, WG&L Financial Reporting & Management.

The Institute of Internal Auditors Research Foundation, *Systems Assurance and Control*, 2003.

Weber, *Information Systems Control and Audit*, Prentice Hall, 1998.

PART IV: BUSINESS MANAGEMENT SKILLS

Bruner, Eaker, Freeman, Spelkman, Teisberg, and Venkataraman, *The Portable MBA*, 4th Ed., John Wiley & Sons, 2002.

Fisher, Ury, and Patton, *Getting to Yes, Negotiating Agreement Without Giving In*, Penguin USA.

Hill, *International Business with Global Resource CD, Powerweb and World Map*, 4th Ed., McGraw-Hill/Irwin, 2002.

Kreitner, *Management*, 9th Ed., Houghton Mifflin Co., 2004.

Kotler, *Marketing Management*, 11th Ed., Prentice Hall, 2002.

PUBLICATIONS AVAILABLE FROM THE IIA

The listing on the previous pages presents only some of the current technical literature available. Quantity discounts are provided. Inquiries should be sent to

Customer Service
Institute of Internal Auditors   Request a current catalog by mail or call
249 Maitland Avenue   (407) 830-7600, ext. 1
Altamonte Springs, FL 32701-4201

Book orders can be placed directly by calling (877) 867-4957 (toll-free) or (770) 442-8633, extension 275.

ORDERING TEXTUAL MATERIAL

The IIA does not carry all of the reference books. Write directly to the publisher if you cannot obtain the desired texts from your local bookstore. Begin your study program with *CIA Review*, Parts I through IV, which most candidates find sufficient. If you need additional reference material, borrow books from colleagues, professors, or a library.

Addison-Wesley Publishing
Company
Reading, MA 01867

Basic Books, Inc.
Harper & Row Publishers
10 East 53rd Street
New York, NY 10022

Business Publications, Inc.
1700 Alma, Suite 390
Plano, TX 75075

The Dryden Press
One Salt Creek Lane
Hinsdale, IL 60521-2902

Harcourt Brace Jovanovich
1250 Sixth Avenue
San Diego, CA 92101

Harper & Row
10 East 53rd Street
New York, NY 10022

Holt, Rinehart, Winston
383 Madison Avenue
New York, NY 10017

Houghton Mifflin Company
One Beacon Street
Boston, MA 02108

Richard D. Irwin, Inc.
1818 Ridge Road
Homewood, IL 60430

Kent Publishing Company
20 Park Plaza
Boston, MA 02116

McGraw-Hill Book Company
1221 Avenue of the Americas
New York, NY 10020

Mitchell Publishing, Inc.
915 River Street
Santa Cruz, CA 95060

Prentice-Hall, Inc.
Englewood Cliffs, NJ 07632

Reston Publishing Company
11480 Sunset Hills Road
Reston, VA 22090

South-Western Publishing
Company
5101 Madison Road
Cincinnati, OH 45227

West Publishing Company
P.O. Box 55165
St. Paul, MN 55101

John Wiley & Sons, Inc.
605 Third Avenue
New York, NY 10016

INDEX

COMPLETE GLEIM CPA SYSTEM with REVIEW ONLINE

All 4 parts, including 5 books, 4 audios, CPA Test Prep software, **Review Online**[1], plus bonus book bag.

☐ $924.95 $ _____

Also available by exam part (Does not include book bag.)				
Auditing ☐ $256.95	Business ☐ $256.95			
Financial ☐ $256.95	Regulation ☐ $256.95	$ _____		

GLEIM CPA SET

All 4 parts, including 5 books, 4 audios, CPA Test Prep software, plus bonus book bag.

☐ $539.95 $ _____

CPA REVIEW

	Online Simulations (Included in Review Online)	Book/Software/ Audio Package Save 20%	Book/Software Package Save 16%	Audio Reviews	Software	Books	
Auditing	☐ @$99.95	☐ @$143.95	☐ @$74.95	☐ @$89.95	☐ @$49.95	☐ @$39.95	$ _____
Business	☐ @$99.95	☐ @$143.95	☐ @$74.95	☐ @$89.95	☐ @$49.95	☐ @$39.95	
Regulation	☐ @$99.95	☐ @$143.95	☐ @$74.95	☐ @$89.95	☐ @$49.95	☐ @$39.95	
Financial	☐ @$99.95	☐ @$143.95	☐ @$74.95	☐ @$89.95	☐ @$49.95	☐ @$39.95	
A System for Success		☐ @$19.95 (FREE with the purchase of any Gleim CPA Review book.)					_____

COMPLETE GLEIM CMA/CFM SYSTEM*

Includes: 5-part set (book, software, and audio), plus bonus book bag.
*11th Edition, Pre-exam changes

☐ $566.95 $ _____

GLEIM 4-Part Set

Includes: 4-part set (book, software, and audio), plus bonus book bag.

☐ CMA@$453.95 ☐ CFM@$453.95 $ _____

CMA/CFM REVIEW

	Book/Software/ Audio Package Save 15%	Book/Software Package Save 10%	Audio Reviews	Software	Books	
Part 1 Eco., Fin., & Mgmt.	☐ @$120.95	☐ @$64.95	☐ @$69.95	☐ @$44.95	☐ @$26.95	$ _____
Part 2CMA Fin. Acc. & Rep.	☐ @$120.95	☐ @$64.95	☐ @$69.95	☐ @$44.95	☐ @$26.95	
Part 2CFM Corp. Fin. Mgmt.	☐ @$120.95	☐ @$64.95	☐ @$69.95	☐ @$44.95	☐ @$26.95	
Part 3 Mgmt. Rep./Behav. Iss.	☐ @$120.95	☐ @$64.95	☐ @$69.95	☐ @$44.95	☐ @$26.95	
Part 4 Dec. Anal. & Info. Sys.	☐ @$120.95	☐ @$64.95	☐ @$69.95	☐ @$44.95	☐ @$26.95	

CIA REVIEW

	Book/Software/ Audio Package Save 19%	Book/Software Package Save 12%	Audio Reviews	Software	Books	
All 4 Parts	☐ @$483.80	☐ @$279.80	☐ @$279.80	☐ @$199.80	☐ @$119.80	$ _____
Part I IA Role in Gov., Risk, Control	☐ @$120.95	☐ @$69.95	☐ @$69.95	☐ @$49.95	☐ @$29.95	
Part II Conducting the IA Engagement	☐ @$120.95	☐ @$69.95	☐ @$69.95	☐ @$49.95	☐ @$29.95	
Part III Bus. Anal. & Info. Tech.	☐ @$120.95	☐ @$69.95	☐ @$69.95	☐ @$49.95	☐ @$29.95	
Part IV Bus. Mgmt. Skills	☐ @$120.95	☐ @$69.95	☐ @$69.95	☐ @$49.95	☐ @$29.95	

EA REVIEW

	Book/Software Package Save 12%	Software	Books	
All 4 Parts	☐ @$279.80	☐ @$179.80	☐ @$119.80	$ _____
Part 1 Individuals	☐ @$69.95	☐ @$49.95	☐ @$29.95	
Part 2 Sole Prop. & Partnerships	☐ @$69.95	☐ @$49.95	☐ @$29.95	
Part 3 Corp./Fid./Est. & Gift Tax	☐ @$69.95	☐ @$49.95	☐ @$29.95	
Part 4 IRS Adm/Other Topics	☐ @$69.95	☐ @$49.95	☐ @$29.95	

"THE GLEIM SERIES" EXAM QUESTIONS AND EXPLANATIONS BOOKS, SOFTWARE, AND CPE[2]

	Book/Software Package (Save 25%)	Software	Books	Books & CPE	
Auditing & Systems	☐ @$29.95	☐ @$20.00	☐ @$19.95	☐ @$200.00	$ _____
Business Law/Legal Studies	☐ @$29.95	☐ @$20.00	☐ @$19.95		
Federal Tax	☐ @$29.95	☐ @$20.00	☐ @$19.95	☐ @$200.00	
Financial Accounting	☐ @$29.95	☐ @$20.00	☐ @$19.95	☐ @$200.00	
Cost/Managerial Accounting	☐ @$29.95	☐ @$20.00	☐ @$19.95		

[1] For more information on our **CPA Review Online**, please visit **www.gleim.com/CPAOL/**

[2] For our online **CPE** courses and course catalog, please visit **www.gleim.com/CPE/**

SUBTOTAL $ _____

Complete your order on the next page. 🐾

GLEIM PUBLICATIONS, INC.

P. O. Box 12848   Gainesville, FL 32604

TOLL FREE:	(888) 87-GLEIM	Customer service is available (Eastern Time):
LOCAL:	(352) 375-0772	8:00 a.m. - 7:00 p.m., Mon. - Fri.
FAX:	(888) 375 -6940 (toll free)	9:00 a.m. - 2:00 p.m., Saturday
INTERNET	www.gleim.com	Please have your credit card ready,
E-MAIL:	sales@gleim.com	or save time by ordering online!

For audio purchases, please select: ☐ CD ☐ Cassette

SUBTOTAL (from previous page) $ _____

Add applicable sales tax for shipments within Florida. _____

Shipping (nonrefundable): **First Item* = $5; each additional item = $1** _____

*Sets and package deals contain multiple items. Each book, audio, and software counts as 1 item; online courses have no shipping charges.

TOTAL $ _____

Fax or write for prices/instructions on shipments outside the 48 contiguous states, or simply order online.

NAME (please print) _____

ADDRESS _____ Apt. _____

(street address required for UPS)

CITY _____ STATE _____ ZIP_____

_____ MC/VISA/DISC _____ Check/M.O.   Daytime Telephone _(_____)_____

Credit Card No. _____ - _____ - _____ - _____

Exp. _____ / _____ Signature _____
     Month / Year

E-mail address _____

1. We process and ship orders daily, within one business day over 98.8% of the time. Call by 3:00 pm for same day service.
2. Please PHOTOCOPY this order form for others.
3. No CODs. Orders from individuals must be prepaid.
4. Gleim Publications, Inc. guarantees the immediate refund of all resalable texts and unopened software and audios if returned within 30 days. Applies only to items purchased direct from Gleim Publications, Inc. Our shipping charge is nonrefundable.
5. Components of specially priced package deals are nonrefundable.

Printed 04/04. Prices subject to change without notice.

For updates and other important information, visit our website.

GLEIM KNOWLEDGE TRANSFER SYSTEMS®

www.gleim.com

The GLEIM CPA System Works!

Just thought I would let you know that I passed all four parts of the CPA Exam during my first attempt! I had only three months to study and a very limited budget. Your program proves that it has the greatest value available anywhere. I had friends who spent over a thousand dollars on other materials and still failed to pass. Thank you for such a great product. I highly recommend it to everyone who is preparing for this challenging experience.

- James G. Vaughn

"I would like to thank you for your CPA Software. It did wonders for me. I passed all 4 parts! In fact, your software was the best of ALL the other companies my friends and I tested. Not just me, but all agreed to that fact. Your CPA products were great. It sure helped me PASS!"

- Faizur Bakshi

I passed the entire CPA exam in November! It was my first attempt and I was really excited about that. I thought the Gleim CPA Review materials worked great. I recommend it to everyone that I know who is studying for the CPA exam. I think it followed the exam format very well and covered all the important material. I liked the multiple-choice questions the most. I just kept going through those questions until I understood the material. As you can see, your software worked for me! I was very pleased with the results. Thanks.

- John J. Hedahl, CPA

I just received notification that I passed all 4 parts of the November 2002 CPA Exam. This was my first time taking the exam. I used Gleim's study materials and I would recommend your product to anyone. There were no surprises on the exam. Gleim Study Materials + Hard Work and Dedication = Passing the CPA Exam on the first try.

- Luis Mendez

GLEIM
KNOWLEDGE
TRANSFER
SYSTEMS®

I passed the CPA exam with the help of Gleim. Thanks for a great product. I've used other products and even went to a review course, but I think Gleim products assisted me in focusing on the areas where I was weak.

- Kathy Napier

268

GLEIM's *ONLINE CPE*

- **Valuable** — Pay as little as $6.00 per hour with our multi-hour packages. Corporate pricing is also available.

- **Flexible** — Choose the courses you would like to complete up to one year after purchasing your CPE hours.

- **Convenient** — Work any place, any time, with one year from beginning a course to complete it.

- **Diverse** — Select from more than 100 separate CPE courses, all meeting NASBA Registry and QAS requirements.

- **Interactive** — Maximize your understanding and knowledge transfer with Gleim's proven format.

GLEIM

provides a wide variety of CPE courses for your needs, in a user-friendly learning format to help enhance your expertise.

FREE *One 4-hour CPE course, including Certificate of Completion.*

(800) 874-5346
www.gleim.com/cpe/

GLEIM
KNOWLEDGE
TRANSFER
SYSTEMS®

GLEIM's *Paper and Pencil CPE*

When online courses are not convenient.

Earn CPE credit using our *Exam Questions & Explanations* series with their respective workbooks.

All GLEIM CPE courses are NASBA Registry and QAS approved.

QUALITY ASSURANCE SERVICE

Gleim Publications, Inc. is registered with the National Association of State Boards of Accountancy (NASBA), as a Quality Service Assurance sponsor of continuing professional education. State boards of accountancy have final authority of the acceptance of individual courses for CPE credit. Complaints regarding QAS program sponsors may be addressed to NASBA,150 Fourth Avenue North, Suite 700, Nashville, TN, 37219-2417. NASBA phone number: 615.880.4200 Web site: www.nasba.org

NATIONAL REGISTRY OF
CPE
SPONSORS

Gleim Publications, Inc. is registered with the National Association of State Boards of Accountancy (NASBA), as a Quality Service Assurance sponsor of continuing professional education. State boards of accountancy have final authority of the acceptance of individual courses for CPE credit. Complaints regarding QAS program sponsors may be addressed to NASBA,150 Fourth Avenue North, Suite 700, Nashville, TN, 37219-2417. NASBA phone number: 615.880.4200 Web site: www.nasba.org

269

GLEIM's *CMA/CFM Review*

Certified Management Accountant
Certified in Financial Management

GLEIM
The First Name in CMA/CFM
Helping CMA and CFM Candidates **PASS**
Since 1980

- Self-study materials provide clear and concise analysis of the CMA and CFM exams.

- Multiple-choice study questions are similar or identical to actual exam questions.

- **GLEIM's** *CMA/CFM Test Prep* software emulates the Prometric testing environment, which gives you experience and promotes confidence with computerized testing.

Save 20%
GLEIM's
complete package

only
$566.95

GLEIM's *EA and CIA Review*

IRS Enrolled Agent

Certified Internal Auditor

- **GLEIM** simplifies the EA and CIA exams by breaking each part down into 10 easy-to-complete study units.

- **GLEIM's** *Test Prep* software enables you to improve your study process and test yourself in an interactive environment with actual exam questions.

Book/software combo package
only **$69**⁹⁵ per part

Book/software/audio package
only **$120**⁹⁵ per part

GLEIM
KNOWLEDGE
TRANSFER
SYSTEMS

www.gleim.com

(800) 87-GLEIM

270

GLEIM's *CPA Review*

GLEIM's *Complete* *CPA Review with Online*

Certified Public Accountant

- **G**LEIM removes the "mystique" of the CPA exam by providing you with the answers, information, and tools you need to arrive at the exam site with a head start, plus the confidence necessary to PASS.

- We guarantee that our review is the easiest to use and the most current with our free e-mail and Internet update services.

- Dr. Gleim has helped candidates pass the CPA exam since 1966. Through his years of experience, he has developed highly effective knowledge transfer outlines to help you pass the CPA exam.

+ CPA REVIEW ONLINE

GLEIM's *Complete CPA Review with Online includes:*

- Extensive Course Outlines that cover the material you need to know to pass.
- Over 5,000 practice multiple-choice questions with thorough answer explanations.
- 150 practice simulations with in-depth answer explanations.

Complete package only **$924⁹⁵**

or $256⁹⁵/part

GLEIM
KNOWLEDGE
TRANSFER
SYSTEMS®

www.gleim.com/CPA/

CIA Review: Part IV, Eleventh Edition, Second Printing -- Please complete and mail to us pages 271 and 272 the week following the CIA exam.

271

Please forward your suggestions, corrections, and comments concerning typographical errors, etc., to **Irvin N. Gleim • c/o Gleim Publications, Inc. • P.O. Box 12848 • University Station • Gainesville, Florida • 32604.** Please include your name and address so we can properly thank you for your interest.

1. _____

2. _____

3. _____

4. _____

5. _____

6. _____

7. _____

8. _____

9. _____

10. _____

11. _____

12. _____

13. _____

14. _____

15. _____

16. _____

17. _____

18. _____

Remember for superior service: Mail, e-mail, or fax questions about our books or software.
Telephone questions about orders, prices, shipments, or payments.

Name: _____

Address: _____

City/State/Zip: _____

Telephone: Home: _____ Work: _____ Fax: _____

E-mail: _____